VOLUME 604   MARCH 2006

THE ANNALS

of The American Academy of Political
and Social Science

ROBERT W. PEARSON, *Executive Editor*

Shelter from the Storm: Repairing the National Emergency Management System after Hurricane Katrina

Special Editor of this Volume

WILLIAM L. WAUGH JR.

Georgia State University

SAGE Publications Ⓢ Thousand Oaks · London · New Delhi

Origin and Purpose. The Academy was organized December 14, 1889, to promote the progress of political and social science, especially through publications and meetings. The Academy does not take sides in controverted questions, but seeks to gather and present reliable information to assist the public in forming an intelligent and accurate judgment.

Meetings. The Academy occasionally holds a meeting in the spring extending over two days.

Publications. THE ANNALS of The American Academy of Political and Social Science is the bimonthly publication of the Academy. Each issue contains articles on some prominent social or political problem, written at the invitation of the editors. Also, monographs are published from time to time, numbers of which are distributed to pertinent professional organizations. These volumes constitute important reference works on the topics with which they deal, and they are extensively cited by authorities throughout the United States and abroad. The papers presented at the meetings of the Academy are included in THE ANNALS.

Membership. Each member of the Academy receives THE ANNALS and may attend the meetings of the Academy. Membership is open only to individuals. Annual dues: $84.00 for the regular paperbound edition (clothbound, $121.00). Members may also purchase single issues of THE ANNALS for $17.00 each (clothbound, $26.00). Student memberships are available for $53.00.

Subscriptions. THE ANNALS of The American Academy of Political and Social Science (ISSN 0002-7162) (J295) is published six times annually—in January, March, May, July, September, and November—by Sage Publications, 2455 Teller Road, Thousand Oaks, CA 91320. Telephone: (800) 818-SAGE (7243) and (805) 499-9774; Fax/Order line: (805) 499-0871; e-mail: journals@sagepub.com. Copyright © 2006 by The American Academy of Political and Social Science. Institutions may subscribe to THE ANNALS at the annual rate: $577.00 (clothbound, $652.00). Single issues of THE ANNALS may be obtained by individuals who are not members of the Academy for $34.00 each (clothbound, $47.00). Single issues of THE ANNALS have proven to be excellent supplementary texts for classroom use. Direct inquiries regarding adoptions to THE ANNALS c/o Sage Publications (address below). Periodicals postage paid at Thousand Oaks, California, and at additional mailing offices.

All correspondence concerning membership in the Academy, dues renewals, inquiries about membership status, and/or purchase of single issues of THE ANNALS should be sent to THE ANNALS c/o Sage Publications, 2455 Teller Road, Thousand Oaks, CA 91320. Telephone: (800) 818-SAGE (7243) and (805) 499-9774; Fax/Order line: (805) 499-0871; e-mail: journals@sagepub.com. *Please note that orders under $30 must be prepaid.* Sage affiliates in London and India will assist institutional subscribers abroad with regard to orders, claims, and inquiries for both subscriptions and single issues.

Printed on acid-free paper

THE ANNALS

© 2006 by The American Academy of Political and Social Science

Editorial Office: 3814 Walnut Street, Fels Institute for Government, University of Pennsylvania, Philadelphia, PA 19104-6197.
For information about membership* (individuals only) and subscriptions (institutions), address:
Sage Publications
2455 Teller Road
Thousand Oaks, CA 91320
For Sage Publications: Joseph Riser and Esmeralda Hernandez

From India and South Asia, write to:
SAGE PUBLICATIONS INDIA Pvt Ltd
B-42 Panchsheel Enclave, P.O. Box 4109
New Delhi 110 017
INDIA

From Europe, the Middle East, and Africa, write to:
SAGE PUBLICATIONS LTD
1 Oliver's Yard, 55 City Road
London EC1Y 1SP
UNITED KINGDOM

*Please note that members of the Academy receive THE ANNALS with their membership.
International Standard Serial Number ISSN 0002-7162
International Standard Book Number 1-4129-4132-6 (Vol. 604, 2006 paper)
International Standard Book Number ISBN 1-4129-4131-8 (Vol. 604, 2006 cloth)
Manufactured in the United States of America. First printing, March 2006.

The articles appearing in *The Annals* are abstracted or indexed in Academic Abstracts, Academic Search, America: History and Life, Asia Pacific Database, Book Review Index,CABAbstracts Database, Central Asia: Abstracts &Index, Communication Abstracts, Corporate ResourceNET, Criminal Justice Abstracts, Current Citations Express, Current Contents: Social & Behavioral Sciences, Documentation in Public Administration, e-JEL, EconLit, Expanded Academic Index, Guide to Social Science & Religion in Periodical Literature, Health Business FullTEXT, HealthSTAR FullTEXT, Historical Abstracts, International Bibliography of the Social Sciences, International Political Science Abstracts, ISI Basic Social Sciences Index, Journal of Economic Literature on CD, LEXIS-NEXIS, MasterFILE FullTEXT, Middle East: Abstracts&Index, North Africa: Abstracts&Index, PAIS International, Periodical Abstracts, Political Science Abstracts, Psychological Abstracts, PsycINFO, Sage Public Administration Abstracts, Scopus, Social Science Source, Social Sciences Citation Index, Social Sciences Index Full Text, Social Services Abstracts, SocialWork Abstracts, Sociological Abstracts, Southeast Asia: Abstracts& Index, Standard Periodical Directory (SPD), TOPICsearch, Wilson OmniFileV, and Wilson Social Sciences Index/Abstracts, and are available on microfilm from ProQuest, Ann Arbor, Michigan.

Information about membership rates, institutional subscriptions, and back issue prices may be found on the facing page.

Advertising. Current rates and specifications may be obtained by writing to The Annals Advertising and Promotion Manager at the Thousand Oaks office (address above).

Claims. Claims for undelivered copies must be made no later than six months following month of publication. The publisher will supply missing copies when losses have been sustained in transit and when the reserve stock will permit.

Change of Address. Six weeks' advance notice must be given when notifying of change of address to ensure proper identification. Please specify name of journal. POSTMASTER: Send address changes to The Annals of The American Academy of Political and Social Science, c/o Sage Publications, 2455 Teller Road, Thousand Oaks, CA 91320.

THE ANNALS

OF THE AMERICAN ACADEMY OF POLITICAL AND SOCIAL SCIENCE

Volume 604   March 2006

IN THIS ISSUE:

*Shelter from the Storm: Repairing the National
Emergency Management System after Hurricane Katrina*
Special Editor: WILLIAM L. WAUGH JR.

Quick Read Synopsis

ON THE COVER: Milvertha Hendricks, 84, (center) waits in the rain with other flood victims outside the convention center in New Orleans, Thursday, Sept. 1, 2005. Officials called for a mandatory evacuation of the city, but many residents stayed in the city and had to be rescued from flooded homes and hotels and remain in the city awaiting a way out. (Associated Press Photo)

FORTHCOMING

Democracy, Crime, and Justice

Special Editors: SUSANNE KARSTEDT
and GARY LAFREE

Volume 605, May 2006

Preface

By
WILLIAM L. WAUGH JR.

Clearly there is plenty of blame to go around for the poor response to Hurricane Katrina and the problems that followed with Hurricanes Rita and Wilma. The disasters were very different in scale; the worst problems experienced with Katrina were not repeated with Rita or Wilma, but serious problems were experienced in each. The Katrina disaster does provide clear lessons on how not to deal with coastal, as well as inland, hazards and how not to respond to catastrophic disasters. Indeed, watching the Katrina disaster unfold was like watching a train wreck in slow motion. Poor planning, poor execution, and a fundamental ignorance of emergency management and disaster behavior on the parts of many policy makers at all levels cost lives and property. The communities along the Louisiana, Mississippi, and Alabama coasts were ill prepared for high winds and storm surge and unprepared to survive on their own while help was mobilized.

The media has certainly drawn attention to the destruction of the nation's capacity to deal with major disasters of all sorts since the attacks on 9/11. The myopic focus of U.S. Department of Homeland Security (DHS) officials on the threat of terrorism led to the dismantling of the Federal Emergency Management Agency (FEMA) and inattention to the more certain threat of natural hazards. FEMA has become the scapegoat for broader policy failures, and in

William L. Waugh Jr. is a professor of public administration in the Andrew Young School of Policy Studies at Georgia State University. He is the author of Living with Hazards, Dealing with Disasters (2000), Terrorism and Emergency Management (1990), and International Terrorism (1982) and coeditor of Disaster Management in the US and Canada (1996), Cities and Disaster (1990), and Handbook of Emergency Management (1990). He serves on the Certified Emergency Manager (CEM) Commission that oversees the national credential for professional emergency managers and on the Emergency Management Accreditation Program (EMAP) Commission that develops standards for and accredits state and local emergency management programs.

DOI: 10.1177/0002716205286067

the rush to fix the problems identified after Katrina, DHS officials are further damaging the nation's system for handling hazards and dealing with disasters. The need to repair the nation's emergency management system is manifest; officials should focus on some of the more obvious failures related to Katrina.

First, it is clear from the Katrina disaster that the failure to mitigate hazards long recognized within the scientific and emergency management communities led to a far larger disaster than would have otherwise resulted from a Category 3 storm. The Army Corps of Engineers, state and local emergency management officials and their FEMA counterparts, and even lay readers of *National Geographic* and *Scientific American* knew that the levee system in southern Louisiana was vulnerable and massive flooding was likely to result from a powerful hurricane. Warnings were issued to public officials years ago, and blame for the failure to reduce the risk is shared by federal, state, and local officials. Funding for levee work was shifted to other priorities, funding for an evacuation study was shifted to other programs, funding for hazard mitigation was shifted to terrorism prevention, and funding for local capacity building was shifted from the more certain natural hazards to the unnatural hazard of terrorism.

Second, an overcentralization of decision making led to long delays in mobilizing and deploying critical human and material resources. The nation's emergency management experts and the disaster relief organizations that normally deal with large-scale disasters were waiting impatiently to be called to duty. Professional emergency managers, search and rescue teams, and other first and second responders had their "go bags" and vehicles packed and ready to go. Approval to mobilize needed National Guard assets was days late. Our federal system contributed to the confusion as well. State officials provided uncertain leadership, and federal officials appeared uncertain as to their legal roles and responsibilities as critical elements in the national emergency management system. National planning was guided by a National Response Plan geared to terrorist attacks involving so-called weapons of mass destruction in which federal officials provide command and control. The plan was inappropriate in a situation in which state and local officials were in the lead.

Third, it was clear from public statements and actions that far too many of the public officials responsible for dealing with the disaster knew little or nothing about emergency management and how to use the nation's emergency management expertise; nor were they surrounded by experts in emergency management to provide advice and counsel. Statements by officials from the White House to the New Orleans city hall did not match the reality playing out in the New Orleans streets and the Superdome or in Mississippi's and Alabama's coastal communities. Assumptions concerning warnings, evacuation, sheltering, and other issues common to disasters demonstrated officials' profound ignorance and lack of leadership. The most obvious faulty assumptions and the most costly in human lives involved evacuation procedure and behavior. Professional emergency managers and disaster scholars know that mandatory evacuation seldom if ever means mandatory. As many as 20 percent of residents typically do not evacuate because they lack the means to do so or choose not to leave because of pets, nonambulatory family members, fear of losing their homes and possessions, or belief that the risk is not as great as officials contend. Ordering people to leave does not work. Evacuation has to be possible and desirable, but it will not be complete in any case. The numbers of residents left at risk should not have been a surprise.

[F]ar too many of the public officials responsible for dealing with the disaster knew little or nothing about emergency management and how to use the nation's emergency management expertise.

There were also faulty assumptions about disaster assistance roles. For example, federal officials argued that state and local officials had unreasonable expectations because the plan says that DHS aid should be ready within seventy-two to ninety-six hours. However, the administrative responsibility to act within seventy-two to ninety-six hours may fail to meet ethical, social, and political responsibilities to act immediately when lives hang in the balance. Expecting individuals and families to survive on their own resources for three or four days generally is reasonable, but it is not practical in circumstances in which victims lack the requisite knowledge and financial resources to do so. The seventy-two-hour rule needs to be shortened, or individuals and communities need to be taught better to be self-sustaining for that long. But while effective public education campaigns to encourage preparedness can reduce the numbers of victims needing rescue, some will always be unprepared to survive until help arrives. The point is that expecting most of the residents to have sufficient food and water for three days is understandable but not reasonable when many, in this case thousands, of people might be without food and water. All-hazards emergency management requires that plans be flexible and that officials adapt and improvise when necessary to save lives and property.

Fourth, failures of leadership were apparent at all levels and contributed to the chaos and resulted in a loss of public confidence. There was no one to provide a focus for the relief effort and to ensure that federal, state, and local operations were coordinated. Indeed, some officials were conspicuously unengaged. No one played the symbolic leadership role that Rudolph Giuliani played in the minutes and hours and days after the World Trade Center attacks. Our system of shared governance means that leadership should come from state, local, and national officials, rather than from a single official. In fact, hundreds of heroes and leaders among the residents and responders helped save lives in flooded and wind-damaged communities, but those charged with responsibility to lead showed little leadership. The question now is whether leadership will emerge to facilitate recovery and to ensure that the risks of similar catastrophes are addressed.

To be sure, the failures are attributable to the confluence of storm, flood, poverty, crime, and intergovernmental complexity. Poor policy decisions decades before Katrina helped elevate the levels of risk along the coastline. DHS's focus on preventing terrorist attacks since 9/11 also diverted attention from the risk of hurricanes, floods, earthquakes, and other more certain natural phenomena and the need to be prepared to deal with disasters of all sorts, including disasters caused by terrorists. And social vulnerability certainly contributed much to the nature of the disaster. Nonetheless, those are not excuses for what happened when Katrina came ashore. The issue now is how to repair the national emergency management system to restore the nation's capacity to deal with catastrophic disasters.

The articles in this volume address some of the more serious issues raised by Katrina, including the responsibility of public officials to ensure that the system works, the president's role in disasters and his role in the Katrina disaster, disaster myths and the erroneous assumptions that underlie our current programs, emergent and prosocial behavior in disasters, individual and community vulnerabilities, the sheltering and housing of very large numbers of evacuees, physical and mental health impacts of disaster, the need to manage hazardous areas better, the need to promote disaster resiliency to facilitate recovery, the need to mitigate hazards and ensure against losses, the need to develop national partnerships for disaster recovery, the need to organize emergency response and emergency management effectively to ensure agility and discipline, and the need to work effectively within the nation's federal system with its shared responsibility for homeland security and emergency management.

The Political Costs of Failure in the Katrina and Rita Disasters

By
WILLIAM L. WAUGH JR.

The Katrina and Rita disasters have raised serious questions about the capabilities of the national emergency management system to handle catastrophic disasters. The system is broken and must be repaired before the next major hurricane, earthquake, volcanic eruption, terrorist attack, or pandemic. The poor disaster responses may have serious political costs for those officials who failed to manage the hazards along the Gulf and/or failed to respond adequately to the storms—or simply appeared to be ineffectual in very dire circumstances. There have already been political casualties among the administrators responsible for managing the responses, and there may well be casualties among the politicians when voters go to the polls. The recommendation to give the military a lead responsibility in catastrophic disaster responses has been met with strong opposition; the issue may broaden the rift between governors' offices and the White House over homeland security and emergency management and broaden the gap between local emergency management imperatives and federal policies.

Keywords: disaster response; hazard mitigation; evacuation; disaster recovery; intergovernmental relations; military roles; Hurricane Katrina; Hurricane Rita

Hurricanes Katrina and Rita will leave political scars, as well as social and economic scars, on the Gulf Coast. Politicians and administrators may pay a high price for failing to deal with the disasters adequately or simply for appearing ineffectual in the days and weeks

William L. Waugh Jr. is a professor of public administration in the Andrew Young School of Policy Studies at Georgia State University. He is the author of Living with Hazards, Dealing with Disasters *(2000),* Terrorism and Emergency Management *(1990), and* International Terrorism *(1982) and a coeditor of* Disaster Management in the US and Canada *(1996),* Cities and Disaster *(1990), and* Handbook of Emergency Management *(1990). He serves on the Certified Emergency Manager (CEM) Commission that oversees the national credential for professional emergency managers and on the Emergency Management Accreditation Program (EMAP) Commission that develops standards for and accredits state and local emergency management programs.*

DOI: 10.1177/0002716205284916

after. The political repercussions from the poor disaster response are already being felt in city halls, county and parish courthouses, state legislatures, governors' offices, and Washington offices and electoral fortunes may suffer when residents have a chance to express their frustration and anger at the polls. The details of what went wrong are slowly coming to light, and those responsible for anticipating the disasters, managing the hazards, preparing for and responding to the disasters, and facilitating the recovery should be held accountable. The "blame game" is an American tradition, but so is the identification of "lessons learned" so that errors are not repeated and successes can be replicated. What went wrong, and how can we repair the nation's emergency management system before the next major hurricane, earthquake, volcanic eruption, catastrophic terrorist attack, or pandemic strikes?

Clearly, Hurricanes Katrina and Rita raise serious questions concerning the capacities of local, state, and federal governments to deal with major hazards and disasters. Obviously, we are not prepared to deal with catastrophic events, including a terrorist attack or an avian influenza pandemic. Katrina and Rita raise long-term questions concerning our capacities to mitigate hazards and deal with disasters. They also raise more immediate and practical questions concerning how to rebuild the infrastructure lost in the storms, facilitate the economic recovery of communities destroyed by the storms, and move evacuees into permanent homes. How will local, state, and federal governments help the businesses, colleges and universities, nonprofit organizations, and families struggling to survive? How will we repair the "cracks in our social foundation" (Langer 2004)—the flaws in the nation's support networks for the poor, elderly, and disabled—that were revealed by the disasters? How can we deal with the racism that contributed to the slow response to devastated African American communities (see, e.g., Gilman 2005). Do troop deployments to Iraq and Afghanistan removed critical National Guard resources that governors depend on in emergencies? What procedural and organizational flaws delayed the dispatch of emergency responders to the disaster area and delayed the delivery of water, food, trailers, and other supplies? The recovery process is also raising questions about the siting of "FEMA cities" for those who lost homes and the recruitment and housing of workers for rebuilding. Recovery, like hazard mitigation and disaster response, is a political process.

Poor implementation of emergency plans, poor communication, and poor decision processes were evident in the lack of congruence between conditions "on the ground" in the disaster areas and local, state, and national decision making. Local, state, and federal leaders appeared disconnected at best and insensitive and incompetent at worse. The news media, too, had problems finding a vantage point from which the scale of devastation could be viewed. Very large sections of the disaster area simply were not accessible to media or rescuers. Thousands of victims saw no rescuers and received no aid for a week or more after the storms passed. All the while, victims, emergency management officials, local emergency responders, and the media waited for the cavalry to arrive—and it did not. Whether reasonable or not, there was some expectation that the cavalry would arrive in helicopters with water, food, tents, and other necessities almost as soon as the storms passed. When that did not happen, Michael Brown, the director of the Federal Emergency Management Agency (FEMA), became the symbol of the failed response. But failure was evident from the city hall level to the White House (Waugh 2005a, 2005b). Indeed, Brown and his predecessor, James Lee Witt, both had warned that FEMA was no longer up to the task of dealing with major disasters because of budget cuts and personnel losses (Strohm 2005b). The critical link between the federal government and state and local emergency management offices was also broken.

Our system for dealing with disaster has to be repaired quickly, and opinions differ fundamentally on how that should be done. President Bush has recommended that the powers of the military be expanded during future catastrophic disasters (Sanger 2005) and even that the military become the nation's lead responder to catastrophic events. But there is strong opposition to "federalizing" natural disaster response and expanding the use of the military (see, for example, GovExec.com 2005). Active duty military troops have been used in past disasters, and they have been considered a critical resource when other resources are outstripped, but questions remain concerning their availability and their training to deal with disasters.

Administration experts recommend that FEMA be removed from the Department of Homeland Security (DHS) to restore its capabilities to deal with natural disasters (see, for example, Kettl 2005; Cigler 2005). It is further argued that the "command and control" orientation of DHS is ill suited to the collaborative and cooperative orientation of the nation's emergency management networks (Waugh 2003; Kettl 2005). Indeed, in many cases, federal officials and agencies interfered with state disaster responses by delaying the deployment of National Guard troops and volunteers (see, e.g., Sentell 2005; Malone 2005). Still other voices argue that the command structures be strengthened to ensure better control and coordination during future catastrophic disasters.

Ironically, following Hurricane Hugo in 1989 and Hurricane Andrew in 1992, FEMA was also criticized for being slow to mount a response. President George H. W. Bush replaced the FEMA director as coordinator of the federal disaster effort in south Florida with Andrew Card, then secretary of transportation. After the Andrew disaster, Congress considered dismantling FEMA during its reauthorization hearings. Fortunately, the agency was reinvented by the Clinton administration and became one of the federal government's biggest successes. FEMA can be reinvented once again, but it is unlikely that that can be done within DHS. The strengths of the old FEMA were in its collaborative relationships with state and local officials and its focus on building local capacities to deal with hazards and disasters. DHS has a different orientation toward public involvement and a different perception of its role in dealing with catastrophic disasters.

The Katrina and Rita disasters have focused public attention on natural and technological hazards, in addition to the threat of terrorism, and on holding public officials accountable for dealing effectively with them. The 2006 elections will show whether political costs accrue for failures during the disasters. That accountability or lack of accountability will likely determine whether the nation's emergency management system will be repaired.

Natural and Man-Made Disaster

The Hurricane Katrina disaster is the largest natural disaster in U.S. history, surpassing the Great San Francisco earthquake and firestorm of 1906 in terms of lives and property lost—and the full costs are not yet known. Like San Francisco, the city of New Orleans experienced two distinct disasters, wind and water damage caused by the hurricane and flooding caused by several levee breaks. Both disasters were in some measure man-made, although the vulnerability of San Francisco was less understood in 1906. Whether the Katrina and Rita disasters will exact the same political costs as the San Francisco disaster is uncertain as yet. After the earthquake, city officials were first cheered for their efforts and then voted from office when the corruption and incompetence of their administration was exposed.

The vulnerability of New Orleans and the Gulf Coast were certainly known well before Katrina began winding her way through the Caribbean. The hazard had been described in government reports, media stories, and academic studies. The risks were outlined in *National Geographic* magazine in October 2004 and *Scientific American* in October 2001. Federal, state, and local emergency management authorities had completed a training exercise, the Hurricane Pam simulation, a year earlier on just such a disaster. While the Pam exercise arrived at somewhat different conclusions concerning the numbers of casualties and amount of damage, the numbers showed a catastrophic event (Beriwal 2005). The scale of the disaster that would result from a real hurricane in that region was not a surprise—or, at least, it should not have been a surprise.

The hazard developed over many decades accompanied by many opportunities to address problem areas such as the levees. The risk was acknowledged periodically. Officials even warned that residents of New Orleans should keep axes in their attics so that they could cut their way through roofs if their homes were flooded. Scars remained from Hurricane Camille's impact along the same coastline in 1969. Residents of Louisiana, Mississippi, and Alabama had ample experience with strong hurricanes. But little was done to address vulnerabilities. There was too little regulation of development along the coast to mitigate wind and surge from major storms, too little investment to ensure that levees were strong enough to survive major storms, too little attention to emergency planning to help get vulnerable populations to safety, and too little attention by public officials and the public to the risk of a strong hurricane. Sorting out the blame for the loss of life and property will take decades; there will be plenty of blame to share among public officials and private individuals.

Local authorities are to blame for poor management of the levee system and poor decision making regarding mass evacuation and mass sheltering. In New Orleans, the evacuation order gave little time to move residents out of the city: two hundred school buses were left to the floodwaters rather than being used to evacuate residents, municipal workers responsible for manning pump stations were evacuated rather than kept at their posts in case of a levee break (Mulrine 2005), and the city's emergency plan was not implemented (ABC News 2005). Similar problems occurred in other jurisdictions in the path of the storm. Where there were emergency operations plans, they were not implemented or were only partially implemented. Many local emergency management and emergency response agencies were simply overwhelmed, often reduced to saving themselves or releasing personnel to save their own families.

The 2006 elections will show
whether political costs accrue for failures
during the disasters. That accountability
or lack of accountability will likely determine
whether the nation's emergency management
system will be repaired.

State officials are to blame for being slow to understand the scale of the disaster. State resources, including National Guard troops and state police, were not deployed as quickly as they might have been. Slow activation of state rescue and relief operations left local emergency managers and first responders on their own. Now state legislatures are investigating the use of the National Guard, particularly with thousands of Louisiana and Mississippi Guard and Reserve troops deployed to Afghanistan and Iraq, and the adequacy of local mass evacuation and other emergency plans.

Federal authorities are to blame for the slow response to state requests for aid and for their reactive posture. Warnings of the impending disaster were given to Secretary Chertoff and top FEMA officials days before Katrina made landfall (Sullivan 2005). Nonetheless, federal officials waited for the states to request aid rather than proactively assisting their state and local counterparts. While Governor Blanco of Louisiana requested federal assistance well before the storm and the levee breaches, assistance was days away. Once the need to act was realized, the federal agencies were slow to deliver aid to victims stranded in New Orleans and other communities, slow to rescue those trapped in homes and hospitals, slow to recover bodies, and slow to deliver trailers to disaster area. Senator Lott of Mississippi complained that twenty thousand trailers were held up in Atlanta waiting for contractors to move them to Mississippi and Louisiana (CNN 2005a). Hundreds of volunteer emergency response and medical personnel were waiting in frustration to be deployed by federal officials.

The networks of local, state, and federal agencies and nongovernmental organizations that make up the national emergency management system were also in disarray. Some agencies, including the American Red Cross, were dissuaded from responding quickly to the disaster because of safety and security concerns. Volunteers were encouraged to wait for officials to ask them to deploy and indicate where the greatest needs were. Some volunteers waited weeks for the call to deploy, even those trained and used by FEMA during the Florida hurricanes in 2004.

Clearly, the national system failed to function as it must, resulting in human and economic costs. More than a thousand people died; bodies are still being found months after the disasters. In the weeks after the storm, problems were evident in the Katrina recovery effort and again when Hurricane Rita made landfall in Louisiana and Texas and Hurricane Wilma made landfall in south Florida. The news media began to focus on the potential for even more calamitous events as Hurricane Victor hit south of the United States and Hurricanes Alpha and Beta passed east of the mainland. Had a major earthquake or a major terrorist attack struck during those weeks, the capacities of the federal government to support emergency response might have been overwhelmed, just as local capacities were overwhelmed by Katrina.

For a time, it appeared that the losses from Katrina would be much worse. Estimates of casualties were in the thousands and FEMA had ordered twenty-five thousand body bags. Estimates of the time to drain floodwaters from New Orleans were from several to many months. Similarly, the potential for Rita to hit Galveston raised the specter of a megadisaster like the 1900 storm that killed as many as eight thousand people. Rita could have been much worse. However, estimates of the economic costs of the storms have grown. The extent of social-psychological damage is still uncertain.

Slow and Disorganized Response

In the hours and days that followed Hurricane Katrina's landfall, more and more attention focused on the slow and inadequate disaster response. The evident lack of understanding of the function and role of emergency management by public officials at all levels was painfully obvious to those within the emergency management professional and disaster research communities. Media criticism focused on FEMA, whereas professional and academic communities largely criticized its parent organization, DHS, and the media. It was frustrating to watch the disaster unfold and to see officials fail to identify and address problems that were obvious to those who understand disasters and emergency response. The news coverage also failed to present a complete picture of the disaster. The coverage did identify some major issues that needed to be addressed, but it also focused too closely on looting and violence. The extent of the violence now appears to have been grossly overblown (Kinney 2005) and, in fact, may have diverted law enforcement and military personnel from rescue to security operations (Pierre and Gerhart 2005).

Much is now known about why the response to Katrina was so inadequate. But questions remain concerning decision processes prior to, during, and soon after the disaster began. Congressional committees are sorting through e-mail messages, documents, public statements, and other materials to determine the timelines for local, state, and federal responses. Committees are examining the more obvious failures to move resources to the disaster areas quickly and focusing on such problems as FEMA's poor resource inventory system. While partisan differences are driving some of the investigations and coloring some of the analyses, there appears to be consensus on some of the basic problems.

Confusion over state and federal roles was a major problem. Homeland Security officials were reluctant to be as proactive as they might be for fear of violating the authority of state officials. State officials were confused by the new federal procedures and structures for dealing with major emergencies and disasters. The National Response Plan (NRP) was newly adopted and not widely understood. The new National Incident Management System (NIMS) was not fully implemented and is not widely understood.

In many respects, the poor emergency response by local, state, and federal agencies was due to the sheer scale of the disaster. Roads were impassable along the coast due to debris and flooding, bridges and roads were destroyed by storm surge and wind, and victims were scattered among and between the hundreds of communities that were in the path of the storm. Access to the disaster area was extremely difficult in many areas and impossible in some. Downed power lines posed risks to those attempting to access or leave the disaster area. Rescue and relief operations were delayed by water and debris and by reports of violence (Pierre and Gerhart 2005). The fact that some communities were not reached for a week or more speaks to the poor preparedness efforts by state and federal authorities. Such delays are not uncommon during major hurricane and earthquake disasters, however, and in fact, some communities in central Florida were not reached quickly during the 2004 hurricanes and during Hurricane Wilma.

The unexpectedly large number of people needing assistance during and immediately following the levee breaches in New Orleans revealed a clear "preparedness divide" (Light 2005), with a very large poor population lacking the resources necessary to evacuate and to survive even a day or two without aid. The debacle in New Orleans revealed, according to Der Spiegel, "America's Dark Underbelly" (Hornig 2005), the large and increasing percentage of poor people in the United States and the underlying racial conflicts associated with poverty and discrimination. Ironically, a report on the increasing poverty in the United States was issued the day that Katrina turned the spotlight on the problem in New Orleans.

Professional emergency managers understand that roughly 80 percent of residents typically respond to evacuation orders. The remaining residents do not have the necessary resources to evacuate, are not mobile enough to evacuate, are caregivers who remain to take care of family members, are unwilling to leave pets or their homes and possessions, or do not believe that the risk is great enough to warrant leaving. Some may not hear or understand the evacuation orders, particularly those who are homeless and are not reached by the media or by emergency warning systems. Some may not understand English. Some may not believe the officials who issue the warnings and order evacuation. When they do evacuate, many do not have the medicines they need under normal circumstances, and many more do not have sufficient medicine to get by for days without assistance. In short, there should always be an expectation that a significant percentage of the residents will not respond to evacuation orders—even mandatory evacuation orders—and an expectation that a significant percentage will need assistance immediately. By contrast, emergency management and Homeland Security officials want individuals and families to have "seventy-two-hour kits" with at least three days' worth of food and water, flashlights, radios, and other essentials. In reality, many Americans live from day to day and do not have the wherewithal to keep three days' worth of food, let alone other supplies, in reserve. In short, expecting emergency responders to arrive as soon as the storm has passed may be unreasonable, but expecting all residents to have three days' worth of supplies is also unreasonable. The desperation among the victims stranded in the Superdome and in neighborhoods in New Orleans became an embarrassment to the nation, but similar situations developed in other communities in Louisiana and Mississippi without receiving the same media coverage. The situation should have been anticipated.

In other respects, the poor emergency response reflected the incomplete implementation of the NRP and the NIMS. The Federal Response Plan (FRP) guided national disaster responses through much of the 1990s and also guided the response to the World Trade Center and Pentagon attacks in 2001. Under FRP, FEMA served as the coordinator of federal response activities, able to call upon twenty-six federal agencies, including the American Red Cross, to provide everything from emergency shelter to unemployment counseling. The presumption was that state and local authorities would be the lead and FEMA would coordinate closely to support their relief efforts. Nongovernmental organizations from the Salvation Army to Pet Rescue served to expand resources to deal with large catastrophes and to address problems that might not be addressed adequately by government agencies (Waugh 2003).

With the creation of the DHS, the role of FEMA changed. No longer a cabinet-level agency, FEMA is dependent upon DHS officials for its budget, spending priorities, and mission priorities. The FEMA budget shrank, FEMA personnel and resources were shifted to counterterrorism programs, and the morale of FEMA personnel suffered (CNN 2005b). The agency is effectively being dismantled with its constituent parts being moved to other parts of DHS. DHS itself is focused on preventing terrorist attacks and is not organized to deal with natural disasters or even terrorist-caused disasters (Waugh and Sylves 2002; Waugh 2005b).

Under the Emergency Management Assistance Compact (EMAC), more than thirty-one thousand personnel were loaned by more than a dozen states for search and rescue, law enforcement, biomedical waste management, firefighting, communications, and other functions. EMAC is a nationwide compact among states administered by the National Emergency Management Association, an association of state emergency management directors, to share resources in major disasters (EMAC 2005). More than seventy-five hundred federal volunteers were enlisted in the response and recovery effort. Michael Brown, director of FEMA, requested two thousand DHS volunteers on August 29 (Pulliam 2005). FEMA has drawn upon volunteers from its own offices, as well as from other federal agencies, in the past and continues to do so. The Medical Reserve Corps and other volunteer groups were also used in the Katrina and Rita responses but, like other volunteers, were only slowly integrated into the relief effort.

Ironically, a report on the increasing poverty in the United States was issued the day that Katrina turned the spotlight on the problem in New Orleans.

The situation along the Mississippi and Alabama coasts did not seem as dire as that in New Orleans, but that was due to the lack of news coverage. Rescue came late to many communities. Emergency supplies reached the rural areas much later than Biloxi, Mobile, and the coastal towns. Local emergency managers were overwhelmed, isolated, with few resources to provide to their residents and the evacuees from the worst-hit areas. Some local emergency management agencies had no food and water for their own personnel.

The slow state and federal response efforts, inadequacy of local resources, limited availability of National Guard troops, and lack of communication within and without their communities contributed to the frustration of local officials. Both Louisiana and Mississippi have large numbers of National Guard and Reserve personnel deployed in Iraq and Afghanistan compared with other states. Close to four thousand Louisiana National Guard and Reserve troops and more than fifty-two hundred Mississippi National Guard and Reserve troops, including many from the communities devastated by Hurricanes Katrina and Rita, were deployed during the disaster (U.S. Department of Defense 2005). Texas's deployment was large, as well. The Guard and Reserves have been vital resources during major disasters, and that was no less true during the Katrina and Rita disasters. By September 4, thirty-five thousand National Guard personnel were involved, and by September 11, fifty thousand National Guard and twenty thousand active-duty personnel became involved in the disaster operation—some under state control and some under federal control (Kitfield 2005). However, the Guard lacked up-to-date communications equipment and had insufficient numbers of trucks, inadequate engineering equipment, and few other resources because of deployments to Iraq and

Afghanistan. National Guard units were using Vietnam-era communications equipment (Moniz 2005).

"FEMA City" Politics and Redevelopment

In Louisiana and Mississippi, restoration of lifelines has been faster than expected, for the most part, although restoration of power has been slow in some areas. Long-term recovery is just getting under way and may take many years. In Louisiana, Governor Blanco appointed an advisory commission, the Louisiana Recovery Authority, to help set priorities for dealing with the 1.5 million Louisianans displaced by Hurricanes Katrina and Rita, eighty-one thousand businesses affected, and two hundred thousand homes destroyed. Tax incentives, more stringent building codes, levee management, takeover of the Orleans Parrish school system, and a comprehensive coastal and hurricane plan have been the major agenda items for the governor and the Louisiana legislature (Alford 2005; Millhollow 2005). Mayor Nagin of New Orleans created a similar commission, and the state and city commissions have established links to facilitate communication (Koppel 2005). However, there are signs that partisan differences may delay the redevelopment effort. Gambling has been a major revenue source for Mississippi, and recovery depends on rebuilding the casinos and reducing their vulnerability to storms. State officials have suggested changes in state law to permit the casinos to be rebuilt on the shoreline, rather than offshore; that suggestion has been met with considerable opposition from those who oppose casinos altogether. Because of the risk in future storms, owners may be reluctant to rebuild their floating casinos because of increased insurance costs.

Recommendations range from rebuilding communities much as they were prior to the disaster to not rebuilding large parts of New Orleans at all to moving most of the development away from the coastlines in Louisiana, Mississippi, and Alabama (see, e.g., Jacob 2005; Dean 2005). Moving to higher ground north of Lake Pontchartrain has been recommended. Buying out those areas most vulnerable to flooding and returning them to marshland has been suggested. Moving port facilities and other industrial facilities further up the Mississippi and away from the Gulf has been suggested. Better land-use planning is a frequent suggestion. The levees are being evaluated to determine how they may be strengthened. Some answers may come from those evaluations, particularly if the cost to strengthen levees is extremely high.

Questions still remain concerning the long-term housing of evacuees, including the use of hotels and motels, apartments, temporary shelters, and dispersed FEMA trailers. The creation of new "FEMA cities" of trailers has been opposed by many communities. Those engaged in rebuilding need temporary housing. Controversy is growing over recruitment of workers from elsewhere, including Mexico, rather than from among New Orleans's displaced workers. The demographic composition of the city is certain to change as many evacuees have said that they do not plan to return. Forty-four percent of those surveyed in Houston shelters in September 2005 said that they plan to relocate permanently, with the overwhelming majority saying that they plan to remain in Houston or elsewhere in Texas (*Washington Post*, Kaiser Family Foundation, and Harvard University 2005). While plans may change, it is likely that many will not return to their hometowns in Louisiana and Mississippi.

Questions also remain concerning the long-term employment of evacuees, including providing housing and employment during the rebuilding of New Orleans and coastal communities and the long-term revitalization of New Orleans and other devastated coastal communities. Rebuilding tax bases is necessary to restore local public services and finance redevelopment. State and local officials are pushing for more use of local resources to rebuild, including contracting with local firms for the rebuilding of schools and infrastructure. Local control or at least direction of recovery is certain to become a contentious political issue and one that will afford local officials opportunity to provide leadership.

Concluding Observations

Hurricane Katrina caused the worst disaster in American history, and Hurricane Rita contributed to the dislocations of residents, loss of property, and disaster response problems. Extensive damage was done to property along the Gulf Coast by storm surge and wind. The scale of the Katrina disaster was such that extraordinary efforts were necessary to preserve life. New Orleans escaped the worst of Katrina's wind and water, but breaches in the levees caused flooding that inundated most of the city. Coastal communities in Alabama, Mississippi, and Louisiana were devastated. The infrastructure along the coastline was severely damaged.

State and local emergency management programs were not up to the tasks of evacuating residents, sheltering and feeding those that remained, conducting search and rescue operations, and initiating the recovery effort. In many cases, local emergency services were not just overwhelmed, they were wiped out. Local first responders, like their neighbors, were struggling to stay alive and, like their neighbors, were often without food or water.

The assumptions upon which local, state, and federal disaster responses were based were seriously flawed. A large percentage of the affected population was much more vulnerable than officials assumed. Poverty and racial distrust complicated the disaster and the response. Confusion over local and state emergency operations plans complicated the evacuations and everything that followed. The New Orleans emergency plan was not implemented. State officials requested federal aid early in anticipation of a catastrophic disaster but were slow to deploy their own resources. Hurricane Rita made landfall along the Texas-Louisiana border, further damaging communities hit by Katrina in Louisiana and precipitating a mass evacuation of residents along the Texas and Louisiana coasts. The evacuation of Houston and neighboring towns revealed serious problems not anticipated in the disaster planning, such as the limited availability of gasoline along the major routes.

Evacuees from the Katrina disaster were again threatened by a major hurricane and joined by a new group of evacuees.

Confusion over the federal role also complicated the responses. The NRP was not activated for the Katrina and Rita disasters, and indeed, it was not activated for the Wilma disaster in Florida weeks later. Poor communication made it difficult for federal, as well as state and local, officials to understand the needs of victims in the disaster area. The expectation that federal resources would not be needed for seventy-two to ninety-six hours was disastrously wrong. The scale of the disaster and the vulnerability of the population required a much faster response.

This might have been the first test of the NRP, had it been activated. It was a test of the ad hoc approach to disaster response that DHS used during the Florida hurricanes in the fall of 2004. In Florida, there was strong incentive to respond swiftly and to return evacuees to their communities as soon as possible because of the election. As many resources as could be found were deployed. Still, serious problems resulted from DHS personnel being unfamiliar with disaster response procedures and unwilling to deal with the media or residents. The lack of access to many communities in central Florida for days after the storms passed was very similar to the experiences in Louisiana, Mississippi, Alabama, and Texas after Katrina and Rita.

There are still active investigations of the disaster assistance provided to areas minimally affected by the hurricanes. An ad hoc response is inadequate in catastrophic and even lesser disasters. The national emergency management system involves networks of local, state, and federal emergency management agencies; nongovernmental disaster relief organizations; private sector organizations; community groups; and volunteers. These networks deal with ordinary and extraordinary disasters and represent the nation's surge capacity in catastrophic disasters. Effective coordination is critical and was lacking from state and federal officials during the Katrina disaster. In some cases, officials interfered with the response by nongovernmental organizations and volunteers.

The response by state and local officials to President Bush's suggestion that the U.S. military assume responsibility for catastrophic disaster responses was quick and unequivocal. The governors of Washington, Mississippi, Michigan, Arkansas, West Virginia, Delaware, and Alabama have criticized the suggestion as a usurpation of state authority (Gouras 2005). The governors of Florida and Arizona criticized the suggestion in testimony before Congress, and the National Governors Association has voiced the objections of its members (Strohm 2005a). In fact, Governor Jeb Bush of Florida accepted the blame for a slow response to Hurricane Wilma after telling federal officials that the state would take responsibility for delivering supplies to storm victims in south Florida (Anderson 2005). The National Emergency Management Association, which is the professional organization for state emergency management directors, has also voiced its opposition. By contrast, the U.S. Conference of Mayors has recommended an expanded military role in disaster response so that cities can have access to military assets earlier and expressed frustration with the slowness with which states have been providing funding to local governments (Wodele 2005). In fact, an annex to the NRP, the Catastrophic Incident Annex, might have been activated to give federal officials authority to respond without state approval (Strohm 2005a), but there are serious concerns about conflicts with state authority. Opposition to President Bush's recommendation concerning the use of the military may well encourage opposition to other recommendations that have extended federal authority over state assets, such as recent recommendations to close Air Guard bases that have roles in state disaster operations (Schmitt 2005).

If Katrina and Rita are to be learning experiences that will reduce the potential for similar response failures, access to information is essential, and an independent analysis of the responses is absolutely essential.

Local officials also are acting on their own to address their own communities' hazards and to prepare their own residents in the absence of effective federal plans and policies. The Katrina disaster has forced state and local officials to examine the potential for catastrophic disaster in their own communities. California officials are concerned about levee breaks and earthquakes; Seattle officials are concerned about vulnerabilities to earthquakes; Montana, Idaho, and Wyoming officials are concerned about an eruption of the Yellowstone volcano; Utah officials are concerned about vulnerabilities to earthquakes; and so on (Murphy 2005). Local and state officials have a political, legal, and ethical obligation to address the hazards that pose serious risk to their own communities, regardless of the priorities of the federal government. There are political costs and, for local officials, potential legal costs that might be exacted if they fail to prepare for and respond adequately to a disaster. A means of addressing the risk of legal liability and mitigating potential political costs is adherence to accepted national standards. In emergency management, the standards for professional development can be found in the Certified Emergency Manager (CEM) program. The CEM is the national credential for professional emergency managers. It is earned by those who have the requisite education, training, experience, and involvement in emergency management. Requirements include breadth of experience, knowledge of emergency management roles and functions, and knowledge of management techniques. At the programmatic level, National Fire Protection Association (NFPA) 1600 has been acknowledged by Congress, the 9-11 Commission, and other bodies as the accepted international standards for emergency management programs. The

Emergency Management Accreditation Program (EMAP) operationalizes and expands the NFPA standards for state and local emergency management programs. The EMAP standards affirm that emergency management programs include the public agencies, nongovernmental organizations, and businesses that constitute the capabilities of states and communities to deal with disasters (Bentley and Waugh 2005). These programs provide benchmarks for professional emergency managers and emergency management programs to ensure that they have the tools to manage risks and to deal with disasters. Interestingly, of the states affected by Hurricanes Katrina, Rita, and Wilma, Florida has the only accredited emergency management program, and it demonstrated its capabilities, albeit with some difficulty, during the 2004 hurricanes and the Wilma disaster.

Sorting out responsibility for the Katrina debacle and problems with the Rita response may be difficult. Congress is having problems getting information from DHS on communications between the department, FEMA, and the White House leading up to, during, and after Katrina's landfall. Similar problems in getting information from DHS were experienced by the 9-11 Commission (Strohm 2005c), and the Government Accountability Office and the Congressional Research Service have also had difficulty extracting responses from DHS (see, e.g., Waugh forthcoming; Strohm 2005c). If Katrina and Rita are to be learning experiences that will reduce the potential for similar response failures, access to information is essential, and an independent analysis of the responses is absolutely essential.

If lessons are not drawn from the Katrina and Rita experiences, corrections will not be made. If officials are not given incentives to repair the national emergency management system, little will be done. For the officials who failed to address the hazards and/or failed to respond adequately, there may be serious political costs. For the communities that fail to mitigate hazards to reduce the likelihood of similar disasters, there may also be serious political and economic costs. The hurricanes have provided a "window of opportunity," and that "window" will begin to close as the memories of the disasters fade.

References

ABC News. 2005. Who's to blame for delayed response to Katrina? September 6. ABCNews.go.com (accessed September 12, 2005).

Alford, Jeremy. 2005. Louisiana lawmakers begin special session on rebuilding. *The New York Times*, November 7. www.nytimes.com (accessed November 7, 2005).

Anderson, Curt. 2005. Gov. Bush takes blame for slow Wilma aid. Yahoo!News, October 26. http://news.yahoo.com (accessed October 27, 2005).

Bentley, Emily, and William L. Waugh. 2005. Katrina and the need for standards in emergency management. *Journal of Emergency Management* 3 (September/October): 3-4.

Beriwal, Madhu. 2005. Hurricanes Pam and Katrina: A lesson in disaster planning. *Natural Hazards Observer*, November, pp. 8-9.

Cigler, Beverly. 2005. FEMA, Homeland Security may need a divorce. CentreDaily.com, October 31. www.centredaily.com (accessed November 7, 2005).

CNN. 2005a. Cut the red tape, Lott says. CNN.com, September 5. www.cnn.com (accessed September 5, 2005).

———. 2005b. A disturbing view from inside FEMA. CNN.com, September 18. www.cnn.com (accessed November 10, 2005).

Dean, Cornelia. 2005. Some experts say it's time to evacuate the coast (for good). *The New York Times*, October 4. www.nytimes.com (accessed October 10, 2005).

EMAC. 2005. Emergency Management Assistance Compact. www.emacweb.org (accessed November 10, 2005).

Gilman, Mils. 2005. What Katrina teaches about the meaning of racism. In *Understanding Katrina: Perspectives from the social sciences*. October. Social Science Research Council. http://understandingkatrina .ssrc.org/Gilman/pf/ (accessed October 11, 2005).

Gouras, Matt. 2005. Governors chafe at greater military role. AP Wire Service, November 4.

GovExec.com. 2005. House leader: Keep feds out of disaster response. GovExec.com, September 26. www.govexec.com (accessed September 28, 2005).

Hornig, Frank. 2005. Katrina fallout: America's dark underbelly. *Der Spiegel*, September 12. www.spiegel.de/ international/spiegel/0,1518,374199,00.html (accessed September 12, 2005).

Jacob, Klaus. 2005. Time for a tough question: Why rebuild? WashingtonPost.com, September 6. www.washingtonpost.com (accessed September 8, 2005).

Kettl, Donald F. 2005. The worst is yet to come: Lessons from September 11 and Hurricane Katrina. Report 05-01. September. Philadelphia: University of Pennsylvania, Fels Government Research Service.

Kinney, Aaron. 2005. Exaggerated stories of hurricane chaos in New Orleans. *Der Spiegel*, October 25. www.spiegel.de/international/0,1518,381618.html (accessed October 26, 2005).

Kitfield, James. 2005. Poor communications slowed military's hurricane response. GovExec.com, September 19. www.govexec.com (accessed October 10, 2005).

Koppel, Lily. 2005. Louisiana governor, under fire, appoints an advisory panel. *The New York Times*, October 18. www.nytimes.com (accessed November 18, 2005).

Langer, Nieli. 2004. Natural disasters that reveal cracks in our social foundation. *Educational Gerontology* 30:275-85.

Light, Paul C. 2005. Homeland Security's extreme makeover. *Christian Science Monitor*, October 12, p. 9.

Malone, Julia. 2005. Disaster help ignored by feds. *Atlanta Journal-Constitution*, November 11, pp. G1, G4.

Millhollow, Michelle. 2005. Session's agenda extensive: Lawmakers feared lack of key issues. 2theadvocate.com, November 2. www.2theadvocate.com (accessed November 2, 2005).

Moniz, Dave. 2005. Guard relief hurt by obsolete equipment. *USA Today*, October 10. http://usatoday.com (accessed October 10, 2005).

Mulrine, Anna. 2005. Lots of blame. USNews.com, September 19. www.usnews.com (accessed September 19, 2005).

Murphy, Dean E. 2005. Storms put focus on other disasters in waiting. *The New York Times*, November 15. www.nytimes.com (accessed November 15, 2005).

Pierre, Robert E., and Ann Gerhart. 2005. News of pandemonium may have slowed aid. *The Washington Post*, October 5. www.washingtonpost.com (accessed October 10, 2005).

Pulliam, Daniel. 2005. Thousands of volunteer feds staff Katrina relief effort. GovExec.com, November 4. www.govexec.com (accessed November 9, 2005).

Sanger, David E. 2005. Bush wants to consider broadening of military's powers during natural disasters. *The New York Times*, September 27. www.nytimes.com (accessed September 27, 2005).

Schmitt, Eric. 2005. States opposing plan to shutter Air Guard bases. *The New York Times*, August 11. www.nytimes.com (accessed August 11, 2005).

Sentell, Will. 2005. Guard's Katrina response questioned. 2theadvocate.com, November 2. www.2advocate .com (accessed November 2, 2005).

Strohm, Chris. 2005a. DHS failed to use Catastrophic Response Plan in Katrina's wake. GovExec.com, October 18. www.govexec.com (accessed October 19, 2005).

———. 2005b. Former FEMA director says agency was gutted. GovExec.com, September 27. www .govexec.com (accessed September 28, 2005).

———. 2005c. Lawmakers threaten subpoenas for Katrina-related documents. GovExec.com, November 2. www.govexec.com (accessed November 9, 2005).

Sullivan, Laura. 2005. Katrina: FEMA official says agency heads ignored warnings. National Public Radio Web site, September 16. www.npr.org (accessed September 26, 2005).

U.S. Department of Defense. 2005. National Guard and Reserve units called to active duty. August 24. www.defenselink.mil/news/aug2005/d20050824ngr.pdf (accessed November 9, 2005).

Washington Post, Kaiser Family Foundation, and Harvard University. 2005. *Survey of Hurricane Katrina evacuees*. September. http://www.kff.org/newsmedia/upload/7401.pdf.

Waugh, William L., Jr. 2003. Terrorism, homeland security, and the national emergency management network. *Public Organization Review* 3:373-85.

———. 2005a. The disaster that was Katrina. *Natural Hazards Observer*, November, pp. 7-8.

———. 2005b. Katrina, Rita, and all-hazards emergency management. *Journal of Emergency Management* 3 (September/October): 1-2.

———. Forthcoming. Terrorism as disaster. In *Handbook of disaster research*, ed. Havidan Rodriguez, E. L. Quarantelli, and Russell Dynes. New York: Springer.

Waugh, William L., Jr., and Richard T. Sylves. 2002. Organizing the war on terrorism. *Public Administration Review* 62 (September): 145-53.

Wodele, Greta. 2005. Mayors' group urges bigger military role in emergency response. GovExec.com, October 24. www.govexec.com (accessed October 27, 2005).

President Bush and Hurricane Katrina: A Presidential Leadership Study

RICHARD T. SYLVES

Hurricane Katrina raised many concerns about presidential management of megadisasters. President George W. Bush has been criticized, and has personally accepted blame, for the failures and shortcomings of governmental response to this disaster. This work draws from government documents and public affairs information to analyze the facts of the event, the policies and organizational alignments in place before the disaster, and the president's performance. This study concludes that how presidents lead, manage federal officials, cope with the news media, address federal-state relations, set the boundaries of civil-military relations, define their policy agendas, and choose political appointees for responsible posts all contribute to their ability, or inability, to address the demands imposed by disasters and catastrophes. In some respects, political, policy, and managerial decisions made by the president and his administration before the disaster seriously impeded the federal government's ability to mitigate, prepare for, and respond to the catastrophe.

Keywords: presidential disaster declarations; catastrophes; incidents of national significance; Hurricane Katrina; Hurricane Wilma; civil-military relations; presidency studies; disaster response; disaster preparedness; national security

"Presidency studies" involves analysis of presidential power and attempts to understand the process of presidential policy making. Many tools of social science have been applied to the study of the presidency, including psychological theories, decision theory, organizational behavior models, sophisticated econometric techniques,

Richard T. Sylves is a professor of political science and senior policy fellow, Center for Energy and Environmental Policy, University of Delaware. He authored The Nuclear Oracles *(1986) and coedited* Cities and Disaster *(1990) and* Disaster Management in the U.S and Canada *(1996). He has conducted funded research with U.S. FEMA, NOAA Sea Grant, and the Public Entity Risk Institute. He is an adviser to the Emergency Management Accreditation Program; was on a National Academy of Science (NAS) panel, "Estimating the Costs of Natural Disasters"; and was a member of the NAS Disasters Roundtable.*

DOI: 10.1177/0002716205286066

26

ANNALS, *AAPSS*, 604, March 2006

historical analysis, and survey research. This study takes a public policy analysis, organizational management, and leadership study approach toward the subject of the Bush administration's handling of Hurricane Katrina and its effects.

Bush and Katrina: The President as Executive

When presidents decide on whether to approve governor requests for declarations of disaster, they have an opportunity to make or shape public policy. For example, since 1950 presidents from Harry S. Truman to George W. Bush have been able to use presidential disaster declaration authority to press forward their respective political ideology on matters of federal-state relations (Sylves and Waugh 1996; Platt 1999). They have been able to do this subtly on a case-by-case basis or overtly after a megadisaster that demands an improved government response.

An example of an overt response would be, for example, how President George W. Bush responded to the 9/11 terror attack by using his executive powers. He used his executive powers to develop his administration's homeland security policy, chiefly through a series of Homeland Security Presidential Directives and by making senior appointments to public management posts integral to homeland security.

An example of a policy change made subtly is the following: in the weeks after Hurricane Katrina in 2005, owing to the displacement of thousands of New Orleans flood victims to other states, President George W. Bush took the unprecedented step of granting presidential disaster declarations to states that hosted Katrina evacuees, even states that had no actual disaster damage from Katrina (U.S. Federal Emergency Management Agency [FEMA] 2005).

President Bush and his administration have made changes in presidential declaration decision making in the months and years after the 9/11 attacks. The administration was pressed to do so by the *9/11 Commission Report* (2004). For example, a new term, "incidents of national significance," now encompasses major disasters or emergencies declared by the president (U.S. Department of Homeland Security [DHS] 2004, 8-9). Incidents of National Significance under the National Response Plan (NRP) are defined as "an actual or potential high-impact event that requires coordination of Federal, State, local, tribal, nongovernmental and/or private sector entities in order to save lives and minimize damage" (DHS 2004, ix). According to the Final Draft of the NRP, issued June 30, 2004, the DHS secretary "can use limited pre-declaration authorities to move initial response resources . . . closer to a potentially affected area" (DHS 2004, 9).

Catastrophic incidents and national security

The NRP adds a new category of incident beyond major disaster and emergency. "Catastrophic incidents" are "any natural or manmade incident, including terrorism, which results in extraordinary levels of mass casualties, damage, or disruption severely affecting the population, infrastructure, environment, economy, and national morale and/or government functions. A catastrophic event could result in sustained national impacts over a prolonged period of time; almost immediately exceeds resources normally available to State, local, tribal, and private sector authorities; and significantly interrupts governmental operations and emergency services to such an extent that national security could be threatened. All catastrophic incidents are considered Incidents of National Significance" (DHS 2004, x).

September 11, 2001, enhanced presidential power, and President Bush took advantage of this to advance his policy of homeland security.

In other words, owing to Bush administration initiatives, presidential declaration authority now concedes openly that disasters may have catastrophic consequences that affect the entire nation, and so presidents may now declare incidents as catastrophes. "All-hazards" emergency management remains a tenet of federal emergency management, but in the past, "all-hazards" meant terrorism was one of many possible agents of disaster or emergency. Today, federal emergency management is predicated on terrorism as a paramount threat while other types of disasters or emergencies occupy diminished positions within the federal emergency management and homeland security community (see Waugh and Sylves 2002).

Since 1950, natural and nonterror human-caused disasters, with the notable exception of civil defense against nuclear attack, were rarely considered matters of national security. Owing to the 9/11 terror attacks, the Bush administration, with the assent of Congress, defined presidential disaster declaration authority as a national security instrument and secondarily as an instrument of federal emergency management. Most of the governmental changes made in response to 9/11 have significantly increased the president's range of authority.

Numerous studies have been published of presidential declarations of major disaster before 2001 (Settle 1990; Sylves 1996; Dymon and Platt 1999; Platt 1999). Since 2001, Relyea has crafted an excellent study regarding the history of presidential emergency powers and the legislative and reorganization issues surrounding formation of the Department of Homeland Security in his "Organizing for Homeland Security" (2003). Presidential disaster declarations interlace many features of federal emergency management. A presidential declaration of major disaster or emergency typically activates the National Response Plan and puts various federal, state, and local agencies to work under the National Incident Management System (NIMS).

The Homeland Security Act of 2002, related laws, and a series of Presidential Homeland Security Directives have forced other changes to both FEMA and the domestic and international world of emergency management. American emergency managers must now learn more about disasters and emergencies outside the United States (Nicholson 2005; Bullock et al. 2005). President Bush has emphasized that the globalization of terror makes this necessary given the disappearance of what was after all an imaginary line between terror attacks on Americans at home and terror attacks on Americans, and American interests, outside the United States. Fewer distinctions are made now between terror attacks inside the United States committed by Americans (e.g., Timothy McVeigh's attack on the Murrah Building in Oklahoma City in 1995) and terror attacks inside America but with origins outside the United States (e.g., Islamic fundamentalist terror attacks on the World Trade Center [WTC] in 1993 and on the WTC and Pentagon in 2001).

The 9/11 disaster centralized presidential authority, as did many previous catastrophic disasters (Kettl 2004). Lawmakers, spurred on by the threat of major terror-caused national crises, granted the president greater powers they believed were needed to address the problems posed by the crises. The president, acting on this opportunity, developed new forms of emergency management authority for his office. President Bush used his presidential declaration decision-making authority to subsume "major disasters" and "emergencies" under the terms "incidents" or "incidents of national significance." This conflated the official definition of disaster (natural or human caused) with any president-perceived threat to the nation. Because the president and his DHS/FEMA officials now label major disasters and emergencies of any type as "incidents of national significance," emergency management is today very much a matter of "national security." The president in effect recruited federal emergency management into the "war on terrorism."

However, the president cannot have missed the significance of Katrina's aftermath; Bush and future presidents facing natural megadisasters may be tempted to federalize the government's response to these megaevents under presidential declarations of "catastrophic disaster." While the Stafford Act of 1988—a measure that set forth modern presidential disaster declaration authority—remains law, the processes by which the president and FEMA/DHS consider governor requests for declarations of major disaster and emergency and the nature of what constitutes a disaster agent have been altered. Most of these changes reflect a preoccupation with homeland security, and this had had ramifications at the state and local levels (explored later in this study).

Hurricane Katrina, like 9/11, represents an epiphenomenon. Katrina may well be the nation's first $100-billion-plus federal payout disaster. The president has suggested that the Katrina recovery may cost as much as $200 billion. However, history shows that presidents tend to demand more spending authority than they actually need to address a megadisaster so that unused spending authority may permit them (via the President's Disaster Trust Fund) to pay federal relief costs of other, subsequent disasters (Sylves 1996).

Political scientist Hugh Heclo (1977) once declared, "How the government performs can be thought of as the product of political leadership times bureaucratic power." At least five general factors contribute to bureaucratic power and shape the pattern of presidential-bureaucratic relations: "the size, complexity, and the dispersion of executive branch power; bureaucratic inertia and momentum; the personnel of the executive branch; the legal position of the executive branch; and the susceptibility of executive branch units to external political power" (Thomas, Pika, and Watson 1993, 239). President Bush, originally an opponent of the proposal to form DHS, has had to cope with the size, complexity, and dispersion of power within DHS. DHS is a mammoth, complex, and organizationally diffuse federal bureaucracy that was less than two years old when Katrina struck. Since 2003, DHS, first headed by former governor Tom Ridge and then by attorney Michael Chertoff, has been put through many reorganizations, president-sanctioned, that have in some ways compromised its ability to manage very large-scale, multistate disasters. President Bush has been extremely successful in appointing highly politically loyal people to senior positions in DHS. Congress, and other outside sources of political power, have until recently been highly deferential to the president's homeland security wishes. To close this section, one needs to understand that September 11, 2001, enhanced presidential power, and President Bush took advantage of this to advance his policy of homeland security. As chief executive, he was able to supervise, and even propose, how the DHS would be formed, what would be included within it, what powers it would have, and who would direct DHS and its constituent parts.

Bush and Katrina: The Presidential Management of Bureaucracy

One of the president's major responsibilities is management of the executive branch of government and many departments and agencies therein. From April 1989 to March 2003, FEMA was an independent agency. Owing to an initiative of President Clinton, the FEMA director was accorded de facto cabinet status for almost eight years. FEMA's cabinet status ended in 2003 when FEMA was folded into DHS (Haddow and Bullock 2003). DHS officials called FEMA, like all agencies folded into DHS, a "legacy" agency. Former FEMA people worked within the Emergency Preparedness and Response Directorate of DHS, but many people and offices of FEMA were transferred either to senior levels of DHS or to DHS offices that had few if any emergency management responsibilities. FEMA was the only component of DHS charged specifically with reducing the losses associated with non-terrorism-related disasters (Platt and Rubin 1999); FEMA has lost significant visibility and financial and human resources in the reorganization. As a small agency within a massive bureaucracy, its activities are now overshadowed by much larger and better-funded entities within DHS (Tierney 2005). Today, FEMA operates as a disaster response agency that reports directly to the secretary of DHS. No longer does FEMA centrally manage disaster mitigation and preparedness.

Hurricane Katrina placed extraordinary demands on an emergency management system implanted into DHS. The fusion of counterterrorism homeland security and emergency management, all-hazards conceived, will continue into the indefinite future and will no doubt be affected again by reforms the president and Congress will make in evaluating the federal government's response to Hurricane Katrina.

Hurricane Katrina devastated the Gulf Coast of Louisiana, Alabama, and Mississippi and triggered the failures of levees surrounding New Orleans. The immensely destructive and widespread hurricane is blamed for more than one thousand deaths and has displaced more than a half a million people for periods ranging from weeks to months. Secretary Chertoff activated the NRP by declaring an "incident of national significance" as a result of the devastation caused by Hurricane Katrina—the first-ever use of this designation. An incident of national significance is a major disaster or emergency that overwhelms the resources of state and local authorities, requiring significant coordination across the federal government. In point of fact, however, president-declared major disasters have long required that the event extends beyond the resources of state and local authorities.

Federal disaster declarations for Katrina covered portions of three states and ninety-thousand square miles of impact area (Press Secretary 2005b). The flaws revealed in after-action reports about the hurricane may highlight aspects of the NRP and NIMS that have to be changed or improved.

The NIMS and NRP no longer assign many predominant emergency management duties and leadership roles to what is left of the former FEMA. This poses problems. Experts in law enforcement, port security, intelligence, border control, immigration, and transportation security tend to see emergency management as an "annex" functional activity of secondary importance. This could not have helped federal response to Hurricane Katrina.

Presidents do possess immense authority to press many agencies of the federal government into action after a disaster. The items below are drawn from a White House Fact Sheet issued about seventeen days after Katrina struck the Gulf Coast (Press Secretary 2005a).

The President announced that the Department of Homeland Security is registering evacuee households in shelters, churches, and private homes near and far from the Gulf Coast. The President has signed an order providing immediate assistance to people from the disaster area. As of today (9/15/05), more than 500,000 evacuee families have received emergency help to pay for food, clothing, and other essentials.

The Department of Health and Human Services has sent in more than 1,500 health professionals along with over 50 tons of medical supplies, including vaccines, antibiotics, and medicine for chronic conditions such as diabetes. The Social Security Administration is delivering checks. The Department of Labor is helping displaced persons apply for temporary jobs and unemployment benefits. And the Postal Service is registering new addresses so that people can get their mail.

The President proposed to create a Gulf Opportunity Zone (GO Zone) to help local economies in Louisiana, Mississippi, and Alabama devastated by Hurricane Katrina. Businesses in the GO Zone would be eligible for the benefits through 2007. The GO Zone will provide tax relief and loans for businesses and entrepreneurs to invest in the region and create jobs. The GO Zone will double small business expensing from $100,000 to $200,000 for investments in new equipment, provide a 50 percent bonus depreciation for all businesses, and extend tax relief to the building of new structures. The GO Zone will also make available loans and loan guarantees for small businesses, including minority-owned enterprises, to get them up and running again. It is this entrepreneurship that will create jobs and opportunity and help break the cycle of poverty.

The President proposed worker recovery accounts to help those who need extra help finding a job. These new Worker Recovery Accounts will provide targeted assistance for those victims of Hurricane Katrina who need extra help finding work. While victims who have lost their jobs are already eligible to receive state unemployment benefits or Disaster Unemployment Assistance for up to 26 weeks, some need more help in their job search. Worker Recovery Accounts will reward work, eliminate red tape, and promote individual choice to help people find work quickly. We also must ensure that as many of the rebuilding jobs as possible go to the people of Louisiana, Mississippi, and Alabama.

Workers will receive flexible assistance to aid in their job search or to pay for retraining. These Accounts, which states will have flexibility to design, will provide up to $5,000 to certain job seekers to allow them to purchase the training or supportive services, such as child care or transportation, they need to get back to work. In addition to whatever services they select, workers will still be able to receive basic employment services from states and One Stop Career Centers. If workers find a job within 13 weeks after starting Unemployment Insurance benefits or Disaster Unemployment Assistance, they may keep the money remaining in their account as an employment bonus.

The President proposed an Urban Homesteading Initiative to provide a new beginning for lower-income evacuees. Homesteading will allow evacuees to occupy a government-owned home at a favorable mortgage rate, in exchange for their personal investment of sweat equity in the property. Under this approach, we will identify property in the region owned by the Federal government, and provide building sites to low-income citizens free of charge, through a lottery. In return, they would pledge to build on the lot, with either a mortgage or help from a charitable organization like Habitat for Humanity. The Department of Housing and Urban Development, in cooperation with other Federal agencies, local governments, and public housing authorities, will support the development of homes on Federal property in New Orleans and cities across the region, and will encourage nonprofit organizations to commit properties as well. Homeownership is one of the great strengths of any community, and it must be a central part of our vision for the revival of this region.

The President has ordered the Department of Homeland Security to conduct an immediate review of preparedness in every major American city. Our cities must have clear and up-to-date plans for responding to natural disasters, disease outbreaks, or terrorist attack. We must have plans to evacuate large numbers of people in an emergency and to provide food, water, and security as needed. In a time of terror threats and weapons of mass destruction, the danger is greater than a fault line or flood plain. Emergency planning is a national security priority.

The Government will learn the lessons of Hurricane Katrina. The response of government at all levels was not equal to the magnitude of Katrina's destruction. Many first responders performed skillfully under the worst conditions, but the coordination at all levels was inadequate. Four years after September 11th, Americans expect better. President Bush takes responsibility for the Federal government's problems, and for its solutions. It is now clear that a challenge on this scale requires greater Federal authority and a broader role for the U.S. Armed Forces—the institution of our government most capable of massive logistical operations on a moment's notice. The President has ordered every Cabinet secretary to conduct a review of the response, and the President will make every necessary change to fully prepare for any challenge of nature or act of evil that could threaten Americans.

Nonetheless, President Bush has approved several reorganizations that have had controversial effects on FEMA and on the nation's system of disaster management. According to Tierney (2005), the decline in FEMA's prestige and influence in the wake of 9/11 has caused great concern among U.S. emergency management experts. Testifying before the U.S. Congress in March 2004, former FEMA director James Lee Witt warned that the nation's ability to respond to disasters of all types has been weakened by some post-9/11 agency realignments. In written testimony regarding the loss of cabinet status for the FEMA director and the current position of FEMA within DHS, Witt stated, "I assure you that we could not have been as responsive and effective during disasters as we were during my tenure as FEMA director, had there been layers of federal bureaucracy between myself and the White House" (Witt 2004). This layering complicated FEMA's management response to Hurricane Katrina. Jane Bullock, who worked at FEMA under five presidents before becoming Witt's chief of staff, remarked, "To deliver resources through heftier departments such as Defense, FEMA must seize the president's attention before disasters happen" (Simendinger 2005).

Presidential management encompasses matters of planning, staffing, and reorganization (Thomas, Pika, and Watson 1993). This article has already examined aspects of planning and reorganization that pertained to the president's management of Katrina. Now, it is necessary to consider staffing.

The president and FEMA directors

Unfortunately, the vast majority of top appointed federal disaster agency managers have lacked emergency management experience before they came to the job (Wamsley, Schroeder, and Lane 1996). An exception was James Lee Witt, an experienced Arkansas state emergency manager who was appointed by President Clinton to head FEMA (1993-2001). Another exception is the current Bush administration FEMA acting director R. David Paulison, formerly a top emergency manager in Miami, Florida. The problem of inexperienced FEMA directors was underscored by the example of Michael Brown, a Bush appointee (2003-2005). Brown was excoriated and forced to resign for his failures in leadership during FEMA's response to Hurricane Katrina.

According to AP Reporter Mark Humphrey, FEMA leaders lack disaster experience and the agency has suffered a "brain drain" since 2001. Five of eight top FEMA officials came to their posts with virtually no experience in handling disasters and now lead an agency whose ranks of seasoned crisis managers have thinned dramatically since the 9/11 attacks. Writing September 9, 2005, Humphrey reported, "FEMA's top three leaders—Director Michael D. Brown, Chief of Staff

Patrick J. Rhode and Deputy Chief of Staff Brooks D. Altshuler—arrived with ties to President Bush's 2000 campaign or to the White House advance operation, according to the agency. Two other senior operational jobs are filled by a former Republican lieutenant governor of Nebraska and a U.S. Chamber of Commerce official who was once a political operative" (MSNBC 2005).

[E]xperts inside and out of government said a "brain drain" of experienced disaster hands throughout [FEMA], hastened in part by the appointment of leaders without backgrounds in emergency management, has weakened the agency's ability to respond to natural disasters.

Meanwhile, veterans such as U.S. hurricane specialist Eric Tolbert and WTC disaster managers Laurence W. Zensinger and Bruce P. Baughman—who led FEMA's offices of response, recovery, and preparedness, respectively—have left since 2003, taking jobs as consultants or state emergency managers, according to current and former officials. Because of the turnover, three of the five FEMA chiefs for natural-disaster-related operations and nine of ten regional directors are working in an acting capacity, agency officials said. Patronage appointment to the crisis-response agency is nothing new to Washington administrations. Inexperience in FEMA's top ranks is emerging as a key concern of local, state, and federal leaders as investigators begin to sift through what the government has admitted was a bungled response to Hurricane Katrina.

"FEMA requires strong leadership and experience because state and local governments rely on them," said Trina Sheets, executive director of the National Emergency Management Association. "When you don't have trained, qualified people in those positions, the program suffers as a whole." Several top FEMA officials are well-regarded by state and private counterparts in disaster preparedness and response. They include Edward G. Buikema, acting director of response since February, and Kenneth O. Burris, acting chief of operations, a career firefighter and former Marietta, Georgia, fire chief (MSNBC 2005).

But scorching criticism was aimed at FEMA Director Michael Brown, who admitted to errors in responding to Hurricane Katrina and the flooding in New

Orleans. The Oklahoma native, fifty, was hired to the agency after a rocky tenure as commissioner of a horse sporting group by former FEMA director Joe M. Allbaugh, the 2000 Bush campaign manager and a college friend of Brown's. DHS spokesman Russ Knocke said Brown has managed more than 160 natural disasters as FEMA general counsel and deputy director since 2001, "hands-on experience [that] cannot be understated. Other leadership at FEMA brings particular skill sets—policy management leadership, for example." The agency has a deep bench of career professionals, said FEMA spokeswoman Nicol Andrews, including two dozen senior field coordinators and Gil Jamieson, director of risk assessment. "Simply because folks who have left the agency have a disagreement with how it is being run does not necessarily indicate that there is a lack of experience leading it," she said. Andrews said the "acting" designation for regional officials is a designation that signifies that they are FEMA civil servants—not political appointees (MSNBC 2005).

Touring the wrecked Gulf Coast with Secretary of Homeland Security Michael Chertoff, Vice President Cheney defended FEMA leaders, saying, "We're always trying to strike the right balance" between political appointees and "career professionals that fill the jobs underneath them." But experts inside and out of government said a "brain drain" of experienced disaster hands throughout the agency, hastened in part by the appointment of leaders without backgrounds in emergency management, has weakened the agency's ability to respond to natural disasters. Some security experts and congressional critics say the exodus was fueled by a bureaucratic reshuffling in Washington in 2003, when FEMA was stripped of its independent cabinet-level status and folded into the DHS. Emergency preparedness has atrophied as a result, some analysts said, extending from Washington to localities. "[FEMA] has gone downhill within the department, drained of resources and leadership," said I. M. "Mac" Destler, a professor at the University of Maryland School of Public Policy. "The crippling of FEMA was one important reason why it failed" (MSNBC 2005).

Richard A. Andrews, former emergency services director for the state of California and a member of the president's Homeland Security Advisory Council, said state and local failures were critical in the Katrina response, but competence, funding, and political will in Washington were also lacking. "I do not think fundamentally this is an organizational issue," Andrews said. "You need people in there who have both experience and the confidence of the president, who are able to fight and articulate what FEMA's mission and role is, and who understand how emergency management works" (MSNBC 2005).

The agency's troubles are no secret (Gilmore 2005). The Partnership for Public Service, a nonprofit group that promotes careers in federal government, ranked FEMA last of twenty-eight agencies studied in 2003. In its list of best places to work in the government, a 2004 survey by the American Federation of Government Employees found that of eighty-four career FEMA professionals who responded, only ten people ranked agency leaders excellent or good. Another twenty-eight said the leadership was fair, and thirty-three called it poor. More than fifty said they would move to another agency if they could remain at the same pay grade, and sixty-seven ranked the agency as poorer since its merger into DHS (MSNBC 2005).

History may prove that Bush administration handling of FEMA after 9/11, through the period of FEMA incorporation into DHS and during Hurricane Katrina, may be one of the most important deficiencies of the federal response to the disaster.

Bush and Katrina: The President and the News Media

For the Bush administration, Hurricane Katrina was a public relations debacle. The timeline presented in the appendix suggests that at many points before, during, and soon after the disaster, President Bush responded too slowly and ineptly. The president may have been poorly advised, may not have been expeditiously informed, or may have been distracted by a vacation or the press of other scheduled duties. News media coverage of disaster has long been shown to have political implications for presidents (Birkland 1997). The appendix provides an exceptionally good running account of what President Bush, White House officials, Secretary Chertoff, and Director Brown did during the days before and after Hurricane Katrina.

The factcheck.org chronology given in the appendix may not be completely fair to President Bush because the selection of quotes sometimes gives the impression that President Bush is not giving the federal response to the hurricane enough of his personal attention. As a head of state, Bush cannot ignore the many duties and obligations of his office, many scheduled weeks or months in advance of the Katrina disaster. However, the account does portray media coverage that discloses problems of mismanagement, slow response, poor federal-state and president-governor cooperation, symbolic activity that exhibits compassion but fails to provide survivors needed relief, and manifestations of protest by people ranging from U.S. senators to the displaced poor of New Orleans. Sadly, the account makes it obvious that the inadequate evacuation and slow response cost some people their lives. The account also reveals a president under siege who eventually chose to apologize to the American public for the deficiencies of the response.

Bush and Katrina: The President and Federal-State Relations

In a news report published September 8, 2005, Homeland Security Secretary Michael Chertoff said that "the crisis showed that the government needs a new plan to deal with ultra-catastrophes. I think that the lesson of this hurricane, which we will clearly look at as we go over an after-action evaluation, is going to be very valuable moving forward." The report disclosed that during an interview on CBS's *Face the Nation*, "Chertoff called Katrina an ultra-catastrophe, but we have to be prepared even for ultra-catastrophes, even things that happen once in a lifetime, or once in a generation" (MSNBC 2005).

A review of the government's NRP shows that DHS has broad authority to respond to catastrophes, even if it means bypassing state and local governments. Moreover, state and local governments have been induced, often through homeland security federal grants, to comply with the uniformity of federal standards governing response to terrorism and other disaster events (U.S. General Accounting Office [GAO] 2005, 2004). What is not clear, according to Strohm (2005), is "whether Chertoff fully utilized that power." The 426-page NRP was approved in December 2004 and put into action for the first time in response to the hurricane. The NRP includes a section, titled the "Catastrophic Incident Annex," that outlines how the government can rapidly deploy "key essential resources" during a crisis, such as medical teams, urban search and rescue teams, transportable shelters, medical supplies, food, and water (Strohm 2005). "A catastrophic incident results in large numbers of casualties and/or displaced persons, possibly in the tens of thousands," the annex states. "A detailed and credible common operating picture may not be achievable for 24 to 48 hours (or longer) after the incident. As a result, response activities must begin without the benefit of a detailed or complete situation and critical needs assessment. Federal support must be provided in a timely manner to save lives, prevent human suffering and mitigate severe damage; this may require mobilizing and deploying assets before they are requested via normal NRP protocols" (Strohm 2005, 1).

The plan gives the Homeland Security secretary the power to bypass the traditional practice of waiting for states to ask for assistance (Strohm 2005). "Standard procedures outlined in the NRP regarding requests for assistance may be expedited or, under extreme circumstances, temporarily suspended in the immediate aftermath of an incident of catastrophic magnitude, pursuant to existing law," the plan states. "Notification and full coordination with states occur, but the coordination process should not delay or impede the rapid mobilization and deployment of critical federal resources" (Strohm 2005, 2).

The timeline presented in the appendix demonstrates that the president and his disaster management leadership group had great problems working with governors in the two most hurricane-ravaged states: Louisiana and Mississippi. These problems were most pronounced in Louisiana and in New Orleans. Weeks after Katrina struck, Hurricane Wilma produced another contest over federal versus state disaster management control.

According to *Wall Street Journal* reporters Block and Schatz (2005), a power struggle unfolded in Florida during Hurricane Wilma. They maintained that this struggle "is shaping a debate about how the country should respond to disasters, both natural and man-made. The big question: Should state or federal authorities be in control of recovery efforts? Giving the debate more urgency are growing concerns about a possible flu outbreak and experts' warnings that next year's hurricane season may be even deadlier than this summer's record-breaking series" (p. 1).

Block and Schatz (2005) reported that the Bush administration says Katrina showed that some states cannot deal with large-scale disasters. DHS, which oversees FEMA, wants to intervene in response efforts and is pressing local officials to vet their emergency plans. DHS is also looking to equip locally based federal employees with cameras and communications gear to provide Washington with real-time disaster information.

Days before Wilma churned through his state, Florida Governor Jeb Bush appeared before Congress alongside the governors of Texas and Arizona. "I can say with certainty that federalizing emergency response to catastrophic events would be a disaster as bad as Hurricane Katrina," he told lawmakers. "If you federalize, all the innovation, creativity and knowledge at the local level would subside" (Block and Schatz 2005, 1). But watching Wilma lurch toward Florida with growing alarm, DHS was not taking any chances. FEMA had taken the brunt of the blame for the slow response to Katrina, culminating in the resignation of its top official, Michael Brown, less than two weeks into the disaster. That was followed by a public outcry for FEMA to act more assertively.

Other nations have sought to offer help to Katrina victims, raising foreign policy issues; some of this help is both problematic and embarrassing for the Bush administration.

For Wilma, federal officials began mobilizing emergency reporting teams and arranged for hundreds of satellite telephones to be sent into the state. Homeland Security Secretary Michael Chertoff hunted for a Coast Guard officer to head up the response, just as he did after Katrina and before Hurricanes Ophelia and Rita (Block and Schatz 2005). As Mr. Chertoff made his plans to assist Florida, the U.S. Northern Command moved to ready the Fifth Army to take over the role of coordinating military assistance in the state. U.S. Northern Command (Northcom) was created after 9/11 as the first standing combat command in the nation since the Civil War. Its role is to coordinate military responses to terrorist attacks in the United States and help states cope with natural disasters.

No one in Florida had requested Northcom's assistance, but neither had anyone in Texas when Hurricane Rita barreled up the Gulf in late September. Nevertheless, the Fifth Army was activated to help run the Rita response. Federal officials urged a hasty mass evacuation from Houston (Block and Schatz 2005). With Wilma, Washington was not asking questions—it wanted control. On October 18, Lieutenant General Robert T. Clark, commander of the Fifth Army at Fort Sam

Houston, Texas, called the head of Florida's National Guard and said he wanted to start flying in equipment to establish a Joint Task Force Command, federal and state officials confirm.

The National Guard chief, Air Force General Douglas Burnett, said in a later interview that he was taken aback. "Did we need a three-star general from Texas to come to direct our response? No, we did not" (Block and Schatz 2005). Without warning federal officials, he announced the creation of "Wilma Command" to oversee the response. It was done according to the rules of Homeland Security's own NIMS, mandated by President Bush after 9/11 to ensure that all levels of government worked from the same playbook. Its bedrock principle: one incident, one commander, no matter how many agencies send help (Block and Schatz 2005).

It is a relatively new process that few state emergency officials have mastered. But Mr. Fugate knew what to do. He said the Wilma Command team would include himself, General Burnett, and Justin DeMello, the head of FEMA in Florida who was close with state officials. Then Mr. Fugate reached off-camera and pulled Mr. Bush into the frame. "I'd now like to introduce the Incident Commander," he said, "The governor of Florida."

"Craig had outmaneuvered them and they knew it," recalled Mr. DeMello, the local FEMA representative. "There was nothing for them to say as under the NIMS they are required to support the incident commander" (Block and Schatz 2005, 1). Mr. Fugate took the three hundred satellite telephones Homeland Security had sent for its reporting teams and gave them to local emergency workers.

Homeland Security officials continued lobbying Florida to allow Mr. Chertoff to name a Coast Guard official as the "principal federal officer." But by October 23, a day before landfall, they had given up. Northcom never activated the Fifth Army (Block and Schatz 2005, 1).

If President Bush supports Secretary Chertoff's efforts to "federalize" future disasters, owing to the alleged shortcomings of state and local governments, Bush must determine whether this is worth alienating many governors (one of whom is his brother) and many federal, state, and local emergency managers. Nothing less than the president's image, prestige, and historical legacy are at stake.

Bush and Katrina: The President and Civil-Military Relations

The nation's experience with Hurricane Katrina highlighted the importance of the National Guard in disasters. Also, since changes made after the 9/11 terror disaster, the active military now has a greater domestic presence and a North American command. In addition, the U.S. Coast Guard, which since March 2003 resides in DHS, has a much higher profile in disaster management. Owing to civilian emergency management problems encountered by FEMA, a Coast Guard admiral was assigned the lead DHS role in managing disaster response operations in and around New Orleans.

President Bush's plan to give the military a larger role in disaster relief faces a number of potential obstacles, according to Pentagon officials and military analysts. Among the hurdles are laws against using active-duty troops for law enforcement, questions about whether the National Guard is overextended because of its responsibilities overseas, and decisions about whether to create specialized military units to handle emergencies including natural disasters and terrorist attacks (Bowman and Gorman 2005). Admiral Timothy J. Keating, who heads Northcom, a newly created military body overseeing homeland defense, has told lawmakers that active-duty forces should be given complete authority for responding to catastrophic disasters. President Bush has already suggested that the military be ready to quarantine cities and states in the event of a flu pandemic.

Local officials, from small-town sheriffs to big-state governors, say Louisiana's problems during Katrina were the exception, not the rule. They say DHS and the Pentagon are overreaching and that a federal takeover of relief work will make matters worse. The head of the Washington state National Guard, Major General Timothy J. Lowenberg, suggested in e-mails to colleagues that Admiral Keating's suggestion amounted to a "policy of domestic regime change" (Block and Schatz 2005).

Similar calls for an expanded role for the armed services after Hurricane Andrew in 1992 largely went nowhere because of quiet opposition from the Defense Department. Bush, in a nationally televised speech from New Orleans, called for "a broader role for the armed forces, the institution of our government most capable of massive logistical operations on a moment's notice," in responding to disasters. Pentagon officials are trying to determine how to put Bush's vision into practice (Bowman and Gorman 2005).

A senior Pentagon official said the military's response to Katrina has been complicated by "archaic laws" that were "difficult to work through." The 1878 Posse Comitatus Act generally bars active-duty military from law-enforcement activities on U.S. soil. The official said he expects the Pentagon to address those and other military issues related to domestic disaster relief in a "more formal way." No deadline has been set for finding answers (Bowman and Gorman 2005). Some military analysts point out that the National Guard and active-duty soldiers often have been used in domestic disasters or disturbances, including riots in the 1960s and Hurricane Andrew in Florida. The biggest lesson learned from Katrina has less to do with changing laws than with coordination and communications between state and local governments and the new DHS, they say.

Anthony Cordesman of the Center for Strategic and International Studies said concerns over Posse Comitatus are misplaced because the president could have declared a national emergency. That would have freed troops to take part in law enforcement and other types of domestic duties. Blum agreed. "Posse Comitatus was not an issue," he said, because tens of thousands of Guard troops streamed into the area, many of them assisting local law enforcement and operating under state law (Bowman and Gorman 2005). About half of the combat units in Iraq are drawn from the Guard, which might need to reduce its overseas responsibilities to devote more personnel to domestic needs. "If not, what level of additional forces is needed?" he asked.

The Guard has about 312,000 soldiers. National Guard troops, who are commanded by a state's governor unless called to federal duty by the president, can perform law-enforcement functions under a state's laws. David Segal, a military sociologist at the University of Maryland, College Park, noted that in 1992, the National Guard in Florida was available for Hurricane Andrew. By contrast, about 60 percent of the Mississippi Guard and 65 percent of the Louisiana Guard were on hand this month because of deployments to Iraq. "In the past, the Guard did not play as large a role in international deployments," Segal said (Bowman and Gorman 2005).

Blum said the Guard can handle international and domestic jobs. "I think the response of the military was more than sufficient, effective and timely for Katrina" and more effective than the response of any other part of the federal government, he said. After Hurricane Andrew, during the administration of Bush's father, proposals were made in Congress that would have broadened the military's role in responding to domestic disasters. They included rolling FEMA into the Defense Department; placing a key portion of FEMA, such as its communications apparatus, in the Defense Department; and increasing the role of the National Guard in emergency response (Bowman and Gorman 2005).

In the end, the only change was the transfer of some emergency functions from FEMA to the National Security Agency to make sure that the government would continue to operate after a disaster, said Gary Wamsley, who was staff director of a 1993 study by the National Academy of Public Administration (NAPA; 1993) that was critical of FEMA's performance. Wamsley said the other proposed changes failed because of quiet opposition by the top ranks at the Pentagon and more vocal protests from state emergency management officials, who feared losing control in a crisis (Bowman and Gorman 2005). Adding the active military to disaster response raises a host of difficult questions, including whether the active military should have shoot-to-kill orders domestically to keep order in a disaster; whether the National Guard or the active military is in charge if both are responding; and what authority governors have in such a situation (Bowman and Gorman 2005).

The slowness of government's emergency response, particularly in areas of New Orleans devastated by levy-failure flooding, and the ensuing blame game, represents a huge public relations setback for the Bush administration. It has also sparked renewed interest in militarizing emergency response, much as happened after Hurricane Andrew (U.S. Congress 1993). Andrew happened near the end of the George H. W. Bush administration, and a new Clinton administration came to office in the winter of 1993 promising major improvements in emergency management. Remember, too, that in 1993 the military, fresh from the first Iraq War and anticipating other international deployments (Bosnia, etc.), actually opposed taking on FEMA's domestic emergency management authority. The military may again step away from assuming civilian emergency management duties, though they may accept invigorated federal support for an enhanced role in short-term emergency response to homeland disasters, particularly through the new North American command.

Katrina has provided an object reminder that natural disasters can be as destructive, or more so, as terror-caused disasters—even the 9/11 disaster. Katrina has also moved natural disaster back onto the public policy agenda, most particularly at the White House level and in Congress. Other nations have sought to offer help to Katrina victims, raising foreign policy issues; some of this help is both problematic and embarrassing for the Bush administration.

For U.S. presidents, there is an unwritten rule book for disaster recovery, and the first rule is "act fast." The second rule is "send it all" because local and state officials are often reluctant to admit they need help.

Emergency management in the United States evolved conjointly, and often unhappily, with civil defense against nuclear attack. In 1993, the shotgun marriage of civil defense and emergency management ended, and emergency management won out. The Nunn-Lugar laws of the mid-1990s, the Oklahoma City bombing in 1995, and the first WTC attack in 1993 provided a comeback of sorts for those touting the threat of weapons of mass destruction. However, it was the terror attack of 9/11 that reintroduced civil defense, now labeled civil security.

The federally led drive to establish the NRP and the NIMS, both heavily pitched on terrorism concerns, is reshaping the state and local conceptualization of what emergency management is. The massive planning and exercise work under the NRP and NIMS may have confounded the federal response to Katrina. The overwhelmingly huge amount of federally required planning paperwork, compounded by federal expectations that state and local emergency managers gear up for an array of about a dozen different types of terror attack scenarios, did little to facilitate intergovernmental response to Katrina. Presidential frustration with the inadequacy of FEMA's response to the Katrina disaster has opened the door to a possible remilitarization of emergency management in some respects, something contemplated even years before Katrina (Healy 2003).

Bush and Katrina: The President and Disaster Policy

Congress approved a measure, which President Bush quickly signed, to provide Katrina-devastated areas with more than $60 billion in assistance. These funds will carry out the first stages of the relief effort and begin the rebuilding. The White House Press Secretary called this an unprecedented response to an unprecedented crisis, which demonstrates the compassion and resolve of our nation (Press Secretary 2005a).

For U.S. presidents, there is an unwritten rule book for disaster recovery, and the first rule is "act fast." The second rule is "send it all" because local and state officials are often reluctant to admit they need help. And the third rule is that presidents are expected to "explain and console." President Clinton and his FEMA director, James Lee Witt, were acknowledged masters. According to Simendinger (2005), it was George H. W. Bush, in regard to Hurricanes Hugo in 1989 and Andrew in 1992, whose experience provided painful lessons about the federal government's bureaucratic intransigence and overdeference to local officials.

"President Clinton learned what happened and never let it happen again," recalled Marlin Fitzwater, former press secretary to Presidents Bush and Reagan. "And the good part is that they learned it for all time and for all the presidents" (Simendinger 2005, 1).

The senior President Bush was not oblivious to the political importance of disasters. Yet he failed to anticipate that his administration was part of the problem. FEMA had been criticized for a sluggish response after Hugo, which struck the Carolinas and claimed eighty-six lives. By the time Andrew destroyed more than one hundred thousand Florida homes two months before the 1992 election, the vulnerabilities of FEMA—which at the time required governors to first request aid—conspired with the shortsightedness of Florida's Governor Lawton Chiles—who initially refused to make the request—to produce a major political setback for George H. W. Bush (Simendinger 2005). Fitzwater said that Clinton rightly went to school on Bush's mistakes. "He, as president, could not afford to wait on governors to develop the response and to make the requests," Fitzwater said. "If you waited a day or two or three, you were too late. You have to get on the ground immediately—and not with checks, but with tents and with food and water" (Simendinger 2005, 2).

Former Presidents George H. W. Bush and Clinton have led a private fund-raising effort that received pledges of more than $100 million to aid the Gulf Coast's recovery from Hurricane Katrina (Press Secretary 2005a). Thus, even former presidents have come to play roles in megadisaster recovery.

Hurricane Katrina, which struck the U.S. Gulf Coast in late August 2005, triggering the failure of the levy system that protected New Orleans, tested the capacity, adequacy, and limits of Bush administration–led disaster policy and management changes made since 9/11. The disaster also represented the supreme test of a president and his administration. When government succeeds in effectively providing help and relief for disaster victims and their devastated state and local governments, a president may garner political credit. As former Clinton administration FEMA official Jane Bullock has said, "Every time we had a disaster, President Clinton's poll numbers went up. They gave him a venue where he was at his best" (Simendinger 2005). However, megadisasters badly managed, and perceived by the media and public to have been badly managed, may produce political losses for a president, as may have been the case for President George W. Bush.

Disasters test presidential leadership and management in extraordinary ways. Some presidents learn lessons from their disaster experience and some do not. The nation is better served by those who learn the lessons of disaster management.

Appendix
Factcheck.org Chronology of Hurricane Katrina Media Coverage

Friday, August 26, 2005—Three Days Prior to Katrina's Louisiana Landfall

Hurricane Katrina strikes Florida between Hallandale Beach and North Miami Beach as a Category 1 hurricane with 80 mph winds. Eleven people die from hurricane-related causes.

- —A Chronology of Hurricane Katrina and its aftermath," Associated Press, 3 Sep 2005.

The storm heads into the Gulf of Mexico and by 10:30 am CDT is reported to be "rapidly strengthening."

- —Hurricane Katrina Special Advisory Number 13," National Hurricane Center, 26 Aug 2005.
- —Louisiana Governor Kathleen Blanco declares a State of Emergency in Louisiana. "Governor Blanco Declares State of Emergency," Louisiana Governor's Office, 26 Aug 2005.

Saturday, August 27, 2005—Two Days Prior

Blanco asks President Bush to declare a State of Emergency for the state of Louisiana due to Hurricane Katrina. Bush does so, authorizing the Department of Homeland Security and FEMA "to coordinate all disaster relief efforts . . ." and freeing up federal money for the state.

- —"Governor Blanco asks President to Declare an Emergency for the State of Louisiana due to Hurricane Katrina," Louisiana Governor's Office, 27 Aug 2005.
- —"Statement on Federal Emergency Assistance for Louisiana," Office of the White House Press Secretary, 27 Aug 2005.

Katrina is a Category 3 storm, predicted to become Category 4. At 4 pm CDT, it is still 380 miles from the mouth of the Mississippi.

- —"Hurricane Katrina Special Advisory Number 18," National Hurricane Center, 26 Aug 2005.

Director of the National Hurricane Center, Max Mayfield, calls the governors of Louisiana and Mississippi and the mayor of New Orleans to warn of potential devastation. The next day he participates in a video conference call to the President, who is at his ranch in Crawford, Texas.

- —Tamara Lush, "For Forecasting Chief, No Joy in Being Right," *St. Petersburg Times*, 30 Aug 2005.

Sunday, August 28, 2005—One Day Prior

1 a.m.—Katrina is upgraded to a Category 4 storm with wind speeds reaching 145 mph.

- —"Hurricane Katrina Special Advisory Number 20," National Hurricane Center, 28 Aug 2005.

7 a.m.—Katrina is upgraded to a "potentially catastrophic" Category 5 storm. NOAA predicts "coastal storm surge flooding of 15 to 20 feet above normal tide levels."

- —"Hurricane Katrina Special Advisory Number 22," National Hurricane Center, 28 Aug 2005.
- —"New Orleans braces for monster hurricane," CNN.com, 29 Aug 2005.

9:30 a.m.—With wind speeds reaching 175 mph, New Orleans Mayor Ray Nagin orders a mandatory evacuation of the city after Governor Blanco speaks with Bush. The evacuation call comes only 20 hours before Katrina would make landfall—less than half the time that researchers had determined was necessary to evacuate the city.

- —Gordon Russell, "Nagin Orders First-Ever Mandatory Evacuation of New Orleans," New Orleans *Times-Picayune*, 31 Aug 2005.
- —Lise Olsen, "City Had Evacuation Plan but Strayed from Strategy," *Houston Chronicle*, 8 Sep 2005.

10 a.m.—NOAA raises their estimate of storm surge flooding to 18 to 22 feet above normal tide levels. The levee protecting New Orleans from Lake Pontchartrain is only 17.5 feet tall; the Mississippi River levee reaches 23 feet.

- —"Hurricane Katrina Special Advisory Number 23," National Hurricane Center, 28 Aug 2005.

The Associated Press reports that New Orleans could become "a vast cesspool tainted with toxic chemicals, human waste and even coffins released . . . from the city's legendary cemeteries."

- "The storm threatened an environmental disaster of biblical proportions, one that could leave more than 1 million people homeless," the AP says.
- —Matt Crenson, "Katrina May Create Environmental Catastrophe on Epic Scale," Associated Press, 28 Aug 2005.

11:31 a.m.—The President—at his ranch in Crawford—speaks briefly to reporters. His statement contains 203 words about Katrina and 819 congratulating Iraqis on their new constitution. "We will do everything in our power to help the people in the communities affected by this storm," he says of the approaching hurricane.

- —"President Discusses Hurricane Katrina, Congratulates Iraqis on Draft Constitution," Prairie Chapel Ranch, Crawford, Texas, 28 Aug 2005.

8:30 p.m.—An empty Amtrak train leaves New Orleans, with room for hundreds of potential evacuees. "We offered the city the opportunity to take evacuees out of harm's way. . . . The city declined," said Amtrak spokesman Cliff Black. The train left New Orleans no passengers on board.

- —Susan Glasser, "The Steady Buildup to a City's Chaos," *Washington Post*, 11 Sep 2005.

Two weeks later, Nagin denies on NBC's *Meet the Press* that Amtrak offered their services. "Amtrak never contacted me to make that offer," the mayor tells host Tim Russert. "I have never gotten that call, Tim, and I would love to have had that call. But it never happened."

- —"Interview with Mayor Nagin," *Meet the Press*, NBC, 11 Sep 2005.

Monday, August 29, 2005—Day of Katrina

6 a.m.—Katrina makes landfall on Louisiana coast as a strong Category 4 storm, with sustained winds of nearly 145 mph and predicted coastal storm surge of up to 28 feet. The National Hurricane Center warns that "some levees in the greater New Orleans area could be overtopped." It says a weather buoy located about 50 miles east of the mouth of the Mississippi river had reported waves heights of at least 47 feet.

- —"Hurricane Katrina Intermediate Advisory Number 26A . . . Corrected," National Hurricane Center, 29 Aug 2005.

8 a.m.—A massive storm surge sends water sloshing up Lake Borgne and the lower reaches of the Mississippi River. Local officials immediately report flooding. Months later, a study sponsored by the National Science Foundation concludes that the storm surge reached approximately 18 to 25 feet, "massively" overtopping levees whose actual height varied between 11 and 15 feet above sea level. A gate tender at one lock station watches from a crows-nest lookout tower as the storm surge rises 5 to 10 feet above the top of the levee system, leaving debris caught high up in the tower. The rushing water caused flood protection to give way entirely in several spots. "The levees in this area, which were largely earthen levees constructed of relatively poor materials, were simply overwhelmed and were massively eroded," the report concludes. It also concludes that a runaway barge, initially suspected of contributing to one breach, was not at fault: "Various barges and other floating structures made contact with the earth levees without causing significant damage."

- —Raymond Seed et al., "Preliminary Report on the Performance of the New Orleans Levee Systems in Hurricane Katrina on August 29, 2005," Center for Information Technology Research in the Interest of Society (University of California, Berkeley), 2 Nov 2005
- —"Testimony of Raymond B. Seed," Committee on Homeland Security and Government Affairs, U.S. Senate, 2 Nov 2005.
- —John McQuaid, "Katrina Trapped City in Double Disasters," New Orleans *Times-Picayune*, 7 Sep 2005.

9 a.m.—The eastern part of the city and Bernard Parish are already flooded several feet deep, even before the eye of the storm has passed. Thousands of survivors are trapped. But

worse flooding is to come: within hours, city canal floodwalls will also collapse and a second, slower wave of flooding will take place.

- —John McQuaid, "Katrina Trapped City in Double Disasters," New Orleans *Times-Picayune*, 7 Sep 2005.

11 a.m.—New Orleans is spared a direct hit, as the center of the storm passes over the Louisiana-Mississippi state line 35 miles away from the city. Maximum sustained winds are now reduced, but still a strong Category 3 storm with 125 mph winds.

- —"Hurricane Katrina Advisory Number 27," National Hurricane Center, 29 Aug 2005.

11:06 a.m.—Bush promotes his Medicare prescription drug benefit at a 44-minute event in El Mirage, Arizona. He devotes 156 words to the hurricane, among them: "I want the folks there on the Gulf Coast to know that the federal government is prepared to help you when the storm passes. I want to thank the governors of the affected regions for mobilizing assets prior to the arrival of the storm to help citizens avoid this devastating storm."

- —"President Participates in Conversation on Medicare," White House, 29 Aug 2005.

Late Morning (exact time uncertain)—The vital 17th Street Canal levee gives way, sending the water from Lake Pontchartrain into the city in a second, slower wave of flooding. A full day will pass before state or federal officials fully realize what is happening.

- —John McQuaid, "Katrina Trapped City in Double Disasters," New Orleans *Times-Picayune*, 7 Sep 2005.

Eventually, engineers will conclude that there was little or no overtopping at these spots, and the best evidence suggests that waters remained 3 to 5 feet below the tops of the walls. The NSF report says "these three levee failures were likely caused by failures in the foundation soils underlying the levees." But is also says the failures could easily have been prevented: "The performance of many of the levees and floodwalls could have been significantly improved, and some of the failures likely prevented, with relatively inexpensive modifications of the levee and floodwall system details." The report's lead author will say these failures are probably due to human error, and possibly to outright malfeasance. Raymond Seed of the University of California, Berkeley, will tell reporters, "It may not have been the result of human error. There's a high likelihood that it was. But we're receiving some very disturbing reports from people who were involved in some of these projects, and it suggests that perhaps not just human error was involved; there may have been some malfeasance. Some of the sections may not have been constructed as they were designed."

- —Raymond Seed et al., "Preliminary Report on the Performance of the New Orleans Levee Systems in Hurricane Katrina on August 29, 2005," Center for Information Technology Research in the Interest of Society (University of California, Berkeley), 2 Nov 2005.
- —"Flawed walls led to flooding in New Orleans," *All Things Considered*, NPR, 2 Nov 2005.
- —John McQuaid, "Mystery Surrounds Floodwall Breaches; Could a Structural Flaw Be to Blame?" New Orleans *Times-Picayune*, 13 Sep 2005.

About 11 a.m. (exact time uncertain)—Roughly five hours after Katrina strikes the coast, FEMA director Michael Brown sends a memo—later obtained and made public by the

Associated Press—requesting an additional 1,000 rescue workers from the Department of Homeland Security "within 48 hours" and 2,000 more within seven days. It is addressed to his boss, Michael Chertoff, Secretary of Homeland Security. Brown refers to Katrina as "this *near* catastrophic event" (our emphasis). He proposes sending the workers first for training in Georgia or Florida, then to the disaster area "when conditions are safe." Among the duties of the workers, Brown proposes, is to "convey a positive *image* of disaster operations to government officials, community organizations and the general public." (Emphasis added.)

- —Michael D. Brown, "Memorandum to Michael Chertoff, Secretary of Homeland Security," 29 Aug 2005.

Later Brown will say FEMA itself has only 2,600 employees nationwide, and normally relies on state workers, the National Guard, private contractors and other federal agencies during disaster relief operations.

- —David D. Kirkpatrick and Scott Shane, "Ex-FEMA Chief Tells of Frustration and Chaos," *New York Times*, 15 Sep 2005: A1.

4:40 p.m.—Bush appears in Rancho Cucamonga, California for another Medicare event. He again devotes a few words to Katrina: "It's a storm now that is moving through, and now it's the time for governments to help people get their feet on the ground. . . . For those of you who are concerned about whether or not we're prepared to help, don't be. We are. We're in place. We've got equipment in place, supplies in place. And once the—once we're able to assess the damage, we'll be able to move in and help those good folks in the affected areas."

- —"President Discusses Medicare, New Prescription Drug Benefits," James L. Brulte Senior Center Rancho Cucamonga, California, 29 Aug 2005.

Time uncertain—Blanco calls Bush, saying, "Mr. President, we need your help. We need everything you've got." Bush later assures her that "help is on the way."

- —James Carney et al., "4 Places Where the System Broke Down," *Time*, 11 Sep 2005.
- —Evan Thomas, "How Bush Blew It," *Newsweek*, 19 September 2005.

Tuesday, August 30, 2005–One Day after Katrina

Dawn—Water has continued to rise overnight and is coursing through the city's central business district, still rising. Eventually, at least 80 percent of New Orleans is under water. Reports of looting surface.

- —John McQuaid, "Katrina Trapped City in Double Disasters," New Orleans *Times-Picayune*, 7 Sep 2005.

11:04 a.m.—In San Diego, California, Bush delivers a 31-minute speech marking the 60th anniversary of the end of World War II. Of Katrina, he says, "we're beginning to move in the help that people need."

- —"President Commemorates 60th Anniversary of V-J Day," Naval Air Station North Island San Diego, California, 30 Aug 2005.

Immediately after the speech, White House Press Secretary Scott McClellan tells reporters that Bush will return to Crawford, then cut short his Texas stay and go to Washington. McClellan says, "This is one of the most devastating storms in our nation's history. I think that's becoming clear to everyone. The devastation is enormous."

- —"Press Gaggle by Scott McClellan," Naval Air Station North Island San Diego, California, 30 Aug 2005.

3 p.m.—With water still pouring into the city, officials report that the Army Corps of Engineers has surveyed the damage to levees and will soon attempt repair. At a Baton Rouge briefing, Sen. Mary Landrieu reports that "most of the roads and highways are impassable, and water is still coming into the city of New Orleans. The water is up to the rooftops in St. Bernard and Plaquemine. We think there may be only one major way into the city right now and it has to be used for emergency personnel to get food and water and rescue equipment to people who are in desperate need." But even now, federal and state officials alike seem unaware of the full extent of the unfolding disaster.

- U.S. Senator David Vitter said of the still-rising water:

Sen. Vitter: In the metropolitan area in general, in the huge majority of areas, it's not rising at all. It's the same or it may be lowering slightly. In some parts of New Orleans, because of the 17th Street breach, it may be rising and that seemed to be the case in parts of downtown. I don't want to alarm everybody that, you know, New Orleans is filling up like a bowl. That's just not happening.

None of the state officials present at the press conference correct the mistaken remark. And Blanco seems puzzled when a reporter asks the governor about the water pollution that will later emerge as a major public health risk:

- Q: Does the water that's downtown—does this represent what everyone feared before the hurricane would come, that you would have this toxic soup that has overrun the city?
- Blanco: It didn't—I wouldn't think it would be toxic soup right now. I think it's just water from the lake, water from the canals. It's, you know, water.
- Q: Well, something could be underneath that water.
- Blanco: Pardon?

- —"The Situation Room; Hurricane Katrina Aftermath; Rescue Efforts and Assessing the Damage," Transcript, CNN, 30 Aug 2005.

Wednesday, August 31, 2005—Two Days After

Morning—Bush, still in Crawford, participates in a half-hour video conference on Katrina with Vice President Cheney (who is in Wyoming) and top aides. Later, he boards Air Force One and flies over New Orleans on his way back to Washington. His press secretary tells reporters: "The President, when we were passing over that part of New Orleans, said, 'It's devastating, it's got to be doubly devastating on the ground.' "

- —"Press Gaggle with Scott McClellan," Aboard Air Force One, En Route Andrews Air Force Base, Maryland, 31 Aug 2005.

Looting intensifies in New Orleans. Nagin orders most of the police to abandon search and rescue missions for survivors and focus on packs of looters who are becoming increasingly violent. The AP reported, "Police officers were asking residents to give up any guns they had before they boarded buses and trucks because police desperately needed the firepower."

- —"Mayor: Katrina May Have Killed Thousands," Associated Press, 31 Aug 2005.

Late Afternoon—Bush, back at the White House, holds a cabinet meeting on Katrina and speaks for nine minutes in the Rose Garden to outline federal relief efforts. He says FEMA has moved 25 search and rescue teams into the area. As for those stranded at the Superdome, "Buses are on the way to take those people from New Orleans to Houston," the President says.

- —"President Outlines Hurricane Katrina Relief Efforts," The Rose Garden, 31 Aug 2005.

Thursday, September 1, 2005—Three Days After

7 a.m.—Bush says "I don't think anybody anticipated the breach of the levees." His remark comes in a live interview on ABC's *Good Morning America*:

- Bush: I want people to know there's a lot of help coming. I don't think anybody anticipated the breach of the levees. They did anticipate a serious storm. These levees got breached and as a result, much of New Orleans is flooded and now we're having to deal with it and will.

- —"Good Morning America," Transcript, *ABC News*, 1 Sep 2005.

Time Uncertain—Red Cross President Marsha Evans asks permission to enter the city with relief supplies, but Louisiana state officials deny permission.

- —"Red Cross: State Rebuffed Relief Efforts: Aid Organization Never Got into New Orleans, Officials Say," CNN.com, 9 Sep 2005.

Thirty-thousand National Guard Troops from across the country are ordered to report to the Gulf Coast, but many do not arrive for several days.

- —"More Navy Ships, National Guard Troops Head to the Gulf Coast," Associated Press, 1 Sep 2005.

The first buses arrive at the Superdome to take evacuees to the Astrodome in Houston, 355 miles away. But the evacuation goes slowly and will take several days.

- —Evan Thomas, "The Lost City," *Newsweek*, 12 Sep 2005.

Associated Press photographer Phil Coale makes an aerial shot of scores of school buses sitting unused in a flooded New Orleans lot. Many will later question why city officials did not use these busses to evacuate residents who lacked transportation prior to the hurricane, or at least move them to higher ground for use later.

- —AP Photo/Phil Coale, "Aerial View of Flooded School Busses," Yahoo News, 1 Sep 2005.

Evening—In a special report that is typical of the picture that television is conveying to the world, CNN Correspondent Adaora Udoji reports: "Three days after Hurricane Katrina, and the situation is getting more desperate by the minute. Thousands are still stranded in misery. . . . They are marching in search of food, water and relief. They're surrounded by a crumbling city and dead bodies. Infants have no formula, the children no food, nothing for adults, no medical help. They're burning with frustration, and sure they have been forgotten."

And CNN's Medical Correspondent, Dr. Sanjay Gupta, reports live from Charity hospital in New Orleans: "It doesn't appear to be safe now, but it seems that a sniper standing atop one of the buildings just above us here and firing down at patients and doctors as they were trying to be evacuated, unbelievable. It just boggles my mind, actually."

- —"Anderson Cooper 360 Degrees, Special Edition: Hurricane Katrina," CNN Transcripts, 1 Sep 2005.

Brown says FEMA officials were unaware for days that—besides the hurricane victims stranded in the Superdome—thousands more had taken refuge in the New Orleans Convention Center nearby. Speaking from Baton Rouge in a live interview with CNN's Paula Zahn, he says:

- Brown: And so, this—this catastrophic disaster continues to grow. I will tell you this, though. Every person in that Convention Center, we just learned about that today. And so, I have directed that we have all available resources to get to that Convention Center to make certain that they have the food and water, the medical care that they need . . .
- Q: Sir, you aren't telling me . . .
- Brown: . . . and that we take care of those bodies that are there . . .
- Q: Sir, you aren't just telling me you just learned that the folks at the Convention Center didn't have food and water until today, are you? You had no idea they were completely cut off?
- Brown: Paula, the federal government did not even know about the Convention Center people until today.

- —Paula Zahn Now, "Desperation in New Orleans; Interview with FEMA Director Mike Brown," Transcript, 1 Sep 2005.

Later, Brown will say he was wrong and that FEMA actually knew about the victims at the Convention Center 24 hours earlier but was unable to reach them until Thursday.

- —David D. Kirkpatrick and Scott Shane, "Ex-FEMA Chief Tells of Frustration and Chaos," *New York Times*, 15 Sep 2005: A1

Evening—Nagin delivers a rambling diatribe in an interview with local radio station WWL-AM, blaming Bush and Blanco for doing too little:

- Nagin: I need reinforcements, I need troops, man. I need 500 buses, man . . .
- I've got 15,000 to 20,000 people over at the convention center. It's bursting at the seams. The poor people in Plaquemines Parish. . . . We don't have anything, and we're sharing with our brothers in Plaquemines Parish.
- It's awful down here, man.
- . . . Don't tell me 40,000 people are coming here. They're not here. It's too doggone late. Now get off your asses and do something, and let's fix the biggest goddamn crisis in the history of this country.

- —"Mayor to Feds: 'Get Off Your Asses,'" Transcript of radio interview with New Orleans' Nagin, CNN.com, 2 Sep 2005.

Friday, September 2, 2005—Four Days After

The Red Cross renews its request to enter the city with relief supplies. "We had adequate supplies, the people and the vehicles," Red Cross official Vic Howell would later recall. Louisiana officials say they needed 24 hours to provide an escort and prepare for the Red Cross's arrival. However, 24 hours later, a large-scale evacuation is underway and the Red Cross relief effort never reaches New Orleans.

- —"Red Cross: State Rebuffed Relief Efforts: Aid Organization Never Got into New Orleans, Officials Say" CNN.com, 9 Sep 2005.

8:02 a.m.—Bush leaves the White House to tour the hurricane area. He says, "A lot of people are working hard to help those who have been affected, and I want to thank the people for their efforts. The results are not acceptable."

- —"President Heads to Hurricane Katrina Affected Areas," The South Lawn, 2 Sep 2005.

10:35 a.m.—Bush, arriving in Alabama to tour the disaster area, says of the FEMA director at a live news conference: "Brownie, you're doing a heck of a job. The FEMA director is working 24—(applause)—they're working 24 hours a day. Again, my attitude is, if it's not going exactly right, we're going to make it go exactly right. If there are problems, we're going to address the problems."

- —"President Arrives in Alabama, Briefed on Hurricane Katrina," Mobile Regional Airport Mobile, Alabama, 2 Sep 2005.

Noon—A convoy of military trucks drives through floodwaters to the convention center, the first supplies of water and food to reach victims who have waited for days. Thousands of armed National Guardsmen carrying weapons stream into the city to help restore order. Commanding is Army Lt. Gen. Russel Honoré, a cigar-chomping Louisiana native who soon wins praise for his decisive style of action.

- —Allen G. Breed, "National Guardsmen Arrive in New Orleans," The Associated Press, 2 Sep 2005.

5:01 p.m.—Bush speaks at New Orleans airport, saying, "I know the people of this part of the world are suffering, and I want them to know that there's a flow of progress. We're making progress."

- —President Remarks on Hurricane Recovery Efforts, Louis Armstrong New Orleans International Airport, 2 Sep 2005.

Saturday, September 3, 2005—Five Days After

10:06 a.m.—Bush announces he is ordering additional active duty forces to the Gulf coast. "The enormity of the task requires more resources," he says in his Saturday radio address. "In America we do not abandon our fellow citizens in their hour of need." He says 4,000 active-duty troops are already in the area and 7,000 more will arrive in the next 72 hours. Those will add to some 21,000 National Guard troops already in the region.

- —President Addresses Nation, Discusses Hurricane Katrina Relief Efforts, The Rose Garden, 3 Sep 2005.

Sunday, September 4, 2005—Six Days After

The President issues a proclamation ordering the US Flag to be flown at half-staff at all federal building until Sept. 20 "as a mark of respect for the victims of Hurricane Katrina."

- —"Proclamation by the President: Honoring the Memory of the Victims of Hurricane Katrina," 4 Sep 2005.

Monday, September 5, 2005—One Week After

U.S. Army Corps of Engineers repair the levee breach on the 17th Street Canal and begin to pump water from the city.

- —"Pumps Begin to Drain New Orleans," CNN.com, 6 Sep 2005.

Tuesday, September 6, 2005—Eight Days After

FEMA asks reporters to refrain from taking pictures of the dead. Reuters quotes a FEMA spokeswoman as sending an email saying, "The recovery of victims is being treated with dignity and the utmost respect and we have requested that no photographs of the deceased be made by the media."

- —Deborah Zabarenko, "Media Groups Say FEMA Censors Search for Bodies," Reuters, 7 Sep 2005

Nagin orders police and law enforcement officials to remove everyone from the city who is not involved in recovery efforts. Despite this order, many residents remain in New Orleans, refusing to leave.

- —Cain Burdeau, "New Orleans Mayor Orders Forced Evacuation," Associated Press, 7 Sep 2005.

Wednesday, September 7, 2005—Nine Days After

FEMA brings in Kenyon International Services from Houston to assist in recovering bodies, many of which have been left in the open since the storm hit. A week later, state and federal officials will still be bickering over who is to pay the $119,000 daily expense of the outside mortuary specialists, and many bodies will still lie uncollected in the open and in drained buildings two weeks after the storm.

- —Michelle Krupa, "Louisiana Hires Firm to Help Recover Bodies; Blanco Says FEMA Moved Too Slowly," New Orleans *Times-Picayune*, 14 Sep 2005.

A bipartisan joint Congressional Committee is announced to investigate the response to Hurricane Katrina at "all levels of government," as federal, state, and local officials continue to blame each other for the slow response in dealing with the aftermath of Hurricane Katrina.

- —"GOP Leaders Agree to Joint Katrina Hearings," CNN.com, 8 Sep 2005.

Friday, September 9, 2005—Eleven Days After

Chertoff removes Brown from his role in managing the Katrina relief effort, and puts Coast Guard Vice Admiral Thad W. Allen in charge.

- —Peter Baker, "FEMA Director Replaced as Head of Relief Effort," *Washington Post*, 10 Sep 2005: A01.

Monday, September 12, 2005—Two Weeks After

Brown resigns as head of FEMA saying, "it is important that I leave now to avoid further distraction from the ongoing mission of FEMA."

- —"Statement by Michael D. Brown, Under Secretary of Department of Homeland Security Emergency Preparedness & Response and Director of the Federal Emergency Management Agency," News Release, FEMA, 12 Sep 2005.

Tuesday, September 13, 2005

11:30 a.m.—Bush takes responsibility for the federal government's failures while speaking at a press conference with Iraqi President Talabani.

Bush: Katrina exposed serious problems in our response capability at all levels of government. And to the extent that the federal government didn't fully do its job right, I take responsibility. I want to know what went right and what went wrong.

- —"President Welcomes President Talabani of Iraq to the White House," The East Room, News Release, 13 Sep 2005.

Thursday, September 15, 2005

Brown, in an interview published in the *New York Times*, says the governor and her staff had failed to organize a coherent state effort in the days after the hurricane, and that his field officers in the city were reporting an "out of control" situation to his superiors. He says he asked state officials, "What do you need? Help me help you. . . . The response was like, 'Let us find out,' and then I never received specific requests for specific things that needed doing." A spokesman for the governor said, "That is just totally inaccurate."

- —David D. Kirkpatrick and Scott Shane, "Ex-FEMA Chief Tells of Frustration and Chaos," *New York Times*, 15 Sep 2005: A1.

8:02 p.m.—Bush says, in a prime-time, televised speech from New Orleans that "the system, at every level of government, was not well-coordinated, and was overwhelmed in the first few days." He says the military should have a greater role in reacting to future large disasters. "Congress is preparing an investigation, and I will work with members of both parties to make sure this effort is thorough." He promises massive aid, tax breaks, and loan guarantees to aid rebuilding, saying that "there is no way to imagine America without New Orleans, and this great city will rise again."

- • —President Discusses Hurricane Relief in Address to the Nation, Jackson Square, New Orleans, Louisiana, 15 Sep 2005.

SOURCE: Available at www.factcheck.org and IAEM Discussion Group: September 16, 2005.

References

Birkland, Thomas A. 1997. *After disaster: Agenda setting, public policy, and focusing events*. Washington, DC: Georgetown University Press.

Block, Robert, and Amy Schatz. 2005. Storm front: Local and federal authorities battle to control disaster relief Florida beat back Washington during Hurricane Wilma; A video-conference coup/Mr. Fugate seizes 300 phones. *Wall Street Journal*, December 8.

Bowman, Tom, and Siobhan Gorman. 2005. Increasing military's role raises questions. *Baltimore Sun*, September 20.

Bullock, Jane A., George D. Haddow, Damon Coppola, Erdem Ergin, Lissa Westerman, and Sarp Yeletaysi. 2005. *Introduction to homeland security*. Boston: Elsevier Butterworth-Heinemann.

Dymon, Ude J., and Rutherford H. Platt. 1999. U.S. federal disaster declarations: A geographical analysis. In *Disasters and democracy: The politics of extreme natural events*, ed. Rutherford H. Platt, 47-67. Washington, DC: Island Press.

Gilmore, J. S., III. 2005. *Management challenges at the Department of Homeland Security: Hearing*. House Homeland Security Committee, Subcommittee on Management, Integration, and Oversight, April 20. 109th Cong., 1st sess., 1-47.

Haddow, George D., and Jane A. Bullock. 2003. *Introduction to emergency management*. Boston: Butterworth-Heinemann.

Healy, G. 2003. Deployed in the USA: The creeping militarization of the home front. Policy Analysis no. 303. December 17. Washington, DC: Cato Institute.

Heclo, Hugh. 1977. *A government of strangers*. Washington, DC: Brookings Institution.

Kettl, Donald F. 2004. *System under stress: Homeland security and American politics*. Washington, DC: Congressional Quarterly Press.

MSNBC. 2005. AP Reporter Mark Humphrey. Updated: 12:11 p.m. ET September 9. Washington, DC: The Washington Post Company.

National Academy of Public Administration (NAPA). 1993. *Coping with catastrophe: Building an emergency management system to meet people's needs in natural and manmade disasters*. Washington, DC: NAPA.

Nicholson, William C., ed. 2005. *Homeland security law and policy*. Springfield, IL: Charles C Thomas.

9/11 Commission Report: Final Report of the National Commission on Terrorist Attacks upon the United States. 2004. New York: Norton.

Platt, Rutherford H. 1999. Shouldering the burden: Federal assumption of disaster costs. In *Disasters and democracy: The politics of extreme natural events*, ed. Rutherford H. Platt, 11-46. Washington, DC: Island Press.

Platt, Rutherford H., and Claire B. Rubin. 1999. Stemming the losses: The quest for hazard mitigation. In *Disasters and democracy: The politics of extreme natural events*, ed. Rutherford H. Platt, 69-107. Washington, DC: Island Press.

Press Secretary, Office of the White House. 2005a. Fact Sheet: President Bush addresses the nation on recovery from Katrina. September 15. http://www.whitehouse.gov/news/releases/2005/09/20050915-7.html (accessed December 21, 2005).

———. 2005b. United States government response to the aftermath of Hurricane Katrina. September 1. http://www.dhs.gov/dhspublic/interapp/press_release/press_release_0727.xml (accessed December 21, 2005).

Relyea, Harold C. 2003. Organizing for homeland security. *Presidential Studies Quarterly* 33 (3): 602-24.

Settle, Allen K. 1990. Disaster assistance: Securing presidential declarations. In *Cities and disaster: North American studies in emergency management*, ed. Richard T. Sylves and William L. Waugh Jr., 33-57. Springfield, IL: Charles C Thomas.

Simendinger, Alexis. 2005. Disaster response threatens to swamp Bush administration. *National Journal*, September 5.

Strohm, Chris. 2005. Daily Briefing—Homeland Security had power to bypass states in hurricane response. *Governing Executive*, September 8.

Sylves, Richard T. 1996. The politics and budgeting of federal emergency management. In *Disaster management in the U.S. and Canada*, ed. Richard T. Sylves and William L. Waugh Jr., 26-45. Springfield, IL: Charles C Thomas.

Sylves, Richard T., and William L. Waugh Jr., eds. 1996. *Disaster management in the U.S. and Canada*. Springfield, IL: Charles C Thomas.

Thomas, Norman C., Joseph A. Pika, and Richard A. Watson. 1993. *The politics of the presidency*. Washington, DC: Congressional Quarterly Press.

Tierney, Kathleen J. 2005. *Recent developments in U.S. Homeland Security policies and their implications for the management of extreme events*. Boulder: Natural Hazards Research and Applications Center, Institute of Behavioral Science, University of Colorado at Boulder.

U.S. Congress. 1993. Senate. Committee on Governmental Affairs. *Hearing on Rebuilding FEMA: Preparing for the Next Disaster*. May 18. 103rd Cong., 1st sess.

U.S. Department of Homeland Security (DHS). 2004. Final Draft: National Response Plan. June 30. http:// www.dhs.gov/interweb/assetlibrary/NRP_Brochure.pdf (accessed December 21, 2005).

U.S. Federal Emergency Management Agency (FEMA). 2005. Declared Disasters Archive. http:// www.fema.gov/news/disasters.fema?year=2005 (accessed December 21, 2005).

U.S. General Accounting Office (GAO). 2004. *Emergency preparedness: Federal funds for first responders*. May 13. GAO-04-788T. Washington, DC: GAO.

———. 2005. *Homeland security: Management of first responder grant programs and efforts to improve accountability continue to evolve*. Statement of William O. Jenkins, Jr., Director of Homeland Security and Justice (GAO). April 12. GAO-05-530T. Washington, DC: GAO.

Wamsley, Gary L., Aaron D. Schroeder, and Larry M. Lane. 1996. To politicize is NOT to control: The pathologies of control in federal emergency management. *American Review of Public Administration* 26 (3): 263-85.

———. 2003. Terrorism, homeland security and the national emergency management network. *Public Organization Review* 3:373-85.

Waugh, William L., Jr., and Richard T. Sylves. 2002. Organizing the war on terrorism. *Public Administration Review* 62:145-53.

Witt, James L. 2004. *Testimony before the Subcommittee on National Security, Emerging Threats and International Relations and the Subcommittee on Energy Policy, Natural Resources and Regulatory Affairs*. March 24.

Metaphors Matter: Disaster Myths, Media Frames, and Their Consequences in Hurricane Katrina

By
KATHLEEN TIERNEY,
CHRISTINE BEVC,
and
ERICA KULIGOWSKI

It has long been understood by disaster researchers that both the general public and organizational actors tend to believe in various disaster myths. Notions that disasters are accompanied by looting, social disorganization, and deviant behavior are examples of such myths. Research shows that the mass media play a significant role in promulgating erroneous beliefs about disaster behavior. Following Hurricane Katrina, the response of disaster victims was framed by the media in ways that greatly exaggerated the incidence and severity of looting and lawlessness. Media reports initially employed a "civil unrest" frame and later characterized victim behavior as equivalent to urban warfare. The media emphasis on lawlessness and the need for strict social control both reflects and reinforces political discourse calling for a greater role for the military in disaster management. Such policy positions are indicators of the strength of militarism as an ideology in the United States.

Keywords: disaster response; disaster management; media reporting on disasters; public response to disasters

Since the inception of the field of social science disaster research in the United States, research has focused on public responses under disaster conditions. Initiated in the late 1940s

Kathleen Tierney is a professor in the Department of Sociology and the Institute of Behavioral Science at the University of Colorado and director of the University of Colorado Natural Hazards Center. She is also a codirector of the National Consortium for the Study of Terrorism and Responses to Terrorism, a Department of Homeland Security academic center of excellence that is headquartered at the University of Maryland.

Christine Bevc is a doctoral student in sociology at the University of Colorado and a graduate research assistant at the Natural Hazards Center. Her research interests include environmental sociology, geographic information science, the quantitative analysis of crisis response networks, and recent trends in emergency management policies and practices.

Erica Kuligowski is a doctoral student in sociology at the University of Colorado and a graduate research assistant at the Natural Hazards Center. Her current research focuses on crisis-related collective behavior, evacuation modeling, and qualitative media analysis.

DOI: 10.1177/0002716205285589

and early 1950s, disaster research in the United States was strongly associated with cold war concerns regarding how the general public might react in the event of a nuclear attack. Federal funding agencies believed that social science research on group behavior following disasters might shed light on such questions as whether people would panic and whether mass demoralization and social breakdown would occur following a nuclear weapons attack (Quarantelli 1987). As studies on public responses in disasters continued, it became increasingly evident to researchers that endangered publics and disaster victims respond and adapt well during and following disasters.

By the 1960s, a body of work had accumulated indicating that panic is not a problem in disasters; that rather than helplessly awaiting outside aid, members of the public behave proactively and prosocially to assist one another; that community residents themselves perform many critical disaster tasks, such as searching for and rescuing victims; and that both social cohesiveness and informal mechanisms of social control increase during disasters, resulting in a lower incidence of deviant behavior than during nondisaster times. Early research on disasters discussed such common patterns as the "expansion of the citizenship role" and "social leveling" to explain public responses to disasters. This literature identified strong situationally induced influences, such as emergent prosocial norms, as factors leading to greater community cohesiveness during disasters. Research indicated that during the emergency period following disasters, earlier community conflicts are suspended as communities unite under conditions of extreme stress. Earlier research also documented the emergence of "therapeutic communities" within disaster-stricken populations, involving victims coming together to provide mutual support to one another (for discussions on these points, see Fritz 1961; Barton 1969; Dynes 1970; Drabek 1986).

Classic research in the disaster field also highlighted contrasts that exist between the realities associated with disaster responses and myths concerning disaster behavior—myths that persist despite empirical evidence to the contrary. The first major article discussing common disaster myths was written by pioneering disaster researchers E. L. Quarantelli and Russell Dynes. That article, titled "When Disaster Strikes (It Isn't Much Like What You've Heard and Read About)," was published in *Psychology Today* in February 1972.

Since the prevalence of disaster myths was first documented, more research has been conducted focusing on such topics as the extent to which the public believes disaster myths (Wenger et al. 1975); the manner in which popular culture—specifically the disaster film genre—both reflects and perpetuates erroneous beliefs about disaster-related behavior (Quarantelli 1985; Mitchell et al. 2000); and the incidence of media accounts featuring disaster myths, relative to other themes (Goltz 1984). Some of this research has focused on how the belief in myths influences individual and organizational decision making in disasters (see Fischer 1998). Other research has pointed to the manner in which media reports can affect public perceptions by amplifying and distorting risk-related information (Kasperson and Kasperson 2005). Outside the field of disaster research, media scholars have also analyzed patterns of reporting in disasters (Smith 1992), as well as how media accounts help to shape public opinion (Walters, Wilkins, and Walters 1989).

[M]essages contained in the mass media and even in official discourse continue to promote ideas that have long been shown to be false in actual empirical research on disasters.

More recent analyses document how mythological beliefs have experienced a resurgence in the aftermath of the September 11, 2001, terrorist attacks (Tierney 2003). Focusing, for example, on the panic myth, the assumption that the public will panic in the event of another terrorist attack, especially one involving weapons of mass destruction, has been taken for granted in media and public policy discourses and is now even reflected in discussions among public health, homeland security, and emergency management professionals. These discourses often conflate the concept of panic with entirely normal and understandable public responses to risk and uncertainty, such as the upsurge of public information seeking in the 2001 anthrax attack. Intensified information seeking under conditions of threat or actual disaster impact, which can give rise to rumors of all types, has long been recognized as an extension of everyday interpersonal communicative practices and is readily explained by theories of collective behavior (Turner 1994). Although such behavior does create challenges for those who must respond to public inquiries, it does not indicate panic.

Similarly, it is well understood that under impending threats, many people who are not directly at risk will try to move out of harm's way, either because they are risk averse or because they do not fully understand or trust the warning information they have received. This sort of behavior, which researchers term the "evacuation shadow" effect, is quite common in threat situations of all types. First documented following the nuclear accident at Three Mile Island (Ziegler, Brunn, and Johnson 1981; Lindell and Perry 1992), the evacuation shadow phenomenon was seen most recently immediately prior to Hurricane Rita. Despite the fact that they are common, and despite the fact that why they occur is well understood, "inappropriate" efforts to seek safety on the part of people whom authorities do not consider at risk have also been seen as indicative of panic.

The panic myth has been consistently reinforced in various ways in the aftermath of 9/11. For example, the American Red Cross is widely viewed as a trusted source of information on disaster preparedness. Yet in 2005, the Red Cross took many researchers and disaster management professionals by surprise by launching a print and electronic media campaign whose theme was "I can't stop a [tornado, flood, fire, hurricane, terrorist attack, etc.] but I can stop panic." The campaign, which was intended to promote household preparedness for extreme events, erred in two ways. First, it conveyed the notion that there is nothing people can do to prevent disasters, which is patently false; and second, it sent a message that panic will invariably break out during disasters and other extreme events and that avoiding panic should be a top priority for the public when disasters strike. (For further discussions in inappropriate uses of the panic concept, see Clarke 2002; Tierney 2003, 2004.)

As the panic example shows, messages contained in the mass media and even in official discourse continue to promote ideas that have long been shown to be false in actual empirical research on disasters. Moreover, since the terrorist attacks of September 11, 2001, these types of messages, which continue to be vigorously challenged by experts, now seem to ring true to many audiences, in part because of the unsubstantiated and arguable but still widely accepted assumption that terrorism-related extreme events are qualitatively different from other types of emergencies and, thus, generate qualitatively different sociobehavioral responses.

Researchers have long pointed out that the belief in myths concerning disaster behavior is not problematic merely because such beliefs are untrue. Rather, these erroneous ideas are harmful because of their potential for influencing organizational, governmental, and public responses during disasters. It has been noted, for example, that incorrect assumptions about the potential for looting and social breakdown can lead to misallocations of public safety resources that could be put to better use in providing direct assistance to victims. Concerns with public panic can also lead officials to avoid issuing timely warnings and to keep needed risk-related information from the public (Fischer 1998). Such actions only serve to make matters worse when threats actually materialize.

We turn next to the substance of this article, which concerns the promulgation of disaster myths by the media during and following Hurricane Katrina. Because analyses on data collected in Katrina's aftermath are still ongoing, the article contains only preliminary observations, presented primarily in the form of examples from major press outlets that illustrate key points. We note also that at this time the media, the research community, and the nation as a whole still do not know with any degree of certainty what actually did happen during the hurricane and in the terrible days that followed. However, we emphasize that even though many questions still remain unanswered, and indeed may never be definitively answered, the images conveyed by the media during that turbulent period left indelible impressions on the public and also provided the justification for official actions that were undertaken to manage the disaster. Moreover, the media vigorously promoted those images even though media organizations themselves had little ability to verify what was actually happening in many parts of the impact region. As the sections that follow show, initial media coverage of Katrina's devastating impacts was quickly replaced by reporting that characterized disaster victims as opportunistic looters and violent criminals and that presented individual and group behavior following the Katrina disaster through the lens of civil unrest. Later, narratives shifted again and began to metaphorically represent the disaster-stricken city of New Orleans as a war zone and to draw parallels between the conditions in that city and urban insurgency in Iraq. These media frames helped guide and justify actions undertaken by military and law enforcement entities that were assigned responsibility for the postdisaster emergency response. The overall effect of media coverage was to further bolster arguments that only the military is capable of effective action during disasters.

What Influences Media Reporting on Disasters?

Discussions on why media portrayals of disasters and their victims so often deviate from what is actually known about behavior during emergencies highlight a number of factors. Some explanations center on reporting conventions that lead media organizations, particularly the electronic media, to focus on dramatic, unusual, and exceptional behavior, which can lead audiences to believe such behavior is common and typical. Other explanations focus on the widespread use of standard frames that strongly shape the content of media messages. Although based on myths about disaster behavior, one such frame, the "looting frame," appears almost invariably in disaster-related reporting. As Fischer (1998) noted in his book on disaster myths,

> Looting is perhaps the most expected behavioral response to disaster. Both print and broadcast media personnel report on the alleged looting incidents, on steps being taken to prevent it, and, alternatively, on how unusual it was for the community in question not to be preyed on by looters. (p. 15)

It is common for both print and electronic media covering disasters to include content indicating that "the National Guard has been brought into (name of community) to prevent looting"—implying that looting would otherwise have been a serious problem without the use of strong external social control. Following circular reasoning, the fact that looting does not occur during a particular disaster event is then attributed to the presence of the National Guard and public safety agencies, even though it is highly likely that looting would never have been a problem in the first place. These types of frames, themes, and content make such a strong impression on audiences in part because they reflect and are consistent with other popular media portrayals of disaster behavior, such as those that appear in disaster films and made-for-TV movies.

In the question-and-answer period following her testimony before the Research Subcommittee of the House Science Committee in November 2005, University of New Orleans sociologist Shirley Laska pointed to another important factor shaping disaster reporting. She noted that while many media outlets often do have science reporters, the media almost universally lack specialists in disaster-related phenomena, particularly those involving individual, group, and organizational behavior. In her comments, Laska recounted the many hours she spent on the telephone with reporters following Hurricane Katrina—interviews that were particularly lengthy because the vast majority of the reporters with whom she spoke lacked even the most basic understanding of societal response and emergency management issues (U.S. Congress 2005). Perhaps this lack of understanding of the fundamentals of disaster-related behavior is one reason why disaster myths and their associated frames have had such a strong influence on media disaster reporting.

Disaster reporting is also linked to what is judged to be newsworthy about particular events. Decisions about what and how much to cover with respect to specific disaster events are often rooted in judgments about the social value of disaster victims and on conceptions of social distance and difference. Thus, the vast outpouring of generosity following the Indian Ocean earthquake and tsunami of December 2004 was driven both by the catastrophic nature of the disaster and by the fact that so many Western tourists happened to be in the impact region when the disaster struck. There was no comparable compassionate response from the West for the victims of the 2005 Pakistan-Kashmir earthquake, despite the fact that the death toll has now exceeded eighty-six thousand and many more victims are expected to die of starvation or freeze to death when winter grips the impact region. Hurricane Wilma battered Cancun for two days and caused widespread devastation, but most U.S. reporting focused on American tourists who were stranded in the region, rather on the challenges faced by Cancun's residents, and reporting on the tragedy in Cancun and its catastrophic aftermath dropped off within a few days after the event, when the tourists had come home safely.

Since the media have a long record of portraying nonmainstream groups, especially minority group members, in stereotypical ways, it should come as no surprise that these same framing conventions would influence reporting on disaster victims in New Orleans following Hurricane Katrina. Indeed, in Katrina's aftermath, among the most widely circulated media images was a set of photographs in which African Americans were consistently described as "looting" goods, while whites engaging in exactly the same behaviors were labeled as "finding" supplies.

Media practices and judgments regarding newsworthiness, as well as media stereotyping, are undeniably important factors in the production of disaster news. At a more macro level, however, media treatments of disasters both reflect and reinforce broader societal and cultural trends, socially constructed metanarratives, and hegemonic discourse practices that support the status quo and the interests of elites. Thus, myths concerning the panicky public, the dangers presented by looters, and the threat disaster victims pose to the social order serve to justify policy stances adopted by law enforcement entities and other institutions concerned with social control (Tierney 2003).

We argue here that media reporting surrounding the Katrina disaster can best be understood from this last-mentioned perspective. In addition to reflecting both standard media reporting conventions and long-standing media biases regarding people of color, disaster reporting also serves broader political purposes. In the following sections, we will provide illustrative materials supporting this point. More specifically, we will argue that post-Katrina reporting led directly to the social construction of negative images of residents of the impact area, particularly African American victims and the very poor. Later shown to be inaccurate, slanted by sources that were themselves biased, and based more on rumor than on direct observation, reports constructed disaster victims as lawless, violent, exploitative, and almost less than human in the days following Katrina. Images of lawlessness and civil unrest were later replaced by media discourse characterizing New Orleans as a "war zone" and framing the challenges faced by emergency responders as not unlike those facing troops battling insurgents in Iraq.

A substantial social science literature points to the marked distinction that exists between how individuals and groups behave during periods of civil unrest and how they behave following disasters.

Both reflecting and further embellishing myths concerning behavior during disasters, media stories influenced officials to adopt unproductive and outright harmful response strategies during the emergency. The stories also served to further bolster claims regarding the need for strong command-and-control procedures and for greater involvement on the part of the military in extreme events ranging from homeland security emergencies to disasters of all types. Set in a broader societal context, media depictions of events as they unfolded during the disaster provided strong evidence for arguments that strict social control should be the first priority during disaster events and that the military is the only institution capable of managing disasters.

Media Reporting and the Social Construction of Looting and Violence in Hurricane Katrina

The preliminary analyses presented here are based on a variety of media sources. News stories focusing specifically on the behavior of victims and the official response to the hurricane were collected from three newspapers: *The New York Times*, *The Washington Post*, and the New Orleans *Times-Picayune*. The period covered spanned the impact period itself and the two weeks following the disaster, from August 29, 2005, to September 11, 2005. In extracting frames and themes from these reports, we used qualitative analytic techniques, rather than quantitatively oriented analytic approaches (see Altheide 1996). We do not argue that the "civil unrest" and "war zone" frames were the only ones employed by the media. Rather, we argue that these frames and their associated discourses were among the most prominent and that they achieved prominence because they were congruent with post-9/11 official discourses regarding how disasters and other extreme events—including in particular those associated with terrorist attacks— should be managed in the United States.

Disaster myths and the social construction of disorder in New Orleans

Rampant looting. As noted in the sections above, the notion that U.S. disasters are followed by looting activity has long been contradicted by empirical evidence. Nonetheless, the media continue to assume that looting and lawlessness are significant elements in the public response to disasters. Media coverage of the behaviors of disaster victims following the hurricane mirrored this assumption. Moreover, particularly in the early days after the hurricane, reports referred to disaster looting behavior in ways that would usually be reserved for describing behavior during episodes of civil unrest.

The distinction between disasters and urban unrest is an important one. A substantial social science literature points to the marked distinction that exists between how individuals and groups behave during periods of civil unrest and how they behave following disasters. When civil disorders occur, looting does break out; indeed, the taking of consumer goods and the destruction of property are hallmarks of modern U.S. "commodity riots," such as the urban riots of the 1960s and the 1992 Los Angeles civil unrest. Such looting is typically carried out by groups from within the riot area (including family groups) and in full view of the media, local residents, and even law enforcement agencies. Riot-related looting behavior develops under the influence of emergent norms that not only permit but actually encourage the taking and destruction of property (Dynes and Quarantelli 1968; Quarantelli and Dynes 1970). However, research also indicates that even during riot situations, looting is selective and usually confined to particular types of stores, such as those carrying retail goods, liquor, and groceries (Tierney 1994). Moreover, studies show that individuals who loot and engage in property violence during episodes of civil unrest do so sporadically, mixing their unlawful behavior with other routine social behavior such as gathering with friends and going home for meals. Looters may or may not share common grievances or reasons for looting; some may see looting as an act of protest or retaliation, while others may view unrest as simply an opportunity to obtain goods for free (Feagin and Hahn 1973; McPhail and Wohlstein 1983; McPhail 1991).

In contrast, research has shown repeatedly that looting is highly unusual in U.S. disasters. When it does occur, it tends to be transient, to be carried out in secret, and to involve isolated groups rather than large numbers of people. Unlike looting during civil disorders, actual and potential disaster-related looting behavior is widely condemned by the residents of affected communities. Signs bearing messages such as "you loot, we shoot," which are often shown in the media following disasters, are not so much indicative of the actual occurrence of looting as they are of strong community norms against looting (Fischer 1998). Community residents also believe looting myths and act accordingly, arming themselves in an effort to prevent looting, even if such behavior has not been reported or verified by official sources. After disasters, individuals returning to their damaged homes and businesses to retrieve items may be mistakenly labeled as looters, as may those who go to others' homes to check to see whether occupants are safe. Overconcern with the possibility of looting often leads community residents to ignore evacuation warnings and remain in their homes to ward off looters—another example of how the belief in myths may actually increase the risk of death and injury in disasters (Fischer 1998; Tierney, Lindell, and Perry 2001).

This is not to say that there have never been instances of large-scale collective looting in U.S. disasters. While vanishingly rare, such episodes have occurred. Perhaps the most notable recent example is the looting that occurred on the island of St. Croix following Hurricane Hugo in 1989. Hugo was a huge storm that caused serious damage and social disruption in many parts of the Caribbean and the southeast, including parts of Puerto Rico and North and South Carolina. However, looting only emerged on St. Croix, not in other hard-hit areas. Because this was such an unusual case, disaster scholar E. L. Quarantelli spent considerable time investigating why looting was a problem on St. Croix but nowhere else Hugo had affected. Based on his fieldwork and interviews, Quarantelli attributed the looting to several factors. First, the hurricane devastated the island, completely destroying the vast bulk of the built environment. Second, government institutions, including public safety agencies, were rendered almost entirely ineffective by the hurricane's severity, so the victims essentially had no expectation that their needs would be addressed by those institutions. Third, victims had no information on when they could expect help to arrive. Equally important, according to Quarantelli, was that the lawlessness that followed Hugo was in many ways consistent with the high rates of predisaster crime on the island and also a consequence of preexisting social inequalities and class and racial resentments, which had long been exacerbated by the sharp class distinctions that characterized the tourist economy on St. Croix (see Quarantelli 2006; Rodríguez, Trainor, and Quarantelli 2006 [this volume]).

It can be argued that the post-Katrina conditions in New Orleans in many ways paralleled the situation on St. Croix following Hugo. Those who were unable to escape the city or find refuge after Katrina struck may well have reached the same conclusions as those who were trapped on St. Croix after Hugo. With homes, property, and livelihoods gone, with no evidence of a functioning governmental system, facing severe danger and hardship, and without having any idea of when help would arrive, many residents might have understandably concluded that they were on their own and that they had best fend for themselves.

Given the utterly miserable conditions the hurricane produced, looting might well have been collectively defined as justifiable by some of those who were forced to remain and await help in New Orleans. Many news reports featured images of desperate residents fanning out through neighborhoods in search of basic necessities such as food, water, diapers, and clothing (Barringer and Longman 2005; Coates and Eggen 2005a). However, as of this writing, no solid empirical data exist regarding how widespread (or rare) looting actually was, who took part in the episodes of looting that did occur, why they were motivated to take part, whether the goods people took could have been salvaged, or how much damage and loss looting actually caused, relative to other losses the hurricane produced. Equally important, whatever lawless behavior may have occurred has not yet been systematically analyzed in the context of "normal" rates of lawbreaking in New Orleans. What do exist are volumes of information on what the media and public officials *believed and communicated* about looting in New Orleans. As discussed below, these reports characterized post-Katrina looting as very widespread, wanton, irrational, and accompanied by violence—in short, as resembling media characterizations of riot behavior. Moreover, the media confined their reporting to the putative lawless behavior of certain categories and types of people—specifically young black males—to the exclusion of other behaviors in which these disaster victims may have engaged during the disaster, producing a profile of looters and looting groups that overlooked whatever prosocial, altruistic behaviors such groups may have undertaken.

More systematic analyses of media looting reports will come later. In this article, we offer a series of representative reports that appeared in *The New York Times*, *The Washington Post*, and the New Orleans *Times-Picayune* as well as from the Department of Defense's American Forces Information Service. We stress that these are typical comments that were made in these media outlets, not unusual ones. The material presented below focuses mainly on the first few days after the hurricane.

From *The New York Times*:

August 31: "These are not individuals looting. These are large groups of armed individuals." . . . "Looting broke out as opportunistic thieves cleaned out abandoned stores for a second night. In one incident, officials said a police officer was shot and critically wounded." (Treaster and Kleinfield 2005)

September 1: "Chaos gripped New Orleans on Wednesday as looters ran wild . . . looters brazenly ripped open gates and ransacked stores for food, clothing, television sets, computers, jewelry, and guns." (McFadden and Blumenthal 2005)

From *The Washington Post*:

August 31: "Even as the floodwaters rose, looters roamed the city, sacking department stores and grocery stories and floating their spoils away in plastic garbage cans. . . . Looting began on Canal Street, in the morning, as people carrying plastic garbage pails waded through waist-deep water to break into department stores. In drier areas, looters raced into smashed stores and pharmacies and by nightfall the pillage was widespread." (Gugliotta and Whoriskey 2005)

September 2: "What could be going through the minds of people who survive an almost biblical tragedy, find themselves in a hellscape of the dead and the dispossessed, and promptly decide to go looting? Obviously not much: Stealing a rack of fancy clothes when there's no place to wear them or a television when there's no electricity does not suggest a lot of deep thought." (Robinson 2005)

From the New Orleans *Times-Picayune*:

August 30: In the midst of the rising water, two men "were planning to head out to the levee to retrieve a stash of beer, champagne, and hard liquor they found washed onto the levee." (MacCash and O'Byrne 2005)

August 30: "Midafternoon Monday, a parade of looters streamed from Coleman's retail store. . . . The looters, men and women who appeared to be in their early teens to mid-40s, braved a steady rain . . . to take away boxes of clothing and shoes from the store." (Philbin 2005)

August 31: "Officials watched helplessly as looters around the city ransacked stores for food, clothing, appliances, and guns." " 'The looting is out of control. The French Quarter has been attacked,' Councilwoman Jackie Clarkson said." (McGill 2005)

Beyond property crime. Not only were the crowds engaging in the collective theft of all types of goods, but their behavior was also violent and even deadly. Media accounts made it seem as if all of New Orleans was caught up in a turmoil of lawlessness.

From *The New York Times*:

September 2: "Chaos and gunfire hampered efforts to evacuate the Superdome, and, the New Orleans police superintendent said, armed thugs have taken control of the secondary makeshift shelter in the convention center. The thugs repelled eight squads of eleven officers each he sent to secure the place . . . rapes and assaults were occurring unimpeded in the neighborhood streets. . . . Looters set ablaze a shopping center and firefighters, facing guns, abandoned their efforts to extinguish the fires, local radio said." (Treaster and Sontag 2005)

September 3: "America is once more plunged into a snake pit of anarchy, death, looting, raping, marauding thugs, suffering infrastructure, a gutted police force, insufficient troop levels and criminally negligent government planning." (Dowd 2005)

From *The Washington Post*:

September 1: "Things have spiraled so out of control [in New Orleans] that the city's mayor ordered police officers to focus on looters and give up the search and rescue efforts." (Coates and Eggen 2005b)

September 3: A firefighter from Long Beach is quoted as saying, "People are taking clothing, liquor, things that aren't life-surviving, material items. I don't have a problem if someone is trying to get food and water, but beyond that, we're bustn' em. . . . What we're getting worried about is people are starting to shoot at us now. . . . That's the lowest form of human being haunting the earth." (Vedantam and Klein 2005)

From the New Orleans *Times-Picayune*:

August 31: According to the New Orleans homeland security chief, "There are gangs of armed men in the city, moving around the city." (*Times-Picayune* 2005a)

September 2: "Governor Kathleen Blanco called the looters 'hoodlums' and issued a warning to lawbreakers: Hundreds of National Guard hardened on the battlefield in Iraq have landed in New Orleans. 'They have M-16s, and they're locked and loaded,' she said." (Breed 2005)

Another graphic *Times-Picayune* story, published on September 1, spoke of gangs looting houses and businesses, robbing people in the street, looting gun stores, stealing guns from Wal-Mart, and assaulting disaster victims (Anderson, Perlstein, and Scott 2005). These media stories, along with stories passed through rumor networks, clearly influenced disaster management decision making. Immediately following the New Orleans levee breach, for example, Louisiana Governor Kathleen Blanco emphasized that search and rescue should take priority over all other emergency activities. However, as the September 1 story above in *The Washington Post* indicates, within three days of the hurricane's impact, she and the mayor of New Orleans ordered public safety officers to pursue lawbreakers, rather than concentrating on lifesaving activities (Coates and Eggen 2005b). This decision directly influenced the survival chances of stranded and dying disaster victims.

The material presented above comes from print media. While we have not attempted to undertake the Herculean task of analyzing electronic media, the Internet, or postings that appeared in the blogosphere, anyone who watched or read these media in the aftermath of Katrina can only conclude that the images of looting and looters these media conveyed were even more extreme. While television news did report extensively on the suffering of Katrina's victims, the intergovernmental disaster response debacle, and other topics, it also featured numerous stories of looting, rape, and lawlessness, continuously "looping" video of the activities of groups that had already become "armed, marauding thugs" in the minds of viewers. Video images also conveyed more powerfully than print media could that the "thugs" who had taken over New Orleans were young black men.

As the emergency continued, all manner of rumors were reported by the media as truth. Readers and viewers were told, for example, of multiple murders, child rape, and people dying of gunshot wounds in the Superdome. These reports were later found to be groundless, but they were accepted as accurate by both media organizations and consumers of news because they were consistent with the emerging media frame that characterized New Orleans as a "snakepit of anarchy," a violent place where armed gangs of black men took advantage of the disaster not only to loot but also to commit capital crimes.

More thoughtful analyses of looting and other forms of disaster-related collective behavior would later emerge in the media (see, for example, an article titled

"Up for Grabs; Sociologists Question How Much Looting and Mayhem Really Took Place in New Orleans," which ran in the *Boston Globe* on September 11, 2005; see Shea 2005). But before these kinds of balanced reports appeared, the "armed thug" frame was already well established. Reports seemed to clearly show that the activities of armed thugs, "the lowest form of human being haunting the earth," had gone well beyond looting for necessities and had spilled over into murder, rape, and acts of random violence (Vedantam and Klein 2005). This frame provided part of the justification for the subsequent governmental response to the Katrina disaster.

Metaphors Matter:
From Civil Unrest to Urban Warfare

The inability of federal, state, and local authorities to respond rapidly and effectively to Hurricane Katrina quickly became a major scandal both in the United States and around the world. In the days immediately following the disaster, the press, the U.S. populace, and Washington officialdom all sought to understand what had gone so terribly wrong with the intergovernmental response to Hurricane Katrina. Within a few days, a broad consensus developed that Michael Brown, the director of the Federal Emergency Management Agency (FEMA), was the individual most responsible for the Katrina debacle. Brown resigned under heavy criticism on September 12, 2005. In the weeks and months following Katrina, the media have continued to report both on Brown's lack of qualifications for his position and on his lack of basic situation awareness during the Katrina disaster. Most recently, stories have focused on e-mails that Brown exchanged with colleagues at the height of the crisis, purportedly showing that he was drastically out of touch with what was actually happening in New Orleans and other areas affected by the hurricane. In the meantime, broader management system failures during Hurricane Katrina became the subject of a congressional investigation.

Even before Brown's resignation, administration officials had likely already concluded that civil authorities were incapable of responding to Katrina and that the military would have to play a significantly larger role than it has traditionally played in U.S. disasters. The president attempted to federalize and militarize the response immediately after the hurricane, but he was rebuffed by Governor Blanco (Roig-Franzia and Hsu 2005). Although the initial federal response to Katrina had been shockingly incompetent, the federal government ultimately did mobilize, and a large component of that mobilization involved military and security resources. Just two days after Hurricane Katrina made landfall in Louisiana and ten days before Brown's resignation, the president had already ordered General Russell Honore, as commander of Joint Task Force Katrina, to coordinate the military's role in rescue and relief activities throughout the Gulf Coast. Within a week (and in some cases, within days), along with first responders from around the United States, military, law enforcement, and private security companies began to converge on the region to provide all forms of assistance and to reinforce overwhelmed state and local public safety forces. They would help restore public order, joining what Governor Blanco had earlier referred to as battle-seasoned Louisiana National Guard forces, "locked and loaded," to put down looting and violence (Breed 2005). When beleaguered FEMA chief Michael Brown was finally recalled to Washington, he was replaced as chief coordinating official in the disaster region not by another civilian official but by Admiral Thad Allen.

[W]hatever lawless behavior may have occurred [in Hurricane Katrina's aftermath] has not yet been systematically analyzed in the context of "normal" rates of lawbreaking in New Orleans.

By the fifth day after the hurricane's landfall in the Gulf region, the number of National Guard and active military deployed in Hurricane Katrina had tripled the number deployed within that same time period following Hurricane Andrew in 1992 (American Forces Information Service 2005a). With the arrival of so many command-and-control-oriented entities into the impact region, the response to Hurricane Katrina, particularly in New Orleans, began to take on a tone not seen in other U.S. disasters. Badges, uniforms, and arms—including assault weapons— were seen on the streets in large numbers. Search and rescue missions in the flooded neighborhoods of New Orleans began to resemble military search and destroy missions, as armed soldiers broke down doors and entered homes in search of stranded victims. In a city already under a strict dawn-to-dusk curfew, the movements of New Orleans residents—described as "holdouts" for their refusal to follow orders to leave their own homes and evacuate the city—were further curtailed, as sheriff's deputies were ordered to "handcuff and 'forcefully remove' holdouts" (Nolan 2005). The militarization of the response now affected even media reporters, as response personnel attempted to limit their access to sites within the city.

Once the looting and civil unrest were perceived to have exceeded the capabilities of local law enforcement, the National Guard were described as having been brought into disaster-stricken areas to help "restore and maintain law and order" to affected areas (Haskell 2005). As more military and law enforcement personnel streamed into Louisiana, and as media reporting continued to emphasize civil disorder and lawlessness, a new "war zone" metaphor began to emerge. First employed by the media, the "war zone" metaphor was quickly reflected in the discourse of both public officials and military personnel who were deployed in the impact region. With so many military and other security personnel on the ground, comparisons to wartime experiences became increasingly common. "I'd thought we'd just entered a war zone" and "the region looks like a war zone" became familiar statements (Alvarez 2005a, 2005b). In interviews, National Guard personnel likened the destruction in the Gulf region to their experiences in the Gulf War. Referring to the extensive building damage, one Guardsman noted that "some of the things you see out here you see in Iraq" (Alvarez 2005a). The extent of the devastation was characterized as shocking even to the "most seasoned veterans of past wars" (American Forces Information Service 2005c).

Within a few days after the hurricane, President Bush and other government officials described themselves as determined to regain control and protect the people from the criminal element through the presence of military forces. For example, on September 3, a *Times-Picayune* story emphasized Mr. Bush's strong law and order stance:

> "What is not working right, we're going to make it right." Referring to rampant looting and crime in New Orleans, Bush said, "We are going to restore order in the city of New Orleans. The people of this country expect there to be law and order, and we're going to work hard to get it. In order to make sure there's less violence, we've got to get food to people. We'll get on top of this situation, and we're going to help the people that need help." (*Times-Picayune* 2005b)

A few days later, the *New York Times* described the warlike conditions in New Orleans in this manner:

> September 11: "Partly because of the shortage of troops, violence raged inside the New Orleans convention center, which interviews show was even worse than previously described. Police SWAT team members found themselves plunging into the darkness, guided by the muzzle flashes of thugs' handguns." (Lipton et al. 2005)

Media also reported that in response to civil unrest at the convention center, one thousand National Guard military police "stormed" the convention center "to thwart a looming potentially dangerous situation" (R. Williams 2005). A National Guard officer explained that "had the Guardsmen gone in with less force, they may have been challenged and innocent people may have been caught in a fight between the Guard military police and those who didn't want to be processed or apprehended" (R. Williams 2005). After military police regained "control" of the convention center, hundreds of disaster evacuees were searched like criminal suspects for guns, illicit drugs, alcohol, contraband, and other items that had been designated as "undesirable" and then sent back into the center to await buses that would take them out of the city (R. Williams 2005).

The increasing threat and the use of military force were presented as key factors in restoring order throughout the Gulf Coast region. On September 3, for example, a news report quoted an Army major general as stating that "once you put soldiers on the streets with M-16s, things tend to settle down" (Alvarez 2005a). On September 4, the *New York Times* reported that "the mere sight of troops in camouflage battle gear and with assault rifles gave a sense of relief to many of the thousands of stranded survivors who had endured days of appalling terror and suffering." In the same article, Louisiana Governor Kathleen Blanco was quoted as stating that

> they [the military] brought a sense of order and peace, and it was a beautiful sight to see that we're ramping up. We are seeing a show of force. It's putting confidence back in our hearts and in the minds of our people. We're going to make it through. (McFadden 2005)

By September 13, the deployment of military personnel in response to Hurricane Katrina, totaling more than seventy-two thousand troops, was the largest for any natural disaster in U.S. history (American Forces Information Service 2005b). According to the media and the military press, military missions included deploying guards at street intersections (Hynes 2005), searching damaged buildings, and reinforcing social control through the use of "security" and "safety" measures.

To media, governmental, and military sources, operations in Louisiana, Alabama, Mississippi, and the rest of the impact region had come to resemble a second Iraq War. Indeed, one military official, presumably equating the disaster impact region with Iraq, was quoted as saying that "we are now fighting on two fronts" (*Times-Picayune* 2005c). A Loudon County, Virginia, sheriff mused upon sending county officers to Jefferson parish near New Orleans, stating, "I almost feel like a father sending his kids off to war or something. Things are becoming more and more violent as people become more desperate" (Laris 2005).

The media emphasized the "war zone" metaphor in multiple articles discussing the response of the people of New Orleans. For example, the *New York Times* described the thoughts of a man who had volunteered his fishing boat to rescue New Orleans residents:

> A shotgun rested in the boat next to Mr. Lovett, who said shots had been fired near him on occasion during the past week. "I don't feel like I'm in the U.S. I feel like I'm in a war. All the guns, the chaos." (Longman 2005)

New Orleans Police Superintendent Eddie Compass spoke with the *Times-Picayune* about the New Orleans Police Department's successful attempts to operate under wartime conditions:

> "In the annals of history, no police department in the history of the world was asked to do what we were asked," Compass said Monday, at the Emergency Operations Center in Baton Rouge. "We won. We did not lose one officer in battle." (Filosa 2005)

Ironically, with the increased presence of the military, the media itself began facing restrictions and threats over its coverage of the hurricane response. The National Guard and law enforcement agencies initiated various strategies to limit journalists' access to places where disaster operations were being carried out. One strategy centered on controlling the movement of journalists within the city of New

Orleans (B. Williams 2005). Response agencies also began refusing media access to the Convention Center and Superdome (B. Williams 2005). When reporters protested, they were faced down by military personnel carrying loaded weapons (B. Williams 2005). As the recovery of bodies began, reporters were told, "No photos. No stories." In an article in the *San Francisco Chronicle*, a soldier was quoted as telling reporters that "the Army had a policy that requires media to be 300 meters—more than three football fields in length—away from the scene of body recoveries" (Vega 2005).

As the quote above indicates, the military's response and reaction to coverage of the deaths from Hurricane Katrina came to eerily resemble the administration's policy in Iraq, which prohibits the media from showing images of dead American soldiers. Reporters were told they would "face consequences" if they took pictures (Vega 2005). In an effort to further contain media coverage, on September 10, 2005, General Honore and Colonel Terry Ebbert announced that the media would have "zero access" to the recovery operations (CNN.com 2005b). The media were granted access to gather information and report on body recovery only after a temporary restraining order was issued at the request of CNN (CNN.com 2005a).

Conclusions and Implications

Myths and their consequences. As the foregoing discussion shows, both media reporting and official discourse following Hurricane Katrina upheld the mythical notion that disasters result in lawlessness and social breakdown. This is not to say that media coverage following Katrina provided nothing helpful or useful to victims, the American public, and audiences around the world. That was certainly not the case. The media devoted enormous resources to covering Katrina and also to performing such services as helping to locate and reunite disaster-stricken households. Reporters worked tirelessly to provide up-to-date information on all aspects of the hurricane.

However, even while engaging extensively in both reporting and public service, the media also presented highly oversimplified and distorted characterizations of the human response to the Katrina catastrophe. Ignoring the diversity and complexity of human responses to disastrous events, media accounts constructed only two images of those trapped in the disaster impact area: victims were seen either as "marauding thugs" out to attack both fellow victims and emergency responders or as helpless refugees from the storm, unable to cope and deserving of charity. These contrasting constructions are reflected in a story that appeared in the *Times-Picayune* on August 30, which discussed Louisiana Governor Blanco's reflection on displaced New Orleans disaster victims:

> Part of the population in the Dome are people "who do not have any regard for others." But many "good people" are also living in the Dome, she said, including mothers with babies. (Scott 2005)

Even as media and official discourses acknowledged that "good people"—mainly women and children—were among those victimized by Katrina, the terms used to describe the behavior of disaster victims in New Orleans, the majority of whom were people of color, were identical to those used to describe individuals and groups that engage in rioting in the context of episodes of civil unrest. Those trapped in New Orleans were characterized as irrational (because they engaged in "senseless" theft, rather than stealing for survival) and as gangs of out-of-control young males who presented a lethal threat to fellow victims and emergency responders. Officials increasingly responded to the debacle in New Orleans—a debacle that was in large measure of their own making—as if the United States were facing an armed urban insurgency rather than a catastrophic disaster. As the situation in New Orleans was increasingly equated with conditions of a "war zone," strict military and law enforcement controls, including controls on media access to response activities such as body recovery, were seen as necessary to replace social breakdown with the rule of law and order.

Once the initial media frenzy finally died down, journalists themselves were among the harshest critics of Katrina reporting. For example, in a September 29 segment that aired on the *NewsHour with Jim Lehrer*, media analysts, a journalist who had covered the Katrina disaster, and a military official were unanimous in their condemnation of how the media promoted myths of looting and violence in stories that were based almost entirely on rumor and hearsay. Noting that media reporters had by and large never actually witnessed lawlessness and violence in New Orleans, *NewsHour* guests gave numerous examples of the ways in which the media fell short of its duty to report facts, as opposed to rumors. One commentator noted that

> The central part of this story, what went wrong at the convention center and the Superdome, was wrong. American media threw everything they had at this story . . . and yet they could not get inside the convention center, they could not get inside the Superdome to dispel the lurid, the hysterical, the salaciousness of the reporting. . . . I have in mind especially the throat-slashed seven-year-old girl who had been gang-raped at the convention center—didn't happen. In fact there were no rapes at the convention center or the Superdome that have yet been corroborated in any way. . . . There weren't stacks of bodies in the freezer. But America was riveted by this reporting, wholesale collapse of the media's own levees as they let in all the rumors, and all the innuendo, all the first-person story, because they were caught up in their own emotionalism . . . [this was] one of the worst weeks of reporting in the history of the American media. (Online NewsHour 2005, 5)

Ways of telling are also ways of not telling, and this same commentator went on to say,

> I think that some of the journalists involved, especially the anchors, became so caught up in their own persona and their own celebrity that they missed important and obvious stories. They failed to report on the basic issues surrounding who deploys the National Guard; they failed to report on why the Salvation Army and the Red Cross were forbidden by state officials to deliver supplies to the Superdome and the convention center. They failed to report what happened to the buses [that were supposed to be used to evacuate residents of New Orleans] . . . they reported panic-inducing, fear-inducing, hysteria-

inducing events: looting, pillaging, murder sprees, sort of the most squalid journalism you could imagine. (Online NewsHour 2005, 7)

Outcomes and consequences of media myths. Despite these and other efforts to criticize the media's performance following Katrina, initial evidence suggests that the media's relentless adherence to disaster myths and to frames emphasizing civil unrest and urban insurgency, along with the strategic response measures these reports justified, had a number of immediate negative consequences. For example, by calling for curfews and viewing all victim movements around the city as suspect, authorities likely interfered with ability of neighborhood residents and family groups to assist one another. Because they focused on combating what the media had constructed as out-of-control looting and widespread violence, officials may have failed to take full advantage of the goodwill and altruistic spirit of community residents and community resources, such as churches and community-based organizations. By reassigning emergency responders from lifesaving activities to law enforcement functions, those in charge of the response placed law and order above the lives of hurricane survivors. By treating disaster victims as thugs engaging in capital crimes at worst and as troublesome "holdouts" at best, responding agencies created conflicts between themselves and disaster victims that might not have developed otherwise and that likely destroyed the potential for the kinds of collaborative partnership activities that major disasters require. Anecdotal reports, not yet verified, also suggest that images of looting and lawlessness may have caused individuals and organizations from outside the affected region to hesitate before mobilizing to disaster sites in the immediate aftermath of Katrina (Laris 2005).

The treatment of disaster victims in New Orleans and other areas affected by Katrina has also reinforced the nation's racial divide. Public opinion polls conducted in the aftermath of Hurricane Katrina reveal stark differences between white and African American perceptions of the governmental response to the disaster. A survey conducted by the Pew Center for the People and the Press in early September found that a majority of those polled disapproved of the government's handling of the Katrina disaster. However, comparisons of black and white responses to the poll revealed very significant opinion differences. For example, 71 percent of blacks thought that the disaster showed that racial inequality is still a major problem in the United States, but 56 percent of white respondents said that was not the case. Two-thirds of black respondents believed that the governmental response would have been swifter had the disaster victims been white, while only 17 percent of whites thought the race of the victims made a difference. The opinions of blacks and whites differed dramatically along other dimensions as well: blacks were much more likely to report feeling angry and depressed after the hurricane; to feel sympathy for those who had been unable to evacuate; and to believe that those who may have looted did so because they needed to survive, not because they were criminals seeking to take advantage of the disaster (although 37 percent of whites expressed the latter view) (Pew Center 2005).

These disparate reactions to the government's handling of Hurricane Katrina have broader implications for other extreme events. If people of color now have such low regard for national leaders and crisis response agencies, and if their faith in mainstream institutions has been so badly shaken by the Katrina disaster, what will be their likely response in future national emergencies, such as an avian flu epidemic? If government leaders, the media, and members of the white majority see African Americans and other people of color as lawless elements who are ready to take advantage of disaster- or terrorism-related social disruption, what extreme measures are they likely to advocate to ensure the maintenance of public security during future emergencies?

Militarism and disasters. Hurricane Katrina showed once again that the potential for catastrophe is present wherever extreme events—natural, technological, or willful—intersect with vulnerable built environments and vulnerable populations. Those left behind in the hurricane's wake were the most vulnerable groups in the impact region—individuals and households that lacked the resources to evacuate or that stayed behind for a variety of other reasons. It was widely understood well before Katrina that New Orleans could not be successfully evacuated in the face of a major hurricane, but few concrete actions had been taken to address the needs of these most vulnerable residents.

Reflecting on the fate of these stranded victims, it is important to note that many of the nation's large urban agglomerations, and their populations, are at risk from future extreme events. These large urban centers include New York City, Los Angeles, the Bay Area of Northern California, and Miami. Highly vulnerable urban places are also home to highly diverse populations, including many who are forced to live in poverty. Will other low-income inner-city communities be seen as potential hotbeds of urban unrest and potential "war zones" in future disasters? Will the same images of violence and criminality that emerged following Katrina be applied, perhaps preemptively, to other large cities affected by extreme events?

Predictably, the failed governmental response to Hurricane Katrina has led to new calls for stronger military involvement in disaster response activities. In Katrina's wake, disasters are now being characterized as best managed not by civil authorities but by entities capable of using force—deadly force, if necessary—to put down civil unrest and restore order in the aftermath of disasters. Military institutions are widely viewed as possessing the resources, logistics capability, and strategic insights required to "get things done" when disasters strike. This militaristic approach stands in sharp contrast with foundational assumptions concerning how disasters should be managed, which emphasize the need for strengthening community resilience, building public-private partnerships, reaching out to marginalized community residents and their trusted institutions, and developing consensus-based coordinating mechanisms at the interorganizational, community, and intergovernmental levels (see Waugh 2000; Haddow and Bullock 2003).

Calls for military control following disasters are not new. Many of the same arguments for greater military involvement were made following Hurricane Andrew, which struck in 1992, and which was followed by failures on the part of the intergovernmental emergency response system that resembled those following Katrina, but on a smaller scale. However, a study later conducted to analyze the response to Andrew and recommend improvements saw no justification for giving broader authority to the military during disasters (National Academy of Public Administration 1993). Even after Katrina, opposition to greater military involvement is widespread. For example, a *USA Today* poll of thirty-eight governors found

---

[I]nitial evidence suggests that the media's relentless adherence to disaster myths and to frames emphasizing civil unrest and urban insurgency, along with the strategic response measures these reports justified, had a number of immediate negative consequences.

---

that only two governors supported the president's proposal that the military take a greater role in responding to disasters (Disaster preparedness 2005). In an Associated Press report on November 4, 2005, Montana governor Brian Schweitzer was quoted as saying that at the upcoming meeting of the Western Governors Association,

> I'm going to stand up among a bunch of elected governors and say, "Are we going to allow the military without a shot being fired to effectively do an end-run coup on civilian government? Are we going to allow that?" We're going to have a little civics lesson for some leaders who are apparently out of touch in the military.

Despite such protests, the concept of military control during disasters continues to gain traction in the aftermath of Hurricane Katrina. Distorted images disseminated by the media and public officials served to justify calls for greater military involvement in disasters. At a broader level, images of disaster victims as criminals and insurgents and of military personnel as the saviors of New Orleans are consistent with the growing prominence of militarism as a national ideology. We do not speak here of the military as an institution or of its role in national defense. Instead, following Chalmers Johnson (2004), we distinguish between the military and *militarism*—the latter referring to an ideology that places ultimate faith in the ability of the military and armed force to solve problems in both the international and domestic spheres. Johnson noted that "one sign of the advent of militarism is the assumption by the nation's armed forces of numerous tasks that should be reserved for civilians" (p. 24) and also that "certainly one of the clearest signs of militarism in

America, is the willingness of some senior officers and civilian militarists to meddle in domestic policing" (p. 119). This is exactly what occurred during Hurricane Katrina—and what may become standard procedure in future extreme events.

It is now common knowledge that in the aftermath of the 2001 terrorist attacks, the Bush administration and some military officials began a reassessment of the *Posse Comitatus* act, which forbids the military to perform policing functions within the United States. This reassessment accompanied the creation in 2002 of the U.S. Northern Command (NORTHCOM), a military force whose purpose is to engage in "homeland defense." A number of analysts, including writers representing conservative think tanks like the Cato Institute, have called attention to the continual expansion of the role of the military in domestic emergency and security operations (Healey 2003). One of the most profound domestic impacts of the so-called war on terrorism is a growing acceptance of the military's involvement in a wide variety of domestic missions, including providing security at the Salt Lake City Olympics, searching for the Washington-area sniper, and now the policing and management of disaster victims.

Disasters can become "focusing events" that bring about changes in laws, policies, and institutional arrangements (Birkland 1997; Rubin and Renda-Tenali 2000). Hurricane Katrina may well prove to be the focusing event that moves the nation to place more faith in military solutions for a wider range of social problems than ever before. If this does turn out to be the case, the media will have helped that process along through its promulgation of myths of lawlessness, disorder, and urban insurgency.

References

Altheide, David L. 1996. *Qualitative media analysis*. Thousand Oaks, CA: Sage.

Alvarez, Steve. 2005a. Alabama guard provides critical disaster response. American Forces Information Service. September 3. http://www.defenselink.mil/news/Sep2005/20050903_2612.html.

———. 2005b. Engineers clear way in Gulf. American Forces Information Service. September 5. http://www.defenselink.mil/news/Sep2005/20050905_2618.html.

American Forces Information Service. 2005a. Day five comparison of troop numbers for Hurricanes Andrew and Katrina. September 5. http://www.defenselink.mil/news/Sep2005/050906-D-6570C-001.jpg.

———. 2005b. Military continues Hurricane Katrina support. September 13. http://www.defenselink.mil/news/Sep2005/20050913_2723.html.

———. 2005c. 139th Airlift Wind aids children and families after Katrina devastation. September 27. http://www.ngb.army.mil/news/story.asp?id=1934.

Anderson, Ed, Michael Perlstein, and Robert Travis Scott. 2005. We'll do what it takes to restore order. *Times-Picayune*, September 1. http://www.nola.com/newslogs/breakingtp/index.ssf?/mtlogs/nola_Times-Picayune/archives/2005_09.html.

Associated Press. 2005. States oppose greater role for military in disasters. November 4. http://www.FoxNews.com.

Barringer, Felicity, and Jere Longman. 2005. Owners take up arms as looters press their advantage. *New York Times*, September 1, sec. A.

Barton, Allen H. 1969. *Communities in disaster: A sociological analysis of collective stress situations*. Garden City, NY: Doubleday.

Birkland, Thomas. 1997. *After disaster: Agenda setting, public policy, and focusing events*. Washington, DC: Georgetown University Press.

Breed, Allen. 2005. National Guardsmen pour into New Orleans. *Times-Picayune*, September 2. http://www.nola.com/newslogs/breakingtp/index.ssf?/mtlogs/nola_Times-Picayune/archives/2005_09.html.

Clarke, Lee. 2002. Panic: Myth or reality? *Contexts* 1 (3): 21-26.

CNN.com. 2005a. Transcript of court proceedings for CNN v. Michael Brown. September 11. http://www.cnn.com/2005/LAW/09/11/katrina.mediaaccess.transcript.

———. 2005b. U.S. won't ban media from New Orleans searches. September 10. http://www.cnn.com/2005/LAW/09/10/katrina.media.

Coates, Sam, and Dan Eggen. 2005a. A city of despair and lawlessness. *The Washington Post*, September 2, sec. A.

———. 2005b. In New Orleans, a desperate exodus; looting persists; mayor fears huge death toll. *The Washington Post*, September 1, sec. A.

Disaster preparedness: Is the U.S. ready for another major disaster? 2005. *CQ Researcher* 15:981-1004.

Dowd, Maureen. 2005. United States of shame. *The New York Times*, September 3, sec. A.

Drabek, Thomas E. 1986. *Human system responses to disaster: An inventory of sociological findings*. New York: Springer-Verlag.

Dynes, Russell R. 1970. *Organized behavior in disaster*. Lexington, MA: Heath Lexington.

Dynes, Russell R., and E. L. Quarantelli. 1968. What looting in civil disturbances really means. *Transaction Magazine* 5 (6): 9-14.

Feagin, Joseph R., and Harlan Hahn. 1973. *Ghetto revolts: The politics of violence in American cities*. New York: Macmillan.

Filosa, Gwen. 2005. New Orleans police chief defends force. *Times-Picayune*, September 5. http://www.nola.com/newslogs/breakingtp/index.ssf?/mtlogs/nola_Times-Picayune/archives/2005_09.html.

Fischer, Henry W., III. 1998. *Response to disaster: Fact versus fiction and its perpetuation: The sociology of disaster*. 2nd ed. New York, University Press of America.

Fritz, Charles E. 1961. Disasters. In *Contemporary social problems*, ed. Robert K. Merton and Robert A. Nisbet, 651-94. New York: Harcourt.

Goltz, James D. 1984. Are the media responsible for the disaster myths? A content analysis of emergency response imagery. *International Journal of Mass Emergencies and Disasters* 2:345-68.

Gugliotta, Guy, and Peter Whoriskey. 2005. Floods ravage New Orleans; two levees give way. *The Washington Post*, August 31, sec. A.

Haddow, George D., and Jane A. Bullock. 2003. *Introduction to emergency management*. New York: Butterworth Heinemann.

Haskell, Bob. 2005. Guard troops put lives on hold to respond to Katrina. American Forces Information Service. September 4. http://www.defenselink.mil/news/Sep2005/20050904_2626.html.

Healey, Gene. 2003. *Deployed in the USA: The creeping militarization of the home front*. Policy Analysis no. 303. Washington, DC: Cato Institute.

Hynes, Kevin. 2005. Security cops patrol devastated Mississippi coast. The National Guard. September 26. http://www.ngb.army.mil/news/story.asp?id=1922.

Johnson, Chalmers. 2004. *The sorrows of empire: Militarism, secrecy, and the end of the republic.*. New York: Metropolitan Books.

Kasperson, Jeanne X., and Roger E. Kasperson, eds. 2005. *Social contours of risk*. Vol. 1, *Publics, risk communication and the social amplification of risk*. London: Earthscan.

Laris, Michael. 2005. Responding with money and ammo; as donations pour in, deputies and equipment set out for stricken Gulf Coast. *The Washington Post*, September 2, sec. A.

Lindell, Michael K., and Ronald W. Perry. 1992. *Behavioral foundations of community emergency management*. Washington, DC: Hemisphere.

Lipton, Eric, Christopher Drew, Scott Shane, and David Rohde. 2005. Breakdowns marked path from hurricane to anarchy. *The New York Times*, September 11, sec. 1.

Longman, Jere. 2005. Rescuers, going door to door, find stubbornness and silence. *The New York Times*, September 5, sec. A.

MacCash, Doug, and James O'Byrne. 2005. Levee breech floods Lakeview, Mid-City, Carrollton, Gentilly, City Park. *Times-Picayune*, August 30. http://www.nola.com/newslogs/breakingtp/index.ssf?/mtlogs/nola_Times-Picayune/archives/2005_08.html.

McFadden, Robert. 2005. Bush pledges more troops as the evacuation grows. *The New York Times*, September 4, sec. 1.

McFadden, Robert, and Ralph Blumenthal. 2005. Bush sees long recovery for New Orleans; 30,000 troops in largest U.S. relief effort; higher toll seen; evacuation of stadium—Police ordered to stop looters. *The New York Times*, September 1, sec. A.

McGill, Kevin. 2005. Officials throw up hands as looters ransack city. *Times-Picayune*, August 31. http://www.nola.com/newslogs/breakingtp/index.ssf?/mtlogs/nola_Times-Picayune/archives/2005_08.html.

McPhail, Clark. 1991. *The myth of the maddening crowd*. New York: Aldine de Gruyter.

McPhail, Clark, and Ronald Wohlstein. 1983. Individual and collective behavior within gatherings, demonstrations, and riots. *Annual Review of Sociology* 9:579-600.

Mitchell, Jerry T., Deborah S. K. Thomas, Arleen A. Hill, and Susan L. Cutter. 2000. Catastrophe in reel life versus real life: Perpetuating disaster myth through Hollywood films. *International Journal of Mass Emergencies and Disasters* 18:383-402.

National Academy of Public Administration. 1993. *Coping with catastrophe: Building an emergency management system to meet people's needs in natural and manmade disasters*. Washington, DC: National Academy of Public Administration.

Nolan, Bruce. 2005. Coming home; thousands return to Jefferson; more rescued in St. Bernard. *Times-Picayune*, September 6. http://www.nola.com/newslogs/breakingtp/index.ssf?/mtlogs/nola_Times-Picayune/archives/2005_09.html.

Online NewsHour. 2005. Katrina media coverage. September 29. http://www.pbs.org/newshour.

Pew Center. 2005. Two-in-three critical of Bush's relief efforts: Huge racial divide over Katrina and its consequences. September 8. Washington, DC: Pew Center for the People and the Press.

Philbin, Walt. 2005. Widespread looting hits abandoned businesses. *Times-Picayune*, August 30. http://www.nola.com/newslogs/breakingtp/index.ssf?/mtlogs/nola_Times-Picayune/archives/2005_08.html.

Quarantelli, E. L. 1985. Realities and mythologies in disaster films. *Communications: The European Journal of Communication* 11:31-44.

———. 1987. Disaster studies: An analysis of the social historical factors affecting the development of research in the area. *International Journal of Mass Emergencies and Disasters* 5 (3): 285-310.

———. 2006. Looting and other criminal behavior in Hurricane Katrina: Atypical and complex but seen before in other catastrophes. Preliminary paper, University of Delaware, Disaster Research Center, Newark. http://www.udel.edu/DRC.

Quarantelli, E. L., and Russell R. Dynes. 1970. Property norms and looting: Their patterns in community crises. *Phylon* 31:168-82.

———. 1972. When disaster strikes (it isn't much like what you've heard and read about). *Psychology Today* 5:66-70.

Robinson, Eugene. 2005. Where the good times haven't rolled. Editorial. *The Washington Post*, September 2, sec. A.

Rodríguez, Havidán, Joseph Trainor, and Enrico L. Quarantelli. 2006. Rising to the challenges of a catastrophe: The emergent and prosocial behavior following Hurricane Katrina. *Annals of the American Academy of Political and Social Science* 604:82-101.

Roig-Franzia, Manuel, and Spencer Hsu. 2005. Many evacuated, but thousands still waiting. *The Washington Post*, September 4, A01.

Rubin, Claire, and Irmak Renda-Tenali. 2000. *Disaster timeline: Selected events and outcomes (1965-2000)*. Arlington, VA: Claire B. Rubin and Associates.

Scott, Robert Travis. 2005. Late Blanco statement. *Times Picayune*, August 30. http://www.nola.com/newslogs/breakingtp/index.ssf?/mtlogs/nola_Times-Picayune/archives/2005_08.html.

Shea, Christopher. 2005. Up for grabs; sociologists question how much looting and mayhem really took place in New Orleans. *Boston Globe*, September 11, sec. E.

Smith, Conrad. 1992. *Media and apocalypse: News coverage of the Yellowstone forest fires, the Exxon Valdez oil spill, and Loma Prieta earthquake*. Westport, CT: Greenwood.

Tierney, Kathleen J. 1994. Property damage and violence: A collective behavior analysis. In *The Los Angeles Riots: Lessons for the urban future*, ed. Mark Baldessare, 149-73. Boulder, CO: Westview.

———. 2003. Disaster beliefs and institutional interests: Recycling disaster myths in the aftermath of 9-11. In *Research in social problems and public policy*, vol. 11, *Terrorism and disaster: New threats, new ideas*, ed. Lee Clarke, 33-51. New York: Elsevier Science.

———. 2004. Collective behavior in times of crisis. Commissioned paper presented at the National Research Council Roundtable on Social and Behavioral Sciences and Terrorism, Meeting 4, "Risk Communication for Terrorism," Washington, DC, National Academies, January 30.

Tierney, Kathleen J., Michael K. Lindell, and Ronald W. Perry. 2001. *Facing the unexpected: Disaster preparedness and response in the United States*. Washington, DC: Joseph Henry Press.

Times-Picayune. 2005a. Blanco says evacuation buses on the way to N.O. August 31. http://www.nola.com/newslogs/breakingtp/index.ssf?/mtlogs/nola_Times-Picayune/archives/2005_08.html.

———. 2005b. Bush stunned by conditions in New Orleans. September 3, sec. A.

———. 2005c. No fatalities reported. September 24. http://www.nola.com/newslogs/breakingtp/index.ssf?/mtlogs/nola_Times-Picayune/archives/2005_09.html.

Treaster, Joseph, and N. R. Kleinfield. 2005. New Orleans is inundated as 2 levees fail; much of Gulf Coast is crippled; toll rises. *The New York Times*, August 31, sec. A.

Treaster, Joseph, and Deborah Sontag. 2005. Despair and lawlessness grip New Orleans as thousands remain stranded in squalor. *The New York Times*, September 2, sec. A.

Turner, Ralph H. 1994. Rumor as intensified information seeking: Earthquake rumors in China and the United States. In *Disasters, collective behavior, and social organization*, ed. Russell R. Dynes and Kathleen J. Tierney, 244-56. Newark: University of Delaware Press.

U.S. Congress. House Science Committee, Subcommittee on Research. 2005. *The role of social science research in disaster preparedness and response.*. Testimony by Shirley Laska, Ph.D. November 10.

Vedantam, Shankar, and Allison Klein. 2005. You wonder why it didn't kill a million; officials upbeat in view of what might have been as survivors recount horror of what is. *The Washington Post*, September 3, sec. A.

Vega, Cecilia M. 2005. As bodies recovered, reporters are told "no photos, no stories." *San Francisco Chronicle*, September 13. http://www.sfgate.com/cgi-bin/article.cgo?file=/c/a/2005/09/13/MNG3HEMQHG1.DTL.

Walters, Lynne M., Lee Wilkins, and Tim Walters, eds. 1989. *Bad tidings: Communication and catastrophe*. Hillsdale, NJ: Lawrence Erlbaum.

Waugh, William L. 2000. *Living with hazards, dealing with disasters: An introduction to emergency management*. New York: M. E. Sharpe.

Wenger, Dennis, James D. Sykes, Thomas D. Sebok, and Joan L. Neff. 1975. It's a matter of myths: An empirical examination of individual insight into disaster response. *Mass Emergencies* 1:33-46.

Williams, Brian. 2005. Making the Quarter rounds. MSN.com, September 7. http://www.msnbc.msn.com/id/9216831/.

Williams, Rudi. 2005. Guard chief describes Katrina response operations. American Forces Information Service. September 4. http://www.defenselink.mil/news/Sep2005/20050904_2613.html.

Ziegler, Donald J., Stanley D. Brunn, and James H. Johnson. 1981. Evacuation from a nuclear technological disaster. *Geographical Review* 71:1-16.

Rising to the Challenges of a Catastrophe: The Emergent and Prosocial Behavior following Hurricane Katrina

By
HAVIDÁN RODRÍGUEZ,
JOSEPH TRAINOR,
and
ENRICO L. QUARANTELLI

Using several data sources including an extensive database of media reports and a series of government documents, but relying primarily on the University of Delaware's Disaster Research Center's field research in the aftermath of Hurricane Katrina, the authors describe the nontraditional behavior that emerged in that catastrophe. They also discuss the prosocial behavior (much of it emergent) that was by far the primary response to this event, despite widespread media reports of massive antisocial behavior. Their study focuses on individual and group reactions in Louisiana during the first three weeks following the hurricane. The authors limit their systematic analyses of emergent behavior to five groupings: hotels, hospitals, neighborhood groups, rescue teams, and the Joint Field Office. Their analysis shows that most of the improvisations undertaken helped in dealing with the various problems that continued to emerge following Katrina. The various social systems and the people in them rose to the demanding challenges of a catastrophe.

Keywords: catastrophe; disaster; emergent groups; organizational improvisation; looting; media; Hurricane Katrina

This article has a dual but related focus. Using several data sources including an extensive database of media reports and a series of government documents, but relying primarily on the University of Delaware's Disaster Research Center's (DRC's) field research in the aftermath of Hurricane Katrina, we describe the nontraditional or new behavior that emerged in that catastrophe. We also discuss the prosocial behavior (much of it emergent) that was by far the primary response to this event, widespread media reports of massive antisocial behavior to the contrary. Our discussions and observations

NOTE: Part of the University of Delaware's Disaster Research Center's field research, following the aftermath of Hurricane Katrina, was partially funded by the Engineering Research Centers Program of the National Science Foundation (NSF), under NSF Award Number 0313747. However, any opinions, findings, conclusions, or recommendations expressed here are those of the authors and do not necessarily reflect those of the NSF.

DOI: 10.1177/0002716205284677

focus on the individual and group reactions in Louisiana during roughly the first three weeks after the hurricane hit.

The Negative Mass Media View

How did people, groups, and organizations in Louisiana react to the impact of Hurricane Katrina in September 2005? One dramatic picture, at least in New Orleans, was continually presented in the mass media coverage. The imagery that spread around the world, through the electronic media in particular, was of a state of anarchy; anomie; chaos; disorganization; regression to animal-like behavior; and a total collapse of social control, agencies, and personnel. This image was conveyed not only by visual but also by verbal means. For example, one cable news anchor reported, "All kinds of reports of looting, fires, and violence. Thugs shooting at rescue crews. Thousands of police and National Guard are on the scene trying to get the situation under control." A reporter responded to that statement with, "As you so rightly point out, there are so many murders that are taking place" (*New York Times* 2005). That same day, a commentator on another cable network said, "People are being raped. People are being murdered. People are being shot. Police officers are being shot" (*New York Times* 2005). In their lead story, a third TV cable network reported, "New Orleans resembled a war zone more than a modern American metropolis" (CNN World News, September 1, 2005). The national TV networks, somewhat less strident, put forward a similar negative image regarding the aftermath of Hurricane Katrina.

In addition, the electronic media disseminated actual comments by the mayor of New Orleans and its police chief that snipers were shooting at helicopters, tourists, and the police; that rival gangs were engaged in shootouts inside the Superdome and the Convention Center; and that there were hundreds of dead bodies lying around. They also quoted the FEMA director saying that his agency was working "under conditions of urban warfare" (CNN World News, September 1, 2005).

The print media was more restrained in its reporting, although there was considerable variation in the tone of the coverage from one newspaper or magazine to

Havidán Rodríguez is the director of the Disaster Research Center and professor in the Department of Sociology and Criminal Justice at the University of Delaware. His areas of interest include social vulnerability, risk communication, and demographic processes and disasters. Along with his colleagues, E. L. Quarantelli and R. R. Dynes, he is editing the Handbook of Disaster Research *to be published by Springer in 2006.*

Joseph Trainor is the projects coordinator at the Disaster Research Center and a Ph.D. student in the University of Delaware Department of Sociology and Criminal Justice. His areas of interest include disasters, organizations, collective behavior/social movements, and deviance.

Enrico L. (Henry) Quarantelli is an emeritus professor (and cofounder) in the Disaster Research Center and professor in the Department of Sociology and Criminal Justice at the University of Delaware. He has undertaken disaster research since 1949, and this year has coedited, with Prof. Ron Perry, What Is a Disaster? New Answers to Old Questions, *published by Exlibris.*

another. They were also the first, within about ten days, to undertake systematic investigation of the validity of earlier reports, and generally concluded that many of them were factually incorrect or had seriously distorted what happened (Dwyer and Drew 2005; Thevenot and Russell 2005). Overall, the national television networks and especially the 24/7 format of cable television were far more important for the overall negative picture that was conveyed than were local and print media. However, only elsewhere do we systematically describe the differentiated mass media coverage (Dynes and Rodríguez 2005; Quarantelli n.d.). For our purposes in this article, we think we have illustrated enough that the initial media imagery stressed the predominance of antisocial behavior going on in Louisiana and particularly in New Orleans.

[E]mergent activities in the impacted region showed a different and opposite pattern to those suggested by the imagery employed by the media outlets.

The major thesis of this article is that emergent activities in the impacted region showed a different and opposite pattern to those suggested by the imagery employed by the media outlets mentioned above. Throughout this article we argue, and provide data to show, that a great variety of new, nontraditional or emergent behavior surfaced in this catastrophic occasion. Not being able to act in traditional ways, most of the citizens and groups in New Orleans as well as the rest of Louisiana rose to the challenge by engaging in primarily new but relevant coping behavior. We also contend that the same was true of outside groups trying to help in the response. As an article on governmental response indicated, "In [the] hurricane's aftermath, agencies made up their missions as they went along" (GovExec 2005). In addition, we suggest that while some antisocial behavior did occur, the overwhelming majority of the emergent activity was prosocial in nature.

Earlier Work on Emergent Behavior

Sociologists have long studied emergent behavior. A subspecialization within the field of sociology is called "collective behavior." This area of study, existing for nearly a century (Park and Burgess 1921), focuses on dynamic social phenomena such as crowds, riots, fads and fashion, panic, revolutions, origins of cults, ephemeral mass actions, and changes in public opinion, among others. The common element in all the behaviors mentioned is that they are primarily of a nontraditional nature and generally arise because the standard ways of acting cannot be followed or are not appropriate for certain occasions.

Moreover, our general theme is as old as the first systematic social science field studies of disasters in the early 1950s. One of the most consistent observations reported by pioneer field researchers was that during the crisis period of disasters, there was a great deal of emergent behavior, both at the individual and group levels. The emergent quality took the form of nontraditional or new behavior, different from routine or customary norm-guided actions. This new behavior was heavily prosocial, helping immensely in coping with the extreme and unusual demands of a disaster situation. But the earliest studies did not go much beyond noting a wide range of emergent features in disaster occasions.

The establishment of the DRC at The Ohio State University in 1963, however, led to a more analytical approach to emergent behavior. The DRC quickly developed a typology of organized behaviors at the time of the crisis period in disasters, which first appeared in a paper (Quarantelli 1966) and later in a book (Dynes 1970). Basically, the model states that organized behavior can involve either regular or nonregular tasks and that the structures to carry out these tasks can either exist before a disaster or come into being after impact. A cross-tabulation of these dimensions produces four types of groups: (1) established groups, *regular tasks and old structures*; (2) expanding groups, *regular tasks and new structures*; (3) extending groups, *nonregular tasks and old structures*; and (4) emergent groups, *new tasks and new structures*.

In the 1970s, this typology was subject to modifications by scholars both within and outside the DRC. For example, Bardo (1978) extended the typology and Quarantelli (1984) attempted to distinguish between emergent behaviors and emergent groups, which resulted in the addition of three new types. Another major step forward occurred in 1987 when Drabek wrote what is still the most extensive theoretical discussion on the topic. Reviewing the existing research, including studies outside of the DRC (e.g., Zurcher 1968; Walsh 1981), he asked such questions as, What is emergence and what emerges? And what are the conditions that lead to emergence? Answers to these questions suggest weaknesses in the traditional DRC typology and later variants.

Almost two decades later, Wachtendorf (2004), using data from her field studies focusing on the organizational response to the 9/11 terrorist attacks in New York City, developed the most sophisticated approach yet. She substituted the term *improvisation* for emergence and indicated three different types of improvisation (which she called reproductive, adaptive, and creative). She also gave some indication of what conditions generate each type.

In looking at emergent behavior in the following sections, we use aspects of all the models just highlighted, and we also attempt to categorize some specific examples.

Data Sources Used

Our data come from two sources. The first as well as the most comprehensive and reliable source is information that DRC teams obtained in the field through quick-response research initiatives following Hurricane Katrina. About three weeks after Katrina hit the Gulf Coast, DRC deployed eight researchers to various places in the impacted region for between five and ten days per team, to engage in several forms of data collection, including interviews ($n = 150$), participant observations, and systematic document gathering. Field teams visited a variety of locations including Houston, Texas (the Astrodome and the Reliant Arena); Mississippi (including Biloxi, Gulfport, Long Beach, and Pass Christian); and Louisiana (including Baton Rouge, New Orleans, and St. Tammany). Specific sites visited included the Joint Field Office (JFO)–the headquarters for the federal response to Katrina—and shelters in the three states. Extensive field observations were also conducted at local response centers, Disaster Recovery Centers, and impacted zones. DRC teams talked to local, state, and federal officials; relief workers; evacuees; and others who responded to the hurricane and consequent flooding. At the time of the writing of this article, the bulk of these data have only been selectively analyzed.

The other sources of data used in this work are accounts or stories by others outside of the DRC. These fall roughly into three general categories:

1. A database of news sources in paper format and/or their Web site equivalent that were collected over the first month of the response. These represent a selected group of both local and national sources and are focused primarily on print media and secondarily on television. It is noteworthy that more than two thousand articles have been collected and catalogued by DRC staff.
2. Reports disseminated by other formal organizations either in printed form or on their Web sites.
3. Stories from other informal sources such as bloggers on the Internet.

For the purpose of this article, special attention was paid to firsthand personal accounts by individuals speaking about their own behavior (and if possible, recorded at the time it was happening). Care was taken to use only stories that seemed valid and reliable. Since we are not writing a social history of specific groups, actual names of organizations or locations are not used except for a few already widely identified in news stories (such as the JFO in Baton Rouge).

The General Framework Used

What happened in New Orleans was a catastrophe rather than a disaster, a distinction reflecting our view that these two happenings are qualitatively different. Six elements capture the major differences between catastrophes and disasters (Quarantelli 2005). In a catastrophe,

1. there is massive physical impact (in contrast to the localized impact in disasters);
2. local officials are unable to undertake their usual work roles (in contrast to this happening only at a small scale in the typical disaster);
3. help will come mostly from more distant areas (in contrast to the massive convergence in disasters from nearby areas);
4. most everyday community functions are sharply and concurrently interrupted (in contrast to this not usually happening in a typical disaster);
5. nonlocal mass media, especially cable TV, socially construct the immediate and ongoing situation (in contrast to the typical disaster, where the greatest attention is by the local media and only incidental and brief reporting is done by cable and national media); and
6. very high-level officials and governmental agencies from the national level become directly involved (in contrast to disasters, where limited and primarily symbolic attention is often given by other than local persons and agencies—community and state).

The importance of the six dimensions mentioned is that they provide the larger social context within which all the emergent phenomena that we describe occurred. In a sense, they are the general conditions that set the stage for emergence. For example, 80 percent of New Orleans was under water (no. 1), and most outside help could only arrive later from more distant areas (no. 3); these elements put tremendous pressure on impacted persons, groups, and organizations to improvise actions that might seem to help in coping with the immediate urgent needs in the crisis.

Different Levels of Description and Analysis

A strong case can be made that as a consequence of the hurricane and subsequent flooding, there was significant disruption across all social levels from individual behavior to that of state governments. So in terms of our framework, we anticipate that similarly, there would be internal and external emergence across all social levels. However, this article limits its systematic analyses to five groupings, based on the amount and validity of the data we had available and our desire to show this phenomenon across the social spectrum. The groupings are hotels, hospitals, neighborhood groups, rescue teams, and the JFO.

Hotels

In this section, we discuss what happened in the major hotels in the New Orleans area, many of them part of national chains such as Hilton, Marriott, Hyatt, and others that cater mostly to tourists and conventioneers (there are about 265 hotels in the area with 38,338 rooms; Hirsch 2005). Overall, much of the improvisation was generally successful in dealing with successive crises and was overwhelmingly prosocial in nature. According to our data, a sequence of events resulted in three different phases or stages in the emergent behavior of the hotels and the people in them.

Traditionally, prior to Hurricane Katrina, hotels—especially high-rise hotels—provided a respite for the vertical evacuation of local citizens. In 2004, when Hurricane Ivan threatened New Orleans, 75 percent of hotel guests in two chain hotels, with a capacity of 2,085 rooms, were local residents. Another hotel housed more than 5,000 locals. Some guests had regularly come to the same hotel over the past twenty years whenever hurricanes threatened the areas (Webster 2005). From a social science perspective, a "disaster subculture" had developed.

The first stage of improvising. The situation and conditions for 2005 were different from previous years. Given what hotel operators observed had happened in Florida the previous year, combined with pressure from local emergency managers to discourage hotels from providing vertical evacuation, and given the weather forecasts that suggested Katrina would be at least a Category 3 hurricane, the major hotels decided that they would not take hurricane-related room reservations during 2005 from local residents. Hotel administrators or managers decided to accept only guests who were stranded but that all other guests should be encouraged to make an attempt to leave the endangered areas. This represented a major shift in organizational behavior, away from the everyday and even the disaster subculture norms.

Hotels ended up with many more guests than they had anticipated, however, because many nonlocal guests, who had intended to leave, found that their airline reservations were cancelled at the last moment. In addition, as in the past, families of hotel employees, a number with pets, sought shelter in these hotels. On Sunday night, hotels boarded up in the usual way, but, atypically, a number had their guests come to windowless ballrooms where blankets and pillows were provided. The impact of the hurricane resulted in broken windows, the disruption of electric power, and a lack of air-conditioning and functioning elevators.

The second stage of improvising. More important, it became clear that floodwaters from the breached levees would become a major problem, preventing hotel guests from driving cars or catching buses to leave the city as well as hampering evacuation efforts at the local level. A major effort in one large hotel to rent buses at a cost of $45 for each guest fell through when the buses were commandeered by the military to evacuate others. So while the creative improvisation more or less handled the initial crisis, a major new crisis was generated by the floodwaters. There was soon a scarcity of food and water in many of the hotels, leading some guests to "loot" basic necessities from machines within hotels and nearby stores. It also became common for hotels to provide each guest with nontraditional necessities such as trash bags.

While they heard many of the rumors about widespread antisocial behavior all around them, in most hotels the guests helped one another and later reported feeling very positive about hotel staff. At the hotel level, the organizational crisis was dealt with relatively quickly as convoys of food and supplies were brought in from other hotels in the same chain and from nearby cities such as Atlanta and Houston. Private security guards also arrived, as well as high-level hotel chain executives and safety engineers. All guests were eventually evacuated, mostly through arrangements made by the hotels. Many hotels using their resources also provided direct immediate relief and help of different kinds for employees' loss of property and personal possessions. There is not much evidence that hotels got help of this kind from sources other than their corporate structures.

The third stage of improvising. After stranded guests had left, the hotels had to adjust to requests made by FEMA and others to rent their rooms to federal employees as well as evacuees. All hotels were booked at 100 percent capacity. DRC field teams were informed by receptionists in more than a dozen hotels that their rooms had been reserved and paid for by FEMA, some until December 2005 and January 2006. Providing semipermanent housing is not a usual tourist hotel function. This forced the hotels to shift to a still different kind of operation; not their preimpact everyday operation; not the no-locals guest operation; not the flood threat operation; but to a new long-term housing operation.

Hospitals

The crisis for hospitals (n = 78 including rehabilitation, psychiatric, and long-term acute care ones; Deslatte 2005) in the New Orleans area was different from that faced by hotels. Simply in terms of everyday operations, all hospitals are required to have disaster plans to maintain accreditation. However, as the DRC has found in its past research on hospitals (see Quarantelli 1997), such plans very seldom deal with the possibility of having to evacuate the hospital if it is impacted in a disaster. Nevertheless, hospitals in southern Louisiana had prior experience with hurricanes, some just as threats, others actually impacting.

Consequently, the initial response of hospitals was to react as they had done in the past. They activated their disaster teams of specially designated physicians, nurses, and other key staff members. Less critically ill patients were discharged. Extra supplies of water, food, blood, and medical supplies were stored on scene. Assuming that electric power might be lost in a major impact, extra fuel was brought in for use by emergency generators. The general expectation was that the hospital would return to more or less normal operations after four days or so.

When the hurricane hit the area, the buildings as a whole suffered little physical damage. The electric power did fail, but that had been anticipated. In most hospitals, the expectation was that normal operations would soon be resumed. For example, as one report stated, "Doctors and nurses in the 12th floor surgical intensive-care unit and elsewhere gave one another high-fives . . . convinced things would return to normal fairly quickly" (Freemantle 2005). It appeared for a few hours that the traditional planning had worked.

Within less than twenty-four hours, however, the floodwaters from the levee breaks created a new kind of crisis. Basements with stored food, water, and fuel, as well as morgues, were inundated; in some hospitals, activities on the first floor had to be moved to higher floors. Telephone systems were erratic at best. As emergency generators ran out of fuel, the water, sewage, and air-conditioning systems failed. Patients who died in the hospitals had to be temporarily stored in stairwells. Eventually, waste of all kinds was strewn almost everywhere. The rising temperatures made most diagnostic equipment inoperable. As a director of emergency medicine indicated, "Above 92 degrees, the lab machines shut down and so did the telephone switches inside the hospital . . . you can't run a CAT scan or an MRI. It's like going back to low-tech medicine" (Schrobsdorff 2005). Regular hospital procedures simply stopped, but personnel improvised to try to provide at least minimum health care. For instance, physicians, nurses, and volunteers fanned patients to keep them cool, sometimes using manually operated devices to keep them breathing.

Overall, much of the improvisation was generally successful in dealing with successive crises and was overwhelmingly prosocial in nature.

In addition to all the mentioned problems were two other complications: very crowded areas and high concern about personal safety. In many cases, more persons arrived at hospitals: some for medical treatment, others just seeking what they saw as a safe place of refuge. In Charity Hospital, for example, at one point there may have been about 350 patients in addition to more than 1,200 staff members, family members of patients, and newly arrived refugees. Also, rumors of widespread antisocial behavior all around them spread among hospital personnel and were believed to be true. This led in some hospitals to staff members being given weapons for protection (it is not clear where such weapons came from). There were also reports (apparently false) of firings at rescue helicopters.

Some hospitals attempted to evacuate—first patients, then the rest of the stranded people in their buildings. One hospital put patients in boats, but these returned when anticipated transportation at higher ground levels never materialized. There was considerable use of helicopters (sometimes from the initiative of a hospital; sometimes they just randomly appeared). Medical personnel found themselves having to make triage decisions in the absence of medical records on whether evacuated patients should be sent to a regular shelter, a special needs shelter, or another hospital. Elsewhere, custodians knocked down light poles and cleared debris to create a makeshift pad for helicopters on the roof of the hospital parking garage. In the same hospital, pharmacists and custodians helped patients in the dark to climb flights of stairs to wait for rescue helicopters (McEnery 2005). Many staff members were doing things that were quite distant from their everyday jobs.

Eventually, all hospitals were completely evacuated except for one that was never flooded. But there was a difference in the coping patterns of some hospitals. Private ones, like the hotels we discussed earlier, with more resources were able to make relatively early arrangements for security personnel and helicopters. Published stories indicate that public hospitals such as Charity and University could not do the same. So in one case, at least, all persons, including all staff members, from a private hospital were totally evacuated, while patients from a public hospital waited in sight of that evacuation but at that time were not picked up.

Overall, hospitals initially responded to the warnings of a hurricane approaching New Orleans with their traditional planning activities. But the rising floodwaters created unforeseen problems that initiated massive but erratic improvisations. These barely coped with the problems and brought most hospitals to a minimally operating but prosocial status until their evacuations brought the crisis to an end.

Local neighborhoods

Apart from improvisations in organizations, there was also very extensive emergent behavior in more informal groupings, especially at the neighborhood level. DRC found instances of emergence in at least four neighborhoods in New Orleans (in Carrollton, Algiers, and in two radically different areas in Uptown). Undoubtedly, there were far more, but informal neighborhood groups, which unlike formal organizations, are less likely to catch mass media attention and seldom produce reports or records.

One group named itself the "Robin Hood Looters." The core of this group consisted of eleven friends who, after getting their own families out of the area, decided to remain at some high ground and, after the floodwaters rose, commandeered boats and started to rescue their neighbors in their working-class neighborhood. For about two weeks they kept searching in the area, although some marooned families absolutely refused to leave their homes. At first they slept on the ground, and then in tents that others brought to them. They foraged for food and water from abandoned homes, and hence their group name. Among the important norms that developed were that they were going to retrieve only survivors and not bodies and that group members would not carry weapons. The group also developed informal understandings with the police and the National Guard who not only gave them ready meals but to whom they also passed on rescued survivors who wanted to leave the area (for further details, see Kiehl 2005). While many of the core members of the group had been childhood friends, and they were very familiar with the area, what they did in this crisis, despite their earlier hurricane experiences, was new for them in every sense of the word. In the DRC typology, this was clearly an emergent group.

In another working-class area in Uptown, a group emerged that gathered their neighbors in a local school. Initially, everyone was invited, but when some "thugs" started to vandalize the building, breaking into vending machines and wielding guns, leaders of the groups expelled them from the school and prevented them from reentering. Before the flooding started, canned flood, cleaning supplies, and a radio and batteries were brought into the school. A classroom was converted into a dining room. At its peak, forty persons slept in the building with men on the third floor and women on the second, using blankets and cots brought from their homes. Those in the school also brought food and liquids to elderly homebound neighbors as well as bringing some of them (eighteen) to the school rooftop to be evacuated by arrangement with Coast Guard helicopters (which also brought in water, food, and clean clothing for those who did not want to leave the school). It appears that at least two hundred people used the school before it was forcefully and fully evacuated by M-16-armed sheriff's deputies from New Mexico, New Orleans' police, and others. Again, the persons in the school were very familiar with the building, and some remembered that it had survived Hurricane Betsy (for more details, see Brewington 2005). This is another emergent group by DRC criteria.

The people in the school, through their radio, heard stories of what supposedly was going on in the Superdome and the Convention Center, which strengthened their determination not to evacuate to those localities. Also hearing the same stories, in a more extensively upscale area of Uptown, some white residents organized themselves into heavily armed groups to protect that locality from rumors about invading gangs of young black men. Other residents in that same neighborhood paid for a team of former Israeli commando units to fly into the area in former Russian attack helicopters (for more details, see Lewis 2005).

While the extent to which and how rumors were a factor in the development of emergent groups in New Orleans will have to await a more systematic and more focused study, the circulating and widely inaccurate stories clearly helped to define the situation many people saw themselves faced with in this catastrophe. The stories added the perceived threat to personal safety to the flood crisis.

Search and rescue teams

Unlike what we have just discussed, emergent behavior also occurred in formal response organizations. The massive impact and subsequent flooding in this catastrophe created a need for a response that many of these agencies had never planned for, as the following examples illustrate.

Our first instance of governmental responder emergence involves the local firefighters and police in Slidell, Louisiana. In informal conversations with DRC field team members, these responders reported that they conducted, with no federal assistance, operations during the first few days after Hurricane Katrina, particularly focusing on door-to-door search and rescue activities within the fifty-five square miles of their community. While responders indicated that their training in previous years was valuable, they were quick to say that following Katrina they had to improvise in many situations, absent previous specific planning for what they actually had to do. The first example they mentioned was that firefighters and police got together to create operational plans on how they would separate the community into grids. Next, they sent scouts out to mark the edges of each grid by spray painting coded symbols on any roadway that crossed a grid line to avoid redundancy, and to make sure that responders knew which grid they were in, in case trouble developed. Finally, they adopted the symbols used by the federal Urban Search and Rescue (USAR) teams to mark every structure on dry land. In terms of the DRC typology, this was an unplanned extending group, involving the use of old structures but for new tasks.

The second phase of this search and rescue effort involved initiating water rescue. For this, the extending group used their personal boats or those of local residents to search inside all the homes that were underwater. While this action was completely unplanned, it did tap into local familiarity and availability of watercraft to engage in a complete search operation over land and water.

There were at least two other examples of emergence in this community. The first was the ad hoc creation of a shelter at the site of an abandoned Wal-Mart. The extending group broke the store door locks off and allowed people inside when they realized that there were no other shelters to which displaced residents could go. Eventually, water and food collected from nearby businesses were also brought by the group members to this temporary shelter.

As a final example of emergent behavior by this group, members mentioned that when their primary communication systems failed, they created a new one by collecting family band radios from local businesses and using them. In this new system, messages were sent out from radio to radio across the jurisdiction until it reached the intended recipient of the message.

Search and rescue was actually undertaken in this catastrophe by a wide variety of groups. As indicated earlier when discussing local neighborhoods, we noted search and rescue was informally carried out by groups in those localities. We have just mentioned formal groups that extended their activities into what was for them nontraditional search and rescue actions. And of course, formal groups were specifically trained and set up to undertake search and rescue, such as the federal USAR teams. Of importance is that our data indicate that all groups undertaking search and rescue in Katrina had to improvise to some degree. Perhaps this stems from the fact that it is almost impossible ahead of time to visualize and therefore to plan for all possible contingencies that have to be faced in a disaster. Also, searching for living persons to prevent their immediate death has a very high priority in all societies, as the recent Indian Ocean tsunami (2004) and the earthquake in Pakistan (2005) showed. This social pressure helps to stimulate the formation of informal groups (nearby friends and neighbors) and encourage improvisation even in formally organized search and rescue groups.

The JFO

The establishment of the JFO is a kind of emergence different from the others we have discussed so far (requiring us to provide far more background information than necessary for what else we have discussed). This is true both in terms of who was involved and how it came about. The catastrophe generated the largest and most complicated mobilization of federal resources and personnel that had ever occurred in the country's history in the face of a national or technological disaster. And even the terrorist attack of 9/11 was more localized than was the direct impact of Katrina on three states and indirect effects on several nearby states, thus occasioning a relatively lesser federal response.

This kind of massive mobilization was neither visualized nor planned for, as far as we know. To be sure, there is a National Response Plan (NRP) but what happened went far beyond what that envisioned. For example, DRC has a document that lists the kinds and levels of response of all the federal cabinet-level organizations and the major independent federal agencies. It is clear from what is reported that many of the activities initiated were of an ad hoc nature and not the result of any preimpact planning or following the NRP (see Bell 2005). There was a degree

---

[I]n all its planning, FEMA did not anticipate that an abandoned shopping mall in Baton Rouge would become the major center for its operations in this catastrophe.

---

of prior planning regarding who was responsible for the coordination across the board of the federal response and indirectly the relationship between the federal level and the state and local levels. Actually, that rested somewhat ambiguously in the Department of Homeland Security (DHS) and the Federal Emergency Management Agency (FEMA). However, in this article we will not examine the structural problems within and between the two organizations; others (e.g., Perrow 2005) have discussed this. While avoiding any analysis of that organizational problem, we can still say that FEMA had the primary responsibility of taking and did take the initial lead role in this disaster; the effectiveness of its response, however, is a topic for another article focusing on the aftermath of Hurricane Katrina. This brings us to what we want to discuss, the physical establishment of and the social features of the JFO.

The physical location of the JFO was in the Bon Marche Shopping Mall in Baton Rouge, the earliest such place in the city. However, the mall had been closed for about five years. It was certainly not a standby site for emergency operations that some government agency had created and clearly did not have the kind of equipment or furnishing typically found in any emergency operations center. Obviously, in all its planning, FEMA did not anticipate that an abandoned shopping mall in Baton Rouge would become the major center for its operations in this catastrophe. While it is not clear at this point who was specifically responsible for and what lay behind the decision to locate in the mall, it was not the result of prior planning but had to be an improvised choice.

Given the deteriorated condition of the mall, many physical improvisations had to take place to turn it into a high-security, massive center of operations. According to the DRC field team, it seemed that the full capacity of the mall was being used for the JFO operations. There were facilities to store an extensive amount of supplies for staff personnel, a security screening facility that would produce (almost instantaneously) official FEMA identification badges with color pictures, and extensive and state-of-the-art computer and communication technology. The DRC was informed that on several occasions there were small fires, power outages, and malfunctioning escalators and elevators at the JFO headquarters given that the facilities were overwhelmed with the massive amount of technology and electronic equipment for which this mall was not structurally prepared. In the past, the DRC has not found that carrying out major maintenance work is a usual requirement at FEMA centers of operation in disasters.

The primary responsibility of the JFO was to plan and coordinate "the efforts of federal, state, and volunteer agencies involved in Louisiana hurricane recovery efforts" (FEMA 2005). A report by Manjot Singh (2005) indicated that "nearly every federal agency from OSHA and the EPA to the Army and Air Force is housed at the JFO here in Baton Rouge. An 'Equal Rights' office was also created to prohibit episodes of discrimination during the relief efforts." Singh additionally reported that an area was also set up for nonprofit organizations, including "America's Second Harvest, Islamic Relief, Red Cross, Salvation Army, and United Sikhs." One DRC field team also observed the presence of many other charitable, religious, and other nongovernmental organizations such as Goodwill, Episcopal Church of World Services, Convoy of Hope, Church of Scientology Volunteer Ministry, and the Adventist Community Services. Also, media representatives had been given space at the JFO facilities, and there was a media monitoring station that JFO personnel used to monitor the most important media and cable reporting of Hurricane Katrina.

DRC was informed that FEMA personnel had arrived from all over the United States and that the agency was trying to minimize their stay and was attempting (although not always successfully) to rotate, on a regular basis, their JFO personnel. Before arriving at the JFO, employees had to be credentialed, trained, and immunized. All personnel admitted to work at the JFO also had to undergo security screening. It appears that the JFO was able (at least partially) to start working in the building about two weeks after the impact of Katrina. About one month later, when DRC field team members did research in it, the JFO was functioning at full capacity with about two thousand federal, state, and local employees.

DRC research team members generated field notes indicating the following:

In the course of several weeks the [JFO] building has been wired to accommodate the increased electrical needs and the computer needs of the personnel. People were sleeping in bunk beds on site, in closets, and in corners of any room. The operation runs 24-7. Maps are hung on almost every wall with every type of imaginable data, from flooded areas to surge areas; total population and population density; number of housing, buildings, and people impacted by Katrina; and comparisons for 100 year events, among others. There is a logistics supply store that is full of materials and supplies, with a sign reminding people to

take only what they need and that this was a "no looting zone." The DRC team also
observed flyers focusing on "stress management," as well as "how to cope with over-
stressed workers," "NIMS training," "ICS training" and other types of training sessions
and opportunities for staff workers.

The JFO had an impressive (and very rapid) convergence of staff, equipment,
and supplies, in what was essentially an obsolete shopping mall. FEMA and other
personnel and staff at the JFO had to be creative and to improvise in response to
the facilities available to them and the dynamic processes that were under way.
Meetings were occurring on an almost continuous basis among and between different staff members, working groups, offices, and organizations; conference calls,
including staff and personnel not only at the JFO but also with the participation of
other personnel located throughout the United States, were also taking place on a
regular basis. Minute-to-minute interactions and meetings, and continuous
requests for information, data, maps, and reports were situations to which all JFO
employees needed to adapt almost instantaneously. In essence, a very complex,
multifaceted, multipurpose, dynamic, and relatively large bureaucracy emerged in
an extremely short time period, requiring not only constant coordination, communication, and interaction but a significant degree of improvisation and creativity.
Without in any way denying that some of what went on at the JFO was both traditional and preplanned, overall, our view was that much of what happened especially in the first few weeks, was of a very emergent nature. In Drabek's (1987)
terms, there was a system emergence; and there were all the kinds of improvisations that Wachtendorf (2004) discussed.

Other illustrations of emergence and improvisations

In concluding this part of the discussion, we want to mention a variety of still
other institutional areas in which major disruptions resulted in emergent coping
behavior and in some cases emergent groups. Area professional sport teams, in the
absence of prior relevant planning, had to change the schedules and locations of
their games. Local scientific researchers in the health area had to try to salvage
their ongoing work: three hundred federally funded National Institute of Health
projects that were disrupted in New Orleans alone (Gardner 2005).

Local traditional religious groups accustomed to providing food and other help
to disadvantaged people on a daily basis in churches and mosques suddenly and
unexpectedly had to take on and train many volunteers (becoming, in the DRC
typology, an expanding group) or to provide new kinds of services (becoming, in
the DRC typology, an extending group). Members of an Internet domain hosting
service located in a skyscraper in the heart of New Orleans not only maintained its
usual services but also extended its activities to setting up a Web message center
freely available to anyone interested, a companion photo gallery, and a live Web
cam site of scenes around their building. They also scrounged for diesel fuel
needed for emergency generators and shared patrol duties in the building
(Broache 2005).

The list could almost be endless because as stated earlier, catastrophes sharply and concurrently disrupted most everyday community functions (no. 4). But a catastrophe also generates emergent behavior in locations far away as outsiders try to help or get involved in some way during the aftermath of the disaster. In fact, we want to illustrate this last point with respect to the operations of the DRC field teams.

Although for the past forty-two years the DRC has undertaken more than 650 field trips collecting perishable data on different kinds of disasters, emergent behavior also characterized its response to the hurricane. For example, having been informed that no lodging facilities were available within a one-hundred-mile radius of Baton Rouge, the DRC assumed the need for camping equipment. Therefore, for the first time in its history, the DRC sent tents, sleeping bags, and other camping material to the Gulf Coast. As it turned out, during our stay in Mississippi and Louisiana, we were greeted by the hospitality and altruistic behavior of colleagues and even strangers. Our research teams spent several nights in the house of a colleague from Louisiana State University; they slept in the facilities of a city hall, in a fire department training facility, and in a Baptist church that not only provided lodging but also meals to our field team. Moreover, in addition to an extensive planning process regarding our research in the impacted regions, the teams also had to develop detailed evacuation plans given that Hurricane Rita was approaching the Gulf Coast during our stay in the region. This was also a new first for the DRC.

Furthermore, despite weeks of intensive preparatory work and the development of a semistructured questionnaire focusing on issues of substantive and theoretical interest to DRC researchers, a team member met with a number of Hispanic immigrants in the field who did not speak English. Thus, she had to translate the questionnaires on site to interview these respondents, who provided detailed information regarding the issues and complexities of undocumented immigrants that had been affected by the catastrophe. So despite the extensive planning process prior to sending the DRC teams into the field, flexibility, innovation, and creativity were instrumental for the success of our research.

The Complexity of Emergence

In this concluding section, we briefly discuss some of the complexities involved in describing and analyzing emergent behavior. In particular, we address two questions. Is "looting" emergent behavior? Is it also antisocial behavior? The answer to these questions is more complex than might be thought at first glance. And we leave aside here that in almost all jurisdictions there is no criminal act that has the label of "looting." Usually, acts of "looting," if taken up by the criminal justice system, are legally treated as instances of burglary.

Emergent behavior is not always legal; this statement is certainly true. However, and more important, it can still be prosocial. We will look at this in terms of the "looting" that occurred in the New Orleans area, and we will see the complexities involved in trying to analyze what went on.

Our analysis draws heavily from a much earlier study of the "antisocial behavior" that occurred after Hurricane Hugo hit the U.S. Virgin Island of St. Croix (see Quarantelli n.d.). There was massive "looting" in that situation, which is the illegal taking of goods and material. The looting was initiated by preimpact delinquent gangs; others later joined in that behavior. However, study after study of the typical natural and technological disaster in the United States and Western Europe have consistently found that looting of any kind is very rare and when it occurs has certain distinctive patterns; mainly it is done covertly, is strongly condemned in the community, is engaged in by few persons, and involves taking advantage of the chance opportunities that occur. In St. Croix, the looting was overt, socially supported, engaged in by many persons often in a group fashion, and involved targeted places to loot (a pattern often found in riot situations).

[T]he behaviors that did appear were overwhelmingly prosocial, making the antisocial behavior seem relatively minor in terms of frequency and significance.

Elements of both patterns emerged in the wake of Hurricane Katrina. The stealing of consumer goods by preexisting delinquent gangs was in the analytical terms of the DRC typology, simply established groups doing on a somewhat larger scale what they do on an everyday basis. Apparently, the pre-Katrina criminal elements were not minor. Estimates by students of the area indicated that as many as twenty thousand participants in the drug culture lived in the area before the hurricane. Thus, in many ways, some of the behavior observed following Katrina was not emergent behavior; doing what one does traditionally is not doing something new.

But after Katrina, other people engaged in the emergent stealing of "necessities." Some of this has also been reported by press and blog sites and is consistent with what the DRC found. Many respondents talking to DRC team members first reported that "looting" behavior had taken place. When asked about the details of such "looting," however, the respondents overwhelmingly indicated that they had only heard that such behavior was occurring but that they had not engaged in it themselves, nor did they know of other persons who had, nor had they directly observe anyone "looting." As we have already indicated in some of our earlier examples of emergent groups and emergent behavior, however, taking necessities was not defined as "looting" (as was also true in St. Croix). Some respondents reported that if they had taken something, it was primarily food and water or a boat to help rescue others who were stranded as a consequence of the flooding (Barnshaw 2005). In a strictly legal sense, such emergent behavior is a violation of the criminal code. But to many people, taking only things that they consider immediate necessities that are often shared with others in similar straights is simply not criminal behavior. (Cases in the literature show that such actions almost never result in legal sanctions.)

However, we should leave open the possibility that more was involved than looting behavior of a traditional kind by organized gangs and the emergent taking of necessities by victims in need. In St. Croix, some "looters" did not fall into either one of these two categories. They were persons who did not engage in everyday criminal behavior yet who did steal more than necessities, for example, consumer goods. It is possible that happened in New Orleans also. Perhaps the documented cases of police officers looting in that city might be instances of this third category. (Officers also did some of the looting in St. Croix.) At the very least, researchers of looting and criminal behavior should examine the obvious complexities of emergent behavior especially in catastrophes rather than crises, a theoretical distinction we have indicated throughout this article is crucial to understanding much of what went on after Hurricane Katrina.

There is also a need to examine more closely a subtle implicit bias, in discussions by disaster researchers, that emergent behavior is always a good thing, in the sense that it provides a better coping mechanism for a crisis than otherwise would have been the case. Our work on Katrina does not fully support that notion. For example, evacuees totally rejected the emergency housing offered them on a tourist cruise ship sent by FEMA to New Orleans. Residents in flooding homes who retreated up into their attics sometimes died. Research is needed on what improvisations work and do not work and why. Overall, emergent behavior, as we saw it in Louisiana, is usually good for those acting in that way, but not always. It is more complex; emergent behavior is a different way of acting, but that does not mean it is necessarily better than other ways.

Concluding Observations

We started our article with a brief description of the antisocial imagery that the mass media initially set forth about what happened after Hurricane Katrina and expressed our doubts about its validity. We then noted that what occurred was a catastrophe rather than just a disaster, that different social factors following Katrina would encourage the emergence of new behaviors to generally cope with new threats and risks. Our examination of five different groupings was intended to illustrate the range of emergent behavior that surfaced. Generally, most of the improvisations undertaken helped in dealing with the various problems that continued to emerge. The various social systems and the people in them rose to the demanding challenges of a catastrophe. Equally as important, the behaviors that did appear were overwhelmingly prosocial, making the antisocial behavior seem relatively minor in terms of frequency and significance.

References

Bardo, John. 1978. Organizational response to disaster: A typology of adaptation and change. *Mass Emergencies* 3:87-104.

Barnshaw, John. 2005. The continuing significance of race and class among Houston hurricane Katrina evacuees. *Natural Hazards Observer* 30 (2): 11-13.

Bell, Peter. 2005. No agency left behind in hurricane relief effort. http:www.govexec.com/story_page.cfm?articleid=32207&printerfrie.

Brewington, Kelly. 2005. A do-it-ourselves shelter shines. http://www.baltimoresun.com/news/nationworld/bal-te.community07sep07,1,2977124.story?ctrack=1&cset=true.

Broache, Anne. 2005. Blog offers rare glimpse inside the chaos. http://news.com.com/2102-1038_3-5846830.html?tag=st.util.print.

Deslatte, Melinda. 2005. Hospitals face struggles in Katrina storm area. http://cms.firehouse.com/content/article/printer.jsp?id=44361.

Drabek, Thomas. 1987. Emergent structures. In *Sociology of disasters: Contributions of sociology to disaster research*, ed. R. Dynes, B. DeMarchi, and C. Pelanda, 259-88. Milan, Italy: Franco Angeli.

Dwyer, Jim, and Christopher Drew. 2005. Fear exceeded crime's reality in New Orleans. *New York Times*, September 29.

Dynes, Russell. 1970. *Organized behavior in disasters*. Lexington, MA: Heath.

Dynes, R., and Rodríguez, H. 2005. Finding and framing Katrina: The social construction of disaster. http://understandingkatrina.ssrc.org.

Federal Emergency Management Agency (FEMA). 2005. Hurricanes Katrina and Rita recovery summary. Press Zoom, October 14. http://presszoom .com/story_112759.html.

Freemantle, Tony. 2005. Hospital's will to survive grew with floodwaters. *Houston Chronicle*, September 18.

Gardner, Amanda. 2005. Katrina leaves scientific research in ruins. http://www.medicinenet.com/script/main/art.asp?articlekey=54885.

GovExec. 2005. In hurricane's aftermath, agencies made up missions as they went along. http://www.GovExec.com.dailyfed/0905/091305cl.htm.

Hirsch, Jerry. 2005. New Orleans' tourist business dealing with big difficult. *Los Angles Times*, September 30.

Kiehl, Stephen. 2005. Some stay to save; some come to see. http://www.baltimoresun.com/news/weather/hurricane/bal-te.tentcity11sep11,1,6007819.story.

Lewis, Michael. 2005. Wading toward home. *New York Times Magazine*, October 9, pp. 44-50.

McEnery, Regina. 2005. How Tulane hospital saved the babies first. *Cleveland Plain Dealer*, September 11.

New York Times. 2005. More horrible than truth: News reports. September 19.

Park, R., and E. Burgess. 1921. *Introduction to the science of sociology*. Chicago: University of Chicago Press.

Perrow, Charles. 2005. Using organizations: The case of FEMA. http://understandingkatrina.ssrc.org/Perrow/.

Quarantelli, E. 1966. Organization under stress. In *Symposium on emergency operations*, ed. Robert Brictson, 3-19. Santa Monica, CA: System Development Corporation.

———. 1984. *Emergent behavior at the emergency time period of disasters: Final report*. Newark, NJ: Disaster Research Center, University of Delaware.

———. 1997. Non-medical difficulties during emergency medical services delivery at the time of disasters. *BC Medical Journal* 39:593-95.

———. 2005. Catastrophes are different from disasters: Some implications for crisis planning and managing drawn from Katrina. http://understandingkatrina.ssrc.org/Quarantelli/.

———. N.d. Notes on antisocial and criminal behavior in disasters, catastrophes and conflict crises: The research evidence. Manuscript.

Schrobsdorff, Susanna. 2005. How two New Orleans hospitals—and two ER physician brothers—endured heat, floods and power outages to treat victims of Katrina. *Newsweek*, September 6.

Singh, Manjot. 2005. Hurricane Katrina—Destruction and devastation. Panthic News, September 18. http://www.panthic.org/news/123/ARTICLE/1788/2005-09-18.html.

Thevenot, Brian, and Gordon Russell. 2005. Rumors of death greatly exaggerated. *New Orleans Time Picayune*, September 26.

Wachtendorf, Tricia. 2004. Improvising 9/11: Organizational improvisation following the World Trade Center disaster. Ph.D. diss., Department of Sociology, University of Delaware, DE.

Walsh, Edward. 1981. Resource mobilization and citizen protest in communities around Three Mile Island. *Social Problems* 29:1-21.

Webster, Richard. 2005. New Orleans-area resident still perceive downtown high-rise hotels as safe havens from hurricanes. *New Orleans City Business*, July 18.

Zurcher, Louis. 1968. Social psychological functions of ephemeral roles: A disaster work crew. *Human Organization* 27:281-97.

Moral Hazard, Social Catastrophe: The Changing Face of Vulnerability along the Hurricane Coasts

By
SUSAN L. CUTTER
and
CHRISTOPHER T. EMRICH

The social vulnerability of the American population is not evenly distributed among social groups or between places. Some regions may be more susceptible to the impacts of hazards than other places based on the characteristics of the people residing within them. As we saw with Hurricane Katrina, when coupled with residencies in high-risk areas such as the hurricane coasts, differential vulnerabilities can lead to catastrophic results. The geographic discrepancies in social vulnerability also necessitate different mitigation, post-response, and recovery actions. Given temporal and spatial changes in social vulnerability in the future, a one-size-fits-all approach to preparedness, response, recovery, and mitigation may be the least effective in reducing vulnerability or improving local resilience to hazards.

Keywords: social vulnerability; spatial inequities; race; class

In 2003 more than 150 million Americans (53 percent of the nation's population) lived in a coastal county, up from 28 percent in 1980

Susan L. Cutter is a Carolina Distinguished Professor and director of the Hazards Research Lab at the University of South Carolina. She has been working in the hazards field for three decades and has published twelve books and more than seventy-five journal articles and book chapters. Her primary research interests are in the area of vulnerability science—what makes people and the places where they live vulnerable to extreי. ˙events and how this is measured and monitored—and spatial social science. She is a fellow of the American Association for the Advancement of Science (AAAS), a former president of the Association of American Geographers, and the founding coeditor of the interdisciplinary journal Environmental Hazards.

Christopher T. Emrich received his Ph.D. in geography at the University of South Carolina, where he specialized in geographic information science and hazards. His primary research interests are in social vulnerability models and metrics and their application to emergency management. In 2004, he worked for FEMA during the Florida hurricane response, where he conducted geographic information system (GIS)–based analyses of recovery operations and mitigation programs. He is the manager of the Hazards Research Lab at the University of South Carolina.

DOI: 10.1177/0002716205285515

(Crossett et al. 2004). This growth is most visible along the nation's hurricane coasts—stretching from Cape Cod to Miami along the Atlantic Ocean and from Brownsville, Texas, to the Florida Keys along the Gulf of Mexico. In addition to the sheer increases in the number of people, the character of coastal residents has changed as well. Instead of seasonal populations, coastal counties now have significant year-round residents—many of them elderly retirees or service industry workers who keep the tourist industry afloat. Coastal residents are more racially and ethnically diverse than in past decades. The expansion of low-wage jobs primarily in the service sector has partially fueled this diversity. Despite our collective prosperity as a nation today, the disparity in incomes between the richest and poorest Americans widens every year. This wealth gap is especially evident in coastal counties, where the rich live right along the shore, and the income gradient decreases with distance away from the water's edge. This disparity in wealth is a significant social problem at the local and regional level. It is also a spatial problem for coastal communities with geographic mismatches between employment opportunities and where workers can find affordable housing that is also built to current code standards.

The American dream of owning a single detached house is beyond the reach of nearly half of the nation's households. Instead, many people turn to manufactured housing or mobile homes to achieve the dream of purchasing their own affordable home. This is especially true among coastal counties in the Gulf and the southeastern United States. Unfortunately, these types of structures are highly vulnerable to severe storms and high winds and actually may increase the risk of damage, along with injury and possibly death, to the people who live in them in hazard-prone areas.

Social Vulnerability Defined

Social vulnerability is the product of social inequalities. It is defined as the susceptibility of social groups to the impacts of hazards, as well as their resiliency, or ability to adequately recover from them. This susceptibility is not only a function of the demographic characteristics of the population (age, gender, wealth, etc.), but also more complex constructs such as health care provision, social capital, and access to lifelines (e.g., emergency response personnel, goods, services) (Cutter 1996; Cutter, Mitchell, and Scott 2000; Cutter, Boruff, and Shirley 2003).

The origins of social vulnerability can be seen in the quality of life and livability studies in the social and behavioral sciences during the 1950s and 1960s. This research attempted to understand the characteristics of places that make them either suitable or less suitable places to reside. The decade of the 1960s and the early 1970s saw a spike in interest by the federal government in the identification of social well-being and progress indicators (U.S. Department of Health, Education, and Welfare 1969; U.S. Office of Management and Budget [OMB] 1973). During this time, research into the social characteristics of people and places began to take shape as a viable and useful way to understand how people might cope with sickness, social problems, and environmental inequities (Maloney 1973; Smith 1973;

Berry 1977). It is this type of research (a combination of demography, sociology, geography, and natural science) that has spawned the current trend in hazards related vulnerability science (Cutter 2003).

Whereas the physical vulnerability can be easily identified using data from past events, the social aspects of hazard vulnerability are a bit more complicated given their temporal and spatial variability.

The built environment also plays a role in social vulnerability, especially the nature and age of the housing stock as noted above (Heinz Center 2002). More generalized characteristics of the built environment such as urbanization, economic vitality, and development help define the livability and quality of life of the community (Pacione 1990, 2003), which in turn influences hazard susceptibility, response, and resilience in the aftermath of a disaster. For example, the preevent trajectory of a community's economic vitality and quality of life almost always continues postevent. If a community were stressed economically and losing population prior to disaster, this trajectory would continue long after the disaster recovery and reconstruction was finished. Disasters magnify the existing social and economic trends in places; they do not fundamentally change them (Kates 1977). So, if we are to make progress in reducing vulnerability, we need to move recovery beyond the status quo to a more sustainable and socially just future.

Hurricane Katrina and the Aftermath

Hurricane Katrina was a wake-up call for the American public. A major hurricane striking New Orleans or nearby was bound to happen and, in fact, was one of the oft-discussed worst-case scenarios by hazards researchers and emergency managers. The ill-fated "Hurricane Pam" training exercise sponsored by FEMA, the series of articles in the *Times-Picayune* in 2002, and provocative essays by researchers (Laska 2004) all highlighted the impending social catastrophe, yet few governmental officials listened or, more important, took action.

The lack of action during the preparedness phase defines an emergency management system that is not functioning at its highest level. When the storm began bearing down along the Gulf Coast, the emergency management system became overwhelmed and simply collapsed, creating the social catastrophe that we saw in New Orleans. While preparedness (including evacuation) was reasonable in some areas along the hurricane's path (Mississippi and Alabama coasts), it was abysmal in other places (the city of New Orleans). Those with resources left in advance of the approaching hurricane; those without (largely the poor, African American, elderly, or residents without private cars) remained, trapped in the rising floodwaters.

Most of our experience with hurricane preparedness, response, and recovery is within a suburban context, not an urban central city. Suburban areas have lower population and housing densities, and the primary mode of transportation is the private automobile. Evacuations from suburban communities are relatively straightforward (albeit traffic congestion is the big problem), with most residents providing their own transportation and seeking shelter out of state or inland with family or friends. Generally, only a small percentage of "special needs" populations require additional assistance in moving out of harm's way—the infirm or some mobility-limited elderly. The evacuations from coastal Mississippi and Alabama reflected more of this suburban experience and went relatively smoothly compared to New Orleans.

Urban places, whether well networked and solidly built or poorly constructed and socially challenging, create new and complex emergency management challenges. Typical large-city problems such as segregation; neighborhood decline; socioeconomic deprivation; and inequities in health, well-being, and health care accessibility have now become central issues for many emergency managers across the nation, necessitating more focus on improving the resilience of the community and its residents—enhancing skills and other attributes known to minimize loss in the first place or to strengthen the capacity to recover.

Many inner-city residents do not have the wealth of their suburban counterparts, do not own a private automobile, and rely almost exclusively on public transportation. In the city of New Orleans, for example, more than fifty-one thousand people or 27 percent of the adult population did not own a car, prompting these residents to seek shelter wherever they could. While not often considered "special needs" by emergency managers and planners, the inner-city poor of New Orleans became the human face of Katrina.

Moral hazards, according to economists, are when insurance changes the behavior of the person being insured. For example, the availability of flood insurance in high-risk, flood-prone areas encourages individuals to build there, despite the known risks. If the insurance was not available and the individual households had to absorb all the losses themselves, they might choose to reside elsewhere, where their investments were more protected. Looking at it differently, the failure of the nation's social safety net despite emergency preparations also created a different moral hazard. With the dysfunctional relief operation, the nation gasped at the sight of people being plucked off of rooftops; the lack of basic food, water, and sanitation at the Superdome and Convention Center; and the general anarchy that befell the city. How could this be America? This socially vulnerable population was exploited even more during the response phase when intergovernmental friction and bureaucratic ineptitude at the local, state, and federal levels delayed relief supplies for up to a week. The preexisting social vulnerabilities gave rise to the social catastrophe; the moral hazard occurred with our collective inability to adequately respond. What good is a federal response plan when it clearly does not work and does not alleviate the suffering of the most vulnerable within our society? What does it say about the adequacy of preparedness when we know so little about the most disadvantaged within the communities—those that require additional assistance to get out of harm's way? How can we mitigate now so that a Katrina-like situation does not occur in the future? How do we know which places are more socially vulnerable than others and where mitigation interventions would be the most beneficial?

Social Vulnerability Metrics and Methods

The development of a social vulnerability metric for U.S. counties has allowed the science of vulnerability to move forward in understanding not only spatial differences in social vulnerability between counties from 1960 to 2000 but has also permitted the temporal analysis of this idea of decreased resiliency within a single county or other political unit. This measure over time is important for understanding the broad impact of disaster mitigation in the United States as well as more localized changes in social vulnerability that are caused by different factors at different spatial and temporal scales.

The theory behind this index of social vulnerability is based in the Hazards of Place Model (Figure 1), which conceptualizes the inputs to social vulnerability within the broader hazards paradigm. Place vulnerability is made up of two main components: those factors of the environment that lead to increased potential for hazardous events to occur, or physical vulnerability (e.g., Do you live in a hurricane area, or near a chemical or nuclear facility?); and those characteristics of the people and places that make them less able to cope with and rebound from disaster events. Whereas the physical vulnerability can be easily identified using data from past events, the social aspects of hazard vulnerability are a bit more complicated given their temporal and spatial variability. How to capture complexity into a single metric or indicator of vulnerability has been difficult.

The Social Vulnerability Index (SoVI)

The SoVI as described by Cutter, Boruff, and Shirley (2003) uses a subset of forty-two socioeconomic, demographic, and built environment variables to capture the level of resilience to hazard events for U.S. counties. This subset of variables was chosen because it encapsulates all of the factors and characteristics found in past research on disaster vulnerability. This set of variables was simplified from a much larger group of census variables culled for each decade from 1960 to 2000. The application of a factor analytical approach to these decadal sets of variables provided a smaller set of independent factors that account for a majority of the overall variance within the data. These component parts can then be appraised and

FIGURE 1
THE CONCEPTUAL FRAMEWORK FOR UNDERSTANDING THE
VULNERABILITY OF PLACES

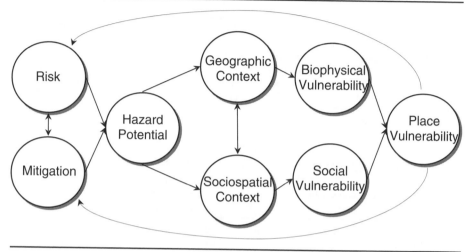

SOURCE: Based on Cutter (1996).

assigned a general socioeconomic or demographic title based on which factors
loaded highest on each component.

There is remarkable consistency (and robustness) in this overall indicator of
social vulnerability. Specifically, the SoVI had a total of eleven to twelve components and explained 74 to 78 percent of the total variation among counties for the
five decades. The most consistent single indicator for all decades was socioeconomic status (Table 1). While there are some minor variations between decades,
socioeconomic status, development density, population age, race/ethnicity, and
gender account for nearly half of the variation in social vulnerability among counties for all U.S. counties.

When applied to the hurricane-ravaged coastal counties/parishes of Louisiana,
Mississippi, and Alabama, the SoVI helps us understand dissimilarities in the ability to adequately respond to and rebound from this disaster, both spatially and tem-
porally. Of particular interest is the differential vulnerability of specific counties/
parishes compared to the others impacted by this storm. This is no more evident
than the disparities between Orleans Parish and the other parishes and counties
hardest impacted by the flooding and storm surge inundation following Hurricane
Katrina. As seen in Table 2, in 2000 Orleans Parish had the highest social vulnerability score of all Katrina-impacted coastal parishes or counties. This was not always
the case. In 1960, both Jefferson and St. Bernard Parishes had higher SoVI scores
than Orleans. However, all the Katrina-affected parishes and counties had lower
overall social vulnerability scores in 2000 than they did in 1960, with one exception:
Orleans Parish. The higher social vulnerability score in 2000 compared to 1960

TABLE 1

CONSISTENCY IN THE SOCIAL VULNERABILITY INDEX (SoVI), 1960-2000

	1960	1970	1980	1990	2000
Percentage variance explained	75.8	74.2	77.5	77.9	78.1
Number of factors	11	12	12	12	11
Most important component (percentage variance explained)	Socio-economic status (17.8)	Socio-economic status (16.1)	Socio-economic status (13.8)	Socio-economic status (13.3)	Socio-economic status (14.7)

TABLE 2

SOCIAL VULNERABILITY SCORES OF COASTAL COUNTIES AFFECTED BY
HURRICANE KATRINA

County/Parish	State	SoVI 2000[a]	Primary Contributing Factors
Baldwin County	AL	−0.69659	Rural agriculture, debt/revenue ratio
Mobile County	AL	0.45640	Race/gendered employment, gender
Jefferson Parish	LA	0.26792	Race/gendered employment, debt/revenue
Lafourche Parish	LA	−0.30376	Debt/revenue ratio, infrastructure employment
Orleans Parish	LA	1.98826	Race/gendered employment, race
Plaquemines Parish	LA	0.96718	Infrastructure employment, rural agriculture
St. Bernard Parish	LA	1.04649	Debt/revenue ratio, infrastructure employment
St. Tammany Parish	LA	−0.54963	Rural agriculture, socioeconomic status
Terrebonne Parish	LA	0.26856	Age, infrastructure employment
Hancock County	MS	−0.82442	Rural agriculture, race
Harrison County	MS	0.16426	Race/gendered employment, gender
Jackson County	MS	−0.24041	Debt/revenue ratio, rural agriculture

a. Standardized scores on Social Vulnerability Index (SoVI) with a mean of 0 and a standard deviation of 1. Positive values indicate higher social vulnerability, while negative values depict lower levels of social vulnerability.

suggests an increase in social vulnerability over time, unlike the other counties in the affected region. This indicates that not only do the persons living in Orleans Parish generally have less ability to cope with major natural disasters than their counterparts in the other parishes, but they also have less ability to rebound from catastrophe than they did in 1960.

What are the primary determinants of the social vulnerability in these counties/parishes? The dominant driving forces behind the social vulnerability of these counties/parishes are race, gender, and class. In addition, two measures of economic vitality were important—rural agriculture and debt/revenue ratio. The dependence on a single-sector economic base such as agricultural provides some vulnerability since there is no alternative source of employment for the community if that sector sustains long-term damage. Similarly, the ratio of local debt to revenue

FIGURE 2
SOCIAL VULNERABILITY OF KATRINA-IMPACTED COASTAL STATES, 1960-2000

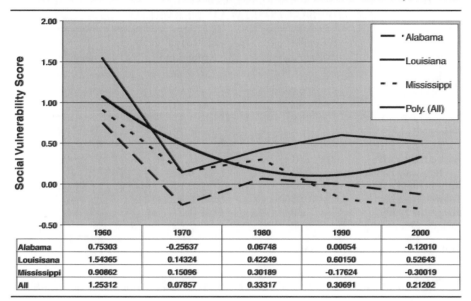

	1960	1970	1980	1990	2000
Alabama	0.75303	-0.25637	0.06748	0.00054	-0.12010
Louisisana	1.54365	0.14324	0.42249	0.60150	0.52643
Mississippi	0.90862	0.15096	0.30189	-0.17624	-0.30019
All	1.25312	0.07857	0.33317	0.30691	0.21202

is also indicative of vulnerability, especially if the debt-to-revenue ratio is high. In Orleans Parish, the primary factors driving social vulnerability are race, class, and gender (Table 2). This is also true for Jefferson Parish, Mobile County, and Harrison County.

Scaling up to the state level, the social vulnerability scores for these three states are similar (Figure 2). Although all three states have seen decreases in social vulnerability since 1960, Louisiana still has an overall higher social vulnerability score when compared to the two other Katrina-impacted coastal states—Alabama and Mississippi. Interestingly, the trend in social vulnerability has been decreasing over time, but in 2000 it took an upward turn.

The SoVI provides a single metric for intrastate and interstate comparisons. It also provides a fundamental grasp of the underlying dimensions that contribute to vulnerability. It is both the aggregate (SoVI score) and disaggregate (individual SoVI components) knowledge that will allow emergency managers, planners, and individuals to help shape the future of hazard mitigation in an attempt to decrease vulnerability and increase the future resilience of these places.

Coastal erosion vulnerability:
The intersection of physical and social indicators

Another way to use the SoVI is to combine it with some physical indicator such as flood potential, storm surge inundation, or coastal erosion. In a pioneering study,

TABLE 3

HURRICANE KATRINA–AFFECTED COASTAL COUNTIES AND THEIR
OVERALL COASTAL VULNERABILITY

County/Parish	Overall Place Vulnerability	Coastal Erosion Index	Social Vulnerability Index
Baldwin County	−0.94	−0.42	−0.52
Mobile County	0.37	0.57	−0.20
Jefferson Parish	0.04	1.15	−1.10
Lafourche Parish	1.09	1.37	−0.28
Orleans Parish	1.38	0.72	0.66
Plaquemines Parish	3.00	2.49	0.51
St. Bernard Parish	1.31	1.76	−0.45
St. Tammany Parish	−0.21	0.17	−0.38
Terrebonne Parish	2.37	2.16	0.21
Hancock County	0.60	0.98	−0.37
Harrison County	1.39	1.55	−0.17
Jackson County	0.46	1.25	−0.78

SOURCE: Based on Boruff, Emrich, and Cutter (2005).

Boruff, Emrich, and Cutter (2005) combined a coastal erosion index developed by the U.S. Geological Survey with a variant of SoVI—a recalculation of social vulnerability derived by comparing the variability in social vulnerability among coastal counties ($N = 213$), not all counties in the U.S. ($N = 3,141$). Looking at all U.S. coastal counties (with the exception of the Great Lakes, Alaska, and Hawaii), the results suggest a highly differentiated pattern of coastal erosion vulnerability along the nation's coastlines. In the Gulf Coast region, for example, the coastal erosion vulnerability is a product of social characteristics, not physical attributes such as mean wave height, rate of sea level rise, and so on. On the other hand, the coastal erosion vulnerability for the Atlantic and Pacific Coast counties was most influenced by physical characteristics.

Two parishes in Louisiana—Plaquemines and Terrebonne—rank in the top ten for the most vulnerable coastal erosion counties in the entire United States. In examining just those counties affected by Hurricane Katrina, physical attributes had more significance than social indicators in determining the overall coastal erosion vulnerability score (Table 3), especially in Plaquemines and Terrebonne. However, in Orleans Parish, social vulnerability and physical attributes had roughly the same impact on the overall coastal erosion vulnerability score.

These are just two illustrations of the spatial dimensions of social vulnerability and the utility of the vulnerability metric known as the Social Vulnerability Index, or SoVI. Simply understanding the characteristics of people and places that lead to increased vulnerability is not enough to curb the escalating losses from natural disasters. What is needed is knowledge about who the most socially vulnerable people are within a population and where those less resilient reside. If we have a spatial understanding of the differences in social vulnerability, policies, procedures, and disaster management protocols can be put into place before an event occurs to minimize the impact of disaster events, thus saving lives and reducing property losses, rather than afterward. It highlights the need for proactive rather than reactive approaches to vulnerability reduction.

Enhancing Resiliency

The stretch of coastline impacted by Hurricane Katrina's storm surge measured more than two hundred continuous miles, from southeast Louisiana, through Mississippi and Alabama, to the Florida panhandle. Although many of the million-dollar houses along this coastline were nearly or completely destroyed from this surge, it was the impact further west and north from the storm surge area that exemplifies the differences in social vulnerability in this disaster. For example, three miles inland from the Grand Strand in Mississippi, people are still trying to live in condemned houses while their more affluent counterparts on the beach have not returned to live in some of the homes that perhaps were only minimally damaged during the hurricane. The people living in the condemned housing have little to fall back on including federal disaster relief, while the beachfront owners have taken a three-month "forced" vacation while the power is restored to their homes and the roads are cleared and repaired. The same could be seen in New Orleans. Those without access to vehicles, proper shelter, food, clothing, and the like paid the price after the storm moved through, while those more affluent were able to evacuate long before impacts were being felt from Hurricane Katrina. Three months after Hurricane Katrina and the failures of the levees in New Orleans, residents in the 9th Ward district were finally allowed into the area to retrieve what was left of their belongings. The more affluent parts of the city (and not surprisingly those less affected by flooding) have had power and water restored for months—a measurable outcome based on the relative social vulnerability of the residents. This scene is played out all along the Gulf Coast in places like Waveland, Pass Christian, and Diamondhead, Mississippi; and in Bayou LaBatre, Coden, and Dauphin Island, Alabama. There will be differential patterns in the recovery of these places.

The SoVI represents an operational protocol for empirically determining social vulnerability. As a single metric, the SoVI is quite robust and consistent over time. It provides a useful tool for comparing one county to another, either within a state or between states. As an overall index with several component parts, the SoVI provides an understanding of the dynamics that factor into the computation of social vulnerability—which factors contribute more, which ones less. The relative importance of each indicator provides the pathway for vulnerability reduction and improvements in the resilience of communities. As such, SoVI presents a tool that will enable planners and developers, city governments, and individuals to make more informed decisions surrounding many aspects of hazard mitigation, preparation, and recovery.

For policy purposes, decreases in overall social vulnerability can be achieved locally by focusing mitigation and planning on the most important component for each community, rather than implementing broad-brush approaches that might miss the more intricate place-based differences in social vulnerability that are present at different localities. For example, a shift from manufactured housing to wood-frame single-unit detached housing built on pilings may be more costly in the short run as the Gulf Coast region rebuilds, yet this type of housing construction may be more sustainable in the longer term. It is not a coincidence that many of the structures that withstood the storm surge and the levee break were some of the older, more historic buildings in the region. The remnants of Hurricane Katrina will be felt for decades along the Gulf Coast. The recovery and reconstruction needs to proceed, but a "one-size-fits-all" strategy is not going to work and may, in fact, exacerbate the preexisting social vulnerabilities found in the region. Greater care and consideration must be taken to derive a socially just recovery and reconstruction of the Gulf Coast.

References

Berry, B. J. L., ed. 1977. *The social burdens of environmental pollution*. Cambridge, MA: Ballinger.

Boruff, B. J., C. Emrich, and S. L. Cutter. 2005. Erosion hazard vulnerability of US coastal counties. *Journal of Coastal Research* 21 (5): 932-42.

Crossett, K. M., T. J. Culliton, P. C. Wiley, and T. R. Goodspeed. 2004. Population trends along the coastal United States: 1980-2008. NOAA/National Ocean Service. http://www.oceanservice.noaa.gov/programs/mb/supp_cstl_population.html.

Cutter, S. L. 1996. Vulnerability to environmental hazards. *Progress in Human Geography* 20 (4): 529-39.

———. 2003. The science of vulnerability and the vulnerability of science. *Annals of the Association of American Geographers* 93 (1): 1-12.

Cutter, S. L., B. J. Boruff, and W. L. Shirley. 2003. Social vulnerability to environmental hazards. *Social Science Quarterly* 84 (1): 242-61.

Cutter, S. L., J. T. Mitchell, and M. S. Scott. 2000. Revealing the vulnerability of people and places: A case study of Georgetown County, South Carolina. *Annals of the AAG* 90 (4): 713-37.

Heinz Center. 2002. *Human links to coastal disasters*. Washington, DC: The H. John Heinz III Center for Science, Economics, and the Environment.

Kates, R. W. 1977. Major insights: A summary and recommendation. In *Reconstruction following disaster*, ed. J. E. Haas, R. W. Kates, and M. J. Bowden, 261-93. Cambridge, MA: MIT Press.

Laska, Shirley. 2004. What if Hurricane Ivan had not missed New Orleans. *Natural Hazards Observer* 29 (2). http://www.colorado.edu/hazards/o/nov04c/html.

Maloney, J. 1973. *Social vulnerability in Indianapolis*. Indianapolis, IN: Community Service Council of Metropolitan Indianapolis.

Pacione, M. 1990. Urban livability: A review. *Urban Geography* 11 (1): 1-30.

———. 2003. Quality-of-life research in urban geography. *Urban Geography* 24 (4): 314-39.

Smith, D. M. 1973. *The geography of social well-being in the United States: An introduction to territorial social indicators*. New York: McGraw-Hill.

U.S. Department of Health, Education, and Welfare. 1969. *Toward a social report*. Washington, DC: Government Printing Office.

U.S. Office of Management and Budget. 1973. *Social indicators, 1973: Selected statistics on social conditions and trends in the US*. Washington, DC: Government Printing Office.

Hurricane Katrina and the Flooding of New Orleans: Emergent Issues in Sheltering and Temporary Housing

By
JOANNE M. NIGG,
JOHN BARNSHAW,
and
MANUEL R. TORRES

Hurricane Katrina created an unprecedented need for sheltering and temporary housing across a four-state area along the Gulf Coast. This article reviews the disaster literature with respect to sheltering and temporary housing and contrasts how these needs actually developed with respect to both the preimpact and postimpact evacuation situations. The article also investigates the ways that intergovernmental planning failed to anticipate the need for shelter/housing solutions or to implement effective measures to put those plans into operation.

Keywords: hurricane; flooding; evacuation; intergovernmental planning; sheltering; temporary housing

Hurricane Katrina resulted in the largest relocation of citizens within the United States since the Dust Bowl of the 1930s. However, the Dust Bowl migration of 300,000 to 400,000 people from the southern plains states to California took place over several years, in comparison to an estimated 1.2 million people who left their homes and communities within hours or days before Hurricane Katrina's landfall along the Gulf Coast on August 29, 2005 (Gregory 1989). Due to the subsequent flooding of New Orleans, the 100,000 to 120,000 residents who remained in the city were rapidly transformed into a second wave of evacuees, greatly intensifying the need for shelter and housing.

This article assesses the adequateness of governmental efforts to provide shelter and housing for thousands of evacuees displaced by Hurricane Katrina. Although this process is ongoing, the data used in this analysis primarily reflect actions taken during the warning and early response periods.[1] Because the largest group of evacuees were from the New Orleans area and because they constituted the largest number of those in "official" shelters (i.e., those facilities that were preidentified and/or run by the Ameri-

DOI: 10.1177/0002716205285889

can Red Cross), we will describe the federal planning processes of the U.S. Department of Homeland Security (DHS) and the Federal Emergency Management Agency (FEMA) and the states of Louisiana and Texas for evacuation, sheltering, and temporary housing. Using these planning documents as "ideal types" (to use Weber's concept) to characterize the way housing issues *were expected to be resolved*, we will then contrast those expectations with the actions that were taken. In other words, we will use evacuation and sheltering/housing processes as a context for explaining how the failure of an unintegrated emergency management system exacerbated threats to the safety, health, welfare, and emotional well-being of evacuees. First, however, we provide an overview of the federal government's plans for responding to large-scale disasters regarding sheltering and temporary housing needs of New Orleans's residents in the hours and weeks following the hurricane.

Emergent Sheltering and Housing Needs: An Overview

On Saturday, August 27, 2005, Max Mayfield, director of the National Hurricane Center, contacted Louisiana Governor Kathleen Blanco and New Orleans Mayor Ray Nagin to express his extreme concern about the immanent threat posed by Hurricane Katrina (Lush 2005). New Orleans is a city below sea level and bordered on three sides by the Gulf of Mexico, the Mississippi River, and Lake Pontchartrain, making it vulnerable to flooding (Eisler and Watson 2005). In response to this information, Governor Blanco declared a state of emergency and Mayor Nagin called for a voluntary evacuation of New Orleans in compliance with the city of New Orleans's and the state of Louisiana's Emergency Response Plans (City of New Orleans Office of Emergency Preparedness 2005; Office of Emergency Preparedness 2005). Implicit in the New Orleans plan and explicit in the Louisiana plan is that "the primary means of hurricane evacuation will be personal

Joanne M. Nigg is a professor of sociology in the Department of Sociology and Criminal Justice and the former director of the Disaster Research Center at the University of Delaware. Since 1976, she has been involved in research on societal issues related to natural, technological, environmental, and human-induced hazards and disasters. She is the author, coauthor, or editor of seven books and more than one hundred articles, book chapters, reports, and papers on individual, organizational, and governmental response to, preparation for, mitigation of, and recovery from natural and technological threats and disasters. She has served as a member of the National Research Council's (NRC's) Board on Natural Disasters as well as the NRC's Committee on Earthquake Engineering. She is also past president of the Earthquake Engineering Research Institute.

John Barnshaw is a doctoral student in the Sociology Program and a graduate researcher at the Disaster Research Center at the University of Delaware. His interests include stratification and inequality in a variety of social contexts ranging from disasters to educational tracking to infectious epidemiology. His most recent disaster research centers on the continuing significance of race and class inequality following Hurricane Katrina.

Manuel R. Torres is a master's student in the Sociology Program and a graduate research assistant at the Disaster Research Center at the University of Delaware. His current research is on the study of interorganizational dynamics in FEMA's Urban Search and Rescue Program.

vehicles" (Office of Emergency Preparedness 2005, 13). Although the state's plan contains a clause for the use of school and municipal buses by volunteer agencies, nowhere in the plan is it specified who is responsible for the logistic coordination of the volunteer agencies for the provision of evacuation transportation (Office of Emergency Preparedness 2005).

On August 28, Mayor Nagin ordered the first mandatory evacuation in the history of the city of New Orleans (Dunne 2005; Russell 2005). Of the more than 460,000 residents of New Orleans, it was estimated that between 100,000 and 120,000 residents did not evacuate prior to Hurricane Katrina for several reasons: they did not have access to personal transportation, they had health conditions that made mobility difficult, they had jobs that required them to remain, or they did not believe the risk from the hurricane was high (Laska 2004; Renne 2005; U.S. Census Bureau 2005).

As Hurricane Katrina quickly escalated to a Category 5 storm on August 28, authorities established the Louisiana Superdome as the "refuge of last resort" for residents unable to evacuate New Orleans (Russell 2005). According to the state of Louisiana's Emergency Operations Plan, a last-resort refuge is

a place for persons to be protected from the high winds and heavy rains from the storm. Unlike a shelter, there may be little or no water or food and possibly no utilities. Thus, a last resort refuge is intended to provide best available survival protection for the duration of the hurricane only. (Office of Emergency Preparedness 2005, 29)

Therefore, according to the state's plan, the Superdome was intended to be used as a refuge of last resort and not necessarily as a mass shelter. Even though the Superdome was considered a refuge of last resort, the Louisiana National Guard delivered three truckloads of ready-to-eat meals and water prior to Katrina's landfall, enough to supply fifteen thousand people for three days (Russell 2005).

For several hours on August 28, buses in New Orleans were deployed to assist transporting nonevacuees (who primarily consisted of residents of the city who had no transportation out of the area and tourists who were stranded when the airport closed) to the Superdome. Despite the fact that the Emergency Operations Plan, developed by the Southeast Louisiana Hurricane Task Force under the auspices of the state's Office of Emergency Planning, called for New Orleans to use several hundred school buses for such an evacuation, these vehicles were not deployed because the city was unable to find drivers (DeBose 2005). By the time Hurricane Katrina made landfall on August 29, an estimated nine thousand residents sought refuge in the Superdome, while an additional three thousand people were housed in forty-five previously identified shelters opened by the American Red Cross (Russell 2005). At this point, it appeared that the Superdome and the much smaller shelters were effectively serving the residents of New Orleans as emergency shelters.

On August 30, however, the levee along the Seventeenth Street Canal was breached, resulting in significant flooding and the relocation of approximately eighteen thousand additional residents to the Superdome and approximately twenty thousand evacuees to the New Orleans Convention Center. Unlike the

Superdome, the Convention Center had not been designated a refuge of last resort, but it became a major emergency shelter for displaced residents (Russell 2005). As conditions deteriorated inside the Superdome and the New Orleans Convention Center and as the numbers of evacuees continued to swell to forty-six thousand between the two sites, Governor Blanco ordered the entire city of New Orleans to be evacuated. Although the media widely reported the deteriorating conditions at both the Superdome and the Convention Center, both FEMA Director Michael Brown and DHS Secretary Michael Chertoff claimed to have no knowledge that the Convention Center was being used as a shelter or that conditions within both facilities were appalling and continuing to worsen until September 1 (O'Brien 2005).

As the orders to relocate evacuees from the Superdome and Convention Center were being given, it was announced that Reliant Park in Houston, Texas, would serve as a site for evacuees from New Orleans (Harris County Joint Information Center 2005c). Reliant Park is a sprawling four-site property located in downtown Houston, consisting of Reliant Stadium (which was not used for evacuees), the Reliant Astrodome, Reliant Arena, and Reliant Center, each of which became large shelters. Additionally, the George R. Brown Convention Center, located approximately six miles from Reliant Park, was also used for evacuees from Louisiana (Barnshaw 2005). The effort to shelter evacuees in Houston was a joint effort coordinated by Houston Mayor William White and Harris County Judge Robert Eckels.

By September 1, this news prompted a convergence at the Superdome where as many as 30,000 to 60,000 people gathered, believing this to be the best place to evacuate from New Orleans and other areas of southeast Louisiana (O'Brien 2005). Later that day, the first busload of evacuees arrived at the Astrodome and Reliant Park in a school bus commandeered by a private citizen (Bryant and Garza 2005). Although the complete evacuation of New Orleans was only expected to last two days, the evacuation took longer than anticipated due to damaged infrastructure and overwhelming throngs of victims seeking exodus from the chaotic scene. By September 2, officials stated that the Reliant Astrodome was holding approximately 15,000 evacuees, while Reliant Arena was sheltering an additional 3,000; Reliant Center would be opened within days and was capable of housing up to 11,000 additional evacuees (Harris County Joint Information Center 2005a). Although comprehensive statistics prior to this period are piecemeal, the four emergency shelters in Texas (Reliant Astrodome, Reliant Arena, Reliant Center, George R. Brown Convention Center) had a peak occupancy of 27,100 evacuees on September 4 and were closed at 7:00 p.m. CDT on September 20, due to the approach of Hurricane Rita (Harris County Joint Information Center 2005b).

Later on September 2, Texas Governor Rick Perry announced an emergency plan that created additional space for 50,000 evacuees in San Antonio and Dallas (Harris County Joint Information Center 2005d). On September 3, a convoy of fifty buses began transporting additional evacuees from Houston to Dallas at such a rate that it was estimated that there were approximately 130,000 evacuees in shelters in Texas, in addition to the estimated 90,000 evacuees already in hotels and private homes in the state (CBS News 2005). By Labor Day, September 6, the date on which the Superdome was completely evacuated, Texas had an estimated 250,000 evacuees, and the state of Texas began requesting further assistance from other states for the remaining 40,000 to 50,000 evacuees from the Gulf Coast region (FEMA 2005b). It is estimated that Arkansas took the majority of the overlap for a total net increase of approximately 100,000 evacuees in various shelters and parks throughout the state, while Oklahoma received at least an additional 20,000 evacuees (FEMA 2005b).

Vertical evacuation, taking shelter from an imminent danger in the upper floors of multistory buildings, has been discussed as an option for people who cannot leave a [threatened] location.

Two weeks after Hurricane Katrina made landfall, twenty-five states were involved in the provision of sheltering for evacuees; and by September 30, evacuees were registered in every state and almost half of the ZIP codes in the United States. Three-quarters of evacuees were staying within 250 miles of their preimpact homes; but tens of thousands were more than one thousand miles away from New Orleans.

Evacuation Planning

Evacuation planning is one of the primary tools that emergency managers use to anticipate removing people from harm's way when a disaster is imminent. Historically, this concept has been used in conjunction with warnings of natural disasters, especially floods, severe storms, hurricanes, and, more recently, tornado events. Due to recent advances in scientific modeling and the development of new technologies, warnings can now be released earlier, providing residents of the potentially effected areas with slightly longer lead times to engage in protective actions.

Recently, two other protective responses to warnings have been proposed as an alternative to horizontal evacuation: vertical evacuation and sheltering-in-place. Vertical evacuation, taking shelter from an imminent danger in the upper floors of multistory buildings, has been discussed as an option for people who cannot leave a location that may become inundated by floodwaters or threatened by hurricane-force winds. The notion is that engineered, high-rise structures can provide adequate short-term protection from these hazards. Vertical evacuation can be thought of as providing a refuge of last resort or as a planned supplement to horizontal evacuation when transportation routes are inadequate for mass egress (Ruch et al. 1991). During the impact of Hurricane Katrina, many tourists were reported to have vertically evacuated to high-rise hotels in New Orleans because their flights had been cancelled and they did not have access to transport out of the city.

Sheltering-in-place is the strategy more often used in instantaneous onset dangers such as tornadoes, hazardous materials incidents, and limited radiological releases. In these instances, people are advised to stay where they are and take precautions to protect themselves by using safe spaces in their residences or businesses and limiting exposure to the hazard. The notion of sheltering-in-place assumes that, if rescue is necessary, people will be moved to safety rather quickly and not left exposed to the elements for days. Given the rapid-onset flooding in New Orleans caused by collapses of the levee along Lake Ponchatrain as well as other sites, sheltering-in-place may have become a death sentence for those who stayed, due to drowning, lack of food and water, or rooftop exposure. Even in mid-November 2005, the death toll from the flooding continues to rise as workers are more thoroughly inspecting homes that had been inundated, finding bodies of people in the attics of their homes where they had retreated from the flood waters, only to be unable to make their way to rooftops.

[In New Orleans,] one in every six people did not have a vehicle available for personal use.

Very little research has actually investigated internal evacuation, that is, the transportation of people to local emergency shelters, either to vertical evacuation facilities or to refuges for sheltering-in-place. To date, planning guidance with respect to internal evacuation focuses almost solely on the identification of structurally sound facilities located in low-risk areas of a community that can be used to provide emergency shelter for short periods of time (usually less than twenty-four hours) to ride out the storm in relative safety. Virtually no planning guidance is available to assist emergency managers in developing transportation strategies for internal evacuation, including how to communicate this information to the public in a timely fashion. Without this type of planning, however, the transportation, medical, social service, and emergency sheltering needs of evacuees cannot be adequately assessed, leaving the most vulnerable evacuees facing severe deprivation, worsening physical and health conditions, potential violence, and even death.

As noted previously, some planning was conducted by the state in concert with the southeast parishes and endorsed by the city of New Orleans, with respect to evacuating people from New Orleans, where one in every six people did not have a vehicle available for personal use. These plans failed, however, in part due to the lack of bus drivers, resulting in people either walking to refuges of last resort or remaining in their own dwellings during the storm and subsequent flood.

If the levees had not failed, this level of planning would probably have been seen as somewhat "successful," despite the lack of transportation and problems with getting supplies to the victims. After all, few casualties have been associated directly with wind or storm surge hazards, and the prehurricane evacuation of approximately 80 percent of the population of New Orleans was remarkable. Once the flooding began, however, the weaknesses of the state and local hurricane plan became apparent.

Planning for Sheltering and Temporary Housing

In the disaster literature, the provision of shelter and housing for victims falls along a continuum from predisaster emergency sheltering to permanent rehousing (Phillips 1992, 1993; Quarantelli 1982, 1991, 1995). The four categories that are usually arrayed along this continuum include emergency shelters, temporary shelters, temporary housing, and permanent (or replacement) housing.

Emergency shelters are intended to provide structurally sound havens for very short periods of less than twenty-four hours during and following the disaster. Refuges of last resort are included in this category. Because these facilities are expected to be used for such a brief time, they are often uncomfortable spaces with few amenities and are sparsely provisioned.

Temporary shelters provide facilities for individuals and families whose homes are without utilities or were damaged to the extent that they are no longer habitable. These temporary living arrangements usually exist for several days to several weeks, depending on how long it takes to find more normal living arrangements. These facilities have adequate sanitation facilities, sometimes food storage and preparation capabilities, and can provide sleeping spaces for a few hundred people at a time. Sometimes these are indoor facilities (school gymnasiums or auditoriums) or tent cities (if the weather is mild enough). These facilities are primarily the responsibility of local governments to identify and, in conjunction with the Red Cross, to operate. The bulk of the research on sheltering has focused on these facilities in the past. There is a consensus among researchers that temporary shelters have been greatly underused, with people staying only for a few days until alternative arrangements could be made. There have been remarkably few instances of temporary shelters failing to satisfy needs of local victims.

Temporary housing is an intermediate stage when victims still cannot return to their damaged homes but need to find interim housing, which allows them to return to their normal functions and tasks. These housing options are usually apartments or rental homes that evacuees use for several weeks to several years until victims can return to their original repaired or totally rebuilt homes. Victims who were renters before the disaster may skip this step entirely if appropriate rental units are available to them on a permanent basis. When rental properties are not available in the disaster-impacted area, FEMA has frequently made mobile homes available as temporary housing options, either situating a trailer on a property owner's lot (seen as more desirable by more property owners) or in mobile home parks that are in the vicinity of the damaged neighborhoods (seen as less desirable from a community planning perspective, but acceptable since local residents can remain in or near the community).

Permanent (or replacement) housing is necessary when victims will never be able to return to their original homes, either because (1) the owners of the victims' rental properties have decided not to rebuild or to replace the rentals with higher-cost dwellings or (2) the victims cannot afford to rebuild their homes. If the vacancy rate in the disaster-affected area is low (as it is in southeastern Louisiana due to widespread damage to the existing housing stock), disaster victims may need to relocate to other cities, counties/parishes, or states.

The unique social impacts created by Hurricane Katrina have created a fifth category of sheltering/housing that has not been considered previously—*long-term sheltering*. Since the city of New Orleans was totally evacuated and residents of that city were bused or flown to temporary shelters in several states without knowing when, or if, they will be able to return, these nonlocal reception centers will have to provide long-term sheltering services for the hurricane/flood victims. It is currently unknown how many of those residents who horizontally evacuated before the hurricane may also be in need of long-term sheltering; however, it should be assumed that most of them have lost their homes and their jobs, making them delayed victims of the hurricane.

Dynamic and fluid sheltering needs. In his review of sheltering and housing needs following disasters, Quarantelli (1982) cautioned that victims do not necessarily progress in a linear fashion through the four sheltering/housing phases discussed above; nor do physical facilities provide only one type of sheltering. Rather, the catastrophic aftermath of Hurricane Katrina reveals the fluid and dynamic sheltering process rendering the four-phase conceptualization somewhat arbitrary along at least three lines. First, in Hurricane Katrina, physical structures provided multiple functions and types of sheltering. The Superdome, for example, served as a refuge of last resort prior to Katrina's landfall, then as an emergency shelter once flooding occurred in New Orleans, and finally as an unplanned temporary shelter for several days because of the delayed postimpact evacuation. Similarly, hotels also underwent a transformation of function. As occupancy increased over time, some hotels—both in and outside the impact area—went from providing emergency shelter to being used as short-term temporary housing, often with financial assistance from FEMA or the American Red Cross. This situation was compounded by Hurricane Rita, which threatened many of the evacuees from Katrina in Louisiana, Mississippi, Alabama, and Texas.

Second, in contrast to previous disasters, Hurricane Katrina provided significant deviation from traditional conceptualizations of temporary sheltering in at least two ways. Due to the catastrophic nature of Katrina and the prolonged inoperability of key geographic locations such as New Orleans, Katrina resulted in an extended dislocation of residents from the impacted area. Unprecedented in previous disasters, Katrina marked the first time evacuees were sent to shelters in other states such as Texas, Oklahoma, Arkansas, and as far away as states on the Pacific Coast. Also unique to Katrina was the extended duration of evacuation. In many previous disasters, the upward limits of evacuees' stays in temporary shelters may be days or a couple of weeks at most; but Katrina-induced flooding caused thousands of evacuees to remain in shelters for weeks or months.

Third, interviews and information gathered from evacuees reveals that transitions were nonsequential for individuals between sheltering stages. While thousands of evacuees transitioned from emergency sheltering to temporary sheltering and then to temporary housing, some transitioned from emergency sheltering to temporary housing, while others transitioned from temporary sheltering and back to emergency sheltering. These instances are indicative of the dynamic and fluid sheltering needs that authorities had to deal with in the complex environment following the hurricane. In some interviews, evacuees reported moving from emergency sheltering to temporary sheltering in mass care facilities, then to hotels, and then back again to mass care facilities as financial resources ran out. In light of recent policy decisions to end the hotel and housing program, likely thousands more will find themselves in a similar transitional stage.

This is not to say that the four-phase typology developed by Quarantelli (1982) should be considered ineffective or ahistorical. It merely highlights emergent areas in sheltering and housing not previously observed and draws attention to the fact that the typology is not mutually exclusive or collectively exhaustive, and as such, further refinement is necessary.

Expectations of Governmental Actions and Resources

We have presented some of the sheltering and housing problems that took place following Hurricane Katrina. Sheltering and housing were, and remain, the principal problem facing all levels of government. What governmental plans were in existence to deal with these short-term problems? Understanding intergovernmental relations is useful for providing a context for the political structure of decisions and understanding how preexisting arrangements facilitate or exacerbate relief provisions and assistance to citizens during a disaster occasion.

The federal context. As a reaction to the September 11, 2001, terrorist attacks, the DHS developed a new federal plan for responding to terrorist attacks, major disasters, and other large-scale emergencies. In December 2004, the National Response Plan (NRP) became effective and was intended to be fully implemented within four months (DHS 2004, ix). The NRP provided the allocation of responsibilities for specific disaster-related tasks across all federal agencies and the American Red Cross (the only nonfederal organization specifically identified as a "primary agency" in the plan). Fifteen tasks, referred to as Emergency Support Functions (ESFs), identify a coordinating agency, a primary agency, and support agencies. For example, ESF no. 6—mass care, housing, and human services—is under the coordination of DHS/FEMA, with DHS/FEMA and the American Red Cross being the primary agencies responsible for carrying out these functions. An additional fifteen federal agencies and two nongovernmental organizations (NGOs) are identified as providing support. With respect to housing, the primary responsibility is "the provision of short- and long-term housing needs of victims" (DHS 2004, EFS no. 6-1). In general, the NRP is intended to provide horizontal coordination among federal agencies, specifying their roles in postdisaster situations.

According to the NRP, a coordinated federal response can be implemented in two ways. The first requires a request from a state's governor if he or she believes that the resources available within the state will be or have been overwhelmed and external resources are needed to limit human suffering. This request for a Presidential Disaster Declaration can be made before the disaster strikes. In the case of Hurricane Katrina, whose speed and force was monitored for days before it made landfall, governors along the Gulf Coast requested such a declaration, knowing the destructive capabilities of the storm. Florida received a declaration on August 28, while the states of Alabama, Louisiana, and Mississippi received declarations on August 29. The second way for federal assistance to be made available to states is by the secretary of the DHS declaring the storm an incident of national significance (INS). Secretary Chertoff formally declared Katrina an INS on August 30, the first time such a designation has been used. Chertoff could have taken this action without receiving requests from the governors anytime before the event, however, but failed to do so despite the computerized models FEMA ran in an exercise a year earlier ("Hurricane Pam") that projected the need for federal resources, especially if the levees failed.

The success of the NRP is predicated on the implementation of the National Incident Management System (NIMS) at all governmental levels (DHS 2004, 1). NIMS provides intergovernmental structure that allows for vertical coordination, resource categorization, a common command structure (the Incident Command System), and the development of communication strategies for identifying and providing resources. NIMS was issued by DHS in March 2004, and all federal agencies were expected to develop a plan for training their personnel by December 2004. By 2007, states would be required to adopt the Incident Command System, begin training their personnel in NIMS concepts, and develop mutual aid agreements. As of May 2005, no date had been set for local government compliance. Clearly, the implementation of the NRP and NIMS was expected to facilitate intergovernmental information gathering and resource provision during major disaster situations.

Although FEMA and the DHS have been engaged in catastrophe planning since 2001, none of the planning exercises have ever seriously addressed the need for long-term sheltering in distant locations, nor has any significant planning guidance on the subject been found (see Clarke [1999] for a critique of catastrophic planning efforts).

However, sheltering and temporary housing were the major problems that had to be addressed by response agencies across all governmental levels due to the evacuation of New Orleans residents. Not only did other Louisiana communities and parishes take in hurricane and flood victims, but other states also established major reception centers for victims, providing temporary shelters as well as temporary housing. The magnitude of this problem overwhelmed all intrastate capabilities to assist victims and also began to strain the resources of nearby states.

This multistate sheltering and relocation of disaster victims had never before been confronted. However, FEMA drew on an initiative that was developed in conjunction with the state of Florida following the 2004 hurricane season when four major hurricanes (Charlie, Frances, Ivan, and Jeanne) crisscrossed the state, leaving thousands of families needing shelter and temporary housing. Drawing on this single-state experience, FEMA established a Housing Area Command (HAC) to expedite the process of developing emergency shelters for those displaced by Hurricane Katrina. The HAC is the "focal point for coordinating the federal response and for maximizing innovation and assistance from donors and businesses" during disaster response (FEMA 2005a). Hurricane Katrina provided the first implementation of the HAC to meet emergency shelter needs after a disaster. The HAC was composed of FEMA representatives, other federal agencies identified in ESF no. 6 (HUD and the Corps of Engineers particularly), the American Red Cross, and members of the private sector. Those corporations represented in the HAC included the Shaw Group Inc., Fluor Group, Bechtel National Inc., CH2M Hill and DewBerry Inc. (FEMA 2005a). Some of these private sector companies received emergency services contracts from FEMA in conjunction with readying shelters.

Hurricane Katrina also provided FEMA with an opportunity to establish the Joint Housing Solution Center (JHSC), a loosely organized, coordinating group to work with local communities to assess their needs for temporary shelters and temporary housing. A plan to establish a JHSC was completed in July 2005, barely a month before Katrina hit. The JHSC is expected to coordinate resources addressing needs in six different areas: bricks and mortar (home design and construction), community services, disaster and recovery policy, housing finance and insurance, community planning, and infrastructure. Although the most pressing concern the JHSC has addressed to date is the need for temporary housing, its major mission is to "facilitate the coordination of re-housing ideas, innovations, strategies, solutions, and resources from all levels of government and all sectors of the society under one roof" (FEMA 2005c). The ultimate goal of the JHSC, then, is to provide resources and housing options with the intent to foster long-term community recovery and redevelopment, not just short-term sheltering and temporary housing. As the federal government's link to local communities, the JHSC is intended to build capacity and develop policy at a regional level, while providing resources to assist them in their rebuilding and planning efforts.

The JHSC is the information-gathering and operational arm of the HAC. To perform this function, several multidisciplinary "strike teams" were formed. These six- to twelve-person teams included planners, architects, engineers, and construction managers who worked with local government representatives and community members to identify sheltering and, more recently, temporary housing needs and to begin to implement solutions.

While these mechanisms sound promising, they did not work effectively for several reasons: they were basically new and untested; they were dealing with four different states at the same time; local officials had no knowledge of, experience with, or role in these types of mechanisms; the HAC made policy in Washington, while the JHSC had to deal with problems in the region; and there was no linkage between the JHSC and FEMA's Individual Assistance program or the Red Cross, which provide money for temporary housing and small home repairs.

The Louisiana context. In attempting to understand why an integrated emergency management system failed to exist before, during, and after Hurricane Katrina, it is important to understand the sociopolitical context and structure of intergovernmental politics in New Orleans, the surrounding parishes, the state of Louisiana, and the U.S. government.

Particularly salient in the case of Hurricane Katrina are the intergovernmental relations between Mayor Nagin, Governor Blanco, and FEMA Director Michael Brown. Before, during, and after Hurricane Katrina, each of these major political figures had varying expectations of the other actors' roles in the response, which on several occasions created ambiguity, confusion, and a misappropriation or underutilization of desperately needed resources. Therefore, it may be illustrative to understand the context and political structure under which these decisions were made and how the actors came to make the decisions they did.

Although the social problems of widespread poverty, racial segregation, underperforming schools, and criminal activity have existed in most large cities such as New Orleans for a considerable time, it was not until Hurricane Katrina disrupted the entire urban system that these structural problems created conditions that drew widespread national media attention. Similarly, the unique tradition of consolidated power in parish presidents, coupled with the historically volatile nature of Louisiana state politics, represents established political conditions that were not sufficiently newsworthy prior to Katrina but that would serve as barriers for effective resource allocation in the impact and postimpact periods. Traditional antagonisms within the Louisiana political milieu were further exacerbated by the introduction of federal actors in the form of President Bush and FEMA Director Michael Brown, who publicly espoused their support for the hurricane and flood victims but were unable to deliver needed resources in a timely manner to reduce suffering.

Following Hurricane Katrina, but during the time that victims were still being rescued from rooftops, the perceived lack of an adequate federal response by Louisiana actors resulted in public displays of frustration and critiques from the bottom up. New Orleans Mayor Nagin, frustrated by his lack of interaction with and resource support from federal officials, stated that they "don't have a clue what's going on down here" (Cable News Network 2005). Similarly, Governor Blanco, who submitted a formal written request to FEMA for specific resources *prior* to Katrina making landfall, reported that she could not get the federal government to respond to her requests (Kettl 2005).

As the federal government's link to local communities, the JHSC [Joint Housing Solution Center] is intended to build capacity and develop policy at a regional level, while providing resources to assist them in their rebuilding and planning efforts.

Unfortunately, in a disaster context such as Hurricane Katrina, the ambiguity, confusion, and lack of intergovernmental coordination resulted in a misappropriation and underutilization of desperately needed resources that put the health and welfare of survivors in jeopardy. Several days after Katrina, essential supplies such as food and water were still not being delivered in sufficient quantities to victims remaining in New Orleans (KVOA-TV 2005). Although the hurricane significantly damaged the region's infrastructure, evidence indicates that the problem may have been exacerbated by various "security measures" enacted to protect the unoccupied areas of New Orleans; for example, truck drivers carrying thousands of bottles of water were prevented from driving into the city because they had not been assigned a necessary "task number" by FEMA, which would allow them to pass through certain security checkpoints (Kettl 2005, 8). Perhaps the most disturbing aspect of the lack of intergovernmental coordination is the realization that the misappropriation and underutilization of strategic resources such as transportation vehicles, boats, helicopters, and first responders may have cost the lives of some citizens in the flooded areas. Five days after Hurricane Katrina, and two days after President Bush announced a massive federal rescue and relief effort, thirty-six hundred troops from the 82nd Airborne were dispatched to the Gulf Coast region to conduct search and rescue activities and to provide security, a delay that federal officials could not explain (Brown, Borenstein, and Young 2005). As retired Army General (and former FEMA Director Julius Becton) noted, "If the First Cav and 82nd Airborne had gotten there on time, I think we would have saved some lives. . . . We recognized we had to get people out, and they had helicopters to do that" (Brown, Borenstein, and Young 2005, 1).

In a harsh media spotlight, the preexisting historical political traditions in Louisiana caused tensions among the different levels of government, further imperiling the health, welfare, and emotional well-being of Hurricane Katrina survivors and facilitating a breakdown of intergovernmental coordination between city, parish, state, and federal actors.

Conclusions

Hurricane Katrina severely taxed the emergency management system of this country and provided insight into how it can be improved to deal with catastrophic situations in the future. These insights fall into three general categories.

Refuges and shelters. Increased attention must be paid to identifying safe refuges of last resort and emergency shelters for larger-scale disasters and catastrophes. Many of the emergency shelters established throughout the city of New Orleans ended up having to be evacuated when the levees failed. Multihazard planning must be taken into consideration when locating these shelters. Guidance needs to be developed on how to staff, provision, and manage refuges and shelters when evacuees may be in the thousands, rather than the hundreds (if that) seen in most disasters.

Temporary migration of evacuees. Katrina pointed out the need not only to prepare an area for a disaster impact but to prepare a region to accommodate the mass, albeit temporary, migration of homeless evacuees. Evacuees quickly taxed the resources of their home states, then adjacent states in the region. Some preplanning for "receptor states" to take in evacuees would lessen the confusion and uncertainty about financial consequences of large-scale disasters for nonimpacted states. The development of policies, similar to mutual aid agreements, might facilitate this process.

Enhanced intergovernmental planning and the role of FEMA. Although there has been an attempt by DHS/FEMA to standardize disaster response procedures through the adoption of the NRP and NIMS, the confusion in response to Hurricane Katrina suggests that one plan may not fit all states equally well. State and local political cultures must be taken into account when considering how these protocols should be implemented. In fact, we would argue that FEMA's regional offices should have a stronger role in working with states to adapt the NRP, NIMS, and other FEMA programs to fit local and state political systems. Perhaps if this had been done, it might not have been necessary to militarize the response in New Orleans. This recommendation, of course, could not be taken without a public discourse about the proper role of FEMA. Since the establishment of DHS, FEMA has been diminished in size, budget and authority; yet it is still the primary civilian agency tasked with all aspects of disaster management. To work with state and local governments to improve their response and recovery capabilities, we believe that enhanced intergovernmental coordination and communication are necessary; and FEMA is the sole federal entity that can currently work with other levels of government to produce this outcome.

Note

1. The Disaster Research Center sent three research teams into Mississippi, Louisiana, and Texas during September 15-30, 2005. One of the major foci for these teams was the collection of data pertaining to sheltering and housing issues. Interviews were conducted with evacuees at Reliant Park in Houston, evacuees in hotels and "official" shelters in Texas and Louisiana, and in churches and other temporary shelters in Mississippi. Interviews were also conducted with Federal Emergency Management Agency, state, and local emergency managers as well as with shelter managers with respect to evacuation, sheltering, and housing issues.

References

Barnshaw, John. 2005. The continuing significance of race and class among Houston Hurricane Katrina evacuees. *Natural Hazards Observer* 30 (2): 11-13.

Brown, Drew, Seth Borenstein, and Alison Young. 2005. Key military help for victims of Hurricane Katrina was delayed. Knight Ridder News Service, September 17. http://www.commondreams.org/headlines05/0917-05.htm (accessed November 12, 2005).

Bryant, Salatheia, and Cynthia Garza. 2005. School bus commandeered by renegade refugees first to arrive at Astrodome. *Houston Chronicle*, September 1. http://www.chron.com/cs/CDA/ssistory.mpl/topstory2/3334317 (accessed November 12, 2005).

Cable News Network. 2005. Mayor to feds: "Get off your asses", September 2. http://www.cnn.com/2005/US/09/02/nagin.transcript/index.html (accessed November 12, 2005).

CBS News. 2005. Katrina disaster blog September 3. *CBS News*, September 4. http://www.cbsnews.com/stories/2005/08/31/katrina/main807164.shtml (accessed November 12, 2005).

City of New Orleans Office of Emergency Preparedness. 2005. Annex I: Hurricanes. *City of New Orleans Comprehensive Emergency Response Plan*. http://msnbcmedia.msn.com/i/msnbc/Components/Interactives/News/US/Katrina/docs/City%20Of%20New%20Orleans%20Emergency%20Preparedness%20%20Hurricanes.pdf (accessed November 12, 2005).

Clarke, Lee. 1999. *Mission improbable: Using fantasy documents to tame disaster*. Chicago: University of Chicago Press.

DeBose, Brian. 2005. Blacks fault lack of local leadership. *Washington Times*, September 10. http://washingtontimes.com/national/20050909-113107-3180r.htm (accessed November 12, 2005).

Dunne, Mike. 2005. State officials urge phase 1 evacuations for low-lying areas. *The Advocate*, July 8. http://www.ohsep.louisiana.gov/newsrelated/StateUrgePhase1.htm (accessed November 12, 2005).

Eisler, Peter, and Tracy Watson. 2005. New Orleans' defenses go only so high. *USA Today*, August 28. http://www.usatoday.com/weather/stromcenter/2005-08-28-katrina (accessed November 12, 2005).

Federal Emergency Management Agency. 2005a. FEMA contracts to provide housing relief for displaced hurricane victims. Press Release, September 8. http://www.fema.gov/news/newsrelease.fema?id=18708 (accessed November 12, 2005).

————. 2005b. Katrina evacuees in Arkansas update. Press Release, September 20. http://www.fema.gov/news/newsrelease.fema?id=19038 (accessed November 12, 2005).

————. 2005c. Working together to rebuild the Gulf Coast. Press Release, November 3. http://www.fema.gov/news/newsrelease.fema?id=20301 (accessed November 12, 2005).

Gregory, James N. 1991. *American exodus: The dust bowl migration and the Okie culture in California*. Cary, NC: Oxford University Press.

Harris County Joint Information Center. 2005a. The Astrodome site is not turning away evacuees. Press Release, September 2. http://www.hcjic.org/news_release.asp?intRelease_ID=1950&intAcc_ID=62 (accessed November 12, 2005).

————. 2005b. Number of citizens. Press Release, September 20. http://www.hcjic.org/default.asp (accessed November 12, 2005).

————. 2005c. Press briefing regarding the transfer of Superdome evacuees to the Houston Astrodome. Press Release, August 31. http://www.hcjic.org/news_release.asp?intRelease_ID=1948&intAcc_ID=62 (accessed November 12, 2005).

————. 2005d. Press conference with Governor Perry. Press Release, September 2. http://www.hcjic.org/news_release.asp?intRelease_ID=1951&intAcc_ID=62 (accessed November 12, 2005).

Kettl, Donald. 2005. Rewiring for success. *Risk Management Review* (Fall): 6. http://grace.wharton.upenn.edu/risk/review/Fall2005.pdf (accessed November 12, 2005).

KVOA-TV. 2005. Five days after Katrina, frustrated refugees still wait for salvation. *KVOA News*, September 3. http://kvoa.com/Global/story.asp?S=3803248 (accessed November 12, 2005).

Laska, Shirley. 2004. What if Hurricane Ivan had not missed New Orleans? *Natural Hazards Observer* 29 (2): 5-6.

Lush, Tamara. 2005. For forecasting chief, no joy in being right. *Saint Petersburg Times*, August 30. http://www.sptimes.com/2005/08/30/State/For_forecasting_chief.shtml (accessed November 12, 2005).

O'Brien, Soledad. 2005. FEMA under fire. CNN Video, September 2. http://www.cnn.com/video/player/player.html?url=/video/bestoftv/2005/09/02/soledad.fema.brown.katrina.cnn (accessed November 12, 2005).

Office of Emergency Preparedness. 2005. State of Louisiana Emergency Operations Plan. http://upload.wikimedia.org/wikipedia/en/3/3c/EOPSupplement1a.pdf (accessed November 12, 2005).

Phillips, Brenda. 1992. Cultural diversity in disasters: Sheltering, housing, and long term recovery. *International Journal of Mass Emergencies and Disasters* 11 (1): 99-110.

————. 1993. Sheltering and housing low income and minority groups after the Loma Prieta earthquake. Paper Presented to the California Seismic Safety Commission, Sacramento.

Quarantelli, Enrico. 1982. General and particular observations on sheltering and housing in American disasters. *Disaster* 6:277-81.

————. 1991. *Patterns of sheltering and housing in American disasters*. Preliminary Paper no. 170. Newark: Disaster Research Center.

————. 1995. Patterns of sheltering and housing in United States disasters. *Disaster Prevention and Management* 4:43-53.

Renne, John. 2005. Car-less in the eye of Katrina. *Planetizen*, September 6. http://www.planetizen.com/node/17255 (accessed November 12, 2005).

Ruch, Carlton, Crane Miller, Mark Haflich, Nelson Farber, Philip Berke, and Norris Stubbs. 1991. *The feasibility of vertical evacuation*. Boulder: University of Colorado Institute of Behavioral Science.

Russell, Gordon. 2005. Nagin orders first-ever mandatory evacuation of New Orleans. *Times-Picayune*, August 28. http://www.nola.com/newslogs/breakingtp/index.ssf?/mtlogs/nola_Times-Picayune/archives/2005_08_28.html#074657 (accessed November 12, 2005).

U.S. Census Bureau. 2005. Fast facts on areas affected by Hurricane Katrina. Press Release, September 6. http://www.census.gov/Press-Release/www/releases/archives/hurricanes_tropical_storms/005672.html (accessed November 12, 2005).

U.S. Department of Homeland Security. 2004. *National Response Plan*. Washington, DC: U.S. Department of Homeland Security.

Weathering the Storm: The Impact of Hurricanes on Physical and Mental Health

The authors briefly review the deaths, injuries, and diseases attributed to hurricanes that made landfall in the United States prior to Hurricane Katrina; recent hurricane evacuation studies and their potential for reducing death, injury, and disease; information available to date about mortality, injury, and disease attributed to Hurricane Katrina; and psychological distress attributable to hurricanes. Drowning in salt water caused by storm surges has been reduced over the past thirty years, while deaths caused by fresh water (inland) flooding and wind have remained steady. Well-planned evacuations of coastal areas can reduce death and injury associated with hurricanes. Hurricane Katrina provides an example of what happens when evacuation is not handled appropriately. Preliminary data indicate that vulnerable elderly people were substantially overrepresented among the dead and that evacuees represent a population potentially predisposed to a high level of psychological distress, exacerbated by severe disaster exposure, lack of economic and social resources, and an inadequate government response.

Keywords   hurricanes; physical health; mental health; evacuation; morbidity; mortality; Hurricane Katrina

By
LINDA B. BOURQUE,
JUDITH M. SIEGEL,
MEGUMI KANO,
and
MICHELE M. WOOD

According to the United Nations Development Programme (UNDP; 2004), four developed nations (the United States, Japan, Australia, and New Zealand) and twenty-nine developing nations have substantial exposure to hurricanes, cyclones, and typhoons. Hurricanes directly affect the public's health by causing deaths, injuries, infectious diseases, and psychological distress. Injuries and diseases that result in serious disability or death are increased to the extent that the health care infrastructure is damaged and public health services are disrupted.

The UNDP (2004, 13) maintains that "human deaths are the most reliable measure of human loss" after a disaster. We suggest that the dependence on mortality rates as the "best" indicator of impact reflects the fact that few studies have attempted to assess the number of injury and disease events that can be directly or

DOI: 10.1177/0002716205284920

indirectly attributed to a given hurricane. This narrow focus on mortality has occurred because of the difficulties both in tracking persons who are injured or diseased and in determining whether the injury or disease of interest can, in fact, be attributed to the index hurricane. Shultz, Russell, and Espinel (2005) noted that "tropical cyclones [hurricanes] have caused an estimated 1.9 million deaths worldwide during the past two centuries and between 300,000 and 500,000 deaths in North America and the Caribbean since the 'discovery' of the Americas in 1492, of which 75,000 occurred during the 20th century" (citing Nicholls, Mimura, and Topping 1995; Rappaport and Fernandez-Partagas 1997, 23). Most deaths have occurred in developing nations, with 42 percent occurring in Bangladesh and 27 percent in India.

The United States and the Caribbean region have experienced many hurricanes during the past twenty years, starting with Hurricanes Elena and Gloria in 1985. The Centers for Disease Control and Prevention (CDC) differentiate between direct mortality caused by the physical forces of a hurricane, primarily flood surges and wind, and indirectly related deaths, caused by unsafe or unhealthy conditions. Shultz, Russell, and Espinel (2005) noted that prior to the development of effective warning, evacuation, and shelter systems, most deaths occurred by drowning in storm surges. Most of the 256 deaths that occurred in Hurricane Camille (1969) were associated with tidal surges, some as high as twenty-five feet. Between 1959 and Hurricane Katrina in 2005, no storms in Japan or the United States (developed countries at high risk of hurricanes, cyclones, and typhoons) resulted in more than 1,000 deaths. During the same time period, fifty high-fatality storms (more than 1,000 deaths) occurred in developing nations of the Asia-Pacific region and sixteen in the Caribbean and Central American area.

Linda B. Bourque is a professor in the Department of Community Health Sciences, associate director of the Southern California Injury Prevention Research Center, and associate director of the Center for Public Health and Disasters at the School of Public Health, University of California, Los Angeles. Her research focuses on community perceptions and responses to disasters, intentional and unintentional injury, and ophthalmic clinical trials.

Judith M. Siegel is a professor in the Department of Community Health Sciences at the School of Public Health at University of California, Los Angeles. She researches the relationship between stress and health, both physical and mental.

Megumi Kano, MPH, is a doctoral student in the Department of Community Health Sciences, UCLA School of Public Health, and a graduate student researcher, at the Southern California Injury Prevention Research Center, UCLA School of Public Health. Awards include the 2005 Chancellor's Dissertation Fellowship at UCLA and a 2005 Pre-Doctoral Fellowship at the National Center for the Study of Terrorism and Responses to Terrorism, University of Maryland.

Michele M. Wood is a teaching fellow at Frontiers in Human Aging (Undergraduate Cluster Program of the College of Letters and Sciences) and a doctoral student at the Department of Community Health Sciences, School of Public Health, at University of California, Los Angeles. Honors include a 2005 Pre-Doctoral Fellowship, National Center for the Study of Terrorism and Responses to Terrorism, University of Maryland, and a 2003-2004 Celia and Joseph Blann Fellowship, School of Public Health, UCLA.

In this article, we will briefly review the deaths, injuries, and diseases attributed to hurricanes that made landfall in the United States prior to Hurricane Katrina; recent hurricane evacuation studies and their potential for reducing death, injury, and disease; information available to date about mortality, injury, and disease attributed to Hurricane Katrina; and psychological distress attributable to hurricanes, including Hurricane Katrina.

United States Hurricanes Pre-Katrina

Consistent with the observations of Shultz, Russell, and Espinel (2005), the number and percentage of deaths attributed to drowning in hurricanes that made landfall in the United States has gradually decreased over the past thirty years, and outbreaks of infectious diseases have been rare. Woshon, Hamilton, et al. (2005) further noted that drowning in salt water caused by storm surges has been reduced, not drowning in fresh water. According to statistics reported by the National Oceanic and Atmospheric Administration (NOAA) Tropical Prediction Center, between 1970 and 1999, only 1 percent of deaths were caused by storm surge, while 59 percent of deaths were caused by fresh water (inland) flooding and 12 percent by wind (as cited in Wolshon, Urbina, et al. 2005, 130).

Between 1959 and Hurricane Katrina in 2005,
no storms in Japan or the United States . . .
resulted in more than 1,000 deaths.

Hurricanes Elena and Gloria, 1985

Hurricanes Elena and Gloria struck the Gulf of Mexico and the Atlantic coast in September 1985. Elena resulted in three storm-related deaths in Mississippi, two in motor vehicle accidents, and one due to electrocution. Visits to emergency rooms increased for approximately one week, but the frequency of total injuries roughly paralleled that of total visits. Gastroenteritis never emerged as a problem during the three-week period of observation (CDC 1986). Gloria resulted in five storm-related deaths in Rhode Island: one from a falling tree, one from a boating accident, two because of lack of electricity, and one because of cardiac arrest while the person cleared debris from a roof. The largest increase in hospital admissions was on the day of the hurricane, with the greatest number of emergency room visits occurring the following day. Of 1,029 patients seen, 484 (47 percent) had sustained injuries. The most common diagnoses were laceration (22 percent), abrasions or contusions (20 percent), sprains (14 percent), and fractures (12 percent). More than half of the records reviewed contained insufficient information to determine whether they were storm related. Eighty-nine (9 percent) of the patients seen had problems clearly related to the storm; 73 had injuries including 26 (36 percent) with lacerations, 11 (15 percent) with fractures, and nine (10 percent) with chain saw injuries. Storm-related injuries were more likely to occur among males (71 vs. 60 percent) and among persons forty to forty-nine years of age (23 vs. 6 percent). Similar emergency room surveillance was conducted in a single Connecticut community of 51,430 residents. When comparing prehurricane to posthurricane periods, emergency room visits and visits for trauma increased, but the distribution of types of visits and the proportion of patients admitted to the hospital did not change. Rates were elevated for corneal abrasion (odds ratio = 3.9) and bee stings (odds ratio = 17.3) and were reduced for psychiatric categories (odds ratio = 0.23).

Hurricane Hugo, 1989

Hurricane Hugo struck Puerto Rico and the Atlantic coast of the United States in 1989. Nine persons died in Puerto Rico, two of whom refused to evacuate, subsequently drowning during the impact phase. Seven deaths were electrocutions, five of which were work related (CDC 1989a, 1989b, 1989c). It was unclear whether influenza-like outbreaks were increased in shelters (CDC 1990). In South Carolina, which was heavily hit by Hurricane Hugo, thirteen persons died during the impact phase, including six who drowned—five while attempting to bring boats inland and one when a storm surge hit a mobile home. Four persons were crushed by mobile homes, one person was crushed by the collapse of a house, and two were crushed by trees. Twenty-two postimpact deaths were recorded including nine in fires, four from electrocutions during cleanup activities, two from falling trees, and one in a chainsaw accident.

In inland North Carolina, 1,090 hurricane-related deaths and injuries were identified and studied. Three of 4 deaths were clearly related to Hurricane Hugo: 1 was caused by a falling tree, and 2 were attributed to drowning in creeks after motor vehicle accidents (Brewer, Morris, and Cole 1993). The number of patients seen in emergency departments was elevated by about 300 above baseline levels of 821 for three days during and following the hurricane, and 30 percent of all emergency department visits were hurricane related. Eighty-eight percent of hurricane-related cases were injuries, with wounds, insect stings, sprains, contusions, and fractures being typical, with wounds and stings accounting for approximately half of the cases. Of 329 wounds caused by cutting and piercing instruments, 135 (41 percent) were caused by chain saws.

Hurricane Andrew, 1992

Following Hurricane Andrew (1992), 462 hurricane-related events[1] were reported in Louisiana by twenty-one of forty-two emergency rooms, five of nine coroner's offices, and two public utilities. Most events occurred after the hurricane (N = 321), 15 occurred before landfall, and 70 occurred during the hurricane. Of the 17 fatalities, 8 occurred before the hurricane, including 6 by drowning, 1 in a motor vehicle accident, and 1 by being crushed during a prehurricane tornado. Of the 445 nonfatal events, 41 percent (N = 184) were cuts, lacerations, or puncture wounds; and 11 percent (N = 49) were strains and sprains, primarily to the upper and lower extremities. Sixty-two illnesses were reported, but no details were provided (CDC 1993a, 1993c).

In contrast to prior hurricanes, most deaths in Florida (Dade County) directly attributable to Hurricane Andrew resulted from blunt trauma or asphyxia, rather than drowning in either a storm surge or flooding (CDC 1992). Nine of the fourteen deaths during the impact phase were caused by blunt or penetrating trauma, four from asphyxia in collapsed buildings, and one from drowning. To control for malaria, dengue, and encephalitis, the density of nuisance mosquito populations was monitored in both Dade County, Florida, and Louisiana (CDC 1993b). Although increased numbers of mosquitoes were found in Louisiana, no increase in diseases associated with mosquito vectors was reported.

Hurricanes Marilyn and Opal, 1995

Hurricane Marilyn resulted in ten deaths in Puerto Rico and the Virgin Islands. The only preimpact death was caused by electrocution, and the death of a 107-year-old woman was attributed to natural causes. The remaining eight deaths occurred in boats, with seven persons drowning and one death by head trauma (CDC 1996a). Hurricane Opal (October 1995) resulted in a total of twenty-seven deaths in Florida (two), Alabama (twelve), Georgia (eleven), and North Carolina (two). One death occurred before the storm, thirteen during impact, and thirteen after impact. Seventy-eight percent (twenty-one of twenty-seven) of the decedents were males.

Of the twenty-seven deaths, twenty-four were considered unintentional while three were attributed to natural causes exacerbated by the hurricane. Thirteen deaths were related to falling trees with nine occurring during impact. Four deaths were attributed indirectly to power outages, including carbon monoxide poisoning (one) and house fires (three). One person drowned in a swollen creek, one was electrocuted while repairing a downed power line, and one suffered massive chest trauma when a tractor being used in cleanup overturned. Most of the 1,084 storm-associated injuries in the U.S. Virgin Islands involved minor wounds (e.g., abrasions, lacerations, puncture wounds) or trauma to the musculoskeletal system (e.g., fractures, sprains, strains, dislocations). In Florida, the only condition that increased in prevalence during and after Hurricane Marilyn was the proportion of health care visits for insect bites (CDC 1996b).

Hurricane Georges, 1998

The contrast between the developed and developing world is clearly seen in reports of mortality and morbidity from Hurricane Georges (1998). In the Dominican Republic, approximately three hundred deaths were reported. Two months after the hurricane, a substantial number of households reported inadequate food, persisting medical needs, and lack of medications. In contrast, only eight deaths, all occurring after impact, were reported in Puerto Rico, with two deaths by carbon monoxide poisoning, four by fire, one by head trauma, and one by electrocution (CDC 1998, 1999).

Hurricane Floyd, 1999

Thirty-five (67 percent) of the fifty-two deaths attributed directly to Hurricane Floyd (1999) in North Carolina occurred on the day of the hurricane. The leading cause of death was drowning (thirty-six), with twenty-four occurring in a motor vehicle, seven in boats, four as a pedestrian, and one in a house. Most drowning occurred in flooded rivers, rather than in storm surges (Dow and Cutter 2000, 152). When emergency department (ED) visits in the following week were compared with the analogous period in 1998, increases were reported in suicide attempts (relative risk = 5.0; confidence interval, 1.4-17.1), dog bites (relative risk = 4.1; confidence interval, 2.0-8.1), febrile illnesses (relative risk = 1.5; confidence interval, 1.3-1.9), basic medical needs (relative risk = 1.4; confidence interval, 1.2-1.8) and dermatitis (relative risk = 1.4; confidence interval, 1.2-1.6). When ED visits during a one-week period one month after Hurricane Floyd were compared with ED visits during the same period in 1998, increases were reported in arthropod bites (relative risk = 2.2; confidence interval, 1.4-3.4), diarrhea (relative risk = 2.0; confidence interval, 1.4-2.8), violence (relative risk = 1.5; confidence interval, 1.1-2.2), and asthma (relative risk = 1.4; confidence interval, 1.2-1.7). Routine surveillance identified outbreaks in shelters of self-limiting gastrointestinal disease and respiratory diseases (CDC 2000).

Hurricane Isabel, 2003

Hurricane Isabel struck the Atlantic seaboard from North Carolina to New Jersey. Forty deaths have been officially attributed to the storm, but no detailed information about either the deaths or injuries has been reported.

2004 hurricane season

The 2004 hurricane season was highly destructive to the state of Florida. Four hurricanes hit Florida, with Hurricane Charley resulting in thirty-five deaths; Hurricane Frances, forty; Hurricane Ivan, twenty-nine; and Hurricane Jeanne, nineteen (Dahlburg 2005). As of September 1, the CDC reported thirty-one deaths from Hurricane Charley (August 13, 2004), with twelve occurring on the first day of the storm, and eight during the next two days (CDC 2004b). Seventy-seven percent (twenty-four of thirty-one) were to males.

Of the thirty-one deaths, twenty-four (77 percent) were classified as unintentional injury, six were attributed to natural causes exacerbated by the hurricane, and one was a suicide. Of the twenty-four deaths attributed to unintentional injury, seventeen deaths, ten on the day of impact, were due to trauma caused by falling trees, flying debris, and destroyed physical structures. As in Hurricane Andrew, only one death was caused by drowning. Other causes of death, all after impact, were carbon monoxide poisoning (three), electrocution (one), and two with multiple causes of death (i.e., trauma and electrocution; carbon monoxide [CO] poisoning and burns).

Successful evacuation of vulnerable areas has the potential to reduce casualties, both fatal and nonfatal, that occur when a hurricane makes landfall.

The Florida Department of Health added thirty questions to the Behavioral Risk Factor Surveillance System (BRFSS) to assess the impact of the hurricanes on state residents (CDC 2005b). All sixty-seven counties in the state were sampled using random digit dialing. Participants included 919 (53.9 percent) persons who lived in the forty-one counties in the direct path of at least one of the four hurricanes, and 787 (46.1 percent) who lived in the twenty-six counties not in the direct path. Physical injuries were reported by 4.6 percent of the first group and 3.8 percent of the second group. Of persons with preexisting health conditions such as diabetes, asthma, or cardiovascular disease, 5.4 percent reported their conditions were made worse by the hurricanes. Of that group, 13.6 percent reported having difficulty getting needed medications, and 9.0 percent reported problems using essential medical equipment. At the time of the interview, 10.7 percent of all respondents reported feelings of nervousness, worry, or anxiety because of the hurricane; while 6.0 percent reported feeling sad or having loss of appetite or difficulty sleeping; and 3.9 percent reported reduced mental ability to work or study.

The most prevalent risk factor for indirect morbidity and mortality following the hurricanes was improper use of portable gas-powered generators. "A total of 167 persons had nonfatal CO poisoning diagnosed during the study period, representing a total of 51 exposure incidents. The number of cases and incidents peaked within three days after landfall of each hurricane" (CDC 2005a). Six persons died in five additional exposure incidents.

Evacuation before Hurricanes

Successful evacuation of vulnerable areas has the potential to reduce casualties, both fatal and nonfatal, that occur when a hurricane makes landfall. During the past decade, research on evacuation behavior and patterns of evacuation has increased substantially. Cutter and colleagues have conducted a series of studies of evacuation in South Carolina prior to tropical storms and Hurricanes Bertha (1996), Fran (1996), Bonnie (1998), Dennis (1999), Floyd (1999), and Irene (1999), with particular attention to the impact of prior repeated calls for evacuation on residents' decisions to evacuate in the future (Dow and Cutter 1998, 2000, 2002). Van Willigen et al. (2005) have examined evacuations in North Carolina before Hurricane Floyd (1999), and Whitehead and colleagues (2000) have examined how evacuation behavior in North Carolina before Hurricane Bonnie (1998) might influence future evacuation behavior. Wilmot and Mei (2004) have developed models of hurricane evacuation based on data collected after Hurricane Andrew (1992), and Prater, Lindell, and colleagues (Lindell, Lu, and Prater 2005; Zhang, Prater, and Lindell 2004) have examined evacuations during Hurricanes Bret (1999) and Lili (2002).

While evacuations have the potential to save lives and reduce injuries, they are costly in time, money, and credibility.

While evacuations have the potential to save lives and reduce injuries, they are costly in time, money, and credibility. Wolshon, Urbina, et al. (2005, 130) estimated that hurricane evacuations "can exceed one million dollars per mile of coastline [evacuated] from direct costs and losses in commerce, tourism, and general productivity." The timing and location of an evacuation order is critical if casualties are to be reduced. If an evacuation is ordered too early, however, the hurricane may change direction such that the evacuation order was either unnecessary or directed populations into areas that were more dangerous than the area that they evacuated. On the other hand, when evacuation orders are too late, dangerous areas may not be completely cleared before the hurricane makes landfall (Urbina and Wolshon 2003). As Dow and Cutter (2000, 146) noted, "A discrepancy between timely and more accurate warnings has received considerable attention. The result is an evacuation policy that is, by design, precautionary, but raises concerns about credibility of the information and its source."

Prior to hurricanes Katrina and Rita, the largest evacuations occurred before Hurricanes Georges (1998) and Floyd (1999) (Wolshon, Hamilton, et al. 2005). These two evacuations resulted in traffic jams throughout the Carolinas, Florida, and Virginia, as 2 million people evacuated, some spending as many as twenty hours in transit. Exacerbating traffic flow was the tendency of South Carolina households to take two cars, to evacuate within a limited time window, and to evacuate only on major interstates. Because 56 percent of coastal South Carolina residents fled the state, with substantial numbers going to North Carolina, this exodus contributed to problems in North Carolina, where landfall and much of the heavy rainfall and flooding occurred (Dow and Cutter 2002).

Between one hundred and two hundred thousand residents of New Orleans were unable or unwilling to evacuate the area, and large portions of the city flooded after *the hurricane had passed through; these facts complicate efforts to assess when and how persons died.*

Despite the substantial problems associated with the Hurricane Floyd evacuation, South Carolina residents, who have experienced numerous voluntary and mandatory orders to evacuate, continue to support evacuation and consider life safety the primary goal of evacuation. At the same time, they want authorities to keep traffic flowing out of the area, and they expect to return home within one or two days, although they recognize that services may not be restored for an additional two or three days (Dow and Cutter 2000). This desire to return before services are fully restored could increase the probability that injuries and deaths will occur during cleanup, particularly if evacuated areas remain flooded.

Although Dow and Cutter (1998) found no associations between demographic characteristics (gender, race, and age) and decisions to evacuate, other researchers report that household size and the presence of children or older persons decreased the probability of evacuation before Hurricane Andrew (Gladwin and Peacock

1997). Van Willigen et al. (2005) reported that younger, low-income African Americans who were not married were more likely to evacuate in Pitt County, North Carolina, before Hurricane Floyd, but possibly the most salient factor was residents' perception that their homes were at risk of flooding. Past experience, perceived safety of residents' homes, anticipated severity of the hurricane, and the location of landfall increased evacuation in the Carolinas (Dow and Cutter 1998); and distance from the nearest body of water influenced evacuation in Hurricane Andrew (Wilmot and Mei 2004).

It appears that mandatory evacuation orders by officials are more effective than voluntary ones in increasing evacuation, but mandatory orders rarely result in bodily removal of persons from their homes by officials. Only 51 percent of Florida respondents reported having an evacuation plan before the 2004 hurricanes (CDC 2004a). Dow and Cutter (2000, 151) suggested that residents of areas like the Carolinas and Florida, where multiple hurricane evacuation orders have been issued over the past few years, pay less attention to what officials say than they did in the past and instead base their decision on what they hear from the media. The Weather Channel and local media are judged the most credible sources of this information. Decisions not to evacuate are influenced by not knowing where to go or how to get there, lack of transportation, the cost associated with evacuation, care for pets, perceived delays in returning home, and perceptions that homes are safe and that the impending hurricane is not sufficiently severe or threatening.

Hurricane Katrina

In June 2002, The New Orleans *Times-Picayune* suggested that efficient evacuation was the key to survival should a major hurricane hit New Orleans and that "for an evacuation of the New Orleans area to work, more than a million people have to travel at least 80 miles over an aging, low-capacity road system to reach high ground and shelter" (McQuaid and Schleifstein 2002). The authors noted that such an evacuation "requires a 72- to 84-hour window," which is substantially longer than the window within which forecasters can accurately predict a storm's track and strength. Such evacuations are highly dependent on private automobiles but, according to the 2000 Census, 27 percent of households in Orleans Parish, Louisiana, did not have an automobile. Wolshon, Urbina, et al. (2005, 136) estimated that 250,000 residents of New Orleans (not including tourists or "special needs" populations) have no means of private transportation and that the total number of buses available (464) could only evacuate 10 percent of those without cars. In fact, no buses were assigned to evacuate residents of New Orleans before Hurricane Katrina, and mandatory evacuation was ordered at 10:00 a.m. on August 28, only twenty hours before the hurricane made landfall at 6:10 a.m. on August 29, and twenty-five hours before the levees began to fail at 11:00 a.m.

Between one hundred and two hundred thousand residents of New Orleans were unable or unwilling to evacuate the area, and large portions of the city flooded *after* the hurricane had passed through; these facts complicate efforts to assess when and how persons died. First, the extensive floods delayed the retrieval of bodies for weeks, which made it difficult to determine both time and cause of death. Second, preliminary information indicates that, in contrast to other recent hurricanes, substantial numbers of persons drowned. It may never be possible to ascertain whether they drowned in storm surges directly associated with the hurricane or in the subsequent flooding associated with the breaks in the levees.

Mortality

As of mid-December 2005, only the state of Louisiana had established an official Web site on deaths attributed to Hurricane Katrina that was updated as deceased were released to families (Louisiana Department of Health and Hospitals 2005). Combining that information with other, less dependable sources, 1,319 deaths had been attributed to Hurricane Katrina, with 1,070 (82 percent) from Louisiana; 228 (17.5 percent) from Mississippi; and a scattering of deaths in Alabama (N = 2), Florida (N = 14), Georgia (N = 2), Kentucky (N = 1), and Ohio (N = 2) (Wikipedia 2005). In addition, 57 evacuees were listed as official deaths, and more than 2,500 persons were listed as missing. In Mississippi, 40 percent (91/228) of deaths occurred to residents of Harrison County, 22.4 percent (51/228) in Hancock County, and 7.5 percent (17/228) in Pearl River County. No additional information was available about deaths of Mississippi residents at the time of this writing. Unlike Louisiana, it is somewhat more likely that the 228 deaths that occurred in Mississippi can be directly attributed to storm surge and wind at the time that the hurricane made landfall.

The Louisiana Department of Health and Hospitals continually updates the status of bodies examined at the St. Gabriel morgue. As of December 16, 2005, 902 of 1,095 recovered bodies had been examined. Of those examined, 97 percent (879/902) of deaths were determined to be storm related; the remaining 23 were listed as coroner's cases, suggesting that death occurred by violence or suspicious means. Of the 879 storm-related deaths, 512 had been identified and released to families, 169 were awaiting release to families, 1 had been identified and was awaiting autopsy, and the identities of 197 were unknown.

Of those that were storm related and who had been released to families, 74 percent (380/512) were residents of Orleans Parish where New Orleans is located; the remaining 132 persons were from Jefferson Parish (n = 26), St. Bernard Parish (n = 94), St. John Parish (n = 1), East Baton Rouge (n = 1), Washington Parish (n = 1), St. Tammany Parish (n = 2), Plaquemines Parish (n = 2), out-of-state (n = 2), and of unknown location (n = 3).

Commentators have speculated that vulnerable, poor African Americans were most at risk of death during and after Hurricane Katrina. By implication, this would suggest that women, African Americans, the elderly, and the young will be overrepresented among the dead. Gender, race, age, and parish of residence were reported for the 512 persons examined and identified at St. Gabriel Morgue, and released to families. When the 380 persons from Orleans Parish were compared to those from other parishes, 53.3 percent of Orleans residents were male as compared to 43.2 percent from other areas (p = .10), and 63 percent were African American as compared to 13.6 percent from other areas (p < .001). When compared with census estimates for 2004, where 46.5 percent of Orleans residents were male and 67.9 percent were African American, males are overrepresented among the identified dead, and African Americans are somewhat underrepresented.

When age is examined, vulnerable elderly are substantially overrepresented among the deceased. Forty-seven percent (239/512) of the deceased were older than seventy-five, and an additional 26 percent (77/285) were between sixty and seventy-five. Among those identified and released to date, only seven were younger than twenty. Age distribution does not differ by parish.

Gender, race, and age also were available for the larger group of 705 bodies that had been examined and identified at St. Gabriel Morgue; this group includes the 512 bodies that had been released and the 170 bodies that had been identified but not yet released. Like the smaller group, males were disproportionately represented among the dead: 51 percent (359/705) were male, 48 percent (339/705) female, and 1 percent (7/705) were of unknown gender. This compares with a state population that is 51.6 percent female. Forty-eight percent (339/705) were African American, which compares with a state population that is 32.5 percent (1,451,944/4,468,976) and a New Orleans city population that is 67.9 percent (302,041/444,515) African American. The single most striking fact, however, is the age of decedents. Sixty-seven percent (475/705) of the dead identified to date at St. Gabriel Morgue were older than sixty, and 44 percent (309/705) were older than seventy-five. Although not reported, these numbers may include 68 persons whose bodies were recovered from four nursing homes in New Orleans and St. Bernard Parish.

According to the New Orleans *Times-Picayune*, deaths in Orleans Parish were caused by drowning and exacerbated medical conditions, while the deaths in St. Bernard Parish are being attributed to drowning in a storm surge that was estimated at more than twenty feet (Warner and Scott 2005).

Morbidity

Reports of physical injuries and disease episodes that occur after disasters, including hurricanes, are always less complete and less accurate than reports of deaths. In the case of Hurricane Katrina, this problem is exacerbated by the wide dispersal of evacuees, particularly those who left New Orleans. As we saw above, physical injuries are the most prevalent casualty after a hurricane, with most injuries occurring as a result of high winds and the collapse and movement of structures, trees, and other debris. Following hurricanes and other natural disasters, the media and others are quick to suggest that survivors are at increased risk of infectious diseases following hurricanes and floods, but in fact, detectable increases have rarely been documented, whether in the United States or elsewhere. To date, the CDC has issued reports on infectious diseases, dermatologic conditions, norovirus outbreaks, vibrio illnesses, and CO poisoning cases attributable to Hurricane Katrina (CDC 2005a, 2005f, 2005d, 2005c, 2005e). A survey of Hurricane Katrina evacuees in Houston shelters has been reported (*Washington Post*, Kaiser Family Foundation, and Harvard University 2005), and assessments of the toxicity of the flood waters in New Orleans has been reported (Pardue et al. 2005).

Vibrio *illnesses*

While cholera is included in the *Vibrio* species, at least seven noncholeragenic *Vibrio* species have been reported as causing illness each year in the United States. Although these organisms are grouped with those that cause cholera, they cause distinctly different illnesses that are usually either food borne or wound associated. Food-borne illness results from eating raw or undercooked shellfish, particularly oysters or other contaminated foods; wound-associated infections result from exposure to seawater or brackish waters where the organism naturally occurs. The most frequently reported posthurricane vibrio illnesses were *V. vulnificus* and *V. parahaemolyticus* wound infections. Eighteen cases were reported in residents of Mississippi ($N = 7$) and Louisiana ($N = 5$); persons displaced from Louisiana to Texas ($N = 2$), Arkansas ($N = 2$), and Arizona ($N = 1$); and a person displaced from Mississippi to Florida ($N = 1$). Ages ranged from thirty-one to eighty-nine, and 83 percent (fifteen of eighteen) were male. Most patients were hospitalized and five died. In 72 percent (thirteen of eighteen), underlying health conditions including heart disease, diabetes, renal disease, alcoholism, liver disease, peptic ulcers, immunodeficiency, and malignancy may have contributed to the severity of the infection.

Four persons, including a two-month-old boy, were reported with non-wound-associated vibrio infection in Mississippi ($N = 2$), Louisiana ($N = 1$), and one person displaced from Louisiana to Arizona. None of these persons died.

On average, 412 cases of noncholeragenic vibrio illnesses were reported each year between 2000 and 2004 in the United States, with an average of 14 reported in Gulf Coast states and 7 being wound related. Clearly, the number of wound-associated cases reported in August and September of 2005 exceeds the average annual rate, and all can be traced to exposure to flood waters after Hurricane Katrina (CDC 2005e).

Infectious diseases and dermatologic conditions among evacuees

A partnership comprised of the *Washington Post*, Kaiser Family Foundation, and Harvard University School of Public Health (2005) conducted a survey of 680 adult evacuees residing in the Houston Reliant Park Complex (Reliant Astrodome and Reliant Center) ($N = 439$), the George R. Brown Convention Center ($N = 152$), five of fourteen Red Cross shelters ($N = 77$), and unrecorded locations ($N = 12$) between September 10 and 12, 2005. Ninety-eight percent of evacuees were from the greater New Orleans area. Sixty-one percent did not evacuate before the storm, giving as their primary reason not having a car or way to leave (36 percent) or underestimating the severity of the storm and its aftermath (29 percent).

Thirty-three percent reported that they had experienced health problems or injuries as a result of the hurricane or flooding. No questions were asked about the health problems or injuries being experienced by evacuees, but the CDC later reported thirty cases of methicillin-resistant *Staphylococcus aureus* dermatologic infections among both child and adult evacuees in Dallas, Texas, and approximately one thousand cases of acute gastroenteritis among evacuees in Louisiana, Mississippi, Tennessee, and Texas during the first three weeks after the hurricane.

Between September 2 and 12, 2005, some 6,500 of the 24,000 evacuees at Reliant Park visited the medical clinic, with 1,169 (18 percent) having symptoms of acute gastroenteritis. Stool samples identified norovirus as the source of infection in 50 percent of cases. Noroviruses are the most common cause of outbreaks of acute gastroenteritis in the United States. Outbreaks are spread through person-to-person contact or from fomites[2] that form in crowded settings, such as cruise ships and shelters. Once an outbreak begins, norovirus is highly contagious, easily transmitted, and remarkably resistant to cleaning agents. No confirmed cases of *Shigella* dysentery, typhoid fever, or toxigenic cholera were identified (CDC 2005d, 2005c).

Surveillance of nonevacuees

CDC, the Louisiana Department of Health and Hospitals, and functioning treatment facilities established an active surveillance system "to detect outbreaks of disease and characterize post-hurricane injuries and illnesses" (CDC 1996a, 1018). Between September 9 and 25, the system had monitored 7,508 reports of health-related events of residents and workers in Jefferson, Orleans, Plaquemines, and St. Bernard Parishes. Retrospective data going back to August 27 were collected when possible. Fifty-five percent (4,169/7,508) of events were illnesses; 26.9 percent (2,018/7,508) were injuries; and 17.5 percent (1,321/7,508) involved medication refills, wound checks, and so forth. Thirty-four percent of events (2,567/7,508) occurred to residents, 13.8 percent (1,037/6,167) to relief workers, and status was unknown for 52 percent (3,904/7,508). The surveillance detected an apparent increase in acute respiratory illnesses over the period while, consistent with data reported after other hurricanes, 35.5 percent (716/2,018) of the injuries reported consisted of cuts, blunt trauma, burns, and environmental exposures; and 23 percent (464/2,018) of falls. Relief workers were significantly more likely than residents to be seen for rashes, such as prickly heat, arthropod bites, and the abrasive effects of wet clothing and moist skin (odds ratio = 1.7; confidence interval, 1.4-2.1).

Carbon monoxide poisoning

CO poisoning primarily occurs when people use portable generators in confined areas. Fifty-one cases of CO poisoning were reported between August 29 and

September 24 in Alabama, Louisiana, and Mississippi. Thirty-eight cases (74.5 percent) occurred within the first week after the hurricane. Five persons died; the forty-six survivors were treated either with hyperbaric oxygen ($N = 37$) or high-flow oxygen ($N = 9$) (CDC 2005a).

Toxicity of flood water

Considerable concern has been expressed about the potential toxicity of the flood waters in New Orleans. The only systematic study reported to date examined samples obtained on September 3 and 7 in the Lakeview district bounded by Lake Pontchartrain to the north and the 17th Street Canal to the west, where one of the levee breaks occurred, and from a comparison site some six to eight miles distant, the Tulane-Gravier neighborhood in the Mid-City district. Areas selected for sampling were determined by accessibility and safety issues (Pardue et al. 2005).

Surface waters were low on oxygen, and samples indicated that levels of lead, arsenic, and chromium exceeded drinking water standards. The floodwater was similar to normal stormwater runoff found both in this area and other areas. "What distinguishes Katrina floodwaters are their large volume and the human exposure to these pollutants that accompanied the flood rather than extremely elevated concentrations of toxic pollutants" (Pardue et al. 2005, 8595). The authors concluded by stating that "although some conclusions can be drawn about the quality of the floodwater based on this data set, more detailed human exposure, waste load allocation, and ecological risk assessment calculations for Lake Pontchartrain should be conducted prior to reaching ultimate conclusions regarding the environmental impacts of Hurricane Katrina" (Pardue et al. 2005, 8598).

Psychological Distress Attributable to Hurricanes

Explanatory models of disaster exposure and psychological distress primarily focus on four critical factors: characteristics of the stressor (disaster), cognitive processing of the traumatic event, individual characteristics, and qualities of the environment (such as social support systems) predisaster and postdisaster (Green et al. 1990). The extant models differ in their emphasis on the various factors, but all attempt to describe the interrelationships between the characteristics of the event and the resources of the individual. These include a conceptual model (La Greca et al. 1996), the conservation of resources theory (Freedy et al. 1992), the social support deterioration deterrence model (Norris and Kaniasty 1996), and an adaptation of stress theory (Folkman et al. 1986). Either in the context of these models or independently, many parameters have been studied as potential predictors of posthurricane distress. Two emerge as stable predictors of distress, severity of exposure and previous mental health problems, whereas most other factors show some inconsistency across studies (Caldera et al. 2001). In regard to outcome, post-traumatic stress disorder (PTSD) has been studied most commonly, using a variety of instruments that have been administered at varying posthurricane intervals. Partly as a function of this variability, estimates of postdisaster PTSD range widely, but collectively, it is reasonable to conclude that hurricanes have a measurable impact on the mental health of children and adults, at least in the short run.

Although the relationship between exposure and distress is robust, intervening individual difference variables, such as coping self-efficacy and optimism, are important in determining degree of distress (Benight et al. 1999). Coping self-efficacy is conceptualized as the individual's perception of his or her ability to manage stressful or threatening environmental demands. Data collected from adults five months after Hurricane Hugo showed that resource loss directly affected level of distress (measured by the SCL-90 and the Impact of Events Scale) and also operated through coping self-efficacy. The extent to which optimism and available support were able to diminish the impact of resource loss depended on the individual's confidence in his or her coping abilities. This study and others emphasize the utility of considering both internal resources (such as optimism) and external resources (social support) in modeling the pathway between disaster exposure and psychological distress.

A number of studies have focused on children in affected communities. In general, increased exposure is associated with increased distress, although most children score in the normal range of distress, and their recovery tends to be relatively rapid. After Hurricane Andrew, the perception of life threat during the hurricane was a stronger determinant of the intrusion and avoidance subscales of the Impact of Events Scale (a measure of PTSD) than the actual number of traumas experienced (Jones et al. 2001), suggesting that children may be less sensitive to loss than adults. Regarding recovery, the proportion of elementary school children scoring in the severe to very severe range of PTSD on the Reaction Index was 30 percent at three months after Hurricane Andrew, 18 percent at seven months, and 13 percent at ten months postdisaster (La Greca et al. 1996). Among the factors that predicted a slow recovery (drop in PTSD score) were intervening, non-hurricane-related life events. Non-hurricane-related life events were as important as hurricane exposure variables in explaining psychological distress in other studies of children, as well (Hardin et al. 1994).

Studies that have collected data on children's postdisaster psychological distress from children's self-report and parents reporting on their children highlight where their perceptions diverge. After Hurricane Hugo, 90 percent of third- to fifth-grade students in high-impact areas scored in the range of severe psychic trauma on the Reaction Index (Belter, Dunn, and Jeney 1991). Parents' report showed a substantial but much smaller proportion of the children (69 percent) could be classified in the severe trauma category. Furthermore, children's trauma was not correlated with any of the objective indices of damage, whereas parents' report on their children's psychological state was correlated with each of the indices of damage, again underscoring that adults are more distressed than their children by tangible resource loss.

Investigations that have included outcomes in addition to PTSD demonstrate a high degree of comorbidity. For example, among Nicaraguan adolescents after

Hurricane Mitch, the comorbidity between PTSD (using the Structured Clinical Interview for *DSM* [SCID], based on *Diagnostic and Statistical Manual of Mental Disorders*, 3rd Revised Edition criteria) and major depression in the most severely affected city was 79 percent (Goenjian et al. 2001). Regressing depression on relevant predictor variables showed that PTSD accounted for 55 percent of the variance. A study of adults (David et al. 1996) yielded similar results (68 percent comorbidity between PTSD and major depression) and, in addition, showed that after adjusting for multiple statistical comparisons, severe damage was the only risk factor that was associated with all of the disorders.

The remainder of this section of the article will attempt to extrapolate to Hurricane Katrina what is known about disasters and mental health. Based on published reports from other disasters, we can offer several predictions about the psychological morbidity associated with Hurricane Katrina. These are discussed in light of the results of a survey conducted between September 10 and 12, 2005, among 680 randomly selected adult evacuees residing in Houston shelters. Interviews were conducted face-to-face, with an estimated 4 percentage point margin of error (*Washington Post*, Kaiser Family Foundation, and Harvard University 2005). The disaster literature shows that vulnerable persons are particularly prone to postdisaster stress, with vulnerability encompassing prior distress, social class, gender, and linguistic or social isolation. Disasters enhance socially structured inequalities already in place (Kaniasty and Norris 1995; Norris et al. 2002; Tierney 2000), particularly among community members who experience chronic adversity (Richmond 1993). Indeed, the most robust relationship in psychiatric epidemiological research is the negative association between socioeconomic status and psychological distress. The overwhelming majority of residents in the most severely affected counties/parishes (Orleans, St. Bernard, East Baton Rouge, and Jefferson Parishes in Louisiana; and Harrison and Hancock Counties in Mississippi) were poor. For example, the median household income in Orleans Parish before Katrina was $27,133, compared to $41,994 for the United States, and rates of poverty in 2000 were more than twice as high in Orleans Parish than in the United States as a whole (27.9 compared to 12.4 percent) (U.S. Census Bureau 2000). Of the evacuees surveyed in Houston (98 percent of whom had evacuated from the Greater New Orleans area), 59 percent reported that their total annual household income before taxes during the prior year was less than $20,000, and 32 percent said it was less than $10,000 (*Washington Post*, Kaiser Family Foundation, and Harvard University 2005). Thus, on this basis alone, one would expect high rates of psychological morbidity.

A second aspect relevant to Katrina is that disasters generate new, secondary stressors that serve as reminders of the trauma (Shaw, Applegate, and Schorr 1996) and further tax coping capacity. Such stressors include but are not limited to lack of food and shelter, relocation, crowding, financial strain, and coping with insurance companies and social services intended to be of assistance to survivors. In terms of financial strain alone, 72 percent of the evacuees surveyed in Houston reported having no insurance to cover their losses, and similar proportions of respondents had no bank accounts from which to withdraw money (68 percent) or any useable credit or debit cards (72 percent) (*Washington Post*, Kaiser Family Foundation, and Harvard University 2005).

Paramount among the secondary stressors that emerge after a disaster is disruption of social networks. In disaster situations, demand for support can exceed a network's capacity to provide support (Kaniasty and Norris 1993; Norris et al. 2002). Instrumental, as opposed to emotional, support is especially important in the face of disaster stressors (Haines, Hurlbert, and Beggs 1999), yet potential support providers may not be in a position to provide instrumental support. After Hurricane Katrina, social networks were disrupted to the extent that individuals waited for days, and often weeks, without knowing the fate of their family members. Two weeks after the hurricane impact, 48 percent of the evacuees surveyed in shelters in Houston reported that they were still trying to find family or friends (*Washington Post*, Kaiser Family Foundation, and Harvard University 2005). Seventy-nine percent of the survey respondents also reported they had no relatives or friends that they could "move in with until you are back on your feet." Communication in all forms was severely impaired, and network members were unable to provide assistance, either because they could not reach the survivors or because they were overwhelmed with their own situation. This predicament is most likely exacerbated in New Orleans where an unusually high number of multigenerational family members reside.

Equally important to support from personal networks was the lack of timely assistance and response from governmental agencies. This has relevance from two perspectives: what is known about the impact of human-initiated disasters and the importance of a speedy return to normalcy. Human-initiated disasters tend to yield higher rates of mental impairment than natural disasters (Norris et al. 2002). Although Hurricane Katrina itself is classified as a natural disaster, human elements were potent, including inattention to preventive maintenance on the levees, poorly coordinated evacuation efforts, and an ineffective and seemingly uncaring postdisaster response. The majority of evacuees (79 percent) surveyed in Houston believed the government response to the hurricane and flooding was "too slow and there's no excuse," 68 percent believed that race and poverty affected the speed of rescue efforts, and 61 percent said their experience made them feel like the government does not care about people like themselves. Beyond the lack of prediction and control that is characteristic of all disasters, human elements in disasters shatter fundamental beliefs about vulnerability, mortality, and human nature, leaving survivors with a sense that their lives have spun out of control (Difede et al. 1979; Ursano, Fullerton, and Norwood 1995) and, in Katrina, that their lives are not valued.

In regard to achieving normalcy, the available literature on postdisaster mental health interventions converges to suggest that resources should be devoted to facilitating a quick return to predisaster conditions and routines in affected communities (Norris, Friedman, and Watson 2002; Sattler et al. 2002; Siegel, Shoaf, and Bourque 2000). This includes restoring utilities, reopening businesses, and reestablishing social services. In the immediate aftermath, survivors of disasters need concrete and timely information on how to find shelter and access other forms of assistance (Joh 1997). In the longer term, to minimize the stress of relocation (Riad and Norris 1996), affected communities need to begin the process of rebuilding both the physical and social infrastructure. Survivors of Katrina are facing a seemingly open-ended time line in their community's return to normalcy. Accordingly, the negative psychological impact is likely to persist as well.

Overall, the data from the Katrina evacuee survey describe a population seemingly predisposed to a high level of psychological distress: a severe disaster exposure, a lack of economic and social resources, and an inadequate government response. Most likely, such distress will be described in future post-Katrina studies that sample from other settings and involve a postdisaster time interval more typical of published research. In the immediate aftermath, however, the evacuees that were housed in Houston were surprisingly resilient. When asked to describe their feelings about their future, a strong majority said they felt relieved (71 percent), grateful (82 percent), and hopeful (87 percent). Most felt that their religious faith had been strengthened by their experience (81 percent). Taken together, these responses most likely reflected their happiness at being alive and removed from any immediate peril. Still, a sizeable minority were depressed (50 percent), angry (39 percent), or frightened (35 percent) about their future. In future investigations of the mental health of Hurricane Katrina survivors, it will be important to document postdisaster experiences, including evacuation, to identify factors that exacerbate or diminish psychological distress following a major disaster.

Summary

The impact of hurricanes, cyclones, and typhoons on physical and mental health differs substantially between developed and developing countries. Within the United States and its territories, an area at high risk of hurricanes, mortality rates have declined over the past century, and the causes of mortality have shifted considerably. Few people drown in a storm surge; rather, they drown in flooded inland rivers and other bodies of water, or die from injuries caused by falling trees, collapsing structures, or other wind-tossed debris. In contrast, mortality in developing countries continues to be high, and a substantial proportion of deaths result from drowning in storm surges.

Deaths that occur during the impact phase could be prevented if officials issued timely evacuation orders and provided transportation for those unable to evacuate and if coastal residents heeded recommendations to evacuate. Preliminary information from Hurricane Katrina suggests that effective evacuation of New Orleans would have reduced postimpact deaths as well as those that occurred as the hurricane made landfall. If vulnerable elderly had been out of the area when the levees failed, death rates would have been substantially reduced.

Postimpact deaths and injuries primarily occur during cleanup activities and as a result of naïve attempts to replace nonfunctioning utilities. Both chain saws and portable generators consistently are reported to be a source of injury, illness, and death following hurricanes. Requirements that residents stay out of evacuated areas until utilities are restored and preliminary cleanup has been completed probably would reduce some of these injuries and deaths, but evacuated residents are anxious to return home both to assess property damage and in an attempt to reestablish the normalcy of prehurricane routines.

Studies of psychological morbidity following hurricanes suggest that distress increases in both children and adults but diminishes with the passage of time. Severity of exposure and prehurricane mental health problems are the most consistent predictors of distress. The wide dispersion of Hurricane Katrina evacuees across the United States, which has disrupted social networks and prevented a return to normalcy, combined with the lack of timely assistance and response from governmental agencies, may exacerbate the mental health problems of victims. Hurricane Katrina was not just a natural disaster. It was also a human-initiated and technological disaster that, for some, may have no foreseeable end.

Notes

1. An event is defined as a reported clinical impression for illness or mechanism of injury for injuries, toxic exposures, or carbon monoxide poisonings.

2. A fomite is an inanimate object, like a used tissue or dish, that transmits an infectious agent from person to person.

References

Belter, R. W., S. E. Dunn, and P. Jeney. 1991. The psychological impact of Hurricane Hugo on children: A needs assessment. *Advances in Behaviour Research & Therapy* 13:155-61.

Benight, C. C., E. Swift, J. Sanger, A. Smith, and D. Zeppelin. 1999. Coping self-efficacy as a mediator of distress following a natural disaster. *Journal of Applied Social Psychology* 29 (12): 2443-64.

Brewer, R. D., P. D. Morris, and T. B. Cole. 1993. Hurricane-related emergency department visits in an inland area: An analysis of the public health impact of Hurricane Hugo in North Carolina. *Annals of Emergency Medicine* 23 (4): 731-36.

Caldera, T., L. Palma, U. Penayo, and G. Kullgren. 2001. Psychological impact of the hurricane Mitch in Nicaragua in a one-year perspective. *Social Psychiatry and Psychiatric Epidemiology* 36:108-14.

Centers for Disease Control and Prevention. 1986. Hurricanes and hospital emergency room visits—Mississippi, Rhode Island, Connecticut. *Morbidity and Mortality Weekly Report* 34:765-70.

———. 1989a. Deaths associated with Hurricane Hugo—Puerto Rico. *Morbidity and Mortality Weekly Report* 38 (39): 680-82.

———. 1989b. Medical examiner/coroner reports of deaths associated with Hurricane Hugo—South Carolina. *Morbidity and Mortality Weekly Report* 38 (44): 759-62.

———. 1989c. Update: Work-related electrocutions associated with Hurricane Hugo—Puerto Rico. *Morbidity and Mortality Weekly Report* 38 (42): 718-25.

———. 1990. Surveillance of shelters after Hurricane Hugo—Puerto Rico. *Morbidity and Mortality Weekly Report* 39:41-42, 47.

———. 1992. Preliminary report: Medical examiner reports of deaths associated with Hurricane Andrew—Florida, August 1992. *Morbidity and Mortality Weekly Report* 41 (35): 641-44.

———. 1993a. Comprehensive assessment of health needs 2 months after Hurricane Andrew—Dade County, Florida, 1992. *Morbidity and Mortality Weekly Report* 42:434-37.

———. 1993b. Emergency mosquito control associated with Hurricane Andrew—Florida and Louisiana, 1992. *Morbidity and Mortality Weekly Report* 42:240-42.

———. 1993c. Injuries and illnesses related to Hurricane Andrew—Louisiana, 1992. *Morbidity and Mortality Weekly Report* 42 (41): 242-43, 250-51.

———. 1996a. Deaths associated with Hurricanes Marilyn and Opal—United States, September-October 1995. *Morbidity and Mortality Weekly Report* 45 (2): 32-38.

———. 1996b. Surveillance for injuries and illnesses and rapid-health-needs assessment following Hurricanes Marilyn and Opal, September-October 1995. *Morbidity and Mortality Weekly Report* 45 (4): 81-85.

———. 1998. Deaths associated with Hurricane Georges—Puerto Rico, September, 1998. *Morbidity and Mortality Weekly Report* 47 (42): 897-98.

———. 1999. Needs assessment following Hurricane Georges—Dominican Republic, 1998. *Morbidity and Mortality Weekly Report* 48 (5): 93-95.

———. 2000. Morbidity and mortality associated with Hurricane Floyd—North Carolina, September-October 1999. *Morbidity and Mortality Weekly Report* 49 (17): 369-72.

———. 2004a. Carbon monoxide poisoning from hurricane-associated use of portable generators—Florida, 2004. *Morbidity and Mortality Weekly Report* 54 (36): 697-700.

———. 2004b. Preliminary medical examiner reports of mortality associated with Hurricane Charley—Florida, 2004. *Morbidity and Mortality Weekly Report* 53 (36): 835-42.

———. 2005a. Carbon monoxide poisoning after Hurricane Katrina—Alabama, Louisiana, and Mississippi, August-September 2005. *Morbidity and Mortality Weekly Report* 54:996-98.

———. 2005b. Epidemiologic assessment of the impact of four hurricanes—Florida, 2004. *Morbidity and Mortality Weekly Report* 54 (28): 693-97.

———. 2005c. Infectious disease and dermatologic conditions in evacuees and rescue workers after Hurricane Katrina—Multiple States, August-September, 2005. *Morbidity and Mortality Weekly Report* 54:1-4.

———. 2005d. Norovirus outbreak among evacuees from Hurricane Katrina—Houston, Texas, September 2005. *Morbidity and Mortality Weekly Report* 54:1016-18.

———. 2005e. Surveillance for illness and injury after Hurricane Katrina—New Orleans, Louisiana, September 8-25, 2005. *Morbidity and Mortality Weekly Report* 54:1018-21.

———. 2005f. *Vibrio* illnesses after Hurricane Katrina—Multiple stages, August-September 2005. *Morbidity and Mortality Weekly Report* 54:928-31.

Dahlburg, John-Thor. 2005. Towns in big storms' path still winded. *Los Angeles Times*, May 30, p. A16.

David, D., T. A. Mellman, L. M. Mendoza, R. Kulick-Bell, G. Ironson, and N. Schneiderman. 1996. Psychiatric morbidity following Hurricane Andrew. *Journal of Traumatic Stress* 9:607-12.

Difede, J., W. J. Apfeldorf, M. Cloitre, L. A. Spielman, and S. W. Perry. 1979. Acute psychiatric responses to the explosion at the World Trade Center: A case series. *Journal of Nervous and Mental Disease* 185:519-22.

Dow, K., and C. L. Cutter. 1998. Crying wolf: Repeat response to hurricane evacuation orders. *Coastal Management* 26:238-52.

———. 2000. Public orders and personal opinions: Household strategies for hurricane risk assessment. *Environmental Hazards* 2:143-55.

———. 2002. Emerging hurricane evacuation issues: Hurricane Floyd and South Carolina 2002. *Natural Hazards Review* 1:12-18.

Folkman, S., R. Lazarus, C. Dunkel-Schetter, A. DeLongis, and R. Green. 1986. The dynamic of a stressful disaster: Cognitive appraisal, coping, and encounter outcomes. *Journal of Personality and Social Psychology* 50:992-1003.

Freedy, J. R., D. L. Shaw, M. P. Jarrell, and C. R. Masters. 1992. Towards an understanding of the psychological impact of natural disasters: An application of the conservation of resources stress model. *Journal of Traumatic Stress* 5:441-54.

Gladwin, H., and W. G. Peacock. 1997. Warning and evacuation: A night for hard houses. In *Hurricane Andrew: Ethnicity, gender, and the sociology of disasters*, ed. W. G. Peacock, B. H. Morrow, and H. Gladwin. New York: Routledge.

Goenjian, A. K., L. Molina, A. M. Steinberg, L. A. Fairbanks, M. L. Alarez, H. A. Goenjian, and R. S. Pynoos. 2001. Posttraumatic stress and depressive reactions among Nicaraguan adolescents after Hurricane Mitch. *American Journal of Psychiatry* 158:788-94.

Green, B. L., J. D. Lindy, M. C. Grace, G. C. Oteser, A. C. Leonard, M. Korol, and M. A. Winget. 1990. Buffalo Creek survivors in the second decade: Stability of stress symptoms over 14 years. *American Journal of Orthopsychiatry* 60:43-54.

Haines, V. A., J. S. Hurlbert, and J. J. Beggs. 1999. The disaster framing of the stress process: A test of an expanded model. *International Journal of Mass Emergencies and Disasters* 17 (3): 367-97.

Hardin, Sally Brosz, Martin Weinrich, Sally Weinrich, Thomas L. Hardin, and Carol Garrison. 1994. Psychological distress of adolescents exposed to Hurricane Hugo. *Journal of Traumatic Stress* 7:427-40.

Joh, H. 1997. Disaster stress of the 1995 Kobe earthquake. *Psychologia* 40:192-200.

Jones, R. T., R. Frary, P. Cunningham, J. D. Weddle, and L. Kaiser. 2001. The psychological effects of Hurricane Andrew on ethnic minority and Caucasian children and adolescents: A case study. *Cultural Diversity and Ethnic Minority Psychology* 7:103-8.

Kaniasty, K., and F. H. Norris. 1993. A test of the social support deterioration model in the context of natural disaster. *Journal of Personality and Social Psychology* 64:395-408.

———. 1995. In search of altruistic community: Patterns of social support mobilization following Hurricane Hugo. *American Journal of Community Psychology* 23:447-77.

La Greca, A., W. Silverman, E. Vernberg, and M. Prinstein. 1996. Symptoms of post-traumatic stress in children after Hurricane Andrew: A prospective study. *Journal of Consulting and Clinical Psychology* 64:712-23.

Lindell, M. K., J. C. Lu, and C. S. Prater. 2005. Household decision making and evacuation in response to Hurricane Lili. *Natural Hazards Review* 6:180-90.

Louisiana Department of Health and Hospitals. 2005. *Vital statistics of all bodies at St. Gabriel morgue.* December 16. http://www.dhh.state.la.us/news.asp?Detail=769 (accessed November 23, 2005).

McQuaid, J., and M. Schleifstein. 2002. *Left behind: Washing away (Part 1).* June 23-27. http://www.nola.com/printer/printer.ssf?/washingaway/harmsway_1.html (accessed November 1, 2005).

Nicholls, R. J. N., N. Mimura, and J. C. Topping. 1995. Climate change in south and south-east Asia: Some implications for coastal areas. *Journal of Global Environment Engineering* 1:137-54.

Norris, F. H., M. J. Friedman, and P. J. Watson. 2002. 60,000 disaster victims speak: Part II. Summary and implications of the disaster mental health literature. *Psychiatry* 65 (3): 240-60.

Norris, F. H., M. J. Friedman, P. J. Watson, C. M. Byrne, E. Diaz, and K. Kaniasty. 2002. 60,000 disaster victims speak: Part I. An empirical review of the empirical literature, 1981-2001. *Psychiatry* 65 (3): 207-39.

Norris, F., and K. Kaniasty. 1996. Received and perceived social support in times of stress: A test of the social support deterioration deterrence *Journal of Personality and Social Psychology* 71:498-511.

Pardue, J. H., W. M. Moe, D. McInnis, J. Thibodeaux, K. T. Valsaraj, E. Maciasz, I. Van Heerden, N. Korevec, and Q. Z. Yuan. 2005. Chemical and microbiological parameters in New Orleans floodwater following Hurricane Katrina. *Environmental Science and Technology* 39 (September): 8591-8599.

Rappaport, E. N., and J. J. Fernandez-Partagas. 1997. History of the deadliest Atlantic tropical cyclones since the discovery of the New World. In *Hurricanes, climate, and socioeconomic impacts*, ed. H. F. Diaz and R. S. Pulwarry. New York: Springer-Verlag.

Riad, J. K., and F. H. Norris. 1996. The influence of relocation on the environmental, social, and psychological stress experienced by disaster victims. *Environment and Behavior* 28:163-82.

Richmond, N. 1993. After the flood. *American Journal of Public Health* 83:1522-24.

Sattler, D. N., A. J. Preston, C. F. Kaiser, V. E. Olivera, J. Valdez, and S. Schlueter. 2002. A cross-national study examining the preparedness, resource loss, and psychological distress in the U.S. Virgin Islands, Puerto Rico, Dominican Republic, and the United States. *Journal of Traumatic Stress* 15:339-50.

Shaw, J. A., B. Applegate, and C. Schorr. 1996. Twenty-one-month follow-up study of school-age children exposed to Hurricane Andrew. *Child and Adolescent Psychiatry* 35:359-64.

Shultz, J. M., J. Russell, and Z. Espinel. 2005. Epidemiology of tropical cyclones: The dynamics of disaster, disease and development. *Epidemiologic Reviews* 27:21-35.

Siegel, J. M., K. I. Shoaf, and L. B. Bourque. 2000. The C-Mississippi scale for PTSD in postearthquake communities. *International Journal of Mass Emergencies and Disasters* 18:339-46.

Tierney, K. J. 2000. Controversy and consensus in disaster mental health research. *Prehospital and Disaster Medicine* 15:181-87.

United Nations Development Programme (UNDP). 2004. *Reducing disaster risk: A challenge for development.* New York: John S. Swift Company.

U.S. Census Bureau. 2000. *The United States Census 2000.* http://www.census.gov/po/www/foia/foiaweb.htm (accessed November 1, 2005).

Urbina, E., and B. Wolshon. 2003. National review of hurricane evacuation plans and policies: A comparison and contrast of state practices. *Transportation Practices Part A* 37:257-75.

Ursano, R. J., C. S. Fullerton, and A. E. Norwood. 1995. Psychiatric dimensions of disaster: Patient care, community consultation, and preventive medicine. *Harvard Review of Psychiatry* 3:196-209.

Van Willigen, M., B. Edwards, S. Lormand, and K. Wilson. 2005. Comparative assessment of impacts and recovery from Hurricane Floyd among student and community households. *Natural Hazards Review* 6:180-90.

Warner, C., and R. T. Scott. 2005. Where they died: When it came to choosing its victims, Hurricane Katrina spared few neighborhoods. In fact, gentility and the lakefront may have suffered as many deaths as the lower 9th. Document no. 10D6ECF050C624C8. *The Times-Picayune*, October 23. http://www.nola.com/printer/printer.ssf?/base/news-4/1130050973 (accessed November 1, 2005).

Washington Post, Kaiser Family Foundation, and Harvard University. 2005. *Survey of Hurricane Katrina evacuees.* September. No. 7401. http://www.kff.org/newsmedia/upload/7401.pdf (accessed November 1, 2005).

Whitehead, J. C., B. Edwards, M. Van Willigen, J. R. Maiolo, K. Wilson, and K. T. Smith. 2000. Heading for higher ground: Factors affecting real and hypothetical hurricane evacuation behavior. *Global Environmental Change Part B: Environmental Hazards* 2:133-42.

Wikipedia Foundation. 2005. *Hurricane Katrina.* http://en.wikipedia.org/wiki/Hurricane_Katrina (accessed November 12, 2005).

Wilmot, C. G., and B. Mei. 2004. Comparison of alternative trip generation models for hurricane evacuation. *Natural Hazards Review* 5:170-78.

Wolshon, B., E. U. Hamilton, M. Levitan, and C. Wilmot. 2005. Review of policies and practices for hurricane evacuation, II: Traffic operations, management, and control. *Natural Hazards Review* 6:143-61.

Wolshon, B., E. Urbina, C. Wilmot, and M. Levitan. 2005. Review of policies and practices for hurricane evacuation, I: Transportation planning, preparedness, and responses. *Natural Hazards Review* 6:129-42.

Zhang, Y., C. S. Prater, and M. K. Lindell. 2004. Risk area accuracy and evacuation from Hurricane Bret. *Natural Hazards Review* 5:115-20.

Challenges in Implementing Disaster Mental Health Programs: State Program Directors' Perspectives

By
CARRIE L. ELROD,
JESSICA L. HAMBLEN,
and
FRAN H. NORRIS

The Crisis Counseling Assistance and Training Program grants supplemental federal funding to states and territories for individual and community crisis intervention services in the aftermath of presidentially declared disasters. Little research has been conducted to evaluate the effectiveness of these services, and few data exist to guide policies and programs. A qualitative study of thirty-eight state program directors (representing 95 percent of all such programs over a five-year period) identified the numerous challenges that states experience when planning, applying for, implementing, maintaining, phasing out, and evaluating these federally funded programs. The results highlighted the importance of including mental health in state-level disaster plans, fostering collaborative relationships across institutions, clarifying program guidelines, sharing innovations across programs, and building state capacity for needs assessment and program evaluation.

Keywords: crisis counseling; disaster mental health; community outreach; indigenous workers; state capacity; disaster preparedness

Federal disaster areas are eligible for a wide range of services, including the Crisis Counseling Assistance and Training Program (CCP), available since 1974 under the Robert T. Stafford Disaster Relief and Emergency Assistance Act (Public Law 100-707). Funded by the Federal Emergency Management Agency (FEMA) and administered by the Substance Abuse and Mental Health Services Administration's (SAMHSA's) Center for Mental Health Services (CMHS), the CCP aims to meet the short-term mental health needs of disaster-stricken communities through a combination of outreach, education, brief counseling services, and referral. Outreach and public education

Carrie L. Elrod, Ph.D., is a community/organizational psychologist and consultant in the area of group and systems dynamics. She wrote an Emergency Response Manual for a Category X airport, developed and implemented training in the areas of emergency response and conflict resolution during emergency response, and led investigative search and recovery teams into active airline disasters. As a researcher, she has developed expertise in

DOI: 10.1177/0002716205285186

serve primarily to normalize reactions and to engage people who might need further care. These roles are often, though not exclusively, performed by paraprofessionals who work throughout the community, including schools, places of worship, and places of work. Crisis counseling helps survivors to cope with current stress and symptoms to facilitate their return to predisaster levels of functioning. Crisis counseling, which is differentiated from treatment in the program model, relies largely on active listening. Counselors are expected to refer clients to other services if the person has or has developed more serious psychiatric problems.

Receipt of funds for crisis counseling is not automatic. Eligible states may apply for the Immediate Services Program (which operates for the first three months postdisaster) and the Regular Services Program (which operates for the next nine months). In these applications, which must be submitted two weeks and two months postdisaster, respectively, states must establish that the need for mental health services is greater than state and local governments can be expected to meet, and they must present a detailed plan about how the grant will enable them to meet these needs. State mental health systems (or their equivalents) serve as host systems upon which funded CCPs are superimposed. These systems are often composed of a variety of local government units, social service agencies, and community-based organizations and are thus inherently complex and challenging to manage. Host systems have preexisting missions and vary in capacity, preparedness, and evalua-

qualitative methodology. With more than twenty-two years' experience as an operational and administrative manager in a corporate environment, she currently provides human technologies training in a variety of settings.

Jessica L. Hamblen, Ph.D., a clinical psychologist, is the deputy for education at the Department of Veterans Affairs National Center for Post-Traumatic Stress Disorder (NCPTSD) and an assistant professor in the Department of Psychiatry at Dartmouth Medical School. She was a coinvestigator of previous studies examining mental health systems' responses to the Oklahoma City bombing and World Trade Center attack. Building upon her past work with New York and Florida, her primary research interests are in developing and evaluating brief cognitive behavioral interventions targeting stress symptoms following disaster.

Fran H. Norris, Ph.D., a community/social psychologist, is a research professor in the Department of Psychiatry at Dartmouth Medical School, where she is affiliated with the National Center for PTSD and the National Consortium for the Study of Terrorism and Response to Terrorism headed by the University of Maryland. She has been the recipient of a number of grants for research, research education, and professional development from the National Institute of Mental Health. Her interests include the mobilization and deterioration of social support after disasters, systems issues in providing disaster mental health services, and the epidemiology of trauma and PTSD. Her disaster studies have focused on such events as Hurricanes Hugo and Andrew in the United States and the 1999 floods and mudslides in Mexico. In 2005, she received the Robert S. Laufer Award for Outstanding Scientific Achievement from the International Society for Traumatic Stress Studies.

NOTE: This work was supported by an interagency agreement between the Substance Abuse and Mental Health Services Administration and the Department of Veterans Affairs National Center for Post-Traumatic Stress Disorder. Please address correspondence to Fran H. Norris, NCPTSD, VAMC 116D, 215 North Main Street, White River Junction, VT 05009; e-mail: fran.norris@dartmouth.edu.

tion expertise, and they are both assisted and constrained by the federal system of emergency management, most specifically, the guidelines of the CCP (Norris et al. 2006, 2005).

Previously published accounts of disaster mental health services and programs have alluded to numerous problems that interfere with the timely or effective delivery of services (Myers and Wee 2005; National Institute of Mental Health 2002). Unsolicited groups of well-meaning volunteers have become one of the major sources of chaos in disaster-stricken settings (Bowenkamp 2000; Gist and Lubin 1999; Hodgkinson and Stewart 1998; Lanou 1993; Sitterle and Gurwich 1998). Less experienced providers may suffer from vicarious trauma, leading to distress, absenteeism, and erosion of staff morale (Call and Pfefferbaum 1999). Staff may self-segregate into those more and less directly affected personally by the disaster (Sitterle and Gurwich 1998). Turf boundaries, communication gaps, confusion, the emotionally stressful nature of disaster work, ambivalence and suspicions regarding outsiders, funding gaps, limited resources, lack of long-term care, and survivor stigma are other problems that may interfere with service delivery (Bowencamp 2000; Canterbury and Yule 1999; Hodgkinson and Stewart 1998; Lanou 1993; Norris et al. 2006, 2005).

Building upon these past writings, the purpose of the present study was to increase understanding of the challenges involved in providing disaster mental health services by capturing the experiences and perspectives of a representative sample of state program directors. CCP directors are the intermediary between a variety of voices speaking for the local community, the state, and the federal government, making their perspectives especially important for understanding the process of implementing a disaster mental health response. In accord with previous writings, we explored issues of preparedness, communication, collaboration, and capacity in considerable depth. The study was based on the assumption that the quality of mental health services provided to disaster victims is based not only on their clinical efficacy but also on the capacity of systems to deliver those services in a timely and effective way.

Method

Sampling procedures: Disasters and directors

To qualify for this study, states must have received Immediate Service Program or Regular Service Program grants between 1996 and 2001, and they must have closed out the grant no later than December 2003. This rule excluded Project Liberty, New York State's response to the terrorist attacks of September 11, 2001, which did not close out until September 2005. States receiving SAMHSA Emergency Response Grants (SERG) over the same time frame were also included. Directors of responses to thirty-seven (of thirty-nine eligible) disasters in twenty-five (of twenty-seven eligible) states participated. A total of thirty-six interviews of thirty-eight people were included in this analysis (one interview was lost due to equipment failure). Most of the responding state agencies existed under the guidance of state divisions or departments of health, mental health, or mental health and substance abuse.

Table 1 shows the states and disasters represented by the research. The types of disasters experienced during this time frame ranged from widespread to contained, natural to human caused, no injuries/deaths to multiple injuries/deaths, single component to multiple components (e.g., hurricane *and* flood), single event to one in a series of events, and short-term to long-term response engagements. The communities involved in these disasters varied in size, location, ethnicity and population distribution, and vulnerability to multiple events.

We interviewed state program directors between May and August 2004, usually in person, by using a semistructured interview protocol consisting of open-ended questions. This protocol was revised from one that had been used in previous case studies of responses to the Oklahoma City bombing (Norris et al. 2005) and the World Trade Center disaster (Norris et al. 2006). Although the job titles of respondents varied across states, the majority of individuals reported their primary function as "administrator." Other descriptors used were coordinator, planner, manager, facilitator, leader, and technical assistance provider. Each brought a different role expectation, background, and sense of mission to the position. Most respondents held an advanced degree related to the mental health field.

Data analysis

All interviews were audiotaped. Transcribed materials (interviews, field notes, and memos) were converted to text files and imported into QSR N6 software for qualitative data analyses. A framework for coding the material was developed based on the concepts of the interview as well as the themes that emerged from previous case studies in Oklahoma City and New York. A code tree was devised containing both the code scheme and operational definitions for each code. Members of the research team met several times during the development of the code tree to ensure its validity and reliability across multiple coders. During these meetings, team members would be asked to code the same short sample passage. Once coded, team members would discuss what code(s) they assigned to the passage and why. These coding strategies were debated until consensus was reached regarding what code should be applied and how it should be operationally defined. Half-day training sessions were then conducted with all coders. Coders consisted of two of the authors, who had also been field researchers for this study, plus two Ph.D.-level qualitative researchers, two Ph.D. candidates with qualitative coding experience, and a master's-level practitioner who had been involved with a previous case study.

Results

Results were organized into a temporal framework proceeding through preparing for the disaster, implementing the response, providing services to the commu-

TABLE 1

STATES AND DISASTER DECLARATIONS
INCLUDED IN THE DIRECTORS' STUDY

State	Event Date	Event Type	Disaster Number[a]	Year of Closeout
Alaska	06-07-96	Fire	1119	2000
Alabama	04-09-98	Tornado	1214	2000
	09-30-98	Hurricane	1250	2001
	12-18-00	Tornado	1352	2002
Arkansas	03-02-97	Tornado	1162	2001
	01-23-99	Tornado and flooding	1266	2001
Colorado	08-01-97	Flooding	1186	2002
District of Columbia	FY 2003	D.C. sniper	SM00164	2003
Florida	01-06-98	Tornado and flooding	1195	2000
	06-18-98	Wildfires	1223	2000
	09-28-98	Hurricane	1249	2001
Idaho	01-04-97	Flooding	1154	2001
Iowa	07-22-99	Flooding	1282	2001
Kentucky	03-04-97	Flooding	1163	2001
Maryland	FY 2003	D.C. sniper	SM00171	2003
Minnesota	04-08-97	Flooding	1175	2001
	04-01-98	Tornado	1212	2000
Missouri	05-12-00	Flooding	1328	2003
Montana	08-30-00	Wildfires	1340	2003
North Carolina	09-16-99	Hurricanes	1292	2002
North Dakota	04-07-97	Flooding	1174	2001
	06-08-99	Tornado	1279	2002
New Jersey	09-18-99	Hurricane	1295	2001
New Mexico	05-13-00	Wildfire	1329	2003
Ohio	03-04-97	Flooding	1164	2001
Rhode Island	02-20-03	Nightclub fire	SM00175	2003
South Dakota	04-07-97	Flooding	1173	2001
	06-01-98	Tornado	1218	2001
Tennessee	01-19-99	Tornado	1262	2001
Texas	08-26-98	Flooding	1239	2001
	10-21-98	Flooding	1257	2001
	04-07-00	Tornado	1323	2003
	06-09-01	Tropical storm	1379	2003
Virginia	09-18-99	Hurricane	1293	2002
	FY 2003	D.C. sniper	SM00163	2003
Wisconsin	05-11-01	Flooding	1369	2003
West Virginia	06-03-01	Flooding	1378	2003

a. These are Federal Emergency Management Agency (FEMA) numbers unless preceded by *SM*, which is used to designate Substance Abuse and Mental Health Services Administration (SAMHSA) emergency grants that are occasionally given to states in the absence of a presidential disaster declaration.

nity within the framework of the CCP model, integrating the CCP into community and state systems, phasing out the response, and evaluating the response.

Preparing for the disaster

Directors' comments about predisaster planning and preparation clustered around three main topics: the presence or absence of a plan, preparatory activities, and predisaster training. Few states had a disaster plan in place prior to the index disaster. Descriptions of plans ranged from nonexistent to fully developed, with those states reporting more frequent or higher-profile disasters also reporting more fully developed disaster mental health plans. Developing a disaster plan was a low priority in states that rarely experienced a disaster. Even so, plans were often described as vague or as still under development. The all-hazards or disaster plans of most states did not include (or only minimally referenced) plans for responding to mental health needs. Programmatic, political, and personal variables were often cited as reasons for poorly developed or nonexistent plans. Respondents who reported experience with a previous event, either as a provider or as a state official, were more likely to report that they felt personally prepared to respond. Feeling prepared to respond to the index disaster was not related to the number of disasters experienced by the state during the five-year sampling frame, the amount of federal dollars received for the disaster, or the type of disaster experienced.

Three elements of preparedness were commonly perceived as necessary for an effective and efficient response. The first element was designation of provisions, ranging from supplies (such as necessary forms, identification badges, writing utensils, updated phone lists) to more substantial resources (such as a designated space to set up a command post, dedicated phone lines, and online technology). The second key element was the need to establish relationships with other agencies (such as the Red Cross and local agencies in the event area). States with the most fully developed plans stressed the need to formalize relationships with memoranda of understanding and the development of councils with representatives of these agencies that met periodically in the absence of an event to discuss roles, response options, and regulatory issues. The third element was plans for having all key decision makers at the strategic command post (federal, state, and local government agencies plus other agencies, such as the Red Cross) to ensure that critical decisions were made in a timely manner.

Training was highlighted as another crucial component of disaster preparation. The FEMA training at Emmitsburg, Maryland, was perceived as vital for helping state directors feel and act prepared once an event occurred. Particularly helpful components of the training included learning from others who had experienced a disaster and assistance with grant writing. FEMA online courses were also cited as useful and convenient. Participants expressed concern about the reduction in the number of times the training is now offered. In addition to federal trainings, trainings were offered by the states. These trainings attempted to build capacity either through train-the-trainer events or through more general trainings to local community agencies. Some respondents reported that they hosted forums and trainings throughout the year during which responding agencies (e.g., Red Cross) would attend and participate in role-plays, tabletop exercises, and disaster response planning sessions. Trainings in Critical Incident Stress Debriefing and

Management (CISD/CISM) techniques were used by many states. Despite research questioning the effectiveness of CISD/CISM, some states believed CISD and CISM trainings are as important to preparing for a disaster as is the FEMA Emmitsburg training.

Implementing the response

The initial phase of a disaster response was described as chaotic due to the many competing needs and priorities of the first week. State leaders found it difficult to attend to the needs and safety of the community while handling the administrative demands that accompany applying for federal funding to support a disaster mental health response. For these reasons, this part of the process was often referred to as "the second disaster," or the "bureaucracy that, although they're trying to help, comes in." One director reported,

> In the first 48 hours, you're not really worrying about how the crisis counseling program should be run. [Y]ou're still in the response mode of responding to that major disaster in the first 48 hours. What you do find yourself worrying about is . . . you got this 14 day dead-line . . . and you worry about . . . getting the information . . . to the right people . . . your local providers, while they are responding.

Additionally, state leaders found the needs assessment problematic as data were described as "anecdotal," "unreliable," and "insufficient."

Several key sources of support were seen as being helpful to the initial response phase. Most state leaders who had attended the FEMA training at Emmitsburg felt somewhat prepared to write the grant application. The CMHS project officer was often cited as another important source of support. Functioning as part of a multidisciplinary team helped states gather information and implement the disaster response. Accessing multiple sources, such as news media (radio, television, Internet, and print), speaking with Chamber of Commerce and public safety representatives, and reading situation reports from workers in the field were cited as useful strategies for obtaining information. Finally, contacting people who had previously been involved in disaster response was always recounted as positive and helpful in educating the state representative and moving the response effort forward.

Providing services within the CCP model

After the first week, interviewees indicated that their attentions were drawn to designing a longer-term response. This process included gaining an understanding of the CCP model that emphasizes outreach, crisis counseling, and referral. Training was an essential aspect of understanding and delivering services within this framework.

Outreach. Outreach was a key component of every CCP and was generally thought to be effective by directors. Outreach is intended as a form of public education where the outreach workers, preferably indigenous, literally go out into the community to educate victims of the disaster regarding what responses they may experience as a victim of the disaster, what types of services are available to them, and where services may be obtained. Directors noted the importance of carefully identifying target populations and employing workers indigenous to those populations.

Unsolicited groups of well-meaning volunteers have become one of the major sources of chaos in disaster-stricken settings.

All states identified target populations, although they varied across communities and across events. Each program recognized the differences in its community population and took great efforts to meet the needs of everyone. Special populations specifically mentioned as adversely affected were older adults, American Indian or Hispanic residents, and children. Other populations mentioned were migrant workers, undocumented aliens, the developmentally disabled, Vietnam veterans, farmers, the homeless, the mentally ill, African Americans, and numerous immigrant populations. Although methods of conducting outreach were fairly standard across programs, strategies were highly dependent on the target population. And although many types of outreach workers were employed across the disasters, indigenous workers were often observed as having the most success in reaching the community's hardest-hit areas. In this context, "indigenous" did not necessarily refer to membership in a minority population, but rather to individuals embedded in the community. One director commented,

> Outreach in a Hispanic neighborhood will work, particularly if you have indigenous people. Door-to-door outreach in the Muslim neighborhood will not work. It's just, it just doesn't work, so you have to come up with other plans . . . your response kind of has to be keyed to . . . who you're dealing with and it's a different approach for different types of communities.

There were several challenges noted regarding outreach. Staff turnover was frequent, most often due to acquiring better jobs, being victims themselves, or suffering burnout. There were some concerns about the use of paraprofessionals for outreach, especially in the area of having "untrained" or unlicensed workers in mental health roles. Another challenge for many state directors was locating victims without the use of the FEMA Registration List. This list contains the names and contact points for individuals who apply for FEMA services. Until the late 1990s, this list was made available to CCP programs as a resource to help program providers locate victims. However, a federal policy change in the late 1990s restricted the availability of the list due to concerns around consumer confidentiality.

Illiteracy and multiple languages in a minority population created potential for gaps in the outreach programs. Sometimes, even indigenous workers did not realize all of the challenges in reaching a diverse population. One interviewee reported,

> So they developed a pamphlet to help deal with some of the stresses and all. . . . And then, after they developed it, they realized upon trying to distribute it, that there were very few of the whole population that could read their own language.

Providing outreach to large groups was challenging as not everyone in a group had the same level of exposure, making it difficult to find a single message acceptable to everyone. Many directors spoke of the discomfort among disaster victims in a group when it became obvious that some had experienced minimal losses while others had endured losses of family members, homes, health, and material possessions.

Some areas and populations simply did not welcome outreach workers and their attempts to help. Sometimes, the resistance was passive and polite; community members simply refused services or said they would consider services later. But occasionally, the resistance was aggressive and hostile. One director described the challenge this way:

> The [outreach workers] were feeling very intimidated . . . by people they were contacting in the areas who had been evacuated . . . I would say more in the working class areas, where, where people just didn't like to be bothered. . . . They weren't received very well, . . . actually, hostile aggressive dogs and people. They were feeling like they didn't have the skills they needed to deal with being met with aggression.

Counseling. Crisis counseling was difficult for directors to define. Although most agreed that crisis counseling is not intended to be therapy, the boundaries of crisis counseling remained blurred across programs and across states. Definitions ranged from "active listening" to "a wellness model" to therapeutic interventions. Because of this, the use of paraprofessionals as counselors (as opposed to outreach workers) was vigorously debated, although most directors thought they could be trained to be effective with supervision. As a result, it is difficult to know exactly what services were being rendered under the auspices of the crisis counseling. One director observed,

> A therapist or traditional mental health person sees the mud covered survivor and . . . is gonna say, "Gee, how does that mud feel?" and the disaster mental health person sees that [same person] and says, "Let's get that mud off of you."

Referrals. Referrals posed a number of challenges. First was the issue of when to refer. Estimates of referrals for each program ranged from "minimal—not enough to count" to "4-7% of all contacts." Most programs observed a formula for when to make a referral. When a person accessed the system a certain number of times and desired more access, they were referred to a professional service. However, there was disagreement regarding the number of visits that would trigger a referral, with the numbers ranging from three times over the course of the program to ten times in a single month. Another strategy for making a referral was the identification of "red flags," such as persons expressing suicidal/homicidal thoughts, new or increased substance abuse, and exacerbation of preexisting mental illness. A final issue focused on system capacity. Most clinical directors expressed sensitivity to the already burdened mental health systems into which contacts were referred; nonclinical directors did not recognize system capacity as a problem. One respondent summarized the dilemma of referrals this way:

> Referral is probably the weakest part of this program because of two reasons. . . . One, you are dealing with paraprofessionals so their ability to . . . actually determine . . . who should be referred. . . . The other problem is you're trying to refer into a system that's already overloaded. . . . It's very hard for my [community mental health system] to get people into their system when there's already a 6-month waiting list for services.

Training. Training was undertaken to ensure compliance with federal program requirements and to enact a quality response. Directors' comments fell into three general categories: (1) the types of training offered, (2) the timing of the training, and (3) the trainers/instructors available to do the training.

There were both federal and state trainings. In many cases, the boundary between federal and state training became blurred, especially in states that experienced multiple disasters, as the state often took the initial training received from the federal agency and offered it down to the provider level. FEMA and CMHS trainings centered on explaining the basics of the Crisis Counseling Program, grant administration, and grant adherence. Issues of concern around the training included the organization of the course content and the level of detail presented. One director commented, "CMHS has a lot of material but they don't have it organized in a way . . . that they can present to states, where it goes from A to Z. Lots of little pamphlets or this is how you do this, but not necessarily something that says this is what you do starting with the event."

Another highlighted the need for clear and succinct training material by saying,

> What I need is a short, sweet, clear . . . bulleted procedure that explains it instead of 85 pages of, "This is something that's expected." What I need is the ability to translate this program clearly, articulately, and quickly so that people can make decisions based on, "Now I understand what you're asking me to do." It needs to be clearer.

One of the biggest challenges in providing training to a large number of people in the smallest amount of time is how to match the course content to the audience. One director recollected,

> The first official kick-off [training] was done by an outside provider that CMHS recom-
> mended, and he was here for 2 days. I was not very happy with it for a lot of reasons. The
> first day, everybody in the community was invited to it, which I thought was sort of crazy,
> but . . . that's what we were told to do. It turned into a debriefing for 300 people. It was just
> a waste of time.

The timing of the training was often cited as a critical factor contributing to
whether the training was considered successful. If offered too soon, staff turnover
left new untrained staff in their place, some workers were too focused on responding to the disaster, and many of the attendees were still coping with their own reactions. This was especially important in smaller programs where staff unavailability
was often cited as a barrier to successful training. If offered too late, many programs reported that their crisis counselor and outreach workers were already out
in the affected areas without clear guidelines; thus, "some of the disaster survivors
started immediately to create a dependency on the program."

Training instructors came from a variety of resources and backgrounds; there
was no apparent consistency, however, across events and/or across states regarding
whom to call for what training. Most of the respondents acknowledged that their
CMHS project officer made them aware of a resource list of "experts" who were
approved to conduct certain types of training. Instructors and the trainings they
conducted from this list were usually acknowledged as very effective. Others
invited trainers with whom they had personal experience or individuals with good
reputations in the field.

A noted strength of the program was being able to develop a team approach to
training. Trainings developed in any part of the state could be taken to other parts
of the state because federal dollars were supporting the training efforts. This effectively facilitated the dissemination of critical information and eliminated the
boundaries that might otherwise have been activated had local dollars been used
for training.

Integrating the CCP into community and state systems

The CCP model focuses on providing a community-level response. Program
directors are confronted with quickly integrating a program into preexisting host
communities and systems of services. The primary challenges in this task are establishing effective and accurate communication; developing collaborative relationships with local agencies as well as other responding agencies; accessing existing
institutions, such as the schools and faith-based organizations; resolving turf issues;
and developing an effective system for acquiring and transferring funds from the
federal authority, to the state coffer, into the CCP, and out to the direct service
providers and agencies.

Communication. Receiving and relaying timely and accurate information is critical to the establishment of the program as a credible and reliable source of information. Additionally, it contributes to relationship building, both between and

within agencies and systems. Both formal and informal methods were used to accomplish this. Methods included the establishment of communication during the year with various agencies through one-on-one conversations, group meetings, teleconferences, and the development of performance contracts with each agency that were reviewed and renewed annually. Although communication during the events was reportedly effective and uneventful, a few directors experienced delays in communication from the federal level (i.e., top-down communication) and conflict in communication at the local level (bottom-up communication). It was not uncommon for a director to report, "The Feds weren't giving us clear messages. Things were always changing, so it looked like we didn't know what we were doing."

The all-hazards or disaster plans of most states did not include (or only minimally referenced) plans for responding to mental health needs.

Collaboration. Most of the directors recognized that the sheer size and scope of disasters demand collaboration between responding and supporting agencies, although most also stated that developing collaboration is neither simple nor without its challenges. As such, developing collaborative relationships is part of planning before, during, and after disasters so that "you won't be out on a limb by yourself."

A few directors indicated that initiating collaborative relationships during the disaster was too late, too time-consuming, and generally nonproductive due to the pressure of each agency trying to respond to the disaster with its own protocol and/ or mission. Most state leaders, however, reported many creative and productive ways of forming relationships that optimized the reach and success of their CCP program. For instance, employing indigenous workers to staff the CCP created instant links to the local community and access to its institutions. Pairing outreach workers with other service delivery agencies and their staff (e.g., Meals-on-Wheels, law enforcement) contributed to the formation of good working relationships between the CCP and other responding programs, plus it increased the outreach impact and the credibility of the CCP by associating the outreach worker with a person already trusted with an ongoing service. One of the best opportunities for forming new relationships was participation on unmet needs committees that brought community and program leaders together in an effort to identify the needs of the community and devise a plan to meet those needs.

Many leaders reflected that a legacy of their program was recognition of the need to have a mental health person "at the table" in disaster preparedness activities. Another legacy was the acknowledgement of the value of developing collaborative relationships before the next event; therefore, leaders found themselves involved in collaborative activities to form new relationships while strengthening old ones.

Developing collaborative partnerships was not without its challenges. Some agencies were resistant. For instance, one community resisted help from the CCP because they wanted to "do it themselves." The director commented,

> It was an agency issue. It was the agency thinking, "We want to do this ourselves," and I kept telling them that you're gonna have to hire somebody. And they kept saying, "No. They're our responsibility. This is our community and . . . we're going to do this," but it didn't work.

Some leaders felt they did not have the skills they needed to develop collaborative relationships with other agencies. One director commented, "If someone could develop a course in how to get people to play well in the sandbox, *that* would have been good training." Some directors remarked that it took time to be recognized as a "player." Several leaders cited how easy it is to ignore the collaborative relationships in the absence of an event. One leader summed up the postdisaster challenges by saying, "Everybody gets busy, and we don't touch base as often as we should, and we're in different buildings. It's difficult."

Access and turf issues. Schools and faith-based organizations served as two primary institutions for gaining access to affected populations. Gaining access to schools was generally difficult, with one director characterizing schools as "an insular societal group." One director summed up the inconsistencies of being able to gain access to the school system this way:

> [Access to schools] varied by area program. In some cases, they had a wonderful relationship with schools, and they would go in and provide information to teachers and in some cases classrooms and in other areas, they could not get a foot in the door, and they weren't considered . . . qualified . . . or the feeling was to address this with the children would increase their anxiety . . .

Barriers included resistance to the idea of having the CCP in the school system and difficulty finding a time to present the program with minimal disruption to the students' schedules. In many cases, the disaster occurred when school was not in session, creating even more challenges to accessing groups of children for outreach. For those programs that were able to access the school system, creativity, persistence, and patience were the keys. These programs used teachers as outreach workers, connected directly with teachers by offering key training, included members of the school system in key multiagency teams, and simply stood by until schools contacted them due to mounting problems with students. One director recounted,

Just as we closed a program down, the principal, who had been saying for weeks . . . that "everything'll be all right as long as we get back on schedule," broke down and said, "Help me." So we went into those schools when the program was over.

Most respondents agreed that faith-based organizations were easier to access than school systems. As collaborative partners, faith-based organizations were key sources for outreach and referral. Although the directors cited many positive aspects regarding the accessibility and participation of the faith-based organizations, directors also reported: difficulties when congregations subscribed to a "just world" paradigm; concern as to how to make referrals to faith-based resources; and some organizations' disinterest in partnering with the CCP.

It is always difficult to have multiple people, agencies, and institutions involved in a systems response and not have insider/outsider or turf issues arise. Turf issues arose between and across state and federal agencies, the military, the Red Cross, local agencies, and providers. Most turf issues revolved around questions of who was in charge and who had ownership of a particular role. One director gave a classic example of turf issues among multiple government and responding agencies by saying,

Because it was a national [site], the Department of [anonymous] assumed they were under control, that they were the incident commander. The fire folks thought they were the incident commander and controlled the incident. Local emergency management in [city] thought they were, and the state's office of emergency management thought they were in charge. The [special population] thought they were in charge of what was going on on their land, and then they found out they really weren't, and then the sheriff in [county], he thought he had control over all of that. Nobody was in charge.

In some cases, turf issues appeared to stem from a common belief that only "locals" could understand their states. The feelings of several directors were captured with this comment:

We're the ones living the disaster. We're the ones on the front lines responding, and we could do a better job of organizing the [response]. They ought to step aside and let somebody else lead the thing.

Although the majority of such comments related to working with the Red Cross, leaders also reported insider/outsider issues between their state and other local responding agencies. Turf issues at the local level centered on geographical and political boundaries, conflict around roles, managing credentialing, and event ownership.

Fiscal issues. Fiscal management was cited as a problem in about half the responses. Although funds arrived quickly from the federal level into the state coffer, the challenge became how to access the funds. As one director observed,

The money doesn't really come to you. It goes first to the state, so then you sort of find out who might be there to talk to you about this. The agencies knew that it was there, that they

had to access it too and then it had to be transferred to [anonymous]. We finally figured out
that there had to be a transfer from [one] Agency to the Department of [anonymous]. . . .
Then educating the financial people and the administrators there that this money was
coming, and that it could be accessed as of a certain date. It was extremely difficult.

State administrative procedures occasionally resulted in a misrepresentation of
the status of the program. A failure to notify programs that extra money had been
approved and deposited occasionally resulted in the closing of programs too early
and the administrative need to account for money that had not been spent and now
had to be given back. Many state systems were not set up for efficient and effective
transfer of these funds. These delays were compounded by subsequent delays in
paying providers. Directors relied on the relationships they had with providers to
begin services, but services were often delayed or stopped when payments did not
arrive in a timely manner. One director reported, "They had to trust me that the
money would eventually get there. [I] have a relationship with them. They trusted
me. They all eventually got funding, but it was slow." Similarly, another said, "Area
programs could do nothing until they got funding. They couldn't get funding for
weeks and weeks because of the state system."

A separate fiscal issue involved the restrictions for the use of the CCP funds.
Concerns were raised about the inability to use the funds for preparedness, administrative costs, food for workers, and program tools such as scrapbooks and event
monuments.

Phasing out the response

By and large, the actual length of the CCPs was described as adequate. Typically, the decision to end a CCP was based on funding or diminished need. In most
cases, community need was determined by feedback from workers in the field.
Very few interviewees stated that the decision to begin phasing down was based on
data. When need continued, directors reportedly requested extensions; however,
this request complicated programs by keeping the end date "up in the air" while
the extension was being considered. One director characterized the close date as a
"moving target." Another observation was that the length of the Immediate and
Regular Services Grants meant that, in the absence of extensions, phase down officially corresponded with the first anniversary of the disaster. This was thought to be
a poor time to end the program as distress often increases and mental health needs
reemerge around the anniversary.

Phasing down a program resulted in job loss for most of the CCP staff. Therefore, phase down was often complicated by the fact that many staff left the CCP for
new positions before the CCP ended. In several cases, directors thought that staffs'
desire to continue the CCP stemmed more from their own needs than from the
actual need of the community.

In general, directors felt prepared to handle the phase down of their programs.
Most directors did not report any issues with the process of close out. A few, however, stated that they wished they had had further guidance. In a few cases, admin-

istrative positions were created or amended to include a disaster coordinator. The majority of directors reported that little was left behind in terms of either infrastructure or educational products. Even when such products were left behind, there were questions as to whether they would actually be used again.

Evaluating the program

Evaluation attempts of any kind were acknowledged as critical but were conducted by only about half of the CCPs. There were no consistent or systematic attempts to evaluate across programs that we studied. Of those that conducted any evaluation, most involved the collection of anecdotal reports or receipt of feedback via newspapers, field reports, field visits, and responding agencies. A few programs attempted surveys, usually conducted by outreach workers without the benefit of training to conduct the survey. Four programs reported that they had contracted evaluations of their program. Of those, only two reported useful findings. Response rates, when reported, were less than 20 percent. A few program directors mentioned resistance surrounding the idea of evaluation. At times, the resistance was related to program members' reluctance to being evaluated or measured, and at other times, the resistance came from the federal level, where an evaluation component was not approved as part of the grant. But several of the directors, understanding the commitment to "do no harm," also recognized the need to know and understand the effectiveness of their program in their community, saying,

> That is an area that I wish, and I know that they are working on this, CMHS really needs to have evaluation as a mandated component of the program, because there's nothing that talks about why this program should continue, why it has continued all this time, what good is it. You know, I find that . . . really bad. It's bad because it can jeopardize the program.

Conclusions and Recommendations

Previous writings on the provision of mental health services in the aftermath of disaster called attention to a wide range of potential challenges. These writings were primarily first-person accounts or were focused on particular responses, with unknown generalizability to other programs. We aimed to expand upon this accumulated clinical wisdom by studying, for the first time, a representative sample of programs, events, and directors. Our study captured responses to thirty-seven different disasters that varied in type, magnitude, scope, and setting. Despite this diversity, program directors showed substantial agreement about the nature of the challenges that states confront in planning, applying for, implementing, maintaining, phasing out, and evaluating crisis counseling programs. The findings from these interviews yielded several recommendations that may improve the rapidity and effectiveness of responses aimed to address the psychosocial needs of disaster victims.

First, it is clear that all states require a disaster plan and that mental health should be an integral part of this plan. Ongoing federal support may be needed for states to become and remain prepared. Plans should include dedicated resources that can be mobilized and accessed immediately. Written mental health response plans may help to ensure knowledge transfer from one event to another and from one person to another. Plans should include a designated disaster mental health coordinator with a clear job description, explicit mechanisms to build capacity by developing collaborative relationships with key agencies, and communication venues. Relationships should be formalized through contracts and/or memoranda of understanding. Special emphasis should be placed on developing partnerships with faith-based communities and schools. The best preparedness training plans include table-top and in vitro exercises.

Particularly helpful components of the [FEMA] training included learning from others who had experienced a disaster and assistance with grant writing.

There are four key recommendations regarding federal trainings for state disaster mental health coordinators. First, it would be helpful to establish a curriculum that progresses through the process of disaster mental health response. Second, instead of having a class each year that focuses on grant writing, an initial grant writing course might be followed by an intermediate or advanced course, as appropriate. Third, it would be helpful to develop online courses that augment the Emmitsburg training. Suggested topics include cultural competence, developing collaborative relationships, writing a disaster mental health response plan, and developing state capacity. Fourth, during the event, states should be provided with a list of trainers that is matched to their event and their audience.

One of the most common recommendations from these directors was a plea to review the grant application process and consider ways to streamline it. Preparing these applications in the midst of the crisis was highly stressful. Many advocated for changing the present needs assessment formula and procedures to make them more compatible with available data. Building state capacity for conducting needs assessment would likewise be helpful.

Several actions would facilitate the implementation and ongoing administration of these programs. First, program manuals should be created that define and clarify the components of outreach, counseling, and referral. Concurrently, training materials should be created that facilitate the understanding of such manuals. States need clear guidelines regarding the appropriate training and use of paraprofessionals as outreach workers and crisis counselors. Some states needed assistance to navigate state regulations that may conflict with the use of paraprofessionals in these roles.

One of the areas of most consistent difficulty was fiscal management. States should be required to address fiscal issues as part of their applications and to have appropriate mechanisms in place for distributing federal funds to the CCP and its providers. Likewise, federal program administrators should increase their capacity to provide technical assistance in this area.

The federal government should also reevaluate policies with respect to program length. A one-year time frame for the Regular Services Program would avoid having phase down co-occur with the first anniversary.

Finally, we recommend a standardized approach to CCP evaluation that depends less on the initiative and expertise of specific programs. This would encompass a set of common tools and procedures and a process of using the evaluation to help guide services. Additionally, exit interviews conducted with state directors once the program phases down would facilitate the federal program's ability to capture and transfer lessons learned from past responses.

This set of recommendations undeniably implies that significant improvements are needed at the federal level to improve the functioning of the program at the state level. In closing, however, we should make two important caveats to this observation. First, it should be remembered that the nature of qualitative research is to explore the issues surrounding a particular program or entity. This often highlights the feedback that may be perceived as negative or "needs improvement." Although this is valuable information, it is important that we not lose the positive responses and aspects of a program or entity. To that end, we want to acknowledge that many positive comments were made throughout the interviews. Directors felt their programs provided adequate reach and quality of service to the victims of their disasters.

Second, it should be acknowledged that several changes in process within the federal program are consistent with the aforementioned recommendations. For example, an operations manual is in production that should provide the temporal program guidance that many of these directors requested. In addition, as a direct result of this study (which was part of a larger retrospective evaluation project commissioned by SAMHSA), a standardized evaluation protocol was enacted across twenty state programs aiming to provide services to victims of Hurricane Katrina. This new policy provided states with common tools, manuals, and procedures and, for the first time, allowed for cross-site analysis of program reach and outputs. Improving understanding of the accomplishments and challenges of past programs should boost the capacity of federal, state, and local leaders to promote the psychosocial recovery of disaster victims.

References

Bowenkamp, Christine. 2000. Coordination of mental health and community agencies in disaster response. *International Journal of Emergency Mental Health* 2:159-65.

Call, John, and Betty Pfefferbaum. 1999. Lessons from the first two years of Project Heartland, Oklahoma's mental health response to the 1995 bombing. *Psychiatric Services* 50:953-55.

Canterbury, Rachel, and William Yule. 1999. Planning a psychosocial response to a disaster. In *Post-traumatic stress disorders: Concepts and therapy*, ed. William Yule. New York: Wiley.

Gist, Richard, and Bernard Lubin. 1999. *Response to disaster: Psychological, ecological, and community approaches*. Washington, DC: Taylor & Francis.

Hodgkinson, Peter, and Michael Stewart. 1998. *Coping with catastrophe: A handbook of post-disaster psychosocial aftercare*. 2nd ed. London: Routledge.

Lanou, Frank. 1993. Coordinating private and public mental health resources in a disaster. Handbook of post-disaster interventions. *Journal of Social Behavior and Personality* 8:255-60.

Myers, Diane, and David Wee. 2005. *Disaster mental health services: A primer for practitioners*. New York: Brunner-Routledge.

National Institute of Mental Health. 2002. *Mental health and mass violence: Evidence based early psychological intervention for victims/survivors of mass violence: A workshop to reach consensus on best practices*. NIH Publication Office no. 02-5138. Washington, DC: Government Printing Office. http://www.nimh.nih.gov/publicat/massviolence.pdf.

Norris, Fran H., Jessica L. Hamblen, Patricia J. Watson, Josef Ruzek, Laura Gibson, Betty Pfefferbaum, Jennifer L. Price, Susan P. Stevens, Bruce H. Young, and Matthew J. Friedman. 2006. Understanding and creating systems of postdisaster care: A case study of New York's mental health system's response to the World Trade Center disaster. In *Mental health intervention following disasters or mass violence*, ed. Elspeth Cameron Ritchie, Patricia J. Watson, and Matthew J. Friedman. New York: Guilford.

Norris, Fran H., Patricia J. Watson, Jessica L. Hamblen, and Betty Pfefferbaum. 2005. Provider perspectives on disaster mental health services in Oklahoma City. In *The trauma of terror: Sharing knowledge and shared care*, ed. Yael Danieli and Daniel Brom. New York: Haywood.

Sitterle, Karen, and Robin Gurwich. 1998. The terrorist bombing in Oklahoma City. In *When a community weeps: Case studies in group survivorship*, ed. Ellen Zinner and Mary Beth Williams. Philadelphia: Brunner/Mazel.

Hurricane Katrina and the Paradoxes of Government Disaster Policy: Bringing About Wise Governmental Decisions for Hazardous Areas

By
RAYMOND J. BURBY

The unprecedented losses from Hurricane Katrina can be explained by two paradoxes. The safe development paradox is that in trying to make hazardous areas safer, the federal government in fact substantially increased the potential for catastrophic property damages and economic loss. The local government paradox is that while their citizens bear the brunt of human suffering and financial loss in disasters, local officials pay insufficient attention to policies to limit vulnerability. The author demonstrates in this article that in spite of the two paradoxes, disaster losses can be blunted if local governments prepare comprehensive plans that pay attention to hazard mitigation. The federal government can take steps to increase local government commitment to planning and hazard mitigation by making relatively small adjustments to the Disaster Mitigation Act of 2000 and the Flood Insurance Act. To be more certain of reducing disaster losses, however, the author suggests that we need a major reorientation of the National Flood Insurance Program from insuring individuals to insuring communities.

Keywords: Hurricane Katrina; disasters; public policy; hazard mitigation; comprehensive plans; building codes; state planning mandate; National Flood Insurance Program

Economic losses from Hurricane Katrina, estimated to be more than \$200 billion, are the largest for any disaster in U.S. history. Katrina captured national and world attention, but it is just the most recent in a series of increasingly severe catastrophic events (Cutter and

Raymond J. Burby is a professor of city and regional planning at the University of North Carolina at Chapel Hill. He is an associate editor of the Natural Hazards Review *and former coeditor of the* Journal of the American Planning Association. *He is the editor of* Cooperating with Nature *(Joseph Henry Press, 1998) and the coauthor of* Making Governments Plan *(Johns Hopkins University Press, 1997) and* Environmental Governance *(Routledge, 1996). Burby is a member of the College of Fellows of the American Institute of Certified Planners. From 1992 to 2000, he was a distinguished professor of city and regional planning and held the DeBlois Chair in Urban and Public Affairs at the University of New Orleans.*

DOI: 10.1177/0002716205284676

Emrich 2005). The 460 presidential disaster declarations of the 1990s were double the number of the previous decade. That trend has continued during the present decade, with 299 disaster declarations through September 2005 (Federal Emergency Management Agency [FEMA] 2005a, 2005b, 2005c). Of the 62 weather-related disasters that have resulted in $1 billion or more in damages over the twenty-five years between 1980 and 2004, a quarter have occurred since 2000 (U.S. Department of Commerce 2005).

In this article, I argue that the extensive damage in New Orleans and the trend in increasing numbers and severity of disasters are the wholly predictable (in fact, predicted) outcomes of well-intentioned, but short-sighted, public policy decisions at all levels of government. These decisions create two paradoxes. One I term the safe development paradox since I show that in trying to make hazardous areas safe for development, government policies instead have made them targets for catastrophes. The second I term the local government paradox since I show that while citizens bear the brunt of losses in disasters, local public officials often fail to take actions necessary to protect them. The consequences of each paradox reinforce the other and in combination lead to a never ending cycle of ever more unsafe urban development and ever larger, ever more catastrophic losses from natural hazards.

The political considerations of the president and Congress that create the safe development paradox are not likely to change. Federal assistance following disasters is likely to increase with increasingly severe disasters, as will federal efforts to make places at risk safer communities in which to live and work. What can change, I argue, is uninformed local government decision making about urban development that results in millions of households and businesses occupying at-risk structures in vulnerable locations. The vehicles for bringing this about are federal policies that (1) require local governments to prepare comprehensive plans that give due consideration to natural hazards and (2) require local governments to assume greater financial responsibility for the consequences of their urban development decision making. Using data on National Flood Insurance Program (NFIP) claims and payments in coastal counties over a twenty-five-year period, I show that comprehensive planning requirements adopted by state governments already have resulted in lower per capita losses from flooding. But less than half of the states require local governments to prepare plans, and fewer than ten states require that plans pay attention to natural hazards.

NOTE: I would like acknowledge the assistance of University of North Carolina at Chapel Hill research assistants Anna Davis, Leanna Hush, and Mary Margaret Shaw in assembling the data used in the statistical analyses of NFIP claims and payments reported here. The article benefited greatly from comments on an earlier draft provided by Philip Berke, Nan Burby, Thomas Campanella, Howard Kunreuther, Peter May, Anthony Mumphrey, Mary Margaret Shaw, and French Wetmore. I am also grateful for assistance provided by the National Science Foundation through research grant CMS-0100012 to the University of North Carolina at Chapel Hill. Of course, the findings and opinions presented here are not necessarily endorsed by the National Science Foundation or those who provided assistance with the research.

The wake of Hurricane Katrina provides an opportunity for the federal government to use the public concern created by the disaster to spur more local governments to prepare comprehensive plans that address hazard mitigation. In addition, if the government reorients the NFIP so that more of the burden of responsibility for insurance coverage is borne by local governments, local officials may become more committed to limiting development in hazardous areas and to mitigating the hazard to existing development at risk (see Burby and May 1998). This article points out several ways the government can accomplish these ends and in doing so erase yet another paradox, noted by Platt (1999, xvii), "On the one hand, the federal government is called upon to assume a major share of state, local and private economic costs of disasters. . . . But on the other hand, the government at all levels is increasingly impotent to demand . . . that local governments and individuals assume the political and financial burdens of curtailing unwise development in hazardous locations."

The article is organized as follows. In the next two sections, I describe the two paradoxes and illustrate them with evidence from policy choices made by federal, state, and local agencies in the New Orleans area over the decades prior to Hurricane Katrina. Next, I examine state requirements for local government planning and building code enforcement as a means of dealing with the adverse consequences of the paradoxes and present empirical evidence on their effects in reducing disaster losses. The article concludes with a brief look at various ways the federal government can increase local government commitment to reducing vulnerability to hazards by (1) requiring that they prepare comprehensive plans with hazard mitigation elements and (2) requiring that they assume more responsibility for insuring private and public property at risk from hazards.

Safe Development Paradox

For most of this century, the federal government has pursued a policy toward the use of hazardous areas that I term safe development. The basic idea is that land exposed to natural hazards can be profitably used if steps are taken to make it safe for human occupancy. The means of achieving this have evolved over time, but they basically include measures to mitigate the likelihood of damage and measures to deal with residual financial risk (see Platt 1999; King 2005). To minimize damage, they include federal financial support for flood and hurricane protection works and beach nourishment, federal requirements through the NFIP for safe building practices such as elevation of construction in flood hazard areas, and federal incentives for local government mitigation efforts through provisions of the Disaster Mitigation Act of 2000 and National Flood Insurance Reform Acts of 1994 and 2004. To minimize the adverse financial consequences for individuals and businesses when steps to make development safe from hazards fail (known technically as residual risk), the federal government has provided generous disaster relief, particularly for homeowners; low-cost loans to ease business recovery; income tax deductions for uninsured disaster losses; and subsidized flood insurance. The costs of these policies to the federal government were estimated conservatively by Conrad, McNitt, and Stout (1998, 5) at $9.5 billion a year (adjusted to 2005 dollars; this amount does not include the cost of lost revenue through tax write-offs and the cost of insurance subsidies).[1] The development stimulus of these policies is further augmented by federal aid that reduces the cost to localities of providing infrastructure in hazardous areas, such as water and sewerage service and highway access (for further discussion of federal incentives for the use of hazardous areas, see H. John Heinz III Center 2000).

The wake of Hurricane Katrina provides an opportunity for the federal government to use the public concern created by the disaster to spur more local governments to prepare comprehensive plans that address hazard mitigation.

The New Orleans metropolitan area's two largest parishes (Jefferson and Orleans) provide examples of federal safe development policies in action. This region is extremely susceptible to floods and hurricanes. Over the twenty-three-year period between 1978 and 2000, the two parishes were exposed to nineteen damaging flood events and eighteen hurricane events, almost one per year (Hazards Research Lab 2005). Given this high level of risk, Congress, following devastating hurricane losses in 1947, authorized federal assistance for levees that would make it possible to convert ninety-six hundred acres from wetland to "productive use." Following even larger flood losses from Hurricane Betsy in 1965 (America's first billion-dollar hurricane), Congress authorized construction of the Lake Pontchartrain and Vicinity, Louisiana, Hurricane Protection Project, which sought to protect virtually all of Orleans Parish and the northern (east bank) portion of Jefferson Parish from storm surge flooding from hurricanes up to a one in two-hundred-year recurrence interval (equivalent to a Category 3 hurricane). It proposed to do this by raising existing levees and constructing new levees along much of the southern shore of the lake. These levees would help prevent a recurrence of the losses experienced from Hurricane Betsy, and, more important, they would facilitate continued urbanization of this very hazardous region. In fact, protection of *existing development* accounted for only 21 percent of the benefits needed to justify the project. An extraordinary 79 percent were to come from *new develop-ment* that would now be feasible with the added protection provided by the improved levee system (Comptroller of the Currency 1976).[2] At about the same time the Corps of Engineers was formulating an improved hurricane protection system, Congress in 1968 passed the National Flood Insurance Act to enable households and businesses to insure their property from flood damages, which most commercial insurance companies refused to cover in standard property insurance policies. This newly available insurance provided another important federal underpinning for continued conversion of wetlands in the parishes to urban uses.

Federal safe development policies had their *intended* effect in easing develop-ment of hazardous areas in Jefferson and Orleans parishes. During the decade after Congress authorized the Lake Pontchartrain hurricane protection project and launched the NFIP, Jefferson Parish added forty-seven thousand housing units and Orleans Parish added twenty-nine thousand. According to Lewis (2003, 76), "the metropolitan area . . . simply exploded into the swamps—first toward the East Bank section of Jefferson Parish; more recently into the eastern reaches of Orleans Parish and beyond." He went on to note that "most of the newly developed land is built on muck and is sinking at various rates. Much of the land is subject to extremely dangerous flooding" (p. 77). Although Hurricane Betsy revealed the potential for widespread flooding of the low-lying areas of both parishes, the con-struction of improved hurricane protection works and availability of flood insur-ance evidently persuaded thousands of households that the region was reasonably safe.

The development of the area east of the Industrial Canal, which contains 50 per-cent of the land area in the City of New Orleans, is a case in point. In 1960, before the new levee plan, eastern New Orleans consisted mostly of wetlands with a few scattered highway commercial activities and subdivisions along Downman Road and the Chef Menteur Highway (U.S. 90), which linked New Orleans to the Missis-sippi Gulf Coast. With the pending construction of the I-10 Twin Span across the east end of Lake Pontchartrain and extension of the interstate through the heart of the area and the decision to extend the city's hurricane protection levee system to the east, the New Orleans City Planning Commission adopted a plan in 1966 call-ing for intensive urban development in what later became known as Planning Dis-trict 9. The *New Century New Orleans Plan* noted,

> Full scale development ensued . . . and concurrent expenditures for streets, parks, schools, and sewerage and drainage was the largest single factor to change the land use profile . . . as well as make the area a significant growth area for the future development of the Metro-politan area . . . the area continued to grow from 1975 to 1985. New subdivisions were developed at a rapid pace . . . (and) major commercial centers developed and prospered. (City Planning Commission 1999, 188)

Further to the east in Planning District 10, the 1970s saw the development of NASA's 830-acre Michoud rocket assembly facility, which is a major employer in the region, and an attempt to build a major new community (Pontchartrain New Town–In Town Plan) with support from the federal new communities program. When the federal program was shut down in 1975, these projects, renamed Orlandia and New Orleans East, proceeded as wholly private ventures that hoped to provide housing for an estimated 250,000 residents. Even though the pace of development slowed after 1985, between 1970 and 2000 this area of former marshes and swamps saw more than 22,000 new housing units built and the city wanted more. In its 1999 *New Century New Orleans Land Use Plan*, the city planning commission argued,

> Moreover, there are extensive opportunities for future development of the vacant parcels that range from single vacant lots to multi-thousand acre tracts. Long term, these development opportunities represent not only population increases but also significant potential employment for the city. (City Planning Commission, 1999, 201)

Ironically, just six years later, the entire area of urban growth the city had been promoting and the Corps protecting for forty years was entirely under water.

As the experience of New Orleans illustrates, federal policy has had its *intended* effect of facilitating and sustaining development in hazardous areas. The paradox is that in trying to make the most hazardous parts of New Orleans safe for urban expansion, it had the *unintended effect* of contributing directly to the devastation of Hurricane Katrina. It did that by increasing the amount of development possible in low-lying, flood-prone areas such as New Orleans East; and, some contend, by providing levee protection and new drainage works to that area of suburban growth, the Corps and city diverted resources that could have been used to improve drainage, pumping capacity, and levees in older areas of the city (see Drew 1984, 1, 10).

Supposedly safe development in New Orleans (and elsewhere) has proven to be unsafe for several reasons including limitations of flood and hurricane protection works and limitations of the NFIP's efforts to control losses through floodplain mapping and regulation of construction practices. Flood control and hurricane protection measures have serious limitations, most of which are not recognized by households and businesses who put themselves at risk by locating in potentially hazardous areas. These limitations include (1) design limits that can lead to levees being overtopped by flood and hurricane events that are larger than they were designed for and (2) design flaws and construction and maintenance shortcomings that lead to protective works being breached when they cannot stand up to the forces exerted by large flood and hurricane events. Both apparently contributed to the levee failures along three New Orleans canals that flooded the city (Carter 2005). This occurrence is not unique inasmuch as FEMA estimated in 1987 that levee overtopping or failure was involved in approximately one-third of all flood disasters. Concern about them is also not recent. Noted geographer Gilbert White observed in 1975 that flood control works "will be of little value if the reduction in damages that they accomplish is more than offset by new damage potential resulting from additional development in floodplains" (p. xviii). This potential was demonstrated by Burby and French (1985), who studied more than twelve hundred communities with flood hazards and found a positive correlation between the degree to which communities used flood control works to limit their vulnerability to flooding and the amount of new development taking place in their flood hazard areas *after* the flood control works were completed.

The NFIP tries to limit flood losses by imposing construction standards that reduce the likelihood of newly constructed buildings being flooded. These standards, which must be adopted and enforced by local governments as a condition for participation in the program, include elevation or flood proofing to the level of floods with a one in one hundred chance of occurring in any given year. For a variety of reasons, that level of protection is not achieved in some cases and even when achieved may not be adequate (see Burby [2002] for a fuller elaboration of these issues). For one, accurate estimation of flood risk is a critical ingredient in regulating the elevation of new development, but the program has had difficulty doing that because it has been unable to update in a timely manner flood insurance rate maps to take into account increased flood risk from sea-level rise, subsidence, coastal erosion, or increased runoff as watersheds develop in urban areas. Flood insurance is available, but buildings are not required to be elevated in areas at risk from dam and levee failure, in areas with localized storm water drainage flooding, or in small watersheds of less than one square mile. As a consequence of these problems, the NFIP has regularly not been able to cover its costs from premiums and has had to borrow from the Treasury. According to Pasterick (1998), operating losses occurred annually between 1972 and 1980 and in the years 1983, 1984, 1989, 1990, 1992, 1993, 1995, and 1996. An operating loss also occurred in 2004, and with more than $22 billion in expected claims from Hurricanes Katrina, Rita, and Wilma in 2005, the program will require an infusion of money from the Treasury that it will not be able to repay from future premium income (Crenshaw 2005, A8). To the degree the program fails to adequately reflect risk in rates and operates at a loss, it subsidizes the occupancy of hazardous areas and facilitates more development than is economically rational.

Furthermore, the basic standard of protection used by the NFIP—the one-hundred-year flood event—may be ill-advised since most flood losses in the United States stem from less frequent flood events. One early study reported that 66 percent of losses in floods come from events with recurrence intervals less frequent than the one-hundred-year flood (Sheaffer et al. 1976). Another study reported that 83 percent of losses from hurricane winds and flooding come from Category 3, 4, and 5 storms, which have recurrence intervals lower than the one-hundred-year event (Pielke and Landsea 1997). Tropical Storm Allison in 2001 flooded forty-five thousand buildings in the Houston area, but only seven thousand were located within one-hundred-year floodplains. In recognition of the limitation of the one-hundred-year flood standard, the Association of State Floodplain Managers (2000) recommends that the five-hundred-year flood be used in regulating the elevation of new urban development.

In addition to limitations in its ability to limit losses to new development, by subsidizing rates for existing development, the program provides little incentive for property owners to take steps on their own to reduce flood vulnerability. House-hold surveys by Burby et al. (1988) and Laska (1991) found that less than 15 per-cent of property owners took action to improve their buildings prior to experienc-ing flood losses (see also, in this volume, Kunreuther [2006]). There are a variety of reasons, in addition to subsidized flood insurance, for this inaction, including misperception and underestimation of the risk of flooding, inability to recover investments in mitigation investments through higher resale values, and budget constraints. For the NFIP, the consequences have been dire since repetitively flooded properties (which account for about 2 percent of all NFIP policies) account for more than 25 percent of claims payments made (see Anderson 2000).

In summary, federal policies have sought to make areas at risk from natural haz-ards safe places for urban development by reducing the degree of hazard and by shielding hazard-area occupants from financial risks of loss. Over time, these poli-cies have facilitated the development of these areas, as illustrated by urban growth in New Orleans, but they have increased the potential for catastrophic losses in large disasters. In this sense, Hurricane Katrina and the flooding of New Orleans could be viewed as an expected consequence of federal policy rather than an aber-ration that is unlikely to be repeated.

Local Government Paradox

Mileti (1999, 66) scrutinized the $500 billion in losses from natural disasters in the United States between 1975 and 1994. He found that a relatively small propor-tion was covered by federal disaster relief and that most losses were not insured. Instead, "losses were borne by victims." Given that the incidence of disaster losses is primarily borne by local residents and businesses, one would expect that avoid-ance of losses would be a high priority for local officials. The paradox is that this is typically not the case.

Prior to being coerced into adopting floodplain management regulations by the National Flood Insurance Act in 1968, virtually no local governments in the United States had adopted building or zoning regulations to minimize flood losses (e.g., see Murphy 1958). Although thousands of governments subsequently adopted the minimum building standards needed to participate, many did not enforce them seriously or take other actions to deal with flood and hurricane risks. In South Carolina, for example, building code violations were found to be an important cause of damages from Hurricane Hugo in 1989 (All-Industry Research Advisory Council [AIRAC] 1989). In south Florida, a quarter of the $16 billion in insured losses from Hurricane Andrew in 1992 were attributed to Dade County's failure to enforce its building code (Building Performance Assessment Team 1992). A study by the Southern Building Code Congress International, Inc. (1992) found that more than half of local building officials surveyed on the Gulf Coast did not under-stand or enforce the provisions of the Southern Building Code related to hurricane wind damage.

Three examples of decision making in the New Orleans area illustrate a lack of local government concern about hazards. Grunwald and Glasser (2005) in an article in the *Washington Post* on the New Orleans levee systems wrote, "Local officials often resisted proposals to protect their communities from storms because they did not want to pay their share of federal projects." Decisions recounted to support this contention include the following. The Orleans Parish Levee Board lobbied the Corps of Engineers for protection to the level of a one-hundred-year, rather than two-hundred-year, hurricane after the local share of the cost of the Lake Pontchartrain and Vicinity Project had escalated many times beyond original estimates. The levee district also opposed hurricane protection floodgates at the mouths of the city's drainage canals, which led to the construction of the walls along

---

[I]n trying to make the most hazardous parts of New Orleans safe for urban expansion, it had the unintended effect *of contributing directly to the devastation of Hurricane Katrina.*

---

the canals that failed in Katrina. As another example of low priority for flood protection, in the early 1980s the Federal Insurance Administration (FIA) launched a subrogation suit for more than $100 million against Jefferson, Orleans, and St. Bernard parishes (subrogation occurs when an insurance entity that pays its insured client for losses then sues the party it contends caused the damages). The FIA contended the parishes caused it to pay excessive flood insurance claims by failing to maintain levees and failing to enforce elevation requirements for new construction, which then led to buildings being flooded and their owners to seek compensation from the federal flood insurance program. The courts ruled in the FIA's favor and ordered the parishes to improve their levee maintenance and enforcement practices (see Malone 1990). As a third example, the City of New Orleans did not update its 1970 comprehensive plan for almost thirty years. When it got around to this in 1999, its *New Century New Orleans Land Use Plan* made absolutely no mention of the extreme flood hazard facing the city, ways of mitigating the hazard through land use or building regulations, or how the city might recover from an event such as Hurricane Katrina.

There are many reasons for the local government paradox. In his national assessment of natural hazards in the United States, Mileti (1999, 160) touched on several of them.

Few local governments are willing to reduce natural hazards by managing development. It is not so much that they oppose land use measures (although some do), but rather that, like individuals, they tend to view natural hazards as a minor problem that can take a back seat to more pressing local concerns such as unemployment, crime, housing, and education. Also, the costs of mitigation are immediate while the benefits are uncertain, may not occur during the tenure of current elected officials, and are not visible (like roads or a new library).

May (1991) noted that these local political factors stem in part from the lack of citizen concern about hazards, which he believes creates a "policies without publics" dilemma that stifles local policy initiatives. In addition, other scholars believe federal encouragement of the intensive use of areas exposed to natural hazards has created a form of "moral hazard" that discourages local governments (and individuals) from taking actions to reduce the risk of loss.

Moral hazard is an insurance term that refers to cases where the availability of insurance protection lowers an insured party's incentive to avoid risk. Insurance companies try to counter this through the use of deductibles, higher insurance rates, and the threat of canceling policies if claims are too frequent. The potential for moral hazard in the federal approach to natural hazards was first noted by the Interagency Floodplain Management Review Committee (1994, 180) following disastrous floods in the upper Midwest in 1993. In commenting on the potential for federal programs to create a form of moral hazard, the committee observed, "Through provision of disaster assistance and, in some cases, enhanced flood protection, the government may in fact be reducing incentives for local governments and individuals to be more prudent in their actions." Also written in 1994, the House Bipartisan Natural Disasters Task Force stated, "If state and local governments believe that the federal government will meet their needs in every disaster, they have less incentive to spend scarce state and local resources on disaster preparedness, mitigation, response and recovery . . . (and) people are encouraged to take risks they think they will not have to pay for" (quoted in Platt 1999, 39). Finally, Mileti (1999, 7) has argued that a "scattershot approach, as well as the federal and state trend to cut risk and assume liability, has undermined the responsibility of local governments for using land-use management techniques to reduce exposures to hazards."[3]

By the 1990s, various federal programs were being adjusted to deal with the moral hazard issue. The Stafford Act in 1988 and more recent Disaster Mitigation Act of 2000 both provide federal assistance for the preparation of state and local hazard mitigation plans and implementation of hazard mitigation projects. Although the Stafford Act has been found to be ineffective in many cases (see Godschalk et al. 1998), some of the problems identified may be countered by the more recent Disaster Mitigation Act of 2000 legislation. A similar effort has been made to counter the potential of the NFIP to foster local complacency toward flood hazards. The Flood Insurance Reform Act of 1994 established incentives for the preparation of floodplain management plans and other flood mitigation measures, and the Flood Insurance Reform Act of 2004 provided tools for dealing with repeatedly flooded properties. However, the degree to which any of these efforts have had an effect on local government commitment to dealing with hazards is not known at this time.

Avoiding the Two Paradoxes

The paradoxes that contributed to the flooding of New Orleans are coming to be widely recognized. An October 2005 analysis by the Brookings Institution Metropolitan Program noted,

> Federal policies and investments in flood protection facilitated development in dangerous locations . . . and failed to discourage floodplain development. . . . [T]he traditional federal deference to state and local land-use planning has meant that federal spending on levees and other protections has been unaccompanied by sensible restrictions on subsequent construction. . . . At the same time, the availability of subsidized federal flood insurance for new development in flood plains . . . also represents a failure of Washington to take the lead in discouraging communities from building in harm's way. (Brookings Institution Metropolitan Program 2005, 23, 25)

It seems obvious that unless the two paradoxes discussed here are addressed directly in federal policy, the devastation brought about by Katrina will be repeated continually across the United States.

Having noted this, it seems to me unlikely that the pork barrel politics that sustain federal investments in flood and hurricane protection, federal disaster relief, and federal insurance subsidies are likely to change even though policy analysts increasingly recognize their adverse effects. What can change is how local governments manage the development and redevelopment of areas at risk. A series of studies supported by the National Science Foundation has shown that through appropriate land-use planning and oversight of development, risk and damages from hazards can be significantly reduced (see Burby, French, and Nelson 1998; Olshansky 2001; Nelson and French 2002; Burby 2005).[4] The difficulty, given the local government paradox, is how to bring this about.

One approach state governments have used is to formulate state building codes and planning policies and to mandate that local governments enforce the codes and prepare comprehensive plans that are consistent with the policies. To determine whether these state requirements are having an effect on loss reduction, I examined the distribution of flood insurance claims and amount of claims payments made by the NFIP in coastal counties of the Atlantic, Gulf, and Pacific states over the twenty-five-year period from January 1, 1978, through December 31, 2002. These states differed significantly in their requirements regarding local enforcement of building codes and local planning for urban development and redevelopment, as shown in Table 1. Six coastal states, including each of those hit by Katrina, required *neither* local code enforcement nor local comprehensive plans. Eight states required local governments to enforce codes or to develop

TABLE 1

STATE REQUIREMENTS FOR LOCAL GOVERNMENT BUILDING
CODE ENFORCEMENT AND COMPREHENSIVE PLANS IN ATLANTIC,
GULF, AND PACIFIC STATES

State Requirements for Local Government Building Code Enforcement and Comprehensive Plans	States (Number of Coastal Counties/Parishes)
No state local government building code enforcement or comprehensive plan requirements	6 states with 58 counties: Alabama (2), Louisiana (25), Mississippi (3), New Hampshire (2), Pennsylvania (3), Texas (23)
State local government building code enforcement requirement but not comprehensive plan requirement	3 states with 37 counties: Connecticut (4), New Jersey (17), New York (16)
State local government comprehensive plan requirement but not building code requirement	5 states with 33 counties: Delaware (3), Georgia (6), Hawaii (5), Maine (10), South Carolina (9)
Both state local government building code and comprehensive plan requirements	10 states with 236 counties: Alaska (19), California (22), Florida (67), Maryland (17), Massachusetts (9) (plan requirement for larger cities and towns), North Carolina (20), Oregon (13), Rhode Island (5), Virginia (46),[b] Washington (17) (plan requirement for high growth counties only)

SOURCE: Schwab (2002).
a. Local governments in seven of these ten states (California, Florida, Maine, Maryland, North Carolina, Oregon, South Carolina) are also required to include a hazards element in the comprehensive plan.
b. Includes independent cities as well as counties.

plans, but not both; and ten states required both local code enforcement and local formulation and adoption of comprehensive plans. Most of the states that required both code enforcement and planning also required that plans address natural hazards.

The number of NFIP insurance claims per capita for compensation of flood damages and the per capita dollar amount of payments made to settle claims were *highest* in states that did not require responsible behavior—neither building code enforcement nor comprehensive plans—from their local governments. They were lowest in states that required one or both from their local governments, as shown in Table 2. The three states hardest hit by Hurricane Katrina left decisions about code enforcement and planning for urban development and redevelopment wholly to local discretion. The consequences for them and the nation have been calamitous. Among all coastal counties, the NFIP experienced thirteen flood-loss claims per thousand residents between 1978 and 2002. In Louisiana, the rate was fifty-five claims per thousand residents of coastal counties, while it was thirty-one and thirty-two in Alabama and Mississippi, respectively. Dollar losses per capita were $133 among all coastal counties. They were $530 per capita in Louisiana, $337 per capita in Alabama, and $277 per capita in Mississippi.

TABLE 2

MEAN PER CAPITA NATIONAL FLOOD INSURANCE PROGRAM (NFIP)
CLAIMS AND PAYMENTS, 1978-2002, IN COASTAL COUNTIES BY PRESENCE
OR ABSENCE OF STATE BUILDING CODE ENFORCEMENT AND
COMPREHENSIVE PLANNING MANDATES

State Requirement	Mean Per Thousand Population	Standard Error	Mean Per Capita ($)	Standard Error ($)
Neither code enforcement nor plan mandate (n = 58)	30	4	299	46
Code enforcement but not plan mandate (n = 33)	11	5	79	31
Plan but not code enforcement mandate (n = 32)	9	3	137	55
Both code enforcement and planning mandated (n = 224)	10	2	99	16
Statistical significance (one-tailed p)				
Code mandate	.007		.001	
Plan mandate	.001		.03	
Code Mandate × Plan Mandate	.003		.009	

The statistical association between state requirements for the preparation of local comprehensive plans and lower per capita NFIP claims and payments continues when adjustments are made for a number of other factors that affect the likelihood of suffering flood damages, including the number of severe weather events experienced over the twenty-five-year period, population size and density, population growth, and the value of homes at risk.[5] However, when these other factors are statistically controlled in multivariate analyses, the impact of planning mandates is lower (a reduction in losses of about 1 percent) and the existence of a building code enforcement mandate is no longer statistically significant. These results are shown in the appendix.

Also revealing is a comparison of Florida and Texas, two states that escaped damage from Hurricane Katrina but are similar in other ways in terms of coastal urbanization and storm history. Texas has chosen to leave decisions about building code enforcement and planning wholly to the discretion of local governments. Florida mandates local code enforcement, and since 1975, it has required the preparation of local comprehensive plans. Florida, but not Texas, requires that comprehensive plans develop and implement objectives for hazard mitigation (see Deyle, Chapin, and Baker 2005). Flood insurance claims from coastal residents between 1978 and 2002 were one per thousand residents in Florida, but twenty-one per thousand residents in Texas. Flood insurance payments per capita were $71 in Florida but $325 in Texas.

Sharing the Burden

In this article, I have argued that two paradoxes help explain the devastation caused by Hurricane Katrina in New Orleans and can be expected to contribute to similar disasters in the future. The *safe development paradox* occurs when federal efforts to make inherently hazardous areas safe for development in fact make them highly susceptible to disasters of catastrophic proportions. In New Orleans, these federal efforts consisted primarily of funding hurricane protection levees and other flood control works to promote urban development in the "protected" areas and the provision of flood insurance at subsidized rates. The *local government paradox* occurs when local governments, whose citizens bear the brunt of human suffering and financial loss when disasters occur, give insufficient attention to threats posed by hazards when they allow the intensive development of hazardous areas. In New Orleans, this paradox is illustrated by the city's facilitation of development in eastern New Orleans and by the Orleans Parish Levee Board's unwillingness to help underwrite the costs of higher levels of flood and hurricane protection.

The two paradoxes help account for the upward spiral in the frequency and magnitude of natural disasters. If this trend is to be slowed or reversed, I believe it will be necessary for local governments to share more of the burden of disasters through careful planning and management of development in hazardous areas and by assuming more of the financial responsibility for development at risk. I have shown that where states have required local governments to prepare and implement comprehensive plans for urban development, losses from flooding are lower than they are when states leave these matters solely to local governments' discretion. State requirements for building code enforcement also may have some effect, although it could not be confirmed in multivariate analyses. Not surprisingly, the states of Alabama, Louisiana, and Mississippi have been noteworthy for their reluctance to interfere in local land-use and development decision making. In contrast, equally flood- and hurricane-prone Florida has demanded local action, and as a result per capita flood losses over twenty-five years have been much lower there.

There are two relatively easy-to-accomplish steps the federal government could take to encourage local governments to prepare comprehensive plans. First, the Disaster Mitigation Act of 2000 could be amended to require that regular mitigation plan updates mandated by the legislation be integrated into local comprehensive plans, where they exist. Without this step, the mitigation plans are likely to be ignored in local government decision making because of the lack of commitment to hazard mitigation activities noted earlier. Many states require that local government land-use and infrastructure decisions be consistent with comprehensive plans. Thus, by incorporating mitigation plans into comprehensive plans, the mitigation plans to some extent would be self-enforcing in the sense that local officials would have to pay attention to them as they make decisions about public investments and development permits. In addition, this would provide a stimulus to broaden the scope of mitigation plans beyond narrow safe development and emergency management considerations.

Second, the Flood Insurance Act could be amended to add the preparation of local comprehensive plans with hazard mitigation provisions as a condition for continued participation in the program. At present, participation in the program is conditioned on local governments' agreement to adopt and enforce building regulations to reduce the likelihood of flood damage. Previous research has shown that local governments with plans are more likely than those without plans to use land-use regulations, in addition to the building regulations, to reduce vulnerability to flooding (Burby and Dalton 1994). Financial assistance could be provided to the states to encourage them to facilitate this through parallel state legislation and to also provide technical assistance to localities.

The major change in approach I have in mind would . . . shift the program from insuring individuals and businesses for flood losses to insuring communities.

The two policy changes suggested above would be beneficial, but given the lack of concern for hazard mitigation revealed by the local government paradox, I believe a sea change in government policy is likely to be needed before the trend in increasing disaster losses can be halted. The major change in approach I have in mind would involve amendment of the Flood Insurance Act to shift the program from insuring individuals and businesses for flood losses to insuring communities (and all of their dwellings and commercial/governmental buildings). With this new approach, flood insurance coverage and premiums would be based on the degree of exposure to loss in jurisdictions (i.e., the aggregate of the current number of dwellings and other buildings located within the five-hundred-year floodplain and other areas at risk of flooding that localities wished to insure plus some set coverage for personal property). Local governments could pay the premiums from general fund revenues, raising tax revenue from all citizens or businesses, but, most likely, they would set up special assessment districts or storm water/flood insurance utilities to raise the required funds from properties that benefit from the flood insurance coverage. Storm water utilities are being used increasingly by localities to fund storm water management activities required by the U.S. Environmental Protection Agency to curb nonpoint source pollution. In cases where local governments refuse to participate, which might be the case when they have few properties at risk or cannot raise the revenue needed to pay flood insurance premiums, state governments could take responsibility for acquiring needed insurance and requiring that both local governments and property owners take steps to reduce their risk of flood loss.

This revolutionary change to the flood insurance program might have a number of benefits:

1. If a community chose to participate in the program, *all* of its flood-prone dwellings and businesses would be covered, which would avoid the problem of a high proportion of properties without insurance as has been the case in many flood disasters. For communities with any degree of flood risk, there would obviously be tremendous political pressure to participate in the program.
2. Incentives for community participation, such as the withholding of disaster relief benefits for the amount of losses that would have been paid by flood insurance if the community were participating in the program, could be created and, with adequate political will, enforced.
3. The cost of insurance coverage could create incentives for state and local governments to reduce the risk of flood loss and the size of the insurance premiums they pay. They also might think more carefully about plans for development and redevelopment of flood hazard areas and be less willing to approve new development in these areas. If communities use some version of a storm water utility to fund insurance premiums, there would be a direct link between flood insurance and local land use and water resources management.
4. The change from an individual- to a community-based program would also make it possible for the NFIP (or private insurance companies) to more precisely align premium amounts with risk and allow the creation of stronger incentives for risk reduction. It could encourage local governments to take steps to reduce risk through retrofit or relocation of properties most at risk of flooding. In addition, it might be possible to begin insuring infrastructure at risk in flood hazard areas, as called for by Platt (1999, 291).

Significant political opposition and government costs could be involved in the transition from the current flood insurance program to this new one. But I suspect that the advantages of wider flood insurance coverage and the benefits in reduced federal flood insurance and disaster assistance costs would outweigh them. In addition, potential state and local opposition might be muted if Congress passes the Safe Communities Act of 2005 (HR 3524, 109th Congress, 1st Session), which authorizes significant financial assistance to help communities integrate hazard mitigation into their ongoing comprehensive planning and urban development decision making. Similar legislation to the Safe Communities Act was recommended by the Interagency Floodplain Management Review Committee (1994, xi) following the 1993 Midwest floods.

Concluding Note

Obviously, before they could be seriously considered, the policy initiatives suggested here would require additional examination of the procedural changes that would be needed to bring them about and in-depth analysis of their benefits and costs and potential for unintended consequences. Nevertheless, there are several reasons for thinking them worth that effort. The policies proposed are cooperative in nature. They are designed to increase local government commitment to hazard mitigation primarily through the creation of new, more powerful incentives. The increased government costs in the short run would be counterbalanced by improved financial security for both citizens and local governments. As local officials take steps to improve safety from hazards, costs would decline over time. In addition, federal financial assistance to meet insurance costs could be provided to particularly poor communities, so that budgetary considerations do not preclude them from insuring their residents. By providing a means to extend flood insurance to *all* local residents and businesses at risk, the suggested policies promise to speed recovery when disasters occur. By strengthening incentives for states and localities to do what they should already be doing on their own initiative—paying systematic attention through existing local planning mechanisms to finding ways to reduce hazards vulnerability—they promise to halt and possibly reverse the trend in increasingly serious natural catastrophes.

Appendix
Factors Associated with Variation in National Flood Insurance Program (NFIP) Claims in Coastal Counties, 1978-2002: Ordinary Least Squares (OLS) Multiple Regression Models

	Number of NFIP Claim Payments Per Capita, 1978-2002[a]			Dollar Amount of NFIP Claim Payments Per Capita, 1978-2002[a]		
	B[b] (SE)	Std B	t-Value	B[b] (SE)	Std B	t-Value
Constant	-3.040 (2.195)		-1.385	-1.198 (2.666)		0.449
State building code enforcement mandate	0.355 (0.345)	.09	1.239	0.396 (0.419)	.09	0.943
State comprehensive plan mandate	-0.859 (0.330)	-.22	-2.604**	-1.111 (0.401)	-.25	-2.770**
Interaction of code enforcement and comprehensive plan mandate	-0.409 (0.438)	-.11	-0.934	-0.106 (0.532)	-.03	-0.200
Control variables						
Number of severe weather events, 1978-2000[c]						
Coastal storms	<0.000 (0.011)	.002	0.046	0.003 (0.013)	.02	0.264
Floods	0.039 (0.013)	.19	3.142***	0.052 (0.015)	.22	3.384***
Hurricanes	0.217 (0.021)	.60	10.455***	0.234 (0.025)	.57	9.287***
Tornadoes	-0.005 (0.011)	-.03	-0.454	-0.015 (0.013)	-.07	-1.109
Thunderstorms	-0.007 (0.012)	-.03	-0.548	-0.009 (0.015)	-.03	-0.637
Property at risk (proxy variables)						
Population, 1980 (log)	-0.233 (0.085)	-.22	-2.750**	-0.065 (0.103)	-.05	-0.631
Population change, 1980-2000 (log)	0.015 (0.024)	.03	0.640	0.025 (0.029)	.04	0.850
Median home value, 1990 (log)	0.535 (0.205)	.16	2.610**	0.434 (0.249)	.12	1.742*
Population density, 1997 (log)	-0.015 (0.060)	-.02	-0.256	-0.177 (0.073)	-.19	-2.435**
Adjusted R^2	.47			.39		
F-value	39.75			19.14		
Significance	.000			.000		
Number of cases	345			340		

a. Natural log values of dependent variables.
b. B-values are unstandardized coefficients.
c. Weather events that resulted in $50,000 or more in property damage. The source of this data is the Hazards Research Lab (2005).
*$p < .05$. **$p < .01$. ***$p < .001$ (one-tailed test).

Notes

1. This estimate was derived from calculations of the average annual costs of federal disaster prepared-ness, response, recovery/reconstruction, and mitigation programs of the following federal departments and agencies: Agriculture, Commerce, Corps of Engineers, Education, FEMA, Interior, and Transportation. It does not include costs borne by state and local governments or private individuals and businesses.

2. Subsequent to authorization of the Lake Pontchartrain project, Congress authorized the Corps to con-struct four additional hurricane projection projects, including one to add to and strengthen levees protecting the west bank sections of Jefferson and Orleans parishes (Carter 2005). However, the Lake Pontchartrain Hurricane Protection Project fell behind its construction schedule, in part because by the 1980s costs of the project had escalated more than 1,000 percent. In addition, according to Grunwald and Glasser (2005, 5), "Local officials resisted the goal of Category 3 protection for their communities as overly extravagant. In 1982, the Orleans Levee District urged the Corps to 'lower its design standards to provide more realistic hur-ricane protection' and argued that 100-year protection would be fine."

3. The potential for moral hazard to undercut local officials' interest in hazard mitigation is based primar-ily on anecdotes and the opinions of various disaster experts. I am unaware of any systematic empirical studies that have demonstrated a link between the provision of disaster relief and a lower degree of local government hazard mitigation activities. In fact, Burby (1991, 109) studied the effects of local government receipt of pub-lic assistance funds following disasters and found that governments that had received federal disaster aid were more, rather than less, likely to take steps to mitigate flood hazards in comparison with governments that had not received federal disaster assistance. They found no effect either way on local government attention to earthquake hazards.

4. The expectation that plans will contribute to a reduction in vulnerability to natural hazards is based on eight considerations: (1) plans provide a systematic way to gather facts about hazards and increase public awareness of them; (2) plans provide a way to systematically examine the adequacy of existing hazard mitiga-tion measures being used; (3) plans enable citizens and local officials to create a vision of hazard resilience and formulate specific policy goals and objectives; (4) plans help to develop consensus about the need to take action to reduce vulnerability and to find courses of action that are politically acceptable; (5) plans improve the likelihood that communities will investigate and use a variety of approaches to hazard mitigation; (6) plans provide guidance to the day-to-day decisions of local officials in approving or disapproving development pro-posals; (7) plans help coordinate the actions of various local government departments that affect vulnerabil-ity; and (8) plans provide the rational nexus between the public interest and governmental actions that is criti-cal in defending them against legal attack. For further elaboration of these benefits of planning, see Burby (2005).

5. Similar findings to these have been reported by Burby (2005) for the impacts of state planning man-dates in reducing private property insurance claims. Also, May and Birkland (1994) and May and Feeley (2000) have shown that state building code enforcement mandates spur responsible local building code enforcement.

References

All-Industry Research Advisory Council (AIRAC). 1989. *Surviving the storm: Building codes, compliance and the mitigation of hurricane damage.* Chicago: AIRAC.

Anderson, Daniel R. 2000. Catastrophe insurance and compensation: Remembering basic principles. *CPCU Journal* 53:76-89.

Association of State Floodplain Managers. 2000. *National program review.* Madison, WI: Association of State Floodplain Managers.

Brookings Institution Metropolitan Program. 2005. *New Orleans after the storm: Lessons from the past, a plan for the future.* October. Washington, DC: Brookings Institution.

Building Performance Assessment Team. 1992. *Preliminary report in response to Hurricane Andrew, Dade County, Florida.* Washington, DC: Federal Emergency Management Agency.

Burby, Raymond J. 2002. Flood insurance and floodplain management: The U.S. experience. *Journal of Environmental Hazards* 3:111-22.

————. 2005. Have state comprehensive planning mandates reduced insured losses from natural disasters? *Natural Hazards Review* 6:67-81.

Burby, Raymond J. (with Beverly A. Cigler, Steven P. French, Edward J. Kaiser, Jack Kartez, Dale Roenigk, Dana Weist, and Dale Whittington). 1991. *Sharing environmental risks: How to control governments' losses in natural disasters.* Boulder, CO: Westview.

Burby, Raymond J., Scott J. Bollens, Edward J. Kaiser, David Mullan, and John R. Sheaffer. 1988. *Cities under water: A comparative evaluation of ten cities' efforts to manage floodplain land use.* Boulder: Institute of Behavioral Science, University of Colorado.

Burby, Raymond J., and Linda Dalton. 1994. Plans can matter! The role of land use plans and state planning mandates in limiting the development of hazardous areas. *Public Administration Review* 54:229-37.

Burby, Raymond J., and Steven P. French. 1985. *Flood plain land use management: A national assessment.* Boulder, CO: Westview.

Burby, Raymond J., Steven P. French, and Arthur C. Nelson. 1998. Plans, code enforcement, and damage reduction: Evidence from the Northridge earthquake. *Earthquake Spectra* 14:59-74.

Burby, Raymond J., and Peter J. May. 1998. Intergovernmental environmental planning: Addressing the commitment conundrum. *Journal of Environmental Planning and Management* 41:95-110.

Carter, Nicole T. 2005. New Orleans levees and floodwalls: Hurricane damage protection. Congressional Research Service Report RS22238. September 6. Washington, DC: Congressional Research Service, Library of Congress.

City Planning Commission, City of New Orleans. 1999. *New century New Orleans, 1999 land use plan, City of New Orleans.* New Orleans, LA: City Planning Commission, City of New Orleans.

Comptroller of the Currency, U.S. General Accounting Office. 1976. *Cost, schedule, and performance problems of the Lake Pontchartrain and vicinity, Louisiana, Hurricane Protection Project.* PSAD-76-161. August 31. Washington, DC: General Accounting Office.

Conrad, David R., Ben H. McNitt, and Martha Stout. 1998. *Higher ground: A report on voluntary buyouts in the nation's floodplains, a common ground solution serving people at risk, taxpayers and the environment.* July. Washington, DC: National Wildlife Federation.

Crenshaw, Albert B. 2005. Flood insurance program seeks more money. *Washington Post*, October 19, p. A8.

Cutter, Susan L., and Christopher Emrich. 2005. Are natural hazards and disaster losses in the U.S. increasing? *EOS, Transactions, American Geophysical Union* 86:381, 388-89.

Deyle, Robert E., Timothy S. Chapin, and Earl J. Baker 2005. Reduced hazard exposure through growth management? An evaluation of the effectiveness of Florida's hurricane hazard mitigation planning mandates. Paper prepared for presentation at the 2005 annual conference of the Association of Collegiate Schools of Planning, Kansas City, MO, October 27-30.

Drew, Christopher. 1984. New, old parts of the city compete for flood protection. *New Orleans Times-Picayune*, January 18, pp. 1, 10.

Federal Emergency Management Agency. 1987. *Reducing losses in high risk flood hazard areas: A guidebook for local officials.* FEMA 116. Washington, DC: FEMA.

————. 2005a. *FEMA disaster costs.* Washington, DC: FEMA. http://www.fema.gov/library/df_7.shtm (accessed October 14, 2005).

————. 2005b. *Total major disaster declarations.* Washington, DC: FEMA. http://www.fema.gov/library/dis_graph.shtm (accessed October 14, 2005).

————. 2005c. *2005 disaster declarations.* Washington, DC: FEMA. http://www.fema.gov/news/disasters.fema?year=2005 (accessed October 14, 2005).

Godschalk, David R., Timothy Beatley, Philip Berke, David Brower, Edward Kaiser, Charles Bohl, and R. Matthew Goebel. 1998. *Natural hazard mitigation: Recasting disaster policy and planning.* Washington, DC: Island Press.

Grunwald, Michael, and Susan B. Glasser. 2005. The slow drowning of New Orleans. *Washington Post*, October 9. http://www.washingtonpost.com/wp-dyn/content/article/2005/10/08/AR2005100801458_pf.html.

Hazards Research Lab. 2005. Spatial hazard events and losses database for the United States, Version 3.1 [Online database]. Columbia: University of South Carolina. http://www.sheldus.org (accessed March 20, 2005).

H. John Heinz III Center for Science, Economics and the Environment. 2000. *The hidden costs of coastal hazards. Implications for risk assessment and mitigation.* Washington, DC: Island Press.

Interagency Floodplain Management Review Committee. 1994. *Sharing the challenge: Floodplain management into the 21st century.* Report of the Interagency Floodplain Management Review Committee to the Administration Floodplain Management Task Force. June. Washington, DC: Government Printing Office.

King, Rawle O. 2005. *Hurricane Katrina: Insurance losses and national capacities for financing risk.* RL33086. September 15. Washington, DC: Congressional Research Service, Library of Congress.

Kunreuther, Howard. 2006. Disaster mitigation and insurance: Learning from Katrina. *Annals of the American Academy of Political and Social Science.* 604:208-27.

Laska, Shirley B. 1991. *Floodproof retrofitting: Homeowner self-protective behavior.* Boulder: Institute of Behavioral Science, University of Colorado.

Lewis, Pierce F. 2003. *New Orleans: The making of an urban landscape.* 2nd ed. Santa Fe, NM, and Harrisonburg, VA: Center for American Places.

Malone, Linda A. 1990. *Environmental regulation of land use.* Deerfield, IL: Clark Boardman Callaghan.

May, Peter J. 1991. Addressing public risks: Federal earthquake policy design. *Journal of Policy Analysis and Management* 10:263-85.

May, Peter J., and Thomas A. Birkland. 1994. Earthquake risk reduction: An examination of local regulatory efforts. *Environmental Management* 18:923-37.

May, Peter J., and T. Jens Feeley. 2000. Regulatory backwaters: Earthquake risk reduction in the western United States. *State and Local Government Review* 32:20-33.

Mileti, Dennis S. 1999. *Disasters by design: A reassessment of natural hazards in the United States.* Washington, DC: Joseph Henry Press.

Murphy, Francis C. 1958. *Regulating flood plain development.* Department of Geography Research Paper no. 56. Chicago: Department of Geography, University of Chicago.

Nelson, Arthur C., and Steven P. French. 2002. Plan quality and mitigating damage from natural disasters: A case study of the Northridge earthquake with planning policy considerations. *Journal of the American Planning Association* 68:194-207.

Olshansky, Robert B. 2001. Land use planning for seismic safety: The Los Angeles County experience, 1971-1994. *Journal of the American Planning Association* 67:173-85.

Pasterick, Edward T. 1998. The National Flood Insurance Program. In *Paying the price: The status and role of insurance against natural disasters in the United States*, ed. Howard Kunreuther and Richard J. Roth Sr., 125-54. Washington, DC: Joseph Henry Press.

Pielke, Roger A. Jr., and Charles H. Landsea. 1997. Normalized hurricane damage in the United States: 1925-1995. Paper presented at the 22nd Conference on Hurricanes and Tropical Meteorology, American Meteorology Society, Fort Collins, CO.

Platt, Rutherford H. 1999. *Disasters and democracy: The politics of natural events.* Washington, DC: Island Press.

Schwab, James. 2002. *Summary of state land use laws.* Tampa, FL: Institute of Business and Home Safety.

Sheaffer, John R., Frederick J. Roland, George W. Davis, Thomas Feldman, and John Stockdale. 1976. *Flood hazard mitigation through safe land use practices.* Prepared for the Office of Policy Development and Research, U.S. Department of Housing and Urban Development. Chicago: Kiefer & Associates.

Southern Building Code Congress International, Inc. 1992. *Coastal building department survey.* Chicago: Natural Disaster Loss Reduction Committee, National Committee on Property Insurance.

U.S. Department of Commerce, National Oceanic and Atmospheric Administration, National Climatic Data Center. 2005. Billion dollar U.S. weather disasters. http://www.ncdc.noaa.gov/oa/reports/billionz.html (accessed October 9, 2005).

White, Gilbert F. 1975. *Flood hazard in the United States: A research assessment.* Boulder: Institute of Behavioral Science, University of Colorado.

Planning for Postdisaster Resiliency

The focus of this article is planning for resiliency in the aftermath of a catastrophe. First, the authors offer their conception of planning for resiliency as a goal for recovering communities, and the benefits of planning in efforts to create more resilient places. Next, they discuss major issues associated with planning for postdisaster recovery, including barriers posed by federal and state governments to planning for resiliency, the promise and risks of compact urban form models for guiding rebuilding, and the failure to involve citizens in planning for disasters. Finally, they discuss lessons from prior research that address these issues and policy recommendations that foster predisaster recovery planning for resilient communities.

Keywords: community resiliency; disaster relief; recovery planning; grassroots organizing; risk reduction; insurance; urban planning

By
PHILIP R. BERKE
and
THOMAS J. CAMPANELLA

The catastrophic aftermath of Hurricane Katrina and Hurricane Rita presents an enormous challenge of rebuilding along the Gulf Coast. Within days after these events, government officials, residents, real estate developers, business owners, architects, and urban designers became engaged in an intense debate about how rebuilding should occur. Critical questions are at the core of the debate: How can we plan for more resilient places that are socially just, economically vital, ecologically compatible, and less vulnerable to future disasters? How can the hundreds of thousands of displaced residents be given a voice in determining the future of their communities? What reforms are needed to federal and state policies that facilitate rather than impede intensive development of hazardous areas?

Predisaster Recovery Planning for Resiliency

Achieving resiliency in a disaster context means the ability to survive future natural disas-

DOI: 10.1177/0002716205285533

ters with minimum loss of life and property, as well as the ability to create a greater sense of place among residents; a stronger, more diverse economy; and a more economically integrated and diverse population (Vale and Campanella 2005). Resiliency also applies to the process of recovery planning in which all affected stakeholders—rather than just a powerful few—have a voice in how their community is to be rebuilt.

Hurricane Katrina opened a window of opportunity for creating more resilient communities. Windows are moments of opportunity when a problem has become urgent enough to push for change of entrenched practices (Birkland 1997). But windows typically do not stay open for long after a disaster. The urgency of residents to get back to their homes coupled with pressure by business owners to return to normalcy builds quickly after a disaster and is amplified by a substantial inflow of capital for reconstruction. A community should be ready with solutions when a window opens while the importance and priority that local officials assign to hazard threats are temporarily elevated.

To take advantage of an open window, a community should have a recovery plan in place long before a disaster strikes. A recovery plan is a policy document that guides short-range emergency and rehabilitation actions (temporary housing, damage assessment, debris removal, restoration of utilities, reoccupancy permitting, reconstruction priorities) and long-range redevelopment decisions (building moratoria, replanning of stricken areas, relocation of housing to safer sites). A well-conceived plan conveys a sense to the public that local officials with recovery responsibilities are organized and in charge because they had the foresight to carefully consider the issues and contingencies throughout the recovery process. Furthermore, by involving and consulting residents in all phases of planning, the predisaster recovery planning process helps create a knowledgeable constituency that is more likely to support redevelopment policies and programs that take effect once a disaster strikes.

Philip R. Berke is a professor of land use and environmental planning, Department of City and Regional Planning at the University of North Carolina at Chapel Hill, and cochair of environmental studies of the Carolina Environmental Program. His current research focuses on building capabilities of disadvantaged communities to respond to environment risk, and evaluating the impacts of compact and low-density sprawl development patterns on watersheds and floodplain environments. He is the coauthor of Urban Land Use Planning, *5th ed. (University of Illinois Press forthcoming) and* After the Hurricane: Linking Recovery to Sustainable Development in the Caribbean *(Johns Hopkins University Press 1997).*

Thomas Campanella is an assistant professor in the Department of City and Regional Planning at the University of North Carolina at Chapel Hill (UNC). His work focuses on the history and design of the urban built environment. He has particular interests in the historical development of the American urban landscape, the design and planning of new towns, and the rapid modernization of China's cities in the post-Mao era. He is a faculty fellow of the Institute for the Arts and Humanities at UNC and a visiting lecturer at Nanjing University's Graduate School of Architecture. He is a recipient of the Spiro Kostof Book Award from the Society of Architectural Historians and the John Reps Prize and de Montequin Prize from the Society for American City and Regional Planning History.

The core purposes of a disaster recovery plan are to (1) offer a vision of the future after a disaster; (2) provide a direction-setting framework (strong fact base, goals, and policies) to achieve the vision; (3) inject long-range resiliency considerations into short-term recovery actions that promote redevelopment that is socially just, economically viable, environmentally compatible, and less vulnerable to hazards, and (4) represent a "big picture" of the community that is related to broader regional, state, and national disaster response and reconstruction policies. To stay relevant, the recovery plan must build in flexibility and be adaptable to the dynamic and changing conditions presented by the recovery process.

In the case of mitigation, a predisaster recovery plan can identify potential sites free of hazards that could serve as relocation zones for developments in hazardous areas that are likely to be significantly damaged during a disaster. Where hazard areas have significant cultural or economic advantages for redevelopment that cannot be foregone, a well-conceived recovery plan can reduce potential losses by including provisions that guide redevelopment to the least hazardous parts of building sites and modify construction and site design practices so that vulnerability is minimized.

Local governments have used two approaches in preparing a predisaster recovery plan. One involves preparing a recovery plan as a stand-alone plan. A stand-alone plan can be easier to revise, has more technical sophistication, is less demanding of coordination, and is simpler to implement. The second entails a recovery plan as one element integrated into a broader comprehensive plan for an entire municipality, county, or region. An integrated plan brings more resources together for implementation, broadens the scope of understanding about interactive effects of recovery issues with other local issues (e.g., transportation, housing, land use, environment), and provides access to a wider slate of planning and regulatory tools. An integrative plan also has the advantage of linking recovery to the broader economic, social, and environmental sustainability concerns of achieving a broader conception of community resiliency. The most effective choice is likely to be preparation of a stand-alone recovery plan in collaboration with preparation of a comprehensive plan, so that their databases, policies, and procedures are compatible.

Evidence is emerging that supports the idea that well-conceived stand-alone plans and elements of comprehensive plans prepared prior to a disaster have a positive influence on facilitating more robust local mitigation practices and reduction in property damage in natural disasters (Berke and Beatley 1992; Burby and May 1997; Deyle and Smith 1994; Mader 1997; Nelson and French 2002; Olshansky and Kartez 1998). These studies also found that stand-alone plans and plan elements are frequently of low quality. Even more problematic, many communities have not given any attention to disaster recovery and mitigation as part of their planning programs. Research findings from multiple surveys of local planners, building inspectors, public works engineers, and residents indicate that respondents are aware of hazards but put a low priority on taking action and have little concern for doing so (Berke 1998). Respondents consistently view natural hazards, especially the long-shot ones posed by low-probability/high-consequence events, as facts of life and acts of nature that are often inexplicable and completely unavoidable. The importance of preparing for a disaster in the distant future and risk-averse action is likely to be eclipsed by more immediate and pressing concerns (street potholes, waste disposal, and crime) that affect people almost daily.

The evidence suggests a need for strong federal and state actions to stimulate local planning for postdisaster recovery and mitigation. As we will discuss, however, the legacy of federal and state policies is seriously flawed in providing support for effective local planning.

Planning for Resiliency: Key Issues

In this section, we discuss three key issues that must be addressed in planning for resiliency on the Gulf Coast: (1) state and federal land use and development policies that have fostered improper rebuilding back in hazardous areas and impede prospects for sensible local predisaster planning; (2) compact urban form models that could enhance resiliency or pose greater risks than prior to the disaster; and (3) the broken promise to involve those citizens most affected by the disaster—the poor—in planning for response and recovery.

State and federal barriers to planning for resiliency

There are significant barriers to effective local planning for mitigation and resiliency in the United States, and especially in the Katrina impact region. As of the late 1990s, only twenty-five states mention that natural hazards should be accounted for in local comprehensive plans in state planning enabling legislation (Schwab 1998). Of these states, only eleven mandate some sort of predisaster and postdisaster planning for natural hazards, either in the form of a hazards element in a comprehensive plan or in the form of hazards-related content in the plan.

Furthermore, the idea of planning as a means for creating more resilient places in the Gulf Coast states is practically nonexistent. In an article included in this special issue, Burby (2006) indicates that except Florida, all Gulf Coast states (Alabama, Georgia, Louisiana, Mississippi, and Texas) have not passed local comprehensive planning mandates. This inaction has deterred adoption of sensible controls on development in high-hazard coastal areas that may have prevented much of the destruction from Katrina. In contrast, Florida has had a strong local planning mandate since the 1970s and has placed considerably more emphasis on requiring local and regional recovery and mitigation planning since Hurricane Andrew in 1992.

States are not the only barrier to local planning. The federal government has had a long history of weak support for planning and strong support for encouraging intensive development in areas exposed to natural hazards. In a penetrating critique of federal hazards policy, Burby et al. (1999) concluded that subsidies for high-hazard development are fostered by greater federal emphasis on risk-reduction and risk-sharing strategies than on risk-avoidance strategies that are premised on proactive land use planning that guide development away from hazardous areas to safer locations. Risk reduction involves fostering high-risk development through federally constructed seawalls, dams, and levees as well as costly beach renourishment schemes that may not provide protection from powerful hazard events. This approach justifies increased levels of development that might not otherwise take place without protective structures. The likelihood of catastrophic losses increases when the structures fail to protect development in the event of a cataclysmic storm like Katrina. Risk sharing involves high-risk development encouraged by generous disaster relief payments; income tax write-offs for lost property; and the thirty-seven-year-old National Flood Insurance Program, which often does not charge high enough premiums to cover storm losses—and now faces a massive deficit due to Katrina and Rita.

Given the nonsupportive federal and state mitigation policy context, prospects for high-quality local recovery plans are low in many parts of the nation.

A fifty-state study by Godschalk et al. (1999) further highlights the limitations of federal hazard mitigation policy. The study concluded that state and local hazard mitigation planning under the Federal Emergency Management Agency's hazard mitigation program needs stronger national policy that supports proactive planning for reconstruction and predisaster mitigation initiatives. Federally supported mitigation efforts at the state and local level tend to be driven by plans hastily prepared during the disaster recovery period rather than before the event when there is time to prepare well-conceived plans. As a result, mitigation efforts were most often scattershot and not based on clear and consistent mitigation priorities.

Given the nonsupportive federal and state mitigation policy context, prospects for high-quality local recovery plans are low in many parts of the nation. It is not surprising that plans for recovery are nonexistent in the disaster-stricken cities and counties of the Gulf Coast.

New Urbanism: A model for creating more resilient communities?

In the wake of Katrina and Rita, there has been increasing attention to how best to rebuild devastated communities. Given the lack of planning in Gulf Coast states, it is no surprise that the coastal areas in these states are poorly planned with limited consideration of development patterns in high-hazard areas. The dominant development pattern has been associated with sprawling, low-density developments caused by expansion of commercial strip development along coastal highways and the outward growth of suburban-style development into rural areas. The increased spread between land uses puts increased pressure to build in environmentally sensitive open spaces (e.g., hazardous areas). Other negative effects include greater auto dependence, more linear feet of roads and sewer and water lines, and possible exacerbation of social inequities by draining fiscal and human resources from older core areas (e.g., New Orleans) to the suburban fringe (Berke, Godschalk, and Kaiser forthcoming).

Compact urban form concepts under the banner of Smart Growth and New Urbanism have emerged to counter the outcomes of this development process. Between its inception in 1986 and 2003, New Urban developments have rapidly expanded throughout the nation with 647 projects completed, under construction, or planned, which include 559,836 dwelling units and 1.56 million residents (Song et al. 2005). New Urbanism has its roots in the dense pedestrian scale towns of the nineteenth century. This compact development pattern mixes different land uses, including homes, shops, schools, offices, and public open spaces. Streets are narrow and pedestrian-friendly (encourages bicycling and walking in place of driving automobiles). Homes punctuated by front porches and short setbacks from streets (not garages and long driveways) encourage street frontage spaces that are designed for people, not automobiles.

A major benefit of New Urbanism is to maximize open space without reducing the number of dwelling units that can be built. The aim is to concentrate development in return for more open space. The high density provides more opportunity to guide development into safe sites while protecting sensitive areas (e.g., wetlands, sand dunes, and riverine floodplains) and avoiding hazardous locations. Other goals include bridging the socioeconomic divides through mixing different housing types that have a wide range of prices, increased access to mass transit, and enhancing overall urban livability and sense of place.

In the wake of Katrina, a variety of national professional organizations like the Congress of New Urbanism and Smart Growth America have called for Gulf Coast states and communities and the federal government to adopt "smart growth" policies that reflect New Urban principles. Mississippi has gone furthest to embrace a vision of redevelopment premised on New Urbanism. The Mississippi Governor's Commission on Recovery, Rebuilding, and Renewal (MGCRRR; 2005) employed a design team to conduct a week-long forum (October 12-17, 2005) to produce New Urban community planning and design tools to guide local and state officials in rebuilding eleven cities in three counties along the entire length of the Mississippi Gulf Coast. The MGCRRR (2005) Web site includes a set of New Urban goals and objectives that cover transportation, affordable housing, land use, resources protection, and utilities that guide rebuilding, as well as maps of local land use design plans that incorporate New Urban concepts.

However, in the rush to prepare recovery plans and design tools, officials may overlook the shortcomings of New Urban development codes involving the lack of attention to conservation and hazardous areas (Berke et al. 2003). New Urban codes support the basic goals of community character, sense of place, and pedestrian movement (Calthorpe 1993; Congress of New Urbanism 2002; Duany Plater-Zyberk and Company 2001) but do not include design standards for natural hazards mitigation as well as other environmental protection concerns (e.g., wildlife habitat and wetland protection, watershed-based zoning, headwater street geometry, and the dimensions of stream buffers) (Berke 2002).

There may be real concern about placing high-density, compact urban forms in harm's way as New Urban developments can lead to greater risk to loss of life and property than low-density development. The MGCRRR (2005) Web site reveals that many of the municipal land use design plan maps illustrate that redevelopment will avoid the highest-risk zones, notably velocity zones on FEMA's flood insurance maps. However, high-density nodes of development that conform to New Urban land use, street, and architectural standards are still placed in flood-prone areas that sustained significant damage from Katrina. These areas will likely be at even greater risk given evidence that the Mississippi coast will be increasingly threatened by sea level rise (Titus and Richman 2001).

Evidence from other locations points to concern with potential increased risk generated by New Urban developments. In a survey of the local planners in charge of permitting for 319 New Urban projects that were identified as under construction or completed, Song et al. (2005) found that 113 (or 35 percent) have some portion of their total footprint in the one-hundred-year floodplain. While this figure indicates the sites that contain floodplains but not whether structures are in the floodplain, the percentage of projects that must deal with flood hazards is significant.

Another case deals with the Envision Utah regional planning effort along the one-hundred-mile-long Wasatch region, which is riddled with earthquake faults, liquefaction prone soils, and landslides. The region currently holds 1.7 million people (including Salt Lake City) and has been experiencing rapid expansion of sprawl. The Envision Utah initiative channels future growth into a series of New Urban developments along the entire region that are denser than conventional developments. However, given the higher densities, these New Urban developments may be at higher risk. Only twelve of the twenty-four major local governments in this region currently use U.S. Geological Survey maps that delineate fault, liquefaction, and landslide hazards in their land use regulations, with the remainder not accounting for the threat in their land regulatory framework, says Gary Christensen, Geologic Manager of the Utah Geologic Survey (interview, September 26, 2003).

Our critique does not mean that we should abandon New Urbanism as the cure of a range of urban issues. In fact, New Urbanism holds considerable promise. Prior research revealed that New Urban developments are considerably more successful than conventional developments in protecting sensitive open spaces (including floodplains), reducing impervious cover that adversely affects watersheds, and using low watershed and wildlife habitat impact design practices (Berke et al. 2003). These successes, however, were dependent on effective local implementation of planning practices that accounted for protection of environmentally sensitive areas. Thus, our concern is with the poor track record of ineffective planning for postdisaster recovery and mitigation in Gulf Coast states that has permitted unbridled coastal development in hazardous areas.

A broken contract: Involving disadvantaged communities

As noted by *Time* magazine (September 2, 2005, 49), "Katrina was in the cards, foreseen and yet still dismissed. That so many officials were caught so unprepared was a failure less of imagination than will." Indeed, the Katrina catastrophe laid bare the deep inequalities of American society. While these inequalities may have been news to some, they were not news to the displaced people at the New Orleans convention center and elsewhere. What was bitter news to them was that their claims of citizenship mattered so little to the institutions charged with their protection. What makes the failure over Katrina so objectionable is the failure of government that should protect them.

---

*[C]itizen participation efforts must
also be made to repair the torn social fabric—
a process that "fundamentally entails
reconnecting severed familial, social and
religious networks of survivors. . ."*

A duty of democratic governance is to consult citizens and involve them in decisions and plans that will affect them. This did not happen with evacuation planning in New Orleans. If the people in the poor wards of New Orleans had been consulted, they would have easily identified its significant weaknesses. Thus, in the wake of Katrina and Rita, one basic test of the rebuilding effort should be, Will the people be fully consulted about the future of their neighborhoods?

Research findings reveal that prospects for well-conceived local mitigation plans and successful implementation increase with broader participation and support of stakeholders who are affected by the outcomes of plans (Burby 2003). The wider the range of participants, the greater the opportunity for public officials to educate a wider array of stakeholders about poorly understood problems and potential solutions. Furthermore, early and ongoing involvement throughout plan making and implementation are important factors in influencing better outcomes (Berke et al. 2002). Residents are more likely to closely track plan implementation efforts when they are active in the early stages of planning and remain involved

through monitoring of the effectiveness of the plan. Early and continuous involvement generates increased commitment and a sense of ownership and control over
policy proposals. Moreover, residents are more likely to be vigilant of ongoing
deliberations and to pressure public officials to offset the influence of traditionally
powerful groups with ties to the real estate industry. Strong participation will help
to ensure that action is taken that is consistent with policy solutions raised in plans,
avoiding a potential mismatch between plans and variances that might eventually
be given during plan implementation.

Research findings also suggest that when issues like predisaster recovery lack
involvement of local people, the formulation of plans and implementation strategies to guide local development decisions is often made without the benefit of local
knowledge and capacities (Healy 1997; Zaferatos 1998). Planning processes
devoid of local involvement often become dominated by technical experts like professional planners, engineers, and biologists (Burby 2003; Dalton 1989). As a
result, the conditions imposed on developments by externally driven plans do not
benefit from local knowledge and may be inconsistent with local values, needs, and
customs. Fundamental questions are then raised about democratic governance,
fairness, and citizen rights to be informed, consulted, and able to freely express
views. Rather than fostering support for government action on disaster recovery
issues, a planning process organized outside the community may create opposition
to plans.

While restoring critical infrastructure and preserving and rebuilding a city's
urban architectural fabric is critical to full recovery, citizen participation efforts
must also be made to repair the torn social fabric—a process that "fundamentally
entails reconnecting severed familial, social and religious networks of survivors,"
often on a grassroots level, neighborhood by neighborhood. Recovering a community in the wake of disaster involves "reconstructing the myriad social relations
embedded in schools, workplaces, childcare arrangements, shops, places of worship, and places of play and recreation" (Vale and Campanella 2005, x). One of the
most formidable challenges facing the disaster-stricken region is that so much of
the communities' social fabric was shredded by the storm and its aftermath. For
example, thousands of families who lived in badly flooded districts such as the
Ninth Ward, Bywater, and New Orleans East were evacuated to places all across
the United States in one of the largest internal migrations of Americans since the
1950s. With every passing day, it becomes less and less likely that these displaced
Orleanians will return home, and that carries profound implications for the recovery of New Orleans as a robust and full-blooded metropolis rather than a kind of
theme park celebrating its former self. Even for the estimated 60 percent of evacuees who have expressed a wish to go home, according to a CNN/Gallup poll conducted in early October 2005, doing so has been held up by a lack of temporary
housing in the city, extensive contamination of neighborhoods, and a general short-
age of goods and services.

In sum, while visions of rebuilt communities can generate inspiration for a
better future, raise the level of discussion, and even offer very worthy solutions, the

best results will only come from a good planning process that is sensitive to the needs and aspirations of those affected by plans. Breaking the hardened cycle of poverty and despair is a major challenge in the postdisaster recovery effort. The real work of healing after Katrina and Rita must be done by residents, public officials, and businesspeople who must plan for the rebirth of their communities. To a large degree, the future confidence and trust in government will depend on local people with the help of supportive national and state governments. The critical issue with any local recovery effort is to get buy-in from the community. It is the community, not outsiders, that should be centrally involved in the recovery effort.

Lessons and Policy Recommendations

We can only hope that Hurricane Katrina, America's most devastating storm in a century, will wrench us to our senses in building more resilient places. In this article, we draw three conclusions. First, plans in place before a disaster make a difference in mitigating risk after a disaster, but many local governments have weak plans and are not committed to disaster recovery and mitigation planning. Weak commitment to planning is especially prevalent among communities struck by Katrina and Rita along the Gulf Coast that lack a supportive culture and tradition in planning.

Second, because communities are reluctant to take action, federal and state governments should play a stronger role to encourage or require local planning for postdisaster recovery and mitigation. However, Gulf Coast states in the Katrina and Rita impact region (Alabama, Georgia, Louisiana, Mississippi, and Texas) have not passed local comprehensive planning mandates and do not require local mitigation and recovery plans. The federal government has provided weak support for proactive planning. Federal policies have emphasized risk reduction (e.g., seawalls, dams, and levees) and risk-sharing strategies (e.g., disaster relief payments, income tax write-offs for lost property, and subsidized flood insurance) rather than risk avoidance strategies that involve land use. These strategies discourage local governments to adopt local controls on development in hazardous areas that may have prevented much of the destruction from Katrina and Rita.

Third, New Urbanism offers a model urban design framework for guiding rebuilding in ways that create more resilient communities. However, without proper planning, this high-density development pattern can lead to greater risk to loss of life and property than predisaster low-density developments. Given the poor track record of ineffective planning for postdisaster recovery and mitigation in Gulf Coast states, rebuilt communities following the New Urban model are likely to have more buildings and people in harm's way compared to predisaster conditions.

Fourth, while federal policy for disaster recovery and mitigation planning needs major reform, and state and local governments must play a more significant role in accepting the risks posed by development in hazardous locations, any change will not be effective without meaningful consultation and participation of citizens in recovery decisions and plans that will affect them. This did not happen with evacuation planning in New Orleans. It may not be happening along the Mississippi coast. The MGCRRR (2005) Web site does not offer much in the way of citizen participation. It simply indicates that participants in Mississippi's New Urban design forum included "state designated representatives from local communities" who will somehow be "plugged in" to "communicate with other residents not present." Achieving grassroots participation is particularly problematic after the recent hurricanes, given the formidable challenge of reconstructing the myriad social relations embedded in schools, workplaces, child care arrangements, shops, places of worship, and places of play and recreation, as well as with outside aid delivery institutions (Vale and Campanella 2005)

We believe that federal disaster policy is in need of major reform. The aims of our recommendations are to encourage state and local governments to take on more responsibility in recovery and mitigation planning and to ensure that meaningful citizen participation is built into such planning.

Reform federal disaster policy

The nation needs a more sustainable approach and a reformed federal-state-local relationship for recovery planning and mitigation. We offer several recommendations.

First, federal policy should focus on performance-based environmental risk reduction targets. The federal government sets performance standard targets for air and water quality—so why not critical environmental risks posed by natural hazards? In threatened drainage basins like the Chesapeake Bay basin, state and local governments are required to prepare nutrient reduction plans to achieve a specific pollutant reduction target within a specified time frame. Given that any community in America will demand aid in an emergency, the federal government should also require every community to produce a meaningful performance-based mitigation and recovery plan. Progress toward meeting the performance target should be monitored on a regular basis. Plans should be adapted if targets are not met. If a community persists in not meeting targets, then it would be ineligible for public disaster assistance aid and mitigation funds. FEMA and states could offer technical assistance to communities on how to conduct risk assessments and monitor changes in risk.

Second, more emphasis should be placed on land use planning in hazardous areas. The federal government sets standards for wetlands and air and water quality—so why not critical land use principles? To be eligible for federal disaster aid and mitigation funds, local governments must produce a land use element as part of their mitigation plans. The land use element must comply with a checklist of steps that specify risk avoidance opportunities that rely on land use planning. Examples include

- high-hazard sending zones where development is to be relocated to low-hazard receiving zones,
- risk avoidance opportunities linked with other local land use concerns such as greenway or beachfront acquisitions that overlap hazard zone areas, and
- stream buffer setbacks that could limit development for water quality purposes and at the same time extend development limits beyond the one-hundred-year floodplain (note that significant damages consistently occur outside the one-hundred-year flood boundary).

The last two examples also would allow for piggybacking mitigation onto more established and higher priority land use issues to be accounted for in local government decision making. Thus, by incorporating mitigation into other land use decisions, mitigation is advanced. States would also have a rule in setting land use standards that fit hazard conditions in each state, and in providing technical assistance to communities.

Third, require local governments to pay a greater share of public infrastructure costs through insurance. Currently, the federal government pays for 75 percent of all local infrastructure damages through public assistance funds. One option is for local governments to purchase infrastructure insurance. Just as private homes and businesses are insured, local governments could insure infrastructure. The premium should be aligned with the level of risk across hazard zones. Many communities have created stormwater utilities with fees based on the amount of impervious surface per residential and commercial property to pay for stormwater infrastructure and stream protection and restoration projects to meet EPA water quality standards under Phases 1 and 2 of the Clean Water Act. It is plausible for these communities to create new utilities or rely on existing ones as a means to cover disaster costs. Another option would be to establish special assessment zones that would levy property taxes in accordance with degree of risk. The additional taxes could pay for infrastructure insurance.

Facilitate a process of inclusion rather than exclusion

We think a crucial recommendation to improve disaster recovery planning and advance more resilient communities entails the federal government requiring that communities take citizen participation seriously. When citizens start to grasp the more resilient and sustainable alternatives for living with hazards, they mobilize and begin to insist that elected officials make decisions leading to long-term resiliency. Active citizens who are deeply involved in planning are important so that aggrandizing real estate interests do not control the recovery process. Another crucial aspect of grassroots participation requires that outside aid delivery organizations (public and private) treat disaster-stricken people as participants in the recovery process, rather than helpless, poor victims. Specific approaches need to be employed in which those with a stake in recovery planning can help develop a bottom-up ability to take collective action.

To illustrate these approaches, we draw a recognized community-based disaster recovery planning effort in an underdeveloped island state of Montserrat in the

Caribbean between 1989 and 1994 (Berke and Beatley 1997). Although the setting is different from the Gulf Coast, parallels can be drawn given that both places have significant poor and disadvantaged populations that were disproportionately affected by the disasters. After hurricane landfall, a collaborative recovery effort evolved between an international nongovernmental organization from Canada, an intermediary nongovernment organization (NGO) from the region with long-standing external ties to foreign donor organizations, and a local community action group. The Canadian NGO sought to provide housing recovery assistance after Hugo by establishing a cooperative arrangement with the intermediary NGO, which had been involved in community development work in a local community

---

The federal government sets standards for wetlands and air and water quality—so why not critical land use principles?

---

for several years before the disaster. The arrangement involved the Canadian NGO providing funds to the intermediary for undertaking reconstruction activities in the community. The intermediary, in turn, worked with the community action group to initiate a new housing assistance program. The intermediary NGO trained local people and provided funds to temporarily employ local people to undertake reconstruction activities. The Canadian NGO also supplied the program with building materials and logistics for transporting the materials. The accomplishments of this program were substantial, with numerous training workshops on carpentry and structural strengthening techniques, twenty homes rebuilt, and many others repaired. Of greatest significance were the long-term development accomplishments. The local visibility and sense of importance of the community action group were raised considerably due to its reconstruction work. The voluntary participation of local people in group activities was also much higher. This strengthened the community action group's capacity to undertake several development projects not directly related to disaster recovery (e.g., new farming practices, building a community center, and improving potable water distribution systems).

According to Briggs (2004), efforts like this one suggest leverage principles for developing more effective participation in the recovery process. Serious application of these leveraging principles should be required in any local recovery planning process. Communities should demonstrate that they have complied with the principles to be eligible for disaster aid and mitigation funds from the federal government.

These principles are fourfold:

First, apply classic lessons in grassroots organizing in new ways to encourage participating and leading new and renewed civic institutions that tackle critical disaster recovery problems. In Montserrat, the local community action group was an important local institution, but it was somewhat limited in resources and capability to deal with the demands of recovery. The disaster opened a window for the local action group to engage local people, and the nonprofit intermediary created links to an outside organization with resources to provide aid. Disasters make clear that we need ways that connect people to immediate problems they need resolved and recognition that these problems are linked to wider social concerns.

Second, help people acquire new civic skills, with special attention to those with low status in the communities. The Montserrat effort included training and other support to help participants with little formal education to acquire and practice civic skills. In a current project supported by FEMA, MDC (a community-building nonprofit organization in Chapel Hill, North Carolina; see MDC 2005) and the Center for Urban and Regional Studies of the University of North Carolina at Chapel Hill (see CURS-UNC 2005) are partnering in an effort to work with seven disadvantaged communities after Hurricane Isabel, which struck the East Coast in 2003. The goal of this project is to support these communities to better cope with hazards and disasters through strategies that seize opportunities in the event of a disaster, reduce poverty, and build inclusive and collaborative ways of doing things. The intent is to create a "community building curriculum" designed to aid disadvantaged communities to cope with threats posed by hazards. The curriculum is designed to teach in ways that support adult learning. Key modules are to include how to build an emergency planning team; develop leadership capacity at the individual, interpersonal, organizational, and community level; conduct a hazard vulnerability assessment; carry out visioning exercises; and link visioning to planning and implementation.

Third, build more extensive networks to accomplish disaster resiliency goals. Formal organizational ties, such as those among nonprofit community groups like churches and self-help economic development cooperatives, and between those groups and external organizations (nonprofits and state and federal government agencies), are vitally important. Networks should relay important information and also be capable of endorsing (or vouching for) those with limited access to funds for rebuilding, political influence, and other disaster assistance resources. In the Montserrat case, the intermediary group provided a key set of links between a local action group and an external aid organization with no history of working together. The intermediary served as an active broker of attention, commitments, and agreement among key participants.

Fourth, build new norms—a culture that values and enables collective action. Actions to build community capability to take action must include cultivation of norms of mutual aid; broadly defined community responsibility and public engagement; and working through differences—helping to address the threads of mistrust, parochialism, and exclusion. In Montserrat, one of the most basic norms was that of cooperating and learning, rather than acting individually. The overarching thrust of the effort was to help build powerful new habits among individuals in the community that emphasized working to integrate community development efforts with long-range disaster recovery efforts. Another norm reflected the local action group's origins in grassroots engagement, which entailed engaging nonexperts in thinking through recovery and development needs and making resource allocations.

Building stronger norms of collective action does not necessarily mean making every decision by committee. Instead, incremental collective steps and steady progress in building networks can lead to a buildup of confidence needed to take bigger, more comprehensive actions aimed at recovery and mitigation planning over time.

In sum, restoring critical infrastructure and preserving and rebuilding a city's urban architectural fabric are critical to full recovery, but efforts must also be made to repair a community's torn social fabric—a process that fundamentally entails reconnecting severed familial, social, and religious networks of survivors at a grass-roots level. In this article, we underscore the fact that cities, towns, and villages are more than the sum of their buildings and infrastructure. They are a tapestry of human lives and social networks that are essential to the heart and soul of the place. Peer into a truly resilient place and you are assured of finding resilient citizens, citizens have who forged bonds in the face of catastrophe and carried the day.

References

Berke, Philip. 1998. Reducing natural hazard risks through state growth management. *Journal of the American Planning Association* 64 (1): 76-88.

———. 2002. Does sustainable development offer a new direction for planning? Challenges for the twenty-first century. *Journal of Planning Literature* 17 (1): 21-36.

Berke, Philip, and Timothy Beatley. 1992. *Planning for earthquakes: Risk, politics and policy*. Baltimore: Johns Hopkins University Press.

———. 1997. *After the hurricane: Linking recovery to sustainable development in the Caribbean*. Baltimore: Johns Hopkins University Press.

Berke, Philip, Neil Ericksen, Jan Crawford, and Jenny Dixon. 2002. Planning and indigenous people: Human rights and environmental protection in New Zealand. *Journal of Planning Education and Research* 22 (2): 115-34.

Berke, Philip, David Godschalk, and Edward Kaiser. Forthcoming. *Urban land use planning*. 5th ed. With Daniel Rodriguez. Chicago: University of Illinois Press.

Berke, Philip, Joseph McDonald, Nancy White, Michael Holmes, Kat Oury, and Rhonda Ryznar. 2003. Greening development for watershed protection: Does New Urbanism make a difference? *Journal of the American Planning Association* 69 (4): 397-413.

Birkland, Thomas. 1997. *After disaster: Agenda setting, public policy, and focusing events*. Washington, DC: Georgetown University Press.

Briggs, Xavier de Souza. 2004. Social capital: Easy beauty or meaningful resource? *Journal of the American Planning Association* 71 (2): 151-58.

Burby, Raymond. 2003. Making plans that matter: Citizen involvement and government action. *Journal of the American Planning Association* 69 (1): 33-49.

Burby, Raymond J. 2006. Hurricane Katrina and the paradoxes of government disaster policy: Bringing about wise governmental decisions for hazardous areas. *Annals of the American Academy of Political and Social Science* 604:171-91.

Burby, Raymond J., Timothy Beatley, Philip R. Berke, Robert E. Deyle, Steven P. French, David Godschalk, Edward J. Kaiser, Jack D. Kartez, Peter J. May, Robert Olshansky, Robert G. Paterson, and Rutherford H. Platt. 1999. Unleashing the power of planning to create disaster-resistant communities. *Journal of the American Planning Association* 65 (3): 247-58.

Burby, Raymond, and Peter May. 1997. *Making governments plan: State experiments in managing land use.* With Philip Berke, Linda Dalton, Steven French, and Edward Kaiser. Baltimore: Johns Hopkins University Press.

Calthorpe, Peter. 1993. *The next American metropolis: Ecology, community, and the American dream.* New York: Princeton Architectural Press.

Congress of New Urbanism. 2002. *New Urban projects on a neighborhood scale in the United States.* Ithaca, NY: New Urban News.

CURS-UNC. 2005. Emergency Preparedness Demonstration Program for Disadvantaged Communities. http://www.planning.unc.edu/grant/fema/about.htm (accessed November 18, 2005).

Dalton, Linda. 1989. The limits of regulation: Evidence from local plan implementation in California. *Journal of the American Planning Association* 55 (2): 161-68.

Deyle, Robert, and Robert Smith. 1994. *Storm hazard mitigation and post-disaster redevelopment policies.* Tallahassee: The Florida State Planning Laboratory, Department of Urban and Regional Planning, Florida State University.

Duany Plater-Zyberke and Company. 2001. *SmartCode.* http:://www.smartgrowth.org (accessed October 1, 2005).

Godschalk, David, Timothy Beatley, Philip Berke, David Brower, and Edward Kaiser. 1999. *Natural hazard mitigation: Recasting disaster policy and planning.* Washington, DC: Island Press.

Healy, Patsy. 1997. *Collaborative planning: Shaping paces in fragmented societies.* London: Macmillan.

Mader, George. 1997. Enduring land use planning lessons from the 1971 San Fernando earthquake. *Earthquake Spectra* 13 (4): 721-33.

MDC. 2005. Disaster Preparedness Demonstration Project. http://www.mdcinc.org/home/ (accessed November 18, 2005).

Mississippi Governor's Commission on Recovery, Rebuilding, and Renewal (MGCRRR). 2005. Mississippi renewal. www.mississippirenewal.com (accessed October 19, 2005).

Nelson, Arthur, and Steven French. 2002. Plan quality and mitigating damage from natural disasters: A case study of the Northridge earthquake with planning policy considerations. *Journal of the American Planning Association* 68:194-207.

Olshansky, Robert, and Jack Kartez. 1998. Managing land use to build resilience. In *Cooperating with nature: Confronting natural hazards with land-use planning for sustainable communities,* ed. Raymond Burby, 167-202. Washington, DC: Joseph Henry Press.

Schwab, Jim. 1998. *Planning for post-disaster recovery and reconstruction.* PAS Report no. 483/484. With Kenneth Topping, Charles Eadie, Robert Deyle, and Richard Smith. Washington, DC: American Planning Association.

Song, Yan, Philip Berke, Allen Serkin, Lisa Crooks, Katherine Hendersen, David Salvesen, and Mark Stevens. 2005. Are New Urbanist communities prone to flood hazard? A reality check of existing New Urban developments. Paper presented at the Association of Collegiate Schools of Planning Conference, Kansas City, MO, October 14-16.

Titus, James, and Charlie Richman. 2001. Maps of lands vulnerable to sea level rise: Modeled elevations along the US Atlantic and Gulf Coasts. *Climate Research* 18:205-28.

Vale, Larry, and Thomas J. Campanella. 2005. *The resilient city: How modern cities recover from disaster.* Oxford: Oxford University Press.

Zaferatos, Nicholas. 1998. Planning the native American tribal community: Understanding the basis of power controlling the reservation territory. *Journal of the American Planning Association* 64 (4): 395-410.

Disaster Mitigation and Insurance: Learning from Katrina

By

HOWARD KUNREUTHER

Hurricane Katrina illustrates the *natural disaster syndrome*. Prior to a disaster, individuals in hazard-prone regions do not voluntarily adopt cost-effective loss reduction measures. The federal government then comes to the rescue with disaster assistance even if it claimed it had no intention of doing so prior to the event. There are a number of reasons why individuals do not protect themselves prior to a disaster. They underestimate the likelihood of a future disaster, often believing that it will not happen to them; have budget constraints; are myopic in their behavior; and/or do not want to be the only one on the block modifying their structure. Given this lack of interest in voluntary protection, benefit-cost analysis can determine when a well-enforced building code would be appropriate. The article concludes by highlighting the importance of public-private partnerships as a way of reducing future disaster losses and aiding the recovery process.

Keywords: disaster insurance; building codes; homeowner motivations; community planning; disaster mitigation; risk assessment

Hurricane Katrina has highlighted the challenges associated with reducing losses from hurricanes and other natural hazards due to what I have termed the "natural disaster syndrome" (Kunreuther 1996). It consists of interconnected ex ante and ex post components. Before a disaster, most homeowners, private businesses, and the public sector do not voluntarily adopt cost-effective loss reduction measures. Hence, the area is highly vulnerable and

Howard Kunreuther is Cecilia Yen Koo Professor; professor of decision sciences and business and public policy; and codirector, Risk Management and Decision Processes Center at the Wharton School of the University of Pennsylvania. His research focuses on decision processes, insurance, low-probability events and decision making, managerial economics, operations management, regulation, and risk assessment.

NOTE: Thanks to Richard Bernknopf, Ray Burby, Hannah Chervitz, and Robert Meyer for helpful comments on an earlier draft of this article. Support from NSF Grant Award no. CMS-0527598 is gratefully acknowledged.

DOI: 10.1177/0002716205285685

unprepared should a severe hurricane or other natural disaster occur. The magnitude of the destruction following a catastrophic disaster, such as Katrina, leads the government to provide liberal relief to victims even if it claimed it had no intention of doing so prior to the event. This combination of underinvestment in protection prior to the event and liberal use of taxpayers' funds after a disaster does not augur well for the future.

One of the reasons for the natural disaster syndrome relates to the decision processes of individuals with respect to low-probability high-consequence events, such as a Category 3 or 4 hurricane. Prior to a disaster, many individuals perceive its likelihood as sufficiently low that they argue, "It will not happen to me." As a result, they do not feel the need to invest voluntarily in protective measures, such as strengthening their house or buying insurance. It is only after the disaster occurs that these same individuals claim they would like to have undertaken protective measures.

The next section examines why individuals do not voluntarily invest in cost-effective mitigation measures. The third section shows how benefit-cost analysis can be used for determining under what situations a well-enforced building code would be appropriate. The fourth section argues for the importance of public-private partnerships for incorporating mitigation measures into a disaster management plan by showing how building codes can be combined with insurance incentives and long-term mitigation loans. The concluding section summarizes the key findings of the article and suggests future research for reducing the natural disaster syndrome.

Why Do Individuals Not Undertake Mitigation Measures Voluntarily?

Extensive evidence indicates that residents in hazard-prone areas do not undertake loss prevention measures voluntarily. A 1974 survey of more than one thousand California homeowners in earthquake-prone areas revealed that only 12 percent of the respondents had adopted any protective measures (Kunreuther et al. 1978). Fifteen years later, there was little change despite the increased public awareness of the earthquake hazard. In a 1989 survey of thirty-five hundred homeowners in four California counties at risk from earthquakes, only 5 to 9 percent of the respondents in these areas reported adopting any loss reduction measures. (Palm et al. 1990). Burby et al. (1988) and Laska (1991) have found a similar reluctance by residents in flood-prone areas to invest in mitigation measures.

In the case of flood damage, Burby (2006 [this volume]) provides compelling evidence that actions taken by the federal government, such as building levees, make residents feel safe when, in fact, they are targets for catastrophes should the levee be breached or overtopped. This problem is reinforced by local public officials who do not enforce building codes and/or impose land-use regulations to restrict development in high-hazard areas. If developers do not design homes so

TABLE 1

EXPECTED BENEFIT-COST RATIO OF INVESTING IN MITIGATION
MEASURES AS A FUNCTION OF TIME HORIZON, PERCEIVED LOSS
REDUCTION, AND PERCEIVED PROBABILITY (p)

| Time Horizon (in Years) | Loss Reduction ($40,000) | |
	$p = 1/100$	$p = 1/300$
1	0.30	0.10
2	0.58	0.19
3	0.83	0.28
4	**1.06**	0.35
5	1.26	0.42
10	2.05	0.68
15	2.54	0.84
20	2.83	0.94
25	3.03	**1.01**

NOTE: Figures in bold reflect the smallest number of years that the benefit/cost ratio exceeds 1.

that they are resistant to disasters and individuals do not voluntarily adopt mitigation measures, one can expect large-scale losses following a disaster, as evidenced by the property damage to New Orleans caused by Hurricane Katrina.

Consider the Adamses, a hypothetical family whose New Orleans home was destroyed by Hurricane Katrina. They have decided to rebuild their property in the same location but are unsure, however, whether they want to invest in a flood-reduction measure (e.g., elevating their home, sealing the foundation of the structure, and/or waterproofing the walls).[1] Suppose that scientific experts have estimated that the annual chances of a severe flood in the area where the Adamses live is 1 in 100. If they invested in a flood mitigation measure, they would reduce damage from this hurricane by $40,000. In other words, the expected annual benefit from investing in such a measure would be $400 (i.e., 1 in $100 \times \$40,000$). The longer the time period T that the Adamses expect to live in their house, the greater the expected benefit from flood-proofing their house. More specifically, let B represent the expected net present value of the benefit of mitigation over the entire time horizon T.[2]

Suppose the extra cost to the Adamses of undertaking flood-proofing measures is $C = \$1,200$. Let T^* represent the minimum number of years for the loss-reduction investment to be cost-effective. In other words, T^* is the smallest time period where $B/C > 1$. The second column in Table 1 depicts the expected benefit-cost ratio as a function of T associated with such an investment if the Adamses' annual discount rate was 10 percent. It is clear that if the family planned to live in their home for more than four years, they would want to flood-proof their house if they were risk-neutral. If the Adamses were risk-averse, then $T^* < 4$ because they would be more concerned with the financial consequences of suffering a large loss from the next disaster and would thus find the expected benefits of mitigation even more attractive than if they were risk-neutral.

The Adams family and other residents of New Orleans could have debated whether to flood-proof their homes prior to Katrina, but suppose they decided not to do so. It is instructive to ask why they chose *not* to adopt cost-effective mitigation measures.

Underestimation or ignoring probabilities

Many individuals perceive the probability of a disaster causing damage to their home as being sufficiently low that they cannot justify investing in mitigation even if they evaluate the risk systematically by comparing the expected benefits with the cost of protection. Suppose that the Adams family perceived the annual chances of a severe flood damaging their home to be 1 in 300 rather than the scientists' estimate of 1 in 100. As shown in the third column of Table 1, the value of T^* is now more than six times higher, so that the Adamses would have to expect to live in their home for at least the next twenty-five years to want to invest in this mitigation measure.[3]

According to the 2004 Housing Survey for the New Orleans Metropolitan Area, the median tenure of occupancy is eleven years for owner-occupied residences, so if most residents with neighboring homes similar to the Adamses misperceived the risk in this manner, they would not want to flood-proof their structure (U.S. Department of Housing and Urban Development and U.S. Census Bureau 2004).

Prior to Katrina, the Adams family did not focus on the likelihood of their house being flooded when making decisions on whether it should be mitigated. As a result, they did not even think about the consequences of future flooding from a hurricane and hence did not make the trade-offs between expected benefits and costs. Magat, Viscusi, and Huber (1987) and Camerer and Kunreuther (1989) provided considerable empirical evidence that individuals do not seek out information on probabilities in making their decisions. Huber, Wider, and Huber (1997) showed that only 22 percent of subjects sought out probability information when evaluating risk managerial decisions. When consumers are asked to justify their decisions on purchasing warranties for products that may need repair, they rarely use probability as a rationale for purchasing this protection (Hogarth and Kunreuther 1995).

Those individuals who seek out information on the likelihood of a severe disaster causing damage to their home may find that experts disagree. For example, different methods for interpreting identical geologic information for earthquake-triggered liquefaction showed significant differences in the probability of the earthquake hazard for the same location (Bernknopf et al. forthcoming). Those who prefer not to think about the hazard may focus on the lowest-probability estimate so they can justify not investing in any protective measures.

Research shows that decision makers use "threshold models," whereby if the probability of a disaster is below some prespecified level, they do not think about the event[4] in making decisions. In a laboratory experiment on purchasing insurance, many individuals bid zero for coverage, apparently viewing the probability of a loss as sufficiently small that they were not interested in protecting themselves against it (McClelland, Schulze, and Coursey 1993). Similarly, many homeowners residing in communities that are potential sites for nuclear waste facilities have a tendency to dismiss the risk as negligible (Oberholzer-Gee 1998). Prior to the Bhopal chemical accident in 1984, firms in the industry estimated the chances of such an accident as sufficiently low that it was not on their radar screen. If the Adams family took this approach, they would not have any interest in investing in a loss mitigation measure no matter how large the savings would be.

Extensive evidence indicates that residents in hazard-prone areas do not undertake loss prevention measures voluntarily.

Short time horizons

In making decisions that involve cost outlays, individuals are often myopic and hence only take into account the potential benefits from such investments over the next year or two. This is one reason that consumers are often reluctant to buy energy-efficient appliances that promise to reduce their monthly electricity bills over the life of the appliance.[5] In the example in Table 1, if the Adams family wanted to recoup their investment in less than four years, then even if they had used the experts' estimate of the risk, they would still not have flood-proofed their house. In one study, subjects indicated the maximum they were willing to pay for such protective measures as investing in a deadbolt lock for their apartment, purchasing a steering wheel club, and strengthening their homes against earthquakes (Kunreuther, Onculer, and Slovic 1998). By varying the number of years that each of the measures provided protection, one could determine how much more the person was willing to invest in the item as a function of time. If a person was willing to pay $50 for a deadbolt lock if he planned to live in his apartment for one year, then he should be willing to pay up to $95.45 if he had a two-year lease and an annual discount rate of 10 percent.

Many of the arguments used by respondents suggest that they focus on the cost of the product in determining how much they are willing to pay to invest in a protective measure and do not take into account the expected benefits over more than one year. These justifications are consistent with experiments by Schkade and Payne (1994) and Baron and Maxwell (1996), which revealed that the willingness to pay for public goods was affected by cost information.

This tendency toward myopia is one of the most widely documented failings of human decision making. As a rule, we have difficulty considering the future consequences of current actions over long time horizons (Meyer and Hutchinson 2001).

As pointed out above, decision makers fail to invest in measures that make their houses more disaster-resistant and underinvest in energy-saving appliances. Patients also undervalue the benefits of exploratory medical testing (Luce and Kahn 1999).

Budget constraints

If the Adams family focuses on the upfront cost of flood-proofing their house and they have limited disposable income after purchasing necessities, then they will not even consider taking this step. Residents in hazard-prone areas have used this argument explicitly for their lack of interest in buying insurance. In focus group interviews to determine factors influencing decisions on whether to buy flood or earthquake coverage, one uninsured worker responded to the question, "How does one decide on how much to pay for insurance?" by responding as follows:

> A blue-collar worker doesn't just run up there with $200 [the insurance premium] and buy a policy. The world knows that 90 percent of us live from payday to payday. . . . He can't come up with that much cash all of a sudden and turn around and meet all his other obligations. (Kunreuther et al. 1978, 113)

The budget constraint for investing in protective measures may extend to higher-income individuals if they set up separate mental accounts for different expenditures. Thaler (1999) suggested that dividing spending into budget categories facilitates making rational trade-offs between competing use of funds and acts as a self-control device. He pointed out that poorer families tend to have budgets defined over periods of a week or a month while wealthier families are likely to use annual budgets. Heath and Soll (1996) provided further evidence on the role of budget categories by showing how actual expenses are tracked against these budgets.

A response by several individuals when asked why they were only willing to pay a fixed amount for a deadbolt lock when the lease for the apartment was extended from one to five years supports this mental accounting argument with respect to budgets. One responder said simply,

> $20 is all the dollars I have in the short-run to spend on a lock. If I had more, I would spend more—maybe up to $50. (Kunreuther, Onculer, and Slovic 1998, 284)

Interdependencies

Suppose the Adams family was considering elevating their house on piles to reduce flood losses from a future hurricane. If none of their neighbors have taken this step, their house would look like an oddity in a sea of homes at ground level. Should the Adamses choose to move, they would be concerned that the resale value of their home would be lower because the house was different from all the others. Given that there is a tendency not to think about a disaster until after it happens, the Adamses may reason that it would be difficult to convince potential buyers that elevating their house should increase its property value.

The question as to how actions of others impact one's own decisions relates to the broader question of interdependencies. If all homes in the neighborhood were elevated, then the Adamses would very likely want to follow suit; if none of them had taken this step, then they would not have an interest in doing so. It is conceivable that if a few leaders in the community elevated their homes, then others would do the same. This type of tipping behavior is common in many situations and has been studied extensively by Schelling (1978) and popularized by Gladwell (2000). Heal and Kunreuther (2005) provided a game theoretic treatment of the topic and indicated that a wide range of problems come under this rubric. They suggested ways to coordinate actions of those at risk ranging from subsidization or taxation to induce tipping or cascading to rules and regulations such as well-enforced building codes.

Disaster assistance

One of the arguments that has been advanced as to why individuals do not adopt protective measures is that they assume liberal aid from the government will be forthcoming should they suffer losses from a disaster. Under the current system of disaster assistance, the governor of the state(s) can request that the president declare a "major disaster" and offer special assistance if the damage is severe enough.

In the case of Hurricane Katrina, Governor Kathleen Blanco declared a State of Emergency on August 26, 2005, and requested disaster relief funds from the federal government on the 28th. President Bush declared a State of Emergency on the 28th (Brookings Institution 2005), an action that frees federal government funds and puts emergency response activities, debris removal, and individual assistance and housing programs under federal control (Congressional Research Service 2005). Under an emergency declaration, federal funds are capped at $5 million. On August 29, in response to Governor Blanco's request, the president declared a "major disaster," allotting more federal funds to aid in rescue and recovery. By September 8, Congress had approved $52 billion in aid to victims of Hurricane Katrina.

Federal disaster assistance may create a type of Samaritan's dilemma: providing assistance ex post (after hardship) reduces parties' incentives to manage risk ex ante (before hardship occurs). If the Adams family expects to receive government assistance after a loss, it will have less economic incentive to invest in mitigation measures and purchase insurance prior to a hurricane. The increased loss due to the lack of protection by residents in hazard-prone areas amplifies the government's incentive to provide assistance after a disaster to victims.

The empirical evidence on the role of disaster relief suggests that individuals or communities have *not* based their decisions on whether to invest in mitigation measures by focusing on the expectation of future disaster relief. Kunreuther et al. (1978) found that most homeowners in earthquake- and hurricane-prone areas did not expect to receive aid from the federal government following a disaster. Burby

(1991) found that local governments that received disaster relief undertook more efforts to reduce losses from future disasters than those that did not. This behavior seems counterintuitive, and the reasons for it are not fully understood. It will be interesting to see whether Hurricane Katrina changes this view given the highly publicized commitment by the Bush administration to provide billions of dollars in disaster relief to victims.

In making decisions that involve cost outlays, individuals are often myopic and hence only take into account the potential benefits from such investments over the next year or two.

Whether or not individuals incorporate an expectation of disaster assistance in their predisaster planning process, a driving force with respect to the actual provision of government relief is the occurrence of disasters where the losses are large (Moss 2002). Following the Alaska earthquake in 1964 where relatively few homes and businesses had earthquake-resistant measures and insurance protection, the U.S. Small Business Administration (SBA) provided 1 percent loans for rebuilding structures and refinancing mortgages to those who required funds through its disaster loan program. Hence, the uninsured victims in Alaska were financially better off after the earthquake than their insured counterparts (Dacy and Kunreuther 1968).

Following Hurricane Betsy, Congress passed the Southeast Hurricane Disaster Relief Act of 1965 (PL 89-339), which authorized the Federal Housing Administration (FHA) and SBA to forgive a part of each loan up to a maximum of $1,800. The forgiveness features were intended to be limited to uninsurable loss or damage. But in practice, anyone who requested forgiveness received it because flood insurance was not available at the time and it was difficult to separate wind damage (normally covered by insurance) from water damage (not covered) (Kunreuther 1973).

The National Flood Insurance Program (NFIP) was established in 1968 to encourage individuals in hazard-prone areas to purchase flood insurance at highly subsidized rates as a way of alleviating the need for disaster assistance. Few individuals voluntarily bought this coverage, so when Tropical Storm Agnes caused more than $2 billion in damage in June 1972, only 1,583 claims totaling $5 million were paid under the NFIP (Kunreuther 1973). Even though flood coverage has been required since 1973 as a condition for a federally insured mortgage, it has been estimated that less than 40 percent of the victims of Hurricane Katrina in Mississippi and Louisiana had flood insurance to cover their losses (Insurance Information Institute 2005). There are at least two issues at play here. The first is that not all flooded areas were determined to be hazard-prone by the Federal Emergency Management Agency (FEMA) (such as the 9th Ward in New Orleans). The second is that even within hazard-prone areas, many homeowners did not have flood insurance coverage.

Summary

The story of the Adams family is one that can be generalized to many residents in hazard-prone areas. There will be a lack of interest in voluntarily adopting loss-prevention measures for several interrelated reasons: an underestimation of the probability of the disaster occurring or even treating the event as if its likelihood was zero, myopic behavior by individuals as reflected in short time horizons for estimating benefits, and interdependencies with neighbors' decisions. There is limited empirical evidence that the expectation or receipt of disaster relief discourages individuals from investing in mitigation measures. However, if victims suffer large losses for which they do not have financial protection, then the government is likely to come to the rescue with significant disaster relief.

Role of Cost-Benefit Analysis (CBA)

The public sector can play an important role in reducing losses from future disasters by examining measures that will be cost-effective from both the residents' perspective and those of the general taxpayer. Consider whether the city of New Orleans should require that homes in flood-prone areas in the metropolitan area be flood-proofed to reduce the likelihood that they would suffer serious disaster losses or whether they should allow the residents to rebuild to pre-Katrina standards by not imposing any building code. The building code would reflect a balance between the costs of flood-proofing structures and the expected reduction in losses from future hurricanes of different intensities that hit New Orleans. Another alternative would be to provide residents whose homes were destroyed with grants and/or low-interest loans and require them to move to other areas and convert the vacated areas to wetlands.

CBA is a systematic procedure for evaluating options, such as the ones specified above. There are different ways to conduct a valid CBA, depending on the information one has and the nature of the problem at hand. A simplified five-step procedure for conducting a CBA is depicted in Figure 1. A more comprehensive approach, which incorporates several additional steps, is discussed in Boardman et al. (2001). Posner (2004) provided a comprehensive analysis of the use of benefit-cost

FIGURE 1
SIMPLIFIED COST-BENEFIT ANALYSIS FOR MITIGATION MEASURES

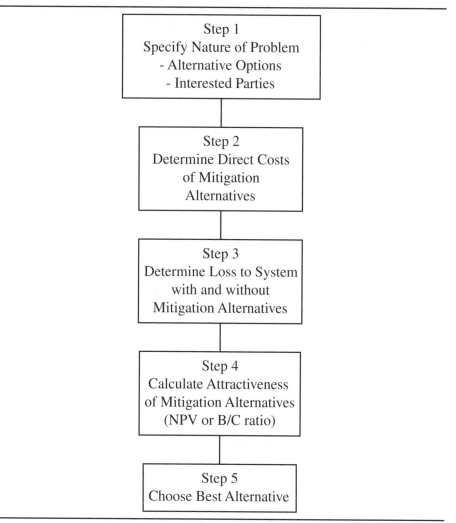

NOTE: NPV = net present value; B/C = benefit/cost ratio.

approaches for determining what measures society will want to invest in for dealing with extremely low-probability catastrophes such as an asteroid hitting land.

The five-step CBA procedure includes defining the nature of the problem, including the alternative options and interested parties; determining the direct cost of the mitigation alternatives; determining the benefits of mitigation, via the difference between the loss to the system with and without mitigation; calculating the attractiveness of the mitigation alternatives; and finally, choosing the best alternative.

Step 1: Specify the nature of the problem

To initiate a CBA, one needs to specify the options that are being considered and the interested parties in the process. Normally, one alternative is the status quo. For the above problem, the status quo refers to allowing homes in New Orleans to rebuild their structures to pre-Katrina standards without having to flood-proof them. The status quo is normally the reference point for evaluating how well other alternatives perform. For this example, there are two alternatives: institute a building code that requires all homes in the Adamses' neighborhood to be mitigated based on their flood risk or provide grants and/or loans to residents in this neighborhood to move to safer areas, creating wetlands in the process.

Each of these options will impact a number of individuals, groups, and organizations in our society. It is important to indicate who will benefit and who will pay the costs associated with each option when undertaking a CBA analysis. These include residents and business owners affected by the hurricane; state and local government agencies that must administer the building code or provide low-interest loans and/or grants; federal agencies that deal with the consequences and losses following a disaster; and the general taxpayer who will bear some of the costs of administering the code, the low-interest loans and/or grants, and the disaster assistance provided by the public sector following a disaster. Depending on the stringency and geographic coverage of mitigation policies and standards for communities, CBA analysis has shown that the spatial heterogeneity of the hazard in a region affects the extent of the regulatory burden and the efficiency of its implementation (Bernknopf et al. 2001).

Step 2: Determine the direct costs of mitigation alternatives

For each mitigation alternative, one needs to specify the direct cost to implement the mitigation measure. For a building code, the property owner incurs the monetary costs associated with making the house more hurricane-resistant. Should residents be required to move to a safer area, the costs include not only the financial expenses of moving but the social and psychological impacts of moving to a new community.

Step 3: Determine the expected benefits of mitigation alternatives

Once the costs are estimated for each mitigation alternative, one needs to specify the potential benefits to each of the interested parties. In the case of the above hurricane risk, one considers either a scenario hurricane event or a set of scenario hurricanes of different magnitude, location, duration, and intensity that affect New Orleans. The damage to the property is then estimated for each alternative option, and the expected benefits are estimated relative to the status quo. For the case where homes are flood-proofed due to a building code, the expected benefits are the reduction in losses from hurricanes of different magnitudes over the life of the home multiplied by the likelihood of each of these hurricanes occurring. The benefits accruing in future years are converted to present value by an appropriate discount rate. Should homes be relocated to safer areas, the expected benefits are computed in a similar manner, except they would then reflect the reduction in damage to these homes from hurricanes of different magnitude because the homes had been relocated to safer areas.

Step 4: Calculate the attractiveness of mitigation alternatives

To calculate the attractiveness of mitigation, the nature of the expected benefits to each of the interested parties is estimated and compared to the upfront costs of mitigation. The impact of a building code could be evaluated by calculating the ratio of the discounted expected benefits to the upfront costs to determine the attractiveness of the alternative as was demonstrated in Table 1 for the Adams family. Whenever this ratio exceeds 1, the alternative is viewed as desirable. Budget constraints may make it difficult for some property owners to incur these extra costs, in which case one may have to consider whether subsidized loans or grants should be provided to these individuals.

A similar analysis could be undertaken for the alternative of moving residents to lower-risk areas. The problem has additional complications since social and psychological costs are involved in relocating to a new area (Heinz Center 2000). For each family, special considerations need to be taken into account, many of which are hard to quantify. Many property owners may resist moving to another area, and it would be difficult to convince them that it is in their best interest to do so. On the other hand, if one only considered the reduction of future disaster losses in the analysis, this alternative may be highly attractive.

Step 5: Choose the best alternative

Once the attractiveness of each alternative is calculated through a net present value calculation or a ratio of the benefits to the costs, one chooses the alternative with the highest benefit-cost ratio. This criterion is based on the principle of allocating resources to their best possible use so that one behaves in an economically efficient manner. As pointed out above, some individuals may perceive themselves as worse off than before and/or feel that they cannot afford the proposed measure.

Incorporating Mitigation into a Disaster Management Program

Suppose that the city of New Orleans decided to impose a building code requiring all homes in the neighborhood where the Adamses live to flood-proof their structures, which would reduce their expected annual flood losses by $275. If the cost of mitigation was $1,200 and the annual discount rate was 10 percent, then Table 1 indicates that each house would only require a four-year lifespan for the expected discounted benefits to exceed the cost of mitigation.

Implementing building codes

The implementation of such a building code is another matter. We have already shown that if families like the Adams family have misperceptions of the probability of a future hurricane, short time horizons, and budget constraints, they will have no interest in adopting the mitigation measure. The challenge in developing a disaster management plan that encourages mitigation measures is to develop approaches that will encourage individuals to want to undertake these measures. This section of the article suggests ways that mitigation can be incorporated as part of a private-public sector partnership for reducing future losses from natural disasters.

Federal disaster assistance may create a type of Samaritan's dilemma: providing assistance ex post (after hardship) reduces parties' incentives to manage risk ex ante (before hardship occurs).

Current federal disaster policy suggests that the public feels some degree of responsibility toward helping victims of natural disasters. Despite the need to limit building in hazard-prone areas, construction has increased radically in coastal areas subject to hurricanes. This construction has increased both property values and buyer attention for these coastal areas. For example, after Hurricane Camille destroyed the Richelieu apartment complex in Pass Christian, Mississippi, in 1969, a shopping center was built in the same location, housing a Winn Dixie and a Rite-Aid, among other retail businesses. Although the shopping center was leveled by Hurricane Katrina, real estate developers already have plans to rebuild on the site, most likely a condominium development this time (Wharton Risk Center 2005).

Development in hazard-prone areas has resulted in skyrocketing disaster costs in recent years starting with Hurricane Andrew in 1992 where the damage was estimated to be $35 billion and culminating in 2005 with Hurricanes Katrina, Wilma, and Rita where insurance claims are estimated to be between $40 and $60 billion and total losses will be considerably higher.

Building codes are often not enforced in hazard-prone areas. Insurance experts have indicated that 25 percent of the insured losses from Hurricane Andrew could have been prevented through better building code compliance and enforcement (Insurance Research Council and Insurance Institute of Property Loss Reduction 1995). Many communities have inadequate staffing and training to enforce these codes effectively. In Dade County, the area struck by Hurricane Andrew, only sixty building inspectors were required to conduct multiple inspections on an average of twenty thousand new buildings each year. This translates into an average of thirty-three inspections per day for each inspector, a near-impossible task when driving time, report writing, and other administrative tasks are taken into account.

Linking mitigation with insurance

In reexamining strategies for reducing losses from disasters in the future, one needs to strike a balance between satisfying the objectives of the individual living in a hazard-prone area and the general public. Banks can play a key role in this regard if

- they require homeowners in hazard-prone areas to purchase insurance coverage against natural disasters, and
- the premiums reflect the risk of living in the area.

Consider the residents of New Orleans, such as the Adams family, who are residing in areas subject to flooding from hurricanes. If they have a federally insured mortgage, banks could require them to purchase flood insurance. Banks could also require that a third-party inspector ensure that structures meet the building code instituted by the city of New Orleans that homes rebuilt after Hurricane Katrina in the neighborhood in which the Adams family lives have to be flood-proofed.

To make the adoption of these mitigation measures financially palatable from the property owner's perspective, banks holding the mortgage on the property could provide funds for this purpose through a home improvement loan with a payback period identical to the life of the mortgage. For example, the mitigation measure considered by the Adams family costs $1,200. A twenty-year loan for $1,200 at an annual interest rate of 10 percent would result in payments of $116 per year. If the annual insurance premium reduction due to the adoption of the mitigation measure is greater than $116, the insured homeowner would have lower total payments by investing in mitigation (Kleindorfer and Kunreuther 1999). In fact, as shown in Table 1, the expected annual savings in reduced wind damage from adopting the mitigation measure was $400. If the insurance premium were reduced by this amount, the annual savings to the property owner would be $284 (i.e., $400 – $116).

A bank would have a financial incentive to provide this type of loan. By linking the expenditure in mitigation to the structure rather than to the property owner, the annual payments are lower and this would be a selling point to mortgagees. The bank will also feel that it is now better protected against a catastrophic loss to the property, and the insurer knows that its potential loss from a major disaster is reduced. The general public will now be less likely to have large amounts of their tax dollars going for disaster relief. A win-win-win-win situation for all!

There is an additional benefit to insurers from having banks ensuring that their mortgagees have met existing building codes. The costs of reinsurance that protects insurers against catastrophic losses should now decrease. If reinsurers know that they are less likely to make large payments to insurers because each piece of property in a region now has a lower chance of experiencing a large loss, then they will reduce their premiums to the insurer for the same reason that the insurer is reducing its premium to the property owner.

Suppose that an insurer had one thousand identical insurance policies in New Orleans, each one of which would expect to make claims payments of $50,000 following a hurricane if homes were not mitigated in the way that the Adamses were considering. The insurer's expected loss from such a disaster would be $50 million. To protect its surplus, suppose the insurer would want to have $25 million in coverage from a reinsurer. Given that the hypothetical hurricane has a 1 in 100 chance of hitting New Orleans, the expected loss to a reinsurer would be $250,000, and the premium charged to the insurer would reflect this. If the bank required that all one thousand homes be flood-proofed to meet the local building code and each homeowner's loss were reduced to $10,000, then the insurer's total loss would be $10 million should all one thousand homes be affected, and it would not require reinsurance. This savings would be passed on to the insurer in the form of a lower premium.

Providing seals of approval

Another way to encourage the adoption of cost-effective mitigation measures is for banks and financial institutions to provide a seal of approval to each structure that meets or exceeds building code standards. Such a seal of approval is likely to increase the property value of the home should the owner want to sell it, by informing the potential buyer that the house is built safely.

Other direct financial benefits result from having a seal of approval. *Fortified...for safer living* is a national new home construction designation program of the Institute for Business and Home Safety (IBHS). *Fortified* techniques and construction materials raise a home's overall disaster resistance above the minimum requirement of building codes. An independent inspector, trained by IBHS, verifies that *Fortified* features have been built into the home. The *Fortified* designation is registered with IBHS and remains with the structure indefinitely (unless major modifications are made). The designation or certain program features may qualify for homeowners' insurance credits in some states.

The success of such a program requires the support of the building industry and a cadre of qualified inspectors to provide accurate information as to whether existing codes and standards are being met. Such a certification program can be very useful to insurers who may choose to provide coverage only to those structures that are given a certificate of disaster resistance.

Evidence from a July 1994 telephone survey of 1,241 residents in six hurricane-prone areas on the Atlantic and Gulf Coasts provides supporting evidence for some type of seal of approval. More than 90 percent of the respondents felt that local home builders should be required to follow building codes, and 85 percent considered it very important that local building departments conduct inspections of new residential construction (Insurance Research Council and Insurance Institute for Property Loss Reduction 1995).

Tax incentives

One way for communities to encourage residents to pursue mitigation measures is to provide them with tax incentives. For example, if a homeowner reduces the chances of damage from a hurricane by installing a mitigation measure, then this taxpayer would get a rebate on state taxes to reflect the lower costs for disaster relief. Alternatively, property taxes could be reduced for the same reason. In practice, communities often create a monetary disincentive to invest in mitigation. A property owner who improves a home by making it safer is likely to have the property reassessed at a higher value and, hence, have to pay higher taxes. California has recognized this problem, and in 1990 voters passed Proposition 127, which exempts seismic rehabilitation improvements to buildings from reassessments that would increase property taxes.

The city of Berkeley has taken an additional step to encourage home buyers to retrofit newly purchased homes by instituting a transfer tax rebate. The city has a 1.5 percent tax levied on property transfer transactions; up to one-third of this amount can be applied to seismic upgrades during the sale of property. Qualifying upgrades include foundation repairs or replacement, wall bracing in basements, shear wall installation, water heater anchoring, and securing of chimneys (Earthquake Engineering Research Institute 1998).

The principal reason for using tax rebates to encourage mitigation is the broader benefit associated with these measures. If a house is not damaged because it is protected in some way, then the general community gains much larger savings than just the reduced damage to the house. For example, residents who would have had to leave their unmitigated homes after a disaster, but who would instead be able to stay there because it was protected, would not have to be fed or housed elsewhere. These added benefits cannot be captured through insurance premium reductions, which normally cover damage only to the property. Taxes are associated with broader units of analysis, such as the community, state, or even federal level. To the extent that the savings in disaster costs accrue to these units of government, tax rebates are most appropriate.

Conclusions and Future Research

Hurricane Katrina has provided additional empirical evidence supporting the natural disaster syndrome. Many victims suffered severe losses from flooding because they had not mitigated their home and did not have flood insurance to cover the resulting damage. As a result, an unprecedented level of federal disaster assistance has been promised to aid these victims.

Those in harm's way have not protected themselves against natural disasters for many reasons. The principal reason is that many individuals believe that the event will not happen to them. In the case of New Orleans, they may have felt that they were fully protected by flood-control measures such as the levees.[6] This has led to increased development in hazard-prone areas without appropriate land-use regulations and well-enforced building codes, as Burby (2006) has demonstrated. In addition, budget constraints and short time horizons may limit people's interest and ability to invest in hazard mitigation measures and desire to purchase insurance.

If we as a society are to commit ourselves to reducing future losses from natural disasters and limit government assistance after the event, we have to engage the private and public sectors in a creative partnership.

If we as a society are to commit ourselves to reducing future losses from natural disasters and limit government assistance after the event, we have to engage the private and public sectors in a creative partnership. This requires well-enforced building codes and land-use regulations coupled with insurance protection. Economic incentives, making these actions financially palatable to property owners, need to be provided in the form of long-term mitigation loans and subsidies to low-income residents of high-hazard areas. The rationale for taking these measures before the next disaster is to avoid the large-scale disaster relief that will otherwise follow. In addition, if structures are well designed and appropriate land-use regulations are in place, injuries and fatalities will be reduced, as will the need to relocate large numbers of victims. These developments could have enormous psychological and sociological implications.

Cost-benefit analysis can play an important role in determining what types of actions the public sector should engage in to reduce future disaster losses. To undertake these analyses, one needs to incorporate the most accurate risk assessments available and recognize the uncertainties that surround them. For example, one of the issues discussed following Hurricane Katrina is whether to rebuild levees and, if so, to what level of protection. This type of decision cannot be evaluated without considering other measures, such as land-use regulations and building codes, for reducing the likelihood of another Katrina should the levees be overtopped or fail due to a severe hurricane.

Finally, one may want to rethink the type of disaster insurance that should be provided to those in hazard-prone areas. It may be useful to revisit the possibility of providing protection against all hazards under a homeowners policy rather than continuing with the separate programs that currently exists for floods and earthquakes. I explore this issue in some detail in another paper (Kunreuther 2006) and contend that a comprehensive natural disaster program provides economic incentives for the private and public sectors to work more closely together so that we can reduce the likelihood of another Hurricane Katrina occurring in our lifetimes as well as those of future generations.

Notes

1. A discussion of alternative flood reduction measures can be found in Laska (1991) and Federal Emergency Management Agency (FEMA, 1998).

2. If the resale value of the house were increased due to mitigation, this would be an additional benefit.

3. Note that we are assuming that they will not recoup some of the cost of mitigation should they sell their house.

4. For a discussion of the use of threshold models of choice in protective decisions, see Camerer and Kunreuther (1989).

5. This myopic behavior could also be explained by a high discount rate. See Hausman (1979) and Kempton and Neiman (1987).

6. FEMA clearly thought that the levees would provide this protection. Otherwise, it would have designated the lower 9th Ward as a hazard-prone area, and residents would have been eligible for flood insurance.

References

Baron, Jonathan, and Nicholas P. Maxwell. 1996. Cost of public goods affects willingness to pay for them. *Journal of Behavioral Decision Making* 9:173-83.

Bernknopf, R. L., L. B. Dinitz, S. J. M. Rabinovici, and A. M. Evans. 2001. A portfolio approach to evaluating natural hazard mitigation policies: An application to lateral-spread ground failure in coastal California. *International Geology Review* 43:424-40.

Bernkopf, R., S. Rabinovici, L. Dinitz, and N. Wood. Forthcoming. The influence of hazard models on GIS-based regional risk assessments and mitigation policies. *International Journal of Risk Assessment and Management*.

Boardman, Anthony, David Greenberg, Aidan Vining, and David Weimer. 2001. *Cost-benefit analysis: Concepts and practice*. 2nd ed. Upper Saddle River, NJ: Prentice Hall.

Brookings Institution. 2005. Hurricane Katrina timeline. http://www.brookings.edu/fp/projects/homeland/katrinatimeline.pdf.

Burby, Raymond J. 1991. *Sharing environmental risks: How to control governments' losses in natural disasters*. With Beverly A. Cigler, Steven P. French, Edward J. Kaiser, Jack Kartez, Dale Roenigk, Dana Weist, and Dale Whittington. Boulder, CO: Westview.

———. 2006. Hurricane Katrina and the paradoxes of government disaster policy: Bringing about wise governmental decisions for hazardous areas. *Annals of the American Academy of Political and Social Science* 604:171-91.

Burby, Raymond J., Scott J. Bollens, Edward J. Kaiser, David Mullan, and John R. Sheaffer. 1988. *Cities under water: A comparative evaluation of ten cities' efforts to manage floodplain land use*. Boulder: Institute of Behavioral Science, University of Colorado.

Camerer, Colin, and Howard Kunreuther. 1989. Decision processes for low probability events: Policy impli-
    cations. *Journal of Policy Analysis and Management* 8:565-92.
Congressional Research Service. 2005. *Federal Stafford Act disaster assistance: Presidential declarations,*
    eligible activities, and funding. Washington, DC: Congressional Research Service, Library of Congress.
Dacy, Douglas, and Howard Kunreuther. 1968. *The economics of natural disasters.* New York: Free Press.
Earthquake Engineering Research Institute. 1998. *Incentives and impediments to improving the seismic*
    performance of buildings. Oakland, CA: Earthquake Engineering Research Institute.
Federal Emergency Management Agency (FEMA). 1998. *Retrofitting: Six ways to prevent your home from*
    flooding. June. Washington, DC: FEMA.
Gladwell, Malcolm. 2000. *The tipping point.* New York: Little, Brown.
Hausman, Jerry. 1979. Individual discount rates and the purchase and utilization of energy-using durables.
    Bell Journal of Economics 10:33-54.
Heal, Geoffrey, and Howard Kunreuther. 2005. You can only die once: Inderdependent security in an uncer-
    tainty world. In *The economic impacts of terrorist attacks*, ed. H. W. Richardson, P. Gordon, and J. E.
    Moore II. Cheltenham, UK: Edward Elgar.
Heath, Chip, and Jack B. Soll. 1996. Mental budgeting and consumer decisions. *Journal of Consumer*
    Research: An Interdisciplinary Quarterly 23:40-52.
Heinz Center. 2000. *The hidden costs of coastal hazards.* Washington, DC: Island Press.
Hogarth, Robin, and Howard Kunreuther. 1995. Decision making under ignorance: Arguing with yourself.
    Journal of Risk and Uncertainty 10:15-36.
Huber, O., R. Wider, and O. Huber. 1997. Active information search and complete information presentation
    in naturalistic risky decision tasks. *Acta Psychologica* 95:15-29.
Insurance Information Institute. 2005. Flood insurance facts and figures. http://www.disasterinformation
    .org/disaster2/facts/flood_insfacts/.
Insurance Research Council (IRC) and Insurance Institute of Property Loss Reduction (IIPLR). 1995.
    Coastal exposure and community protection: Hurricane Andrew's legacy. Wheaton, IL: IRC; Boston:
    IIPLR.
Kempton, Willett, and Max Neiman, ed. 1987. *Energy efficiency: Perspectives on individual behavior.* Wash-
    ington, DC: American Council for an Energy Efficient Economy.
Kleindorfer, Paul, and Howard Kunreuther. 1999. The complimentary roles of mitigation and insurance in
    managing catastrophic risks. *Risk Analysis* 19:727-38.
Kunreuther, Howard. 1973. *Recovery from natural disasters: Insurance or federal aid?* Washington, DC:
    American Enterprise Institute for Public Policy Research.
———. 1996. Mitigating disaster losses through insurance. *Journal of Risk and Uncertainty* 12:171-87.
———. 2006. Comprehensive disaster insurance: Has its time come? In *Risk and disaster: Lessons from*
    Hurricane Katrina. Philadelphia: University of Pennsylvania Press.
Kunreuther, Howard et al. 1978. *Disaster insurance protection: Public policy lessons.* New York: John Wiley.
Kunreuther, Howard, Ayse Onculer, and Paul Slovic. 1998. Time insensitivity for protective measures. *Jour-*
    nal of Risk and Uncertainty 16:279-99.
Laska, Shirley B. 1991. *Floodproof retrofitting: Homeowner self-protective behavior.* Boulder: Institute of
    Behavioral Science, University of Colorado.
Luce, Mary Frances, and Barbara Kahn. 1999. Avoidance or vigilance? The psychology of false-positive test
    results. *Journal of Consumer Research* 26:242-59.
Magat, Wes, W. Kip Viscusi, and Joel Huber. 1987. Risk-dollar tradeoffs, risk perceptions, and consumer
    behavior. In *Learning about risk*, ed. W. Viscusi and W. Magat, 83-97. Cambridge, MA: Harvard Univer-
    sity Press.
McClelland, Gary, William Schulze, and Don Coursey. 1993. Insurance for low-probability hazards: A
    bimodal response to unlikely events. *Journal of Risk and Uncertainty* 7:95-116.
Meyer, Robert, and Wes Hutchinson. 2001. Bumbling geniuses: The power of everyday reasoning in multi-
    stage decision making. In *Wharton on making decisions*, ed. S. Hoch and H. Kunreuther, with R. Gun-
    ther. New York: John Wiley.
Moss, David. 2002. *When all else fails: Government as the ultimate risk manager.* Cambridge, MA: Harvard
    University Press.

Oberholzer-Gee, Felix. 1998. Learning to bear the unbearable: Towards an explanation of risk ignorance. Mimeograph, Wharton School, University of Pennsylvania.

Palm, Risa, Michael Hodgson, R. Denise Blanchard, and Donald Lyons. 1990. *Earthquake insurance in California: Environmental policy and individual decision making.* Boulder, CO: Westview.

Posner, Richard. 2004. *Catastrophe: Risk and response.* New York: Oxford University Press.

Schelling, Thomas. 1978. *Micromotives and macrobehavior.* New York: Norton.

Schkade, David, and John Payne. 1994. How people respond to contingent valuation questions: A verbal protocol analysis of willingness to pay for an environmental regulation. *Journal of Environmental Economics and Management* 26:88-109.

Thaler, Richard. 1999. Mental accounting matters. *Journal of Behavioral Decision Making* 12:183-206.

U.S. Department of Housing and Urban Development and U.S. Census Bureau. 2004. *Current Housing Reports, Series H170/04-30, American Housing Survey for the New Orleans Metropolitan Area: 2004.* Washington, DC: U.S. Department of Housing and Urban Development and U.C. Census Bureau.

Wharton Risk Center. 2005. Lessons from Katrina: Déjà vu all over again. *Risk Management Review,* fall, p. 5.

The Primacy of Partnership: Scoping a New National Disaster Recovery Policy

Hurricane Katrina is widely perceived as a threshold-crossing event, capable of bringing about changes in public policy comparable with those that followed the terrorist attacks of September 11, 2001. Headline-grabbing proposals for improving the leadership of disaster-management organizations divert attention from a task of greater importance: the nourishment of partnerships among different stakeholder groups. Such partnerships have previously been organized around common material interests. Stronger and more enduring partnerships might better be based on ideas that capture shared ambiguities of hazard, as well as material interests. Lay publics need to be engaged with contradictory concepts that exist across the full range of environmental and societal contexts in which hazards are embedded. The process of recovery from Katrina presents social scientists with an opportunity to extend inquiry and partnerships into new arenas that have the potential to sharpen intellectual understanding as well as to address needed policy reforms.

Keywords: Katrina; leadership; partnership; national project; urban functions; interpretation; surprise; contingency

By
JAMES K. MITCHELL

The terrorist attacks of September 11, 2001, precipitated a revolution in U.S. disaster policy making and hazards management (Demuth 2002; Kershaw 2005). On one hand, they propelled public concerns about the safety of Amer-

James K. Mitchell is a professor of geography at Rutgers University. Born in Northern Ireland, he is a fellow of the American Association for the Advancement of Science and author of more than 130 professional works on the human dimensions of environmental hazards. He has also led National Research Council postdisaster survey teams, advised hazard policy bodies on four continents, chaired the International Geographical Union's Study Group on the Disaster Vulnerability of Megacities, and founded the international journal Global Environmental Change.

NOTE: This article integrates and extends a critique of hazards management that has been developed in recent oral presentations, some of which have also been published in summary form (Mitchell 2004, 2005a, 2005b, 2005c, 2005d).

DOI: 10.1177/0002716205286044

TABLE 1

SHIFTS IN THE BALANCE OF U.S. HAZARDS POLICIES AFTER 9/11

From	Toward
Hazard events and causal contexts	Hazard events
Risk agents and vulnerability factors	Risk agents
Reaction and anticipation	Reaction
Technological and behavioral fixes	Technological fixes
Centralized and decentralized decision making	Centralized decision making
Experts and laypersons	Experts
Emergency management and hazard mitigation	Emergency management
Transparency	Secrecy

ican communities firmly onto the national policy agenda (Eisinger 2004; Savitch 2003) and impelled a major governmental reorganization that created the Department of Homeland Security. On the other hand, these same changes profoundly unsettled the existing systems for managing natural, technological, and social hazards by abruptly reversing beneficial trends in policy and management that had been gathering momentum for decades.

In the latter part of the twentieth century, shifts in the emphasis of public policy had increasingly favored a broad engagement between society and hazard. Lay populations were encouraged to take more responsibility for protecting themselves against environmental threats, especially through anticipatory long-term measures directed against context-driven forces that increased human vulnerability. But in the wake of 9/11, there was a sudden return to older and narrower approaches that reinforced reactive emergency responses by specially trained experts, whose first preference was to apply technological controls to the immediate physical agents of risk (see Table 1).

Much has been written about this transformation by researchers in the social sciences as well as by professional hazards managers (Flynn 2004; Mitchell 2003; Perrow 2005; Tierney 2005; Waugh and Sylves 2002; Waugh 2004). That literature is occasionally optimistic, as when analysts look toward the potential benefits of heightened public attention to safety, but mostly it conveys a sense of disappointment and disapproval about the regressive changes that were adopted. This is not the place to revisit the literature or the debates that it sparked, except as a point of departure for the present article. Many critics of the post-9/11 policy shifts expected that serious flaws in the contemporary hazards management system would be revealed by subsequent non-terrorism-related disasters. Hurricane Katrina provided a test of those beliefs.

Unfortunately, those who perceive Katrina as a wake-up call that will dispel the illusions of recently adopted hazards management policies and set us on the road to more realistic alternatives may find that this unprecedented disaster is an unreliable harbinger, not least because it has opened the door to proposals that would undermine carefully built systems of partnership without which any future hazard management system is unlikely to succeed. These partnerships exist in a myriad of forms that bring together different levels of government, bridge the divide between public and private sectors, merge the contributions of disciplines and professions, and seek to close the gap between experts and laypersons.

For hazards professionals, the trick has always been to promote community sensitivity to risks and vulnerabilities without unduly stifling actions that serve other valuable goals.

To some observers, Katrina was a general indictment of existing arrangements that were supposed to provide safety and assuage loss, most especially the failure of public institutions to discharge their mandated responsibilities. Influential critics have promoted visions of no-nonsense leaders imbued with new authority to cut through the inherent messiness of disasters and clear the way for centrally controlled, rapid response teams of experts from the military and other action-oriented institutions, who will implement measures that are simultaneously prompt, effective, efficient, and just. Beguiling though such man-on-horseback solutions might seem to be, they divert attention away from notions of partnership that have proven their value in reducing hazards and are particularly well suited to the complexities of contemporary American life. Amid the societal and environmental uncertainties of the new century and the emergence of new threats that are generated by international forces, as well as national and subnational ones, such partnerships may also hold the keys to human survival. It will be important for Americans to pay close attention to the construction of new partnerships as they embark on the process of recovery from one of the country's epic natural disasters (Etkin 2005).

Katrina:
An Exceptional Disaster

When a final accounting of its impacts and consequences becomes available, Hurricane Katrina is likely to be without peer among the sudden onset disasters of North America. Other extreme events have killed more people,[1] have more radically transformed physical landscapes,[2] and have obliterated more settlements,[3] but there has been nothing quite like the scope, scale, and combination of effects that followed in Katrina's wake. For an affluent developed society like the United States, this event is truly exceptional, whether measured by the size of the impacted population,[4] the dimensions of the affected area,[5] the degree to which buildings and infrastructure were destroyed or rendered unusable,[6] the dispersion of displaced people,[7] the range and scale of the economic costs,[8] the number of jobs lost,[9] the duration of the emergency period,[10] the starkness of the vulnerability and loss gaps that separate more privileged victims from less privileged ones,[11] or the extent of public interest in mass media coverage.[12] Taken together, the combination of problems and consequences is unprecedented. New Orleans, one of America's most distinctive and cherished major cities (Colten 2005), has been so heavily damaged as to be uninhabitable by most of its people for months to years, maybe permanently for a majority. Sober analysts have suggested that a rebuilt New Orleans might have to be a much smaller place, in light of the inherent vulnerabilities of its site and the cost—as well as the complexity—of making it safer. Lesser cities like Biloxi and Gulfport have also been grievously stricken, together with a much larger number of towns and rural communities in an extended coastal arc that cuts across three of the poorest U.S. states.[13] Now, in Katrina's aftermath, Americans face a recovery job of heroic proportions.

To that task they bring a considerable fund of knowledge about disasters and the process of recovery. It might be said that the United States possesses one of the world's most disaster-intimate cultures, as remarkable in its own way as those of countries like China, Japan, and the Netherlands whose engagements with natural hazards are widely acknowledged (Elvin 2004; Reuss 2002). Despite a relatively brief history of urbanized settlement, Americans have compiled an impressive record of rehabilitating, replacing, and extending communities devastated by earthquakes, fires, floods, and storms.[14] In addition to New Orleans, the histories of many U.S. cities pivot around major natural disasters that turned out to be regenerative events, including among others Charleston, South Carolina (1886 earthquake); Johnstown, Pennsylvania (1889 dam-burst-related flood); Galveston, Texas (1900 hurricane); San Francisco (1906 earthquake); Pueblo, Colorado (1921 flood); Santa Barbara, California (1925 earthquake); Pittsburgh, Pennsylvania (1936 flood); Bar Harbor, Maine (1947 forest fire); Hilo, Hawaii (1960 tsunami); Anchorage, Alaska (1964 earthquake); and Grand Forks, North Dakota (1997 flood and fire).[15] When (man-made) urban fires are included, the list of regenerative urban disasters includes most of the East Coast metropolises (e.g., Boston, New York, Baltimore) as well as other large cities like Chicago and Seattle, Washington. However, compared with Katrina, in none of these cases were so many people directly affected, nor such large costs incurred, nor was the spread of impacts so pervasive and prolonged.

Despite the country's intimacy with natural disasters and its record of successful recovery, the size and complexity of post-Katrina recovery tasks is daunting, combining a signal urban catastrophe with general regionwide devastation. This helps to explain why some commentators have labeled Katrina a "megadisaster" or a "megacatastrophe" (King 2005; Sylves 2005; Litan 2005), in other words, a phenomenon that calls for public engagement on a wholly different plane from the floods and storms of the past.[16] Perhaps the most appropriate models for such a new departure might be found outside the United States in responses to disasters like the 1953 floods in the Rhine delta region of the Netherlands and the 1959 typhoon that struck Nagoya, Japan. Both of those events became the focus of *national* campaigns to lower the threshold of acceptable losses by fundamentally reconfiguring each country's hazard management system.[17] Within the larger Gulf Coast region, the more focused reconstruction problems that face New Orleans are perhaps on a par with the postearthquake plight of Tokyo-Yokohama, Japan, in 1923; Tangshan, China, in 1976; Kobe, Japan, in 1995; or with the post–World War II reconstruction tasks of European and Japanese cities (Mitchell 1996, 1999, 2004; Vale and Campanella 2005; Inam 2005; Schneider and Susser 2003). In these cases too, recovery generally became a national, rather than a state or local, priority. It was also a task that remained in the public spotlight for a decade or more after the destructive events.

In the pages that follow, recovery issues pertinent to New Orleans are highlighted because it faces the biggest and most complex recovery problems of any Katrina-impacted community. The New Orleans experience has exposed a major gap between knowledge and praxis that calls for thinking outside the box of existing policy and conventional practice. This facilitates a generic discussion about innovative conceptions of recovery. The prospect of a global future that will likely contain more megadisasters and other surprises requires no less.

Recovery

Recovery is the process by which a stricken community binds up its wounds, reasserts order, and acquires or reacquires preoccupations beyond those of the disaster itself.[18] Paradoxically, therein lies a danger, for the further the disaster experience recedes from present consciousness, the more likely its lessons will be neglected or lost, thereby paving the way for another disaster. For hazards professionals, the trick has always been to promote community sensitivity to risks and vulnerabilities without unduly stifling actions that serve other valuable goals.

As knowledge about appropriate adjustments to hazard has grown and management skills have increased, conceptions of recovery have changed. Early in the twentieth century, recovery was a hoped-for state whose attainment might be sought by public leaders, in a loosely organized way, but without any guarantees of success. Thereafter, it gradually became an activity managed by professionals who sought to return communities to "normal" as quickly as possible. (This was also the thrust of broader national recovery policies instituted during the Great Depression in the United States and in the years immediately after World War II for Europe and Japan.) Later still, the objective became achievement of a "new normalcy" because it was recognized that there was no going back to a predisaster state. During the 1990s, the characterization of recovery as a series of discrete but overlapping stages was replaced by the notion of recovery as a continuing opportunity-seeking process (Mileti 1999, 229-30). Finally, as hazards theorists and managers sought to link their work with the movement for sustainable development, a new concept of "holistic disaster recovery" emerged. Such is the reigning policy orthodoxy in New Zealand, where it is now enshrined in a national recovery strategy (New Zealand, Ministry of Civil Defence and Emergency Management 2005). There, recovery is viewed as one element in a comprehensive framework for managing disasters that also includes mutually supportive activities of risk reduction, increased readiness, and improved response. Recovery is further subdivided into five separate components that address the physical environment, infrastructure, psychosocial dimensions, attributes of community, and the economy, respectively.

If Hurricane Katrina had affected New Zealand rather than the United States, it would have triggered a comprehensive national policy on disaster recovery that lays out a broad clear path for the stricken area, and the nation as a whole, to follow. Since Americans lack such a policy, they have the additional burden of sorting out how to approach the task of recovery as well as what to do when appropriate procedures have been agreed to. In practice, this has been a matter of local-scale initiatives undertaken by municipal governments working in collaboration with private sector institutions and the federal government. If typical historical precedents are followed in the wake of Katrina, there will be a period of more or less frenzied improvisation amid conflicts about legitimacy, authority, jurisdictions, interests, values, and visions of the future interspersed with calls for an epochal figure (or his institutional equivalent) to appear and sort matters out. While it is entirely possible that a program of informed, efficient, and just action might arise out of this process—and that its outcome might be exemplary—much more likely is a process of muddling through that is not informed by the best available knowledge, does little to mitigate future risks, and adds to the burdens of those who suffered the most during the disaster. In light of these deficiencies, it may now be time to institute a formal national policy for disaster recovery. This might take account of super-disasters, as well as those of lesser magnitude, and it might include policies that address impacts that are national—perhaps even global[19]—in scope as well as those that affect local communities. Such a discussion has largely been missing from public discourse in the wake of Hurricane Katrina.

Leadership

After Katrina there have been many suggestions both for how to proceed with the tasks of recovery and for how to change societal arrangements for coping with the threat of future disasters. Prominent among these are calls for improved leadership during emergencies. Such calls tend to emphasize certain qualities of crisis leaders (e.g., courage, vision, steadfastness of purpose, willingness to take risks when information is uncertain) and certain attributes of optimal emergency decision-making systems (e.g., unambiguous centralized authority, clearly designated areas of responsibility, agreed chains of communication and command, etc.) A typical example is a recent speech by Tom Kean, former governor of New Jersey and cochairman of the National Commission on Terrorist Attacks. In it, Kean remarked that the nation's preeminent need, after Katrina—as it was in the wake of 9/11—is for a single person or entity that would be clearly in charge during emergencies and through which all of the important decisions would flow.[20]

The potential for a crisis to elevate a competent leader to a position of eminence among peers can produce a lack of congruence between the interests of the public and the interests of the leader, perhaps with disastrous results for both.

Governor Kean is not alone in calling for strong centralized leadership as a sine qua non of disaster management. The same notion is shared by many who have offered opinions about Katrina in the mass media, in public opinion polls, and elsewhere. For example, a recent Pew Center national poll (released September 6, 2005) showed that leadership by U.S. President Bush, Louisiana Governor Kathleen Blanco, and New Orleans Mayor Ray Nagin was a focal point of criticism by sizeable majorities of respondents (see http://people-press.org/reports/display.php3?ReportID=255). Editorials and opinion columns in many U.S. newspapers offered similar assessments, sometimes—as in the case of a *Washington Post* article on the U.S. Coast Guard—using the performance of emergency-response agencies that were deemed to have done well in Katrina, to highlight the failures of others—like the Federal Emergency Management Agency (FEMA).[21] The overseas press was even more trenchant about flaws in leadership during Hurricane Katrina.[22] Representatives of varied U.S. interests from nongovernmental organizations to emergency response professionals to erstwhile national political notables also weighed in with critiques of leadership and calls for the replacement of key personnel.[23]

While skillful leadership is undeniably helpful in the often-confused circumstances of an ongoing emergency, its significance is easy to misinterpret and to overstate. This is so for several reasons.

First, humans have a well-documented tendency to commit the "fundamental attribution error" by attaching disproportionate importance to individuals as causal agents and by downplaying the role of structural or contextual factors (Jones and Harris 1967; Ross 1977). This is particularly true when a complex problem that was long in the making and global in scope is crystallized in a particular place during a moment of crisis. Problems, and responses to problems, become personified in prominent individuals or salient groups, though many other factors may be just as important. After 9/11, the demonization of Osama bin Laden and the enhanced stature of Mayor Rudolf Giuliani, as well as the "heroes" of New York City's police and fire departments, are cases in point.[24]

Second, crises tend to constrain decision choices that are available to leaders. Challenges are often reduced to immediate issues, but a shorter agenda with a narrower range of alternatives does not guarantee a better outcome. This problem is familiar to students of hazard, who realize that anticipatory hazard mitigation is not only a bigger, slower, and less glamorous process than reactive emergency management but also one that offers greater payoffs for society as a whole. Yet mitigation has proven to be a hard sell for hazards researchers and managers to political leaders. Few leaders appear willing to look past emergencies to tackle the causes of disasters before they gestate rather than the impacts after they occur. Progress toward mitigation has often come in the form of pressures that arise outside government in the civic sector of society or in the scientific community. In other words, an emphasis on (political) leadership as the key to effective hazard management is likely to bias the scope of problem solving toward measures that can be accomplished quickly and with maximum public visibility but not necessarily optimal results.

Third is the matter of luck; planning for improved leadership during crises is highly problematic, given the unpredictability of extreme events. In crises, leaders stand out from their peers in part because they were lucky enough to have been presented with a challenge that was denied to the others. Many politicians, who know just how important it is to confront a great crisis if one wishes to be considered a great leader, appreciate this point (Clinton 2004). The potential for a crisis to elevate a competent leader to a position of eminence among peers can produce a lack of congruence between the interests of the public and the interests of the leader, perhaps with disastrous results for both. Moreover, the criteria for evaluating leadership are difficult to anticipate in advance of an emergency. Individuals who prevailed in past emergencies might perform significantly better or worse under a slightly different set of circumstances.

Fourth and finally, while leadership is not the same as mastery, emergencies have often generated pressures to adopt "command and control" procedures that encourage centralization and standardization of disaster norms. In these circumstances, militarized models of leadership are often promoted as substitutes for civilian alternatives (Wright 1997). With recent renewed calls for increased military supervision of disaster relief and recovery tasks, they are once again up for broader consideration. Yet disasters are inherently fluid situations that, severally, resist control, carry with them the contextual baggage of the local predisaster society, and throw up emergent new social formations that may or may not become permanent (Drabek and McEntire 2002; Wachtendorf and Kendra 2005). They also generate many kinds of victims with different needs and interests that require help that can only be provided by a vast range of civilian organizations, few of whom are either familiar with (or necessarily sympathetic toward) military-style management. The weighing and balancing of multiple demands—both for imme-diate action and long-term plans—are more apt to require satisfying negotiation and mediation skills than optimizing commands.

Without belaboring the point, these examples suggest that the capacity for sound leadership during emergencies is a provisional attribute whose mobilization and application are deeply contextualized and therefore hardly a reliable basis on which to establish policies for coping with future disasters. While it would be fool-ish to ignore the importance of leadership, it is both facile and thoroughly mislead-ing to view leadership as a panacea for what is already—and for other reasons—a faltering American public engagement with natural hazards and disasters.

Partnership

The welter of criticisms about leadership flaws during Katrina may blind us to the even more important role of partnership as a policy instrument for address-ing natural hazards and disasters. Partnership is at the heart of American hazards management policies, and it is also the pivotal concept in reforms of those policies that have been proposed—though less often implemented—for many years (Etkin 2005).

In the United States and other parts of the world, some of the biggest barriers to improved policies for the reduction of hazards have been the modest size and im-permanence of the supporting political constituencies. After major disasters, calls for immediate public actions are commonplace, and the will to undertake them is abundant. But at other times, there is usually no great public clamor for more effective programs to prevent, avoid, or reduce risks and vulnerabilities. As a re-sult, hazards management has usually been the preserve of a relatively small range of people who are permanently and directly involved with the study or implemen-tation of programs that regulate risks and assist victims. Typically these include experts in government agencies, academia, humanitarian organizations, and non-governmental entities as well as a limited range of others in private institutions such as electrical utilities, real estate development firms, or insurance companies. It is one of the signal achievements of this modest constituency that they have man-aged to persuade public leaders to work toward the adoption of anticipatory hazard mitigation programs in place of reactive disaster relief ones.[25] In this task, they have been mightily assisted by formal or informal partnerships that permit these inter-est groups to combine and lever their separate contributions and to reach out to others who were previously uninvolved. In less than two decades, the notion of partnership has become deeply embedded in the hazards community, and it is now commonly accepted that policy making and management should involve repre-sentation of all so-called stakeholders.

Partnership, in its broadest sense, refers to mutual cooperation and shared responsibility among individuals or groups that pursue a common goal. It is a pow-erful concept that informs many aspects of human life and stands as a central meta-phor of governance in the United States and many other democracies.[26] For exam-

SAGE Publications

2455 Teller Road • Thousand Oaks, CA 91320 • U.S.A.
PHONE: (800) 818-7243 or (805) 499-9774 • FAX: (805) 499-0871
E-MAIL: journals@sagepub.com
WEBSITE: www.sagepublications.com

1 Oliver's Yard • 55 City Road • London EC1Y 1SP • U.K.
PHONE: +44 (0) 20-7324-8500 • FAX: +44 (0) 20-7324-8600
E-MAIL: subscription@sagepub.co.uk
WEBSITE: www.sagepublications.co.uk

HO3409

FOR MORE INFORMATION ABOUT THIS JOURNAL, TO SIGN UP FOR E-MAIL OR PRODUCT ALERTS, TO VIEW A SAMPLE ISSUE ONLINE, OR TO SUBSCRIBE, PLEASE VISIT: http://theannals.sagepub.com OR FILL OUT THIS POSTCARD AND RETURN IT TO Ⓢ SAGE PUBLICATIONS.

THE ANNALS OF THE AMERICAN ACADEMY OF POLITICAL AND SOCIAL SCIENCE-PAPERBOUND

Frequency: 6 Times/Year

The Annals of the American Academy of Political and Social Science-Paperbound (J295) ISSN: 0002-7162

Please start my subscription to The Annals of the American Academy of Political and Social Science.

In North America, South America, Central America, the Caribbean, and Asia

☐ Individuals (Print only): $84 *
☐ Single Copy Price: Individuals (Print only): $34
☐ Institutions (Combined print & online): $577
☐ Single Copy Price: Institutions (Print only): $102

In the United Kingdom, Europe, Australasia, the Middle East, and Africa

☐ Individuals (Print only): £55 *
☐ Single Copy Price: Individuals (Print only): £22
☐ Institutions (Combined print & online): £373
☐ Single Copy Price: Institutions (Print only): £66

* (All individual subscriptions are handled through the Annals of the American Academy of Political and Social Science at www.aapss.org)

Name

Title/Department

Address

Address

City/State or Province / Zip or Postal Code / Country

Phone

E-mail

Subscriptions will begin with the current issue, unless otherwise specified. Customers outside of the United States will receive their publications via air-speeded delivery.

NO POSTAGE
NECESSARY
IF MAILED
IN THE
UNITED STATES

BUSINESS REPLY MAIL
FIRST-CLASS MAIL   PERMIT NO. 90   THOUSAND OAKS, CA

POSTAGE WILL BE PAID BY ADDRESSEE

SAGE PUBLICATIONS
PO BOX 5084
THOUSAND OAKS CA 91359-9989

ple, the need for partnership is stated or implied in founding documents of the U.S. republic and reaffirmed in national myths and societal traditions. The assertion of rights to diverse national goals (e.g. life, liberty, and the pursuit of happiness) encourages mechanisms of mediation and compromise that open the constitutional door to partnership.[27] The federal structure of national, state, and local governments; the division of powers among legislative, executive, and judicial branches; and the principle of checks and balances all imply a need for bridges between different political constituencies. Institutional cooperation is also required because of the vast size, heterogeneity, and dynamism of the country.

Recently, the importance of partnership as an institutional operating principle has been underlined in domestic debates about federalism, immigration, multiculturalism, and civic society as well as international debates about climate change, sustainable development, the restructuring of nation-states into supranational economic and political associations, democratization, and human rights, among other topics. Burgeoning trends in globalization also reveal a need for collective solutions to shared problems that transcend narrow jurisdictions or interests, while in the realm of intellectual inquiry the die seems cast ever more strongly in favor of team research, interdisciplinary thinking, and collaborative enterprise. None of these endeavors is conceivable without partnerships, albeit of differing kinds.

Partnership has long been a central motif of U.S. public policies formulated in response to natural hazards, disasters, and catastrophes.[28] The fragmented nature of societal responsibilities for the making and implementation of hazards policies virtually compels the use of partnership mechanisms (May and Williams 1986). Just by itself, the role of the federal government is enormously complex. As one prominent analyst has noted,

> Over the past fifty years the United States Congress has created a legal edifice of Byzantine complexity to cope with natural disasters. The federal disaster apparatus includes laws, agencies, programs, policies, and strategies, many of them intended to operate in "partnership" with state and local governments, non-governmental organizations, and the private sector. Federal assistance is provided under approximately fifty different laws and executive orders to households, businesses, farms, states, municipalities, special districts, and non-governmental organizations. (Platt 2000)

It is no accident that FEMA's Strategic Plan was titled "Partnership for a Safer Future" or that FEMA entered into "Performance Partnership Agreements" with other organizations (Godschalk et al. 1999, 59) or that the notion of partnership has been central to many of the programs for managing specific hazards (e.g., tsunamis, landslides, floods) or to programs dealing with cross-cutting sectoral responsibilities like hazard mitigation, disaster relief, and emergency management (Bernard 2005; Byman et al. 2000; Mileti 1999, 159; National Research Council 2000, 25; National Research Council 2004). Partnerships are also central to the broad field of natural hazard insurance, especially the path-breaking National Flood Insurance Program (Changnon and Easterling 2000; Grossi and Kunreuther 2005; Kunreuther 2000; Meyer 1997), and they are considered central to any future system for the financing of recovery from megadisasters (Comerio 1998, 252). Likewise, beginning in the late 1990s during an era of governmental restructuring, *public-private partnerships* have been widely touted as a path-breaking institutional innovation that brings a wide range of stakeholders into a policy-making apparatus that once was dominated by political leaders, bureaucrats, disaster management professionals, and scientists.

Partnership is at the heart of American hazards management policies, and it is also the pivotal concept in reforms of those policies that have been proposed—though less often implemented—for many years.

To some extent, the need for partnership is a function of increasing societal complexity. This puts a premium on coordinating the actions of many different institutions and formal or informal groups. For example, since its inception FEMA has been tasked with the preeminent role of coordinating the responses of other agencies that have their own more limited spheres of action. The need for improved coordination has also been a theme of both the 9/11 terrorist attacks and Hurricane Katrina. The Final Report of the National Commission on Terrorist Attacks upon the United States (the 9/11 Commission) contains forty-one different recommendations, of which at least sixteen focus on coordination, sharing, connectivity, consolidation, integration, joint or common action, and other synonyms for working together in partnerships. Similar kinds of issues have also figured prominently in the aftermath of Hurricane Katrina. For example, thirteen of thirty essays that appear on the Social Science Research Council's Katrina Web page highlight issues of coordination (Alexander 2005; Dynes and Rodríguez 2005; Frymer, Strolovitch, and Warren 2005; Fussell 2005; Graham 2005; Hurlbert, Beggs, and Haines 2005; Krause 2005; Lakoff 2005; Mitchell 2005b; Molotch 2005; Quarantelli 2005; Tierney 2005; Wachtendorf and Kendra 2005). The prominence that is accorded to coordination and the associated need for improved collaboration reflect the difficulties that are experienced by a complex large society during a period of rapid change, when existing institutions are stressed by unfamiliar problems and by demands for action that press against the limits of their capabilities.

For all its potency, the notion of partnership is all too often interpreted in a prosaic way that robs it of the potential to be a sustaining instrument for change. It is most often conceived as a union of people who share common interests in the management of hazards. However, interest-centered forms of partnership tend to last only as long as the groups that come together share those interests. Once the circumstances that favor a convergence of interests no longer exist—whether due to a switch of parties in power, or a grassroots shift in political ideology, or a surprising external shock that destabilizes taken-for-granted assumptions, or for some other reason—then the dependent partnerships are likely to weaken and disappear. In short, partnerships that are solely marriages of interests are easily sundered by events; those based on something more substantial—like expansive, compelling ideas—are likely to prove more durable.

Consider, for example, the enduring vitality of the concept of *hazard*. It is a union of two separate but interrelated ideas, namely, risk and vulnerability—each of which has spawned its own tributary disciplines, professions, institutions, and user groups. To grasp the dynamism of the underlying interaction is not only to find common ground among the diverse interest groups but is also to perceive the potential for a vastly expanded range of managerial responses around which nuanced policies can be constructed and adjusted, irrespective of the interests at stake. *Sustainable development* is another idea with legs. It synthesizes the concerns of two fundamentally important fields of endeavor—ecology and economics—while also offering the notion of transgenerational equity as a counterweight to short-term decision making that ignores long-term constraints on survival. Though no panacea, sustainability has become a concept that few leaders can now afford to ignore, whatever their political inclinations. These two examples of complex but elegant ideas illustrate how contradictions and ambiguities that would otherwise be causes for division among interest groups can be captured and harnessed to serve unifying generative purposes. Partnerships based on this kind of divergent but synthetic thinking are likely to be more resilient than those that rest on simpler notions of self-interest. The hazards community would be well served by encouraging movement in that direction.

Beyond Sustainability:
Partnerships of Knowledge and Ideas

The concept of sustainable development addresses one pair of human goals that have frequently been in tension, namely, the desire for environmental stability and the desire for economic growth. Under the sustainability rubric, safety from hazard is implied, insofar as long-term survival means that short-term perturbations can be borne without permanent destruction. However, such perturbations still occur, and they can inflict substantial losses; absolute safety in the face of all extreme events is not guaranteed. Indeed, small-scale perturbations are necessary for the greater, longer-term good. In accord with theories of complex adaptive change, small-scale shocks may be useful both as tests of societal resilience and as events that build capacity for absorbing or rebounding from bigger shocks. Principles of self-organization, emergence, and vulnerability are characteristic of such systems (Comfort 1999; Holling 2001; Kates et al. 2001; Turner et al. 2003).

Hazards mitigation is the strategy by which safety considerations have been introduced into sustainability planning protocols (Mileti 1999). But the post-9/11 shift in U.S. hazards policies that brought emergency management to the forefront of public attention also marginalized mitigation as a preeminent policy instrument, thereby jeopardizing the usefulness of sustainable development policies as tools of hazard management. At some point in the future, national leaders may again promote mitigation policies, but until then, it may be worthwhile to look elsewhere for alternatives that are capable of comprehensively engaging society with hazard. Moreover, sustainable development is only one conceptual stop on the way to a better fit between society and nature. In the paragraphs that follow, several possibilities for thinking beyond sustainability are suggested. These are organized around four different themes: (1) linking recovery to other national policy goals, (2) opening a dialogue between sustainability and surprise, (3) taking account of multiple functions that hazardous places must serve, and (4) accommodating contradictory interpretations of hazard. They are in no way intended to diminish the desirability of sustainability as a public goal but are viewed as logical extensions and corollaries that need to be assessed and debated now, in the context of recovery from Katrina and in preparation for future megadisasters.

Recovery in the context of national projects

The first strategy for creating partnerships of ideas about recovery is already being followed in a variety of countries around the world, though—at least explicitly—not in the United States. In China, Canada, New Zealand, and other places, disaster recovery is being linked with broader national and international projects of governance. In each of these cases, the approaches that are under way go well beyond adopting new public policies to encouraging deep-seated shifts in the way people think about—and act—toward hazards. Public institutions are being reinvented to better cope with future hazards and disasters, and new programs or policies are being negotiated within larger frameworks of public choice.

For example, in Canada there is a continuing debate about shifting the emphasis from postdisaster relief to anticipatory hazard mitigation. Like the similar debate that began in the United States about a decade ago (and is now—seemingly—in cold storage), there is much discussion about horizontal collaboration among departments and agencies as well as new institutional arrangements that involve public-private partnerships. But unlike the prior U.S. debate, Canadians are not just focusing on arguments about reducing government spending, increasing the economic efficiency of hazard control measures, and protecting critical infrastructures; many are also paying significant attention to larger constitutional and moral issues raised by a shift toward mitigation (Henstra and McBean 2004).

New Zealanders have gone considerably further down the road toward institutional innovations than Canadians. For example, in Wellington the national government has adopted a "holistic" strategy for disaster recovery, one that recognizes the need for combined attention to the recovery of ecosystems and the recovery of economies as well as infrastructures, buildings, and human victims. The mere fact that New Zealand has a strategy for disaster recovery puts it ahead of most countries; its commitment to a holistic strategy sets it even further apart from existing international norms. Moreover, because sustainability is the guiding principle of all public actions taken during the recovery phase of disasters, hazards policy making is now in the vanguard of a broad movement to reframe the entire spectrum of New Zealand governance around the notion of sustainable development.

In China, the central government is actively upgrading its disaster relief and mitigation apparatus so that some of the benefits of very rapid economic development can be channeled into making possible a transition from the country's customary high disaster death tolls to low ones. Scientific and technological innovations are expected to play an important role in this transformation via improved instrumentation of hazard monitoring, enhanced forecasts and warnings, and faster—and better-targeted—disaster relief, among others. But the central concern of Chinese hazards managers is how to come to terms with the vast societal transformation sweeping the country. Unlike the United States, they recognize the need to redesign the delivery of government-provided disaster services because patterns of risk and vulnerability and perceptions of acceptable risk are being changed both by the process of economic globalization and by the appearance of a widening gap that separates poor and underprivileged citizens from everybody else.

In Europe the challenges are different, but the approach is no less ambitious. Here the basic task is to initiate a continent-wide integrated hazards response strategy for a vastly expanded European Union whose members had previously felt no need to go beyond the existing programs of national governments. Improved education and communication about hazards is at the heart of the new policy process because European leaders have very much embraced the notion of a "Risk Society" where the first task of governance is to manage various kinds of threats to human welfare. A very prominent role is being accorded to electronic information technologies. These include GIS and remote sensing systems, networked and digitized atlases, information clearing houses, Internet sites, online conferencing, e-mail discussion groups, peer-to-peer messaging, and real-time computer-assisted emergency management systems. Part of the attraction of these technologies is that they are not burdened by a conflicted history of previous uses in different national jurisdictions that would now have to be laboriously renegotiated in the new pan-European setting. In this case, improved information exchange is not just an end in itself; it is the main mechanism for encouraging a sense of common identity and purpose among a large and diverse range of organizations and governments that share wide-ranging concerns about hazards.

All of these examples suggest a common trend toward very broad analyses of emerging disaster problems, analyses that situate hazards management in the context of wider debates about appropriate policies for environment and society during an era of fundamental change. By framing hazards variously within expansive contexts of constitutionality, morality, sustainability, sociocultural change, technological revolution, and geopolitical transformation, the countries just mentioned are also pointing the direction in which hazard-focused partnerships might evolve most effectively in the future. The way lies open for disaster recovery specialists to

---

[P]artnerships that are solely marriages of interests are easily sundered by events; those based on something more substantial— like expansive, compelling ideas—are likely to prove more durable.

---

make common cause with groups that are already part of these broader contexts, thereby expanding the constituency for improved management of hazards.

Surprises complicate recovery

The second strategy for creating a partnership of ideas about recovery extends the dialectical principle that is at the core of sustainable development thinking by adding other interacting variables that compete with the notion of sustainability. For example, *surprises* bring the relationship between sustainability and hazard into central focus. Disaster recovery cannot be solely a matter of building toward a sustainable future; it must also address unexpected contingencies.

History contains many examples of disaster recovery plans that were upset by subsequent events unconnected with the disasters. Often the outcomes were ambiguous; sometimes they were deleterious or felicitous. For example, in 1976 when the city of Tangshan was destroyed by the twentieth century's most deadly earthquake, the socioeconomic transformation of China that began with Premier Deng Xiaoping's administration was not yet on the horizon. After it arrived in the mid-1980s, the resulting boom helped speed the physical reconstruction of Tangshan and made possible the provision of long-term aid to victims. More important, it also encouraged leaders to readjust the city's initial economic recovery targets upward to previously unimagined heights. In the process, Tangshan became an award-winning model of innovative postdisaster recovery and one of the most vibrant urban centers of the new China (Mitchell 2004). Without the larger socioeconomic transformation, it is questionable that Tangshan's recovery would have proceeded either as fast or as successfully as it did.

TABLE 2
SURPRISES THAT CHANGED HAZARDS POLICIES

Type	Locus	Dates	Impacts
Economic transformation	China	Post 1972, especially after 1980	Accelerated recovery of Tangshan
Sustainable development	Global	Post 1987, especially after Rio Declaration and Agenda 21 (1992)	Increased salience of land use change and behavioral fixes
Global climate change	Global	Post 1988, especially after Kyoto Protocol (1992)	Increased salience of physical risks
Political restructuring	Europe	Post 1951, especially after fall of Berlin Wall (1989) and publication of Agenda 2000 (1997)	Increased preferences for electronic decision-support systems
War on Terror	Subglobal	Post-9/11	Narrowed range of choice and increased salience of emergency management

Other post-1980 surprises have had contrasting impacts on the context of hazard management and disaster recovery (see Table 2). Since 1988, the emergence of global climate change as a policy issue has boosted the salience of planning for increasing atmospheric risks, among them the prospect of more numerous, stronger, or longer-lasting hurricanes, like the kind that affected the United States during 2004 and 2005. Conversely, from the late 1980s onward, the sustainable development movement has fostered environmentally sensitive designs for living that would reduce societal vulnerabilities and mitigate new risks. The sudden end of the cold war also had unanticipated fallout for hazards managers. A spate of requests for membership in the European Union arrived from states that were accustomed to relatively frequent natural disasters.[29] As described above, leaders of the EU rushed to craft a continent-wide hazards management system where none had previously existed. In an attempt to quickly ramp up awareness and coping capacity, the emerging system now places a premium on risk education and real-time electronic-information-based decision support systems. Finally, the post 9/11 international War on Terror has brought emergency management back to center stage and fed new concerns about the vulnerability of society to human-created environmental hazards.

Other surprises have also jostled the locus of hazard management. These include the Chernobyl and Bhopal technological disasters, global pandemics (e.g., HIV-AIDS, SARS, avian flu), emergent social movements (e.g., human rights, feminism, environmental justice), and the IT (information technology) revolution. Taken together, such surprises suggest an important principle for the design of disaster recovery policies and programs. Recovery cannot be thought of simply as a managed process that moves society toward a desired state; recovery is also likely to be affected by disjunctive changes that are both unprecedented and pivotal for the success of the recovery strategy. Hence, it will be necessary for recovery planners and managers to hone their capacities for managing surprising contingencies as well as their skills for achieving sustainability goals. The bifurcated task of seeking sustainability while managing contingencies that challenge assumptions about recovery is another example of the dualistic thinking that epitomizes a partnership of ideas.

Diverse functions need to be recovered

The third strategy for partnering ideas about recovery pivots on the concept of place and recognizes that hazardous *places where people live serve many different functions* that are vulnerable to risks in different ways. The manner in which these functions are addressed and the degree to which they meet human needs creates a unique context within which issues of hazard and disaster recovery are negotiated.

New Orleans amply illustrates the multifunctional nature of large cities. Just as it occupies a site and structures that provide a modicum of security in an uncertain hazardous environment, New Orleans also inspires musical and culinary creativity that nourish a unique culture. In other words, the city of New Orleans functions as both a shelter and a muse. Performance is also a signal characteristic of New Orleans life. Vernacular lifestyles as well as celebrity ones are confirmed, expressed, and renegotiated through performances, sometimes ritualized (e.g., Mardi Gras, second lining) but often more casual. Unscripted performances of everyday life in buildings, parks, and streets vie with the scripted behaviors on which the city's tourist industry so often relies. More than most others, this is a city that has tested the limits of social control and cherishes an ebullient, wayward self-image. It is also a city with a flawed learning relationship to hazard. Whereas some other communities (e.g., San Francisco [Platt 1999]) have pioneered a continuing series of institutional adjustments to hazard and become laboratories for developing new ones, New Orleans has had a fitful engagement with incident natural risks. Sometimes the city has developed effective adjustments such as drainage and pumping stations during the late nineteenth and early twentieth centuries or the evolution of raised housing that took account of ground subsidence and flooding (*Times-Picayune*, October 30, 2005)

Doubtless there are many urban functions, but for the purposes of this analysis, the most important fall under a half-dozen headings. *Material and economic functions* involve the accumulation of resources and subsequent conversion into products or services that sustain the physical fabric of the built environment and the livelihoods of human populations. *Metabolic functions* involve natural and human-modified life-support systems (i.e., ecosystems) including—among others—those that generate, nurture, circulate, and absorb air, water, biota and wastes. *Learning*

TABLE 3

URBAN FUNCTIONS, MODELS/METAPHORS, AND VULNERABILITY

Function	Model	Vulnerability
Material-economic support	Machine	Design and performance failures
Metabolism	Organism	Threats to life-support systems
Learning	Information network, brain, mind	Lack of stimuli; barriers to knowledge acquisition and exchange
Performance	Theater, carnival, sport	Rejection or breakdown of accepted behavior norms
Creativity	Muse, palimpsest	Rigid repressive conformance with narrow expectations; sanctions against experimentation and risk taking
Regulation	Command, control, negotiation, and incentive systems	Failures of trust, authority, and coercion; neglect of alternative courses of action

functions stimulate citizens and challenge them to adopt behaviors that are appropriate for the continuously shifting mix of urban experiences, expectations, inducements, and constraints. *Performance functions* are served by actions undertaken for purposes of role clarification, identity confirmation, novelty, and experimentation rather than for purposes of direct adaptation and survival. Communities allow humans to enact, inscribe, confirm, and test identities and roles as well as to probe the limits of permissible action. By means of such experiences, new norms and other emergent attributes of urban culture are incubated for the future. *Creative expression functions* are associated with the cultivation of intellectual, artistic, and spiritual values. *Regulatory functions* seek to order the complexity of urban living so that a vast range of competing activities and objectives can be accommodated within the same limited territorial space.

Each type of function is linked with a characteristic metaphor or model. In urban contexts, material and economic functions are usually associated with models of *cities as machines*. Metabolic functions are reflected in models of *cities as organisms*. Learning functions find expression in models of *cities as information exchange networks*. Performance functions are addressed via models of *cities as performances* (e.g., theaters, carnivals). Creative expression functions are associated with the notion of *cities as muses*. Regulatory functions are addressed through models of *cities as power structures and regulated places* (e.g., characterized by different mixes of hegemony, autonomy, dependence, and territoriality).

Sustainable development accommodates a dialogue between models of cities as machines and cities as organisms. But this does not take account of the other functions, all of which are vulnerable to risks that arise in nature as well as society. Table 3 summarizes the main relationships between functions, models, and vulnerabilities in urban communities. The vulnerability of cities as machines is signaled by the failure of their physical components to perform according to design specifications. The vulnerability of cities as organisms involves threats to life-support systems rather than to technologies. The vulnerability of cities as information exchange networks is mobilized by impaired learning about ongoing and forthcoming changes, on the part of their inhabitants, managers, and leaders. These include barriers that affect knowledge acquisition and communication, gaps that separate decision makers from the consequences of their actions, and failures to develop institutional memories and reflexive feedback mechanisms, among others.

Disaster recovery cannot be solely a matter of building toward a sustainable future; it must also address unexpected contingencies.

The vulnerability of cities as performances is more difficult to measure, but it implies propensities toward the reduction of societal experimentation, the discouragement of nonnormative behaviors, and restrictions on the range of publicly permissible actions in common urban spaces. Performances that are tolerated rather than embraced, or are contested, controversial, deviant, liminal, or otherwise marginal, are likely to be vulnerable in this sense. Tendencies toward routinization, surveillance, pejorative labeling/scapegoating, censorship, and rigid orthodoxy are clues to performance vulnerability. The vulnerability of cities as muses is also difficult to measure. Changes that disconnect and isolate intellectual creativity from policy making are particularly damaging. On one hand, cities are repositories of irreplaceable cultural treasures whose societal value is out of all proportion to their monetary worth. Many societies go to extraordinary lengths to safeguard such heritage objects. On the other hand, analysts cannot assume that physically disruptive global changes will necessarily place a damper on future artistic and intellectual creativity. The opposite may be more likely. Creative responses—both practical and symbolic—are often at the core of public policies for the memorialization and recovery of disaster-stricken communities. Finally, in the present era of vast sociocultural and political ideological changes, the vulnerability of cities as regulatory systems is not just a theoretical abstraction. No longer can it be assumed that existing systems of governance provide stable and effective frameworks for coping with wrenching global changes. The palette of alternatives is broad. Within the past century, social movements and political revolutions have promoted many species of public regulation including imperialism, nationalism, liberalism, fascism, social-ism, communism, welfare-stateism, and neoliberalism. Different systems have at-tempted to reorganize basic relationships between individuals, economies, poli-ties, and societies, thereby altering the process of urbanization and bequeathing legacies that are likely to persist for decades to centuries thereafter. All such regu-latory systems are vulnerable to the extent that they are not capable of accommo-dating surprises and/or resolving the multiple contending demands of increasingly heterogeneous urban constituencies. In the wake of a catastrophe like Katrina, it is to be expected that most or all of these vulnerabilities will be mobilized, if not directly by the extreme event, then indirectly by cascading consequences.

It is time for disaster recovery specialists to add other functions to the material and metabolic ones that are currently the focus of sustainable development and to explore the context of vulnerability as it pertains to these functions. This will pro-vide the knowledge base that must precede the crafting of new public policies for disaster recovery that address the full spectrum of urban habitability and gover-nance issues.

Forging common actions
in spite of different interpretations

The fourth strategy for partnering ideas in support of recovery policies builds upon the notion that individuals construct a coherent picture of the world by syn-thesizing many different, often-contradictory, interpretations of perceived reality. This shifts discourse away from an exclusive concern for reducing uncertainty to also address issues characterized by ambiguity. We should not expect that ambigu-ity will be removed; rather it is the recognition and accommodation of enduring ambiguities, incommensurables, and paradoxes that is at the very heart of the human experience. This is as true for hazards as it is for other societal phenomena. The various means by which interpretations are formed and defended against alternative meanings will not be explored in this article, but a brief introduction to this theme is appropriate.

Multiple interpretations of hazard events may be held by a single individual or by different groups or institutions. For example, among others a hurricane like Katrina may be simultaneously regarded as a disaster, a natural experiment, an aesthetic spectacle, a manifestation of divine power, an indicator of anthropogenic climate change, a mechanism of societal differentiation, a test of societal resilience, a device for redistributing economic and political resources, a fortuitous oppor-tunity for mischief making, and an entertaining or cathartic diversion. Although multiple interpretations have probably always existed, they now take on added importance because this is an era when challenges to the legitimacy and/or domi-nation of science and other sources of intellectual authority occur with increasing frequency. Hence it becomes much more difficult to put one exclusive reference frame around a situation that might once have been unambiguously labeled a hazard.

At present, the attention of hazards researchers and management professionals is monopolized by the notion of disasters as public policy problems that need to be managed or resolved. Yet this is only a sometime concern of most laypersons. Furthermore, this focus ignores the fact that different interpretations create different constituencies that may become allies if areas of conceptual overlap, convergence, or mutuality can be identified and exploited. In a few cases, tacit cooperation exists across these kinds of interpretational divides. For example, disaster victims are primary sources of information for hazards researchers, and the knowledge that scientific researchers acquire is often shared with victims or applied to victim-support programs. But the potential for making common cause between groups that view hazard through the lens of science and those that employ paradigms of aesthetics has not been explored to any significant degree. Nor have overlaps and interactions between hazard viewed as entertainment and hazard viewed as stimulus to risk-taking behavior, or as cathartic therapy or any of the other interpretative tropes that are employed by laypersons. The way lies open for a major constituency-building effort by proponents of hazard management if the managers grasp the potential for new partnerships between different interpretive paradigms.

Conclusions and Implications

The central argument of this article is that partnerships are essential to the American system of hazard management and are also increasingly important components in the hazard management systems of other countries. Moreover, partnerships will become more important to humankind everywhere as a diverse and interdependent world confronts new kinds of threats, old risks that are resurfacing (because they have been left unattended for too long), new vulnerabilities driven by globalization, and the accelerating dynamism of contemporary society, as well as surprises that can only be imagined at present.

To address these challenges, it will be necessary to increase the size and permanence of hazard as an item on the human agenda. At the moment, leaders attempt this by drawing on public anxieties about new threats and failures in existing risk management systems to craft more powerful public institutions that specialize in the management of certain risks (especially terrorism) and employ narrowly targeted policies for that purpose. By itself, that approach is unlikely to meet with much success because it segregates engagement with hazard to the realm of professional experts, because an atmosphere of crisis cannot be maintained indefinitely, and because too many of the institutions that we rely on to protect us against risks—or to recover from disasters—are heterogeneous, nonspecialized entities that address multiple goals on a broad front. They are, in effect, mirrors of the increasingly global society that Americans—and many others—inhabit.

Far from narrowing and specializing, we need to maintain and expand the range of alternative coping measures available to humans. Humans owe an enormous debt to the cumulative availability of more and more means of managing hazards over the past century. As a result, we can now put together many different combinations of ways to prevent, avoid, and reduce disasters. One of the most disturbing trends of the years since 9/11 has been the tendency to turn away from that heritage and put more of our eggs in fewer baskets, especially baskets that are concerned with terrorism risk reduction. Social scientists should be concerned to encourage the use of all proven alternatives wherever possible. In the twenty-first century, many of the new hazards that we will face will take a long time to reach maturity and will be subject to numerous reinterpretations as we learn more about them. This is as true of terrorism as it is of risks connected with human-driven climate changes or megadisasters like Katrina. Moreover, if—as our national leaders suggest—we are in for a long War on Terror, one that will likely span several presidential cycles, there will be every reason to keep the mix of alternative disaster management approaches as rich and variable as possible because we will have no way of knowing when presently neglected ones will become useful.

What is most needed is a way of broadening the discourse about recovery and bringing more people into it. We can wait for catastrophes and hope to prolong public involvement in hazards management decisions that are taken in their wake, or we can begin to lay the basis for an alternative approach that would permanently expand the calculus of decision making and call into play unorthodox constituencies, different kinds of knowledge about hazards, and different meanings of hazards.

In support of these ends, much greater effort should be directed toward harnessing the enormous potential for collective action against hazard that is available through the medium of partnerships. What is proposed herein is a strategy that broadens the notion of partnership by fostering new concepts that involve the linking of reciprocal—often contradictory—*ideas and ideals*, as well as by optimizing human *interests* that are likely to be more ephemeral. Four sets of principles are suggested as bases for this endeavor. These involve (1) coordinating community recovery with important projects on the national policy agenda, (2) building contingency management for environmental hazards into sustainable development strategies, (3) expanding the number and variety of community functions served by recovery programs, and (4) incorporating groups that hold different (and at times contradictory) interpretations of hazards that transcend the rubric of hazard as a public policy problem.

All of these activities call for greater investment in scientific knowledge about the human engagement with hazards and the larger context of relationships between societies and environments. None of them can be accomplished quickly, but several are already under way; there is little doubt that the knowledge base will grow substantially in the near future. At least in one respect, the lesson of Hurricane Katrina seems clear: changes to existing policies for the management of acute environmental hazards and disasters are necessary, and the momentum to bring them about is present. The question that remains to be answered is whether Americans will abandon the flexible, broad-based, partnership-based approach that has served so well and is so promising for the future and retreat to narrower, expediency-driven alternatives that neither reduce uncertainty nor transcend the ambiguities that are an increasing part of the hazards that will challenge us in the twenty-first century.

Notes

1. Hurricane Katrina inflicted fewer deaths (c. 1,300 in Louisiana and Mississippi) than several American disasters, including the 1900 Galveston hurricane (c. 8,000 dead), the 1906 San Francisco earthquake (3,000-6,000 dead), the 2001 collapse of the World Trade Center (c. 2,750 dead), the 1928 Lake Okeechobee (Florida) floods (c. 2,500 dead), and the 1889 Johnstown flood (c. 2,200 dead). Although an estimated 6,644 people are listed as missing after Katrina, about 1,300 of whom lived in the hardest-hit areas, it is believed that a majority of the missing are likely to be alive (USA Today, November 21, 2005).

2. Earthquakes, volcanic eruptions, landslides, and coastal erosion probably have greater capacity than floods to irrevocably change the physical landscape and deny the use of sites previously occupied by humans. The Alaska earthquake of 1964 deformed about fifty thousand square miles of (mostly unpopulated) land in the state's southern districts. Detectable amounts of ash from the 1980 eruption of Mount St. Helens covered about twenty-two square miles, some to a depth of hundreds of feet.

3. Many small towns and villages (none containing more than 1,000 people) were abandoned or relocated after the 1964 Alaska earthquake, including, among others, Valdez, Girdwood, Portage, Chenega, and Afognak. During the past sixty years, the largest settlement in the United States abandoned after a natural disaster is believed to be Vanport, Oregon, a dormitory community occupied by war industry workers and their families that succumbed to floods on the Columbia River in 1948. At its peak, Vanport held about 40,000 people, but only 18,500 were still in residence when its protective dyke failed.

4. At least 4.4 million lived in areas covered by federal disaster declarations 1603 (Louisiana), 1604 (Mississippi), and 1605 (Alabama), issued on August 29, 2005. A much larger population throughout the United States experienced indirect effects as a result of sheltering victims or paying higher fuel costs triggered by damage to Gulf Coast oil refineries, for example.

5. Approximately 31,000 square miles of territory in 49 counties of Louisiana, Mississippi, and Alabama were covered by federal disaster declarations 1603, 1604, and 1605. By comparison, the celebrated 1927 Mississippi floods affected about 27,000 square miles. Neither event comes near to the record-setting Midwest floods of 1993, which covered 270,000 square miles of (mostly agricultural) land in 534 disaster-designated counties spread across nine states. In that event, federally designated disaster areas included all of Iowa, 62 percent of Missouri, 58 percent of Wisconsin and North Dakota, 52 percent of South Dakota, 46 percent of Nebraska, 40 percent of Minnesota, 25 percent of Illinois, and 22 percent of Kansas (Lott 1994).

6. The National Association of Home Builders estimates that 350,000 homes were destroyed and around half a million are damaged but repairable. This is twelve times the number destroyed in any previous U.S. natural disaster (Nation's Building News, October 10, 2005).

7. A month after Katrina, more than 450,000 evacuees remained in Red Cross shelters or hotel rooms paid for by the Red Cross in twenty-four states (National Geographic 208, no.6 [December 2005]: 10). A map of Katrina's diaspora published in the New York Times (October 2, 2005) shows that of 1,356,704 applications for aid submitted to FEMA by September 23, 2005, 86 percent came from people who had relocated to places in Louisiana, Mississippi, Texas, and Alabama. But more than 35,000 families had relocated more than one thousand miles from the impacted Gulf Coast region, including a small number in Alaska and Hawaii.

8. Recent estimates by government agencies and the insurance industry indicate that the costs of immediate relief may be as much as $60 billion and of long-term reconstruction and recovery in the vicinity of $150 billion (Associated Press, October 6, 2005). It seems likely that this will be the largest payout for losses incurred due to a single disaster in the history of the global insurance industry.

9. At least 363,000 jobless claims related to Katrina were filed by the beginning of October 2005. (Associated Press, October 6, 2005). Unemployment rates among the 800,000 evacuees identified by the U.S. Bureau of Labor Statistics were 24.5 percent overall during October 2005 with higher rates recorded among blacks (41.5 percent) and Hispanics (42.1 percent) than whites (17.5 percent). See http://www.epi.org/content.cfm/webfeatures_snapshots_20051109.

10. At the time of writing (late November 2005), some aspects of the first (emergency) phase of this disaster have been completed (e.g., search and rescue, emergency medical care) but others (e.g., debris clearance, emergency feeding and housing) are not yet at an end nearly three months after the hurricane struck. The second postdisaster phase (repair and rehabilitation) is under way for some damaged buildings and infrastructure, but the task is far from complete. Only one in seven of New Orleans's residents have returned to the city; a full accounting of the dead and missing has not yet been completed.

11. Social Science Research Council, "Understanding Katrina: Perspectives from the Social Sciences," http://understandingkatrina.ssrc.org/.

12. During the past twenty years when systematic surveys of public interest in mass media reporting have been compiled, Hurricane Katrina has been outranked by stories about five other events. In declining salience, these are the *Challenger* space shuttle (July 1986), the 9/11 terrorist attacks (September 2001), the San Francisco earthquake (November 1989), the high price of gasoline (September 2005), and the Rodney King verdict and riots (May 1992) (Pew Center for People and the Press 2005).

13. Among the fifty U.S. states, Mississippi ranks fiftieth in per capita income and forty-ninth in median household income, while Louisiana ranks forty-seventh on both of these indicators, just ahead of West Virginia and Arkansas. Alabama is somewhat better off (thirty-eight and forty-second, respectively). However, with a few exceptions (e.g. Wilkinson and Greene Counties, Mississippi), the coastal municipalities that bore the brunt of Katrina's losses are not as poor as parishes and counties located further inland. Fishing and the oil and gas industry are heavily concentrated in coastal regions of Louisiana, while the gambling and resort industries have benefited coastal Mississippi during the past two decades.

14. There is also a fund of experience with other hazards. Although drought is not a sudden-onset hazard, there has been a long-term American engagement with the semiarid edges of the ecumene (inhabited earth). From Frederick Jackson Turner's "frontier thesis" (Block 1980) to Frank and Deborah Popper's notion of the "Buffalo Commons" (Popper and Popper 2004), the theme of colonization and abandonment of risky places in the Great Plains' fluctuating environment has been a prominent element of cultural ecology. In this respect, the national experience with natural hazards bears comparison with those of other "settler societies" like Australia, New Zealand, South Africa, and Canada and perhaps even Israel or the USSR during Nikita Khrushchev's "Virgin Lands" program. Engagement with wildfires in temperate zone forests also constitutes a part of the American experience with natural hazards that is shared with other countries—in this case northern parts of Scandinavia, Russia, and China (Manchuria) as well as places characterized by Mediterranean vegetation and climate regimes (e.g., Iberia, southern France, Greece).

15. Some of these places were also repeatedly stricken by lesser events, and many other U.S. cities suffered heavy losses to particular neighborhoods.

16. The term "megacatastrophe" entered the literature of hazards management during the 1990s, especially after hurricane Andrew (1992) produced record-setting insurance losses in Florida (Kunreuther and Roth 1998). Since then the global reinsurance industry has been particularly concerned about the likelihood that such a disaster will exceed its capacity to provide subscribers with adequate reimbursement, and some experts have identified financing as the main obstacle to ensuring recovery (Comerio 1998, 239).

17. However, neither of these events is a perfect analogue for Katrina's combination of a big city catastrophe (New Orleans) set within vast regional devastation. No large cities were overwhelmed in the 1953 Dutch floods, and the worst effects of the Ise Bay typhoon were largely confined to the immediate vicinity of Nagoya.

18. Among hazards professionals, recovery is usually portrayed as a series of overlapping stages that begin with managing the ongoing emergency and end with memorialization and betterment projects that may not conclude until decades after the disaster.

19. For discussions about the increasingly geographic scale and global reach of disasters, see Walker (2005); Feinstein International Famine Center, "Disaster Globalization: Evaluating the Impact of Tsunami Aid," Tufts University (2005), http://nutrition.tufts.edu/pdf/research/famine/disaster_globalization.pdf; and the forthcoming Third Annual MaGrann Research Conference, "The Future of Disasters in a Globalizing World," to be held at Rutgers University, New Brunswick, NJ, April 21-22, 2006.

20. "Terrorism: Are We Safe Yet?" lecture by Tom Kean, 2005 Clifford P. Case Professor of Public Affairs, Rutgers University, Piscataway, NJ, October 24, 2005.

21. Stephen Barr, "Coast Guard's Response to Katrina a Silver Lining in the Storm (September 6, 2005), http://www.washingtonpost.com/wp-dyn/content/article/2005/09/05/AR2005090501418.html.

22. See especially comments reported by the British Broadcasting Corporation (September 5, 2005), http://news.bbc.co.uk/1/hi/world/americas/4216142.stmby; and the news digest magazine *World Press* (September 3, 2005), http://www.worldpress.org/Americas/2142.cfm.

23. See John Graham, "It's All about Leadership," http://www.sierraclub.org/pressroom/speeches/2005-09-11johngraham.asp; "Boston Homeland Security Chief Stresses Leadership," Harvard School of Public Health (September 30, 2005), http://www.hsph.harvard.edu/now/sep30/homeland_security.html; and Al Gore, "The Time to Act Is Now: The Climate Crisis and the Need for Leadership" (November 4, 2005), http://www.salon.com/opinion/feature/2005/11/04/gore/.

24. The tendency to focus on the behavior of certain individuals or groups in disaster has a parallel in the social amplification of selective information about disasters (Pidgeon, Kasperson, and Slovic 2003).

25. It was not always thus. In the United States, the emphasis on partnership began as an offshoot of a campaign to reinvent government that started twenty years ago under the Reagan administration, accelerated in the 1990s during Bill Clinton's presidency, and culminated in a series of Public-Private Partnership 2000 Forums held in Washington, D.C., between 1997 and 1999 (Kettl 1994; see also http://www.usgs.gov/ppp2000/).

26. Meanings that attach to the word "partnership" vary among states and—even more so—among nations. Partnership might refer to amity and brotherhood (as in the French constitutional imperative of *fraternité*), or efficiency-through-cooperation (as in the Canadian constitutional dedication to "good government"), or what some psychotherapists call self-actualization (as in the American "pursuit of happiness"), or even to a synthesis of all these ideas.

27. The sometimes incompatible national aspirations of other Western democracies such as France (liberty, equality, friendship) and Canada (peace, order, good government) also ensure a role for partnership as a constitutional instrument.

28. Nor is the principle of partnership confined to U.S. hazard management systems. It has also been adopted by international hazards management agencies and developing countries (El-Masri and Tipple 2002; Kreimer and Arnold 2000; Pelling 2003, 89-90).

29. Several Eastern European states were subsequently admitted to the EU, including the former German Democratic Republic, the Czech Republic, Slovakia, Hungary, Poland, Romania, and Bulgaria. The possibility that Turkey, Ukraine, and other territories of the former USSR may also be admitted to the EU has raised the stakes for hazard policy making even further.

References

Alexander, David. 2005. *Symbolic and practical interpretations of the Hurricane Katrina disaster in New Orleans*. New York: Social Science Research Council. http://understandingkatrina.ssrc.org/.

Bernard, E. N. 2005. The U.S. National Tsunami Hazard Mitigation Program: A successful state-federal partnership. *Natural Hazards* 35 (1): 5-24.

Block, Robert H. 1980. Frederick Jackson Turner and American geography. *Annals of the Association of American Geographers* 70 (1): 31-42.

Byman, Daniel, Ian O. Lesser, Bruce Pirnie, Cheryl Benard, and Matthew C Waxman. 2000. *Strengthening the partnership: Improving military coordination with relief agencies and allies in humanitarian operations*. Santa Monica, CA: Rand Corporation.

Changnon, Stanley A., and David R. Easterling. 2000. Disaster management: U.S. policies pertaining to weather and climate extremes. *Science* 289 (5487): 2053-2055.

Clinton, Bill. 2004. *My life*. New York: Knopf.

Colten, Craig E. 2005. *An unnatural metropolis: Wresting New Orleans from nature*. Baton Rouge: Louisiana State University Press.

Comerio, Mary C. 1998. *Disaster hits home: New policy for urban housing recovery*. Berkeley: University of California Press.

Comfort, Louise K. 1999. *Shared risk: Complex systems in seismic response*. New York: Pergamon.

Demuth, Julie L., ed. 2002. *Countering terrorism—Lessons learned from natural and technological disasters: A Summary to the Natural Disasters Roundtable*. Washington, DC: National Academy Press. http://www.nap.edu/books/NI000412/html/R1.html.

Drabek, T. E., and D. A. McEntire. 2002. Emergent phenomena and multi-organizational coordination in disasters: Lessons from the research literature. *International Journal of Mass Emergencies and Disasters* 20 (2): 197-224.

Dynes, Russell R., and Havidán Rodríguez. 2005. *Finding and framing Katrina: The social construction of disaster.* New York: Social Science Research Council. http://understandingkatrina.ssrc.org/.

Eisinger, Peter. 2004. The American city in the age of terror: A preliminary assessment of the effects of 9/11. Presented at the Urban Affairs Association Meetings, Washington, DC, March 30–April 3.

El-Masri, Souheil, and Graham Tipple. 2002. Natural disaster, mitigation and sustainability: The case of developing countries. *International Planning Studies* 7 (2): 157-75.

Elvin, Mark. 2004. *The retreat of the elephants: An environmental history of China.* New Haven, CT: Yale University Press.

Etkin, David, ed. 2005. *Reducing risk through partnerships: Proceedings of the 1st CRHNet Symposium.* Winnipeg, Manitoba: Canadian Risk and Hazards Network.

Flynn, Stephen. 2004. *America the vulnerable: How our government is failing to protect us from terrorism.* New York: HarperCollins.

Frymer, Paul, Dara Z. Strolovitch, and Dorian T. Warren. 2005. *Katrina's political roots and divisions: Race, class, and federalism in American politics.* New York: Social Science Research Council. http://understandingkatrina.ssrc.org/.

Fussell, Elizabeth. 2005. *Leaving New Orleans: Social stratification, networks, and hurricane evacuation.* New York: Social Science Research Council. http://understandingkatrina.ssrc.org/.

Godschalk, David, Edward J. Kaiser, David J. Brower, Philip R. Berke, and Timothy Beatley. 1999. *Natural hazard mitigation.* Washington, DC: Island Press.

Graham, Stephen. 2005. *Cities under siege: Katrina and the politics of metropolitan America.* New York: Social Science Research Council. http://understandingkatrina.ssrc.org/.

Grossi, Patricia, and Howard Kunreuther, eds. 2005. *Catastrophe modeling: A new approach to managing risk.* New York: Springer.

Henstra, D., and G. McBean. 2004. *The role of government in services for natural disaster mitigation.* February. Toronto, Canada: Institute for Catastrophic Loss Reduction.

Holling, C. S. 2001. Understanding the complexity of economic, ecological and social systems. *Ecosystems* 4 (5): 390-405.

Hurlbert, Jeanne S., John J. Beggs, and Valerie A. Haines. 2005. *Bridges over troubled waters: What are the optimal networks for Katrina's victims?* New York: Social Science Research Council. http://understandingkatrina.ssrc.org/.

Inam, Aseem. 2005. *Planning for the unplanned: Recovering from crises in megacities.* New York: Routledge.

Jones, E. E., and V. A. Harris. 1967. The attribution of attitudes. *Journal of Experimental Social Psychology* 3:1-24.

Kates, Robert W., William C. Clark, Robert Corell, J. Michael Hall, Carlo C. Jaeger, Ian Lowe, James J. McCarthy, Hans Joachim Schellnhuber, Bert Bolin, Nancy M. Dickson, Sylvie Faucheux, Gilberto C. Gallopin, Arnulf Grübler, Brian Huntley, Jill Jäger, Narpat S. Jodha, Roger E. Kasperson, Akin Mabogunje, Pamela Matson, Harold Mooney, Berrien Moore III, Timothy O'Riordan, and Uno Svedlin. 2001. Environment and development: Sustainability science. *Science* 292:641-42.

Kershaw, Patricia Jones, ed. 2005. *Creating a disaster resilient America: Grand challenges in science and technology. Summary of a workshop of the Disasters Roundtable.* Division on Earth and Life Studies, National Research Council. Washington, DC: National Academies Press.

Kettl, Donald F. 1994. Reinventing government? Appraising the National Performance Review. A Report of the Brookings Institution's Center for Public Management. CPM 9402. Washington, DC: Brookings Institution.

King, Rawle O. 2005. *Hurricane Katrina: Insuring losses and national capacities for financing disaster risk.* September 15. CRS Report for Congress no. RL 33086. Washington, DC: Congressional Research Service, Library of Congress.

Krause, Monica. 2005. *New Orleans: The public sphere of the disaster.* New York: Social Science Research Council. http://understandingkatrina.ssrc.org/.

Kreimer, Alcira, and Margaret Arnold, eds. 2000. *Managing disaster risk in emerging economies.* Washington, DC: World Bank.

Kunreuther, H. 2000. Insurance as a cornerstone for public-private sector partnerships. *Natural Hazards Review* 1:126-36.

Kunreuther, Howard, and Richard J. Roth Sr. 1998. *Paying the price: The status and role of insurance against natural disasters in the United States.* Washington, DC: National Academies Press.

Lakoff, Andrew. 2005. *From disaster to catastrophe: The limits of preparedness.* New York: Social Science Research Council. http://understandingkatrina.ssrc.org/.

Litan, Robert E. 2005. Sharing and reducing the financial risks of future mega-catastrophes. Economic Studies Working Paper, November 11, Brookings Institution, Washington, DC.

Lott, J. N. 1994. The US summer of 1993: A sharp contrast in weather extremes. *Weather* 49 (11): 370-83.

May, P. J., and W. Williams. 1986. *Disaster policy implementation: Managing programs under shared governance.* New York: Plenum.

Meyer, B. 1997. The insurance of natural hazards: Proposals to an appropriate risk partnership between insurers, reinsurers, the government and the policyholders. *Insurance: Mathematics and Economics* 19 (3): 266.

Mileti, Denis. 1999. *Disasters by design.* Washington, DC: Joseph Henry Press.

Mitchell, James K., ed. 1996. *The long road to recovery: Community responses to industrial disaster.* Tokyo: United Nations University Press.

———, ed. 1999. *Crucibles of hazard: Mega-cities and disasters in transition.* Tokyo: United Nations University Press.

———. 2003. The fox and the hedgehog: Myopia about homeland vulnerability in US policies on terrorism. *Terrorism and Disaster: New Threats, New Ideas. Research in Social Problems and Public Policy Volume* 11:53-72.

———. 2004. Reconceiving recovery. In *NZ Recovery Symposium proceedings, July 12-13*, ed. Sarah Norman, 47-68. Wellington, New Zealand: Ministry of Civil Defence and Emergency Management.

———. 2005a. Comments on the symposium. In *Reducing risk through partnerships: Proceedings of the 1st CRHNet Symposium*, ed. David Etkin, 40. Winnipeg, Manitoba: Canadian Risk and Hazards Network.

———. 2005b. *Empowering knowledge: A modest proposal for a broader social science research agenda in the wake of Katrina.* New York: Social Science Research Council. http://understandingkatrina.ssrc.org/.

———. 2005c. An expanded perspective on partnerships for the reduction of hazards and disasters, 1st annual CRHNet Symposium, Winnipeg, Manitoba, Canada, November 18-22, 2004. In *Reducing risk through partnerships: Proceedings of the 1st CRHNet Symposium*, ed. David Etkin, 37-38. Winnipeg, Manitoba: Canadian Risk and Hazards Network.

———. 2005d. We're not in Kansas any more: Some guides for science and technology inputs to hazard management in the 21st century. In *Creating a disaster-resilient America: Grand challenges in science and technology*, 11. Washington, DC: National Academies Press. http://www.nap.edu/books/0309096634/html/11.html.

Molotch, Harvey. 2005. *Death on the roof: Race and bureaucratic failure.* New York: Social Science Research Council. http://understandingkatrina.ssrc.org/.

National Research Council. 2000. *Risk analysis and uncertainty in flood damage reduction studies.* Committee on Risk-Based Analysis for Flood Loss Reduction, Water Science and Technology Board, Commission on Geosciences, Environment, and Resources. Washington, DC: National Academy Press.

———. 2004. *Partnership for reducing landslide risk: Assessment of the National Landslide Hazards Mitigation Strategy.* Committee on the Review of the National Landslide Hazards Mitigation Strategy, Board of Earth Sciences and Resources, Division on Earth and Life Studies. Washington, DC: National Academies Press.

New Zealand, Ministry of Civil Defence and Emergency Management. 2005. *Focus on recovery: A holistic framework for recovery in New Zealand.* Wellington: New Zealand Ministry of Civil Defence and Emergency Management.

Pelling, Mark. 2003. *The vulnerability of cities: Natural disasters and social resilience.* London: Earthscan.

Perrow, Charles. 2005. *Play it again, FEMA.* New York: Social Science Research Council. http://understandingkatrina .ssrc.org/.

Pew Center for People and Press. 2005. Huge racial divide over Katrina and its consequences: Two-in-three critical of Bush's relief efforts. Press Release. September 8. http://people-press.org/reports/pdf/255.pdf.

Pidgeon, Nick, Roger E. Kasperson, and Paul Slovic, eds. 2003. *The social amplification of risk*. New York: Cambridge University Press.

Platt, R. 1999. Natural hazards of the San Francisco Bay mega-city: Trial by earthquake, wind, and fire. In *Crucibles of hazard: Mega-cities and disasters in transition*, ed. James K. Mitchell. Tokyo: United Nations University Press.

———. 2000. Extreme natural events: Some issues for public policy. Presented at Extreme Events Workshop, Boulder, CO, June 7-9.

Popper, Deborah E., and Frank J. Popper. 2004. The Great Plains and the Buffalo Commons. In *WorldMinds: Geographical perspectives on 100 problems*, ed. Donald Janelle, Barney Warf, and Kathy Hansen, 345-49. New York: Kluwer Academic.

Quarantelli, E. L. 2005. *Catastrophes are different from disasters: Some implications for crisis planning and managing drawn from Katrina*. New York: Social Science Research Council. http://understandingkatrina .ssrc.org/.

Reuss, Martin. 2002. Learning from the Dutch: Technology, management and water resource development. *Technology and Culture* 43 (3): 465-72.

Ross, L. 1977. The intuitive psychologist and his shortcomings: Distortions in the attribution process. In *Advances in experimental social psychology*, vol. 10, ed. L. Berkowitz, 173-220. New York: Academic Press.

Savitch, H. V. 2003. Does 9-11 portend a new paradigm for cities? *Urban Affairs Review* 39:103-27.

Schneider, Jane, and Ida Susser, eds. 2003. *Wounded cities: Destruction and reconstruction in a globalized world*. Oxford: Berg.

Sylves, Richard T. 2005. Revolution needed in U.S. emergency management, EIIP (Emergency Information Infrastructure Project) Virtual Forum Presentation. September 15. http://www.emforum.org/vforum/ lc050914.htm.

Tierney, Kathleen. 2005. *The red pill*. New York: Social Science Research Council. http:// understandingkatrina.ssrc.org/.

Turner, B. L., II, Roger E. Kasperson, Pamela A. Matson, James J. McCarthy, Robert W. Corell, Lindsey Christensen, Noelle Eckley, Jeanne X. Kasperson, Amy Luers, Marybeth L. Martello, Colin Polsky, Alexander Pulsipher, and Andrew Schiller. 2003. Science and technology for sustainable development special feature: A framework for vulnerability analysis in sustainability science. *Proceedings of the National Academy of Science* 100 (14): 8074-79.

Vale, Lawrence J., and Thomas J. Campanella, eds. 2005. *The resilient city: How modern cities recover from disaster*. Oxford: Oxford University Press.

Wachtendorf, Tricia, and James M. Kendra. 2005. *Improvising disaster in the city of jazz: Organizational response to Hurricane Katrina*. New York: Social Science Research Council. http://understandingkatrina .ssrc.org/.

Walker, Peter. 2005. Disaster globalization: Evaluating the impact of tsunami aid. Policy Briefing Paper, Feinstein International Famine Center, Tufts University. http://nutrition.tufts.edu/pdf/research/famine/ disaster_globalization.pdf.

Waugh, William L. 2004. Terrorism, homeland security and the national emergency management network. *Public Organization Review* 3:373-85.

Waugh, William L., Jr., and Richard T. Sylves. 2002. Organizing the war on terrorism. *Public Administration Review* 62:145-54.

Wright, W. E. 1997. Incorporating military civil affairs support into domestic disaster management. *International Journal of Mass Emergencies and Disasters* 15 (2): 283-92.

Agility and Discipline: Critical Success Factors for Disaster Response

By
JOHN R. HARRALD

For more than thirty years, the U.S. emergency management community has been increasing its ability to structure, control, and manage a large response. The result of this evolution is a National Response System based on the National Response Plan and the National Incident Management System that is perceived to have failed in the response to Hurricane Katrina. Over the same period, social scientists and other disaster researchers have been documenting and describing the nonstructural factors such as improvisation, adaptability, and creativity that are critical to coordination, collaboration, and communication and to successful problem solving. This article argues that these two streams of thought are not in opposition, but form orthogonal dimensions of discipline and agility that must both be achieved. The critical success factors that must be met to prepare for and respond to an extreme event are described, and an organizational typology is developed.

Keywords: response; critical success factors; agility; improvisation; discipline

Extreme events such as the September 11, 2001, attacks on the United States, the December 2004 Sumatra earthquake and Indian Ocean Tsunami, Hurricane Katrina, and the October 2005 Pakistan earthquake produce catastrophic immediate impacts and cause long-term disruption of economic and social systems. With the exception of the 9/11 attacks, these

John R. Harrald is the director of the George Washington University (GWU) Institute for Crisis, Disaster, and Risk Management and a professor of engineering management in the GWU School of Engineering and Applied Science. He is the executive editor of the Journal of Homeland Security and Emergency Management. *He has been actively engaged in the fields of emergency and crisis management and maritime safety and port security and as a researcher in his academic career and as a practitioner during his twenty-two-year career as a U.S. Coast Guard officer, retiring in the grade of captain. He received his B.S. in engineering from the U.S. Coast Guard Academy, an M.S. from the Massachusetts Institute of Technology where he was an Alfred P. Sloan Fellow, and an MBA and Ph.D. from Rensselaer Polytechnic Institute.*

DOI: 10.1177/0002716205285404

events exceeded our ability to organize and execute coordinated, effective response and relief efforts. The national response system crafted over the past three years by the U.S. Department of Homeland Security (DHS) was tested for the first time when Hurricane Katrina struck the Gulf Coast. Hurricane Katrina was a catastrophic event because it was actually two disasters. Comfort (2005, 5) noted that "the first phase, the hurricane, could legitimately be called a natural disaster, as it was generated by meteorological activity beyond human control. The second phase, the breach of the levees and ensuing flood, can only be acknowledged as a man made disaster, after years of neglected maintenance of the levee system, inadequate public education regarding the risk and severity of hurricanes in the region, and inadequate planning and preparedness training across jurisdictional levels . . . city, parish state, and federal." The second phase destroyed the capability of state and local government and overwhelmed the federal response.

The perceived failure of the response system shocked the nation. As we face the reality that we are vulnerable to threats of terrorist attacks and to natural hazards that can surpass the impact of these historic events, it is appropriate to ask how we organizationally prepare for, respond to, and recover from extreme events in ways that minimize the disruption to and maximize the resiliency of our social and economic systems.

This article reviews the nature of the challenge presented by extreme events; describes the recent U.S. experience in developing plans and procedures for managing these events; offers a critical success factor approach to preparing for, responding to, and recovering from events with potential catastrophic impacts; and offers an organizational typology based on the orthogonal dimensions of discipline and agility.

Three themes from the organizational and emergency management literature describe the essential elements of organizing for and coordinating the massive effort required to respond to an extreme event. These themes are as follows:

- There is a trade-off between command and control requirements necessary for mobilizing and managing a large organization and the need to ensure broad coordination and communication.
- Extreme events present unforeseen conditions and problems, requiring a need for adaptation, creativity, and improvisation while demanding efficient and rapid delivery of services under extreme conditions.
- Diverse organizations must achieve technical and organizational interoperability requiring common structure and process while absorbing and interacting with thousands of spontaneous volunteers and emergent organizations.

The answer proposed in this article is that these are all needed and that the implied trade-offs are false choices. This article argues that designers of organizational systems for emergency response, like designers of software systems, must ensure both discipline (structure, doctrine, and process) and agility (creativity, improvisation, and adaptability).

Extreme Events

The context of the arguments in this article is the context of extreme events that require a coordinated federal response to avoid catastrophic failures resulting from the overwhelming of state and local resources. As stated by Roberts (2005, 4), this is one of the primary reasons that a federal government exists.

---

*The national television reportage
largely defined the New Orleans catastrophe,
particularly since there was no
significant federal or state presence
in the city for days after the flooding.*

The Catastrophic Annex to the National Response Plan (NRP; DHS 2004b) describes the attributes of an extreme event from the perspective of its demands on emergency management. These attributes remarkably described the actual impacts experienced in the aftermath of Hurricane Katrina:

- *"The response capabilities and resources of the local jurisdiction (to include mutual aid from surrounding jurisdictions and response support from the State) may be insufficient and quickly overwhelmed. Local emergency personnel who normally respond to incidents may be among those affected and unable to perform their duties."* The New Orleans leaders, emergency managers, and first responders were all victims. The police and firefighters that responded were themselves homeless and were not reinforced by state and federal resources for days.
- *"A catastrophic incident may cause significant disruption of the area's critical infrastructure, such as energy, transportation, telecommunications, and public health and medical systems."* The total loss of infrastructure in New Orleans is one of the main discriminators between this event and prior near-catastrophic events in U.S. history such as Hurricane Andrew and the Northridge earthquake. Post-9/11 infrastructure protection investments have focused on increasing the security of infrastructure, not in increasing its resilience.
- *"A detailed and credible common operating picture may not be achievable for 24 to 48 hours (or longer). As a result, response activities must begin without the benefit of a detailed or complete situation and critical needs assessment."* The failure to obtain situational awareness during Katrina is well documented, as is the failure to act creatively and quickly based on incomplete information. The total breakdown of emergency communications was a key part of this failure.
- *"Federal support must be provided in a timely manner to save lives, prevent human suffering, and mitigate severe damage. This may require mobilizing and deploying assets before they are requested via normal NRP protocols."* FEMA coordinated a massive mobilization

effort. The need to deploy assets, other than search and rescue, outside of normal protocols apparently was not recognized.

- *"Large numbers of people may be left temporarily or permanently homeless and may require prolonged temporary housing."* The peak shelter population was more than 250,000 people; today more than 125,000 evacuees are in temporary shelter, and many of them will require extended housing assistance. We are only now developing a long-term housing and recovery strategy.
- *"A catastrophic incident may produce environmental impacts . . . that severely challenge the ability and capacity of governments and communities to achieve a timely recovery."* Much of southern Louisiana, including New Orleans and Lake Pontchartrain, is an environmental disaster area, including oil spills approaching the volume of the *Exxon Valdez* spill, and the federal involvement in the environmental cleanup will last years.
- *"A catastrophic incident has unique dimensions/characteristics requiring that response plans/strategies be flexible enough to effectively address emerging needs and requirements."* The DHS has spent years developing a common, national approach to incident management through the creation of the NRP, the National Incident Management System (NIMS; DHS 2004a), and the National Preparedness Goals. This emphasis on structure and process may have diminished our ability to react creatively and adaptively.
- *"A catastrophic incident results in large number of casualties and/or displaced persons, possibly in the tens of thousands."* Although the number of deaths due to the flooding of New Orleans were less than initial estimates, the Katrina death toll was approximately thirteen hundred and was the largest experienced from a natural disaster since the Galveston Hurricane of 1900. Three months after the storm, there is still no plan of how to deal with the dispersion of hundreds of thousands of residents from New Orleans and Southern Louisiana.
- *"A catastrophic incident may occur with little or no warning. Some incidents, such as rapid disease outbreaks, may be well underway before detection."* The National Hurricane Center provided ample warning for Hurricane Katrina, allowing for evacuations and other preparations. The second disaster, the failure of the New Orleans levees and the inundation of 80 percent of the city, although predicted by many experts, occurred with little or no warning and surprised residents, government leaders, and responders alike. Due to complete communication failures, the failures of the levees was not known to emergency managers until hours after they occurred.
- *"Large scale evacuations, organized or self directed, may occur. The health-related implications of an incident aggravate attempts to implement a coordinated evacuation management strategy."* The first evacuation of New Orleans was the large-scale evacuation and dispersal of approximately 80 percent of the city's population prior to the storm. This evacuation was conducted primarily by automobile and was relatively successful from the perspective of numbers evacuated, but it left the poor, the sick, and the disabled in the city to fend for themselves. The second evacuation was the ad hoc evacuation of the flooding victims; the lack of coordinated strategy and tactics and the severe health and safety impacts were widely reported.

Henry Quarantelli (2005) described the attributes of a catastrophic event that impact the social structure of the community:

- *"Most or all of the community-built environment is heavily impacted."* Quarantelli pointed out that Hurricane Katrina flooded 80 percent of New Orleans.
- *"Local officials are unable to undertake their usual work role, and this often extends into the recovery period. Many leadership roles may have to be taken by outsiders to the community."* Police and fire personnel were victims of Katrina, and vehicles and operations centers were destroyed. The mayor of New Orleans was forced to establish city offices in Baton Rouge.

- *"Help from nearby communities cannot be provided."* In Katrina, all surrounding communities were, themselves, devastated.
- *"Most, if not all, of the everyday community functions are sharply and concurrently interrupted."* The result is the emergence of decentralized decision making, and the idea that there could be any centralized control imposed on these disparate decisions and varying community activities flies in the face of what researchers have found in crises.
- *"The mass media system constructs catastrophes even more than they do disasters."* There is also "far less of the normal filtering and screening of stories especially in the electronic media." The national television reportage largely defined the New Orleans catastrophe, particularly since there was no significant federal or state presence in the city for days after the flooding.
- *"The political arena becomes even more important. National government and very top officials become involved."* Within days, the perceived failure of the federal response had become a major political issue, resulting in the personal involvement of President Bush and the eventual replacement of FEMA Director Michael Brown.

Responding to Extreme Events

In spite of all efforts to reduce threats and hazards, and to minimize our vulnerability to extreme events, these events will occur. When such an event does occur, the response and recovery effort requires an extensive commitment of funds and organizational resources. For an event such as Katrina, the response and recovery effort eventually requires the contributions of hundreds of organizations and hundreds of thousands of people. Figure 1 shows that compared to the preevent investment in resources devoted to managing risk and preparing for response, the postevent organizations are large and complex. Figure 1 also shows that the response phase can be subdivided into four subphases reflecting the evolution of objectives and functions over time. The initial response is conducted by resources on the ground reacting to the situation created by the event, while external resources are mobilized. An integration phase is required to structure these resources into a functioning organization capable of identifying needs and providing services that are beyond the capability and capacity of the early responders. If the mobilization and integration are successful, a production phase is reached where the response organization is fully productive, delivering needed services as a matter of routine. These three phases are analogous to the processes of "storming," "forming," "norming," and "performing" that are experienced by any stranger group tasked to solve unanticipated problems (Tuckman 1965). Finally, the large external presence is diminished during a demobilization and transition to recovery stage. In an extreme event, a significantly large external recovery force is required for an extended period of time. The planning for and transition to this force must be managed. The success factors in each stage are linked; success in one phase is a precondition for success in the next.

The critical success factor approach, developed by MIT's Jack Rockhart (Rockhart and Bullen 1981; Rockhart 1979, 1981; Carali et al. 2004), can be used to describe the essential factors that must occur in each of these phases. *Critical success factors* are those few key areas of activity in which favorable results are absolutely neces-

FIGURE 1
STAGES OF A DISASTER RESPONSE: ORGANIZATIONAL SIZE VERSUS TIME

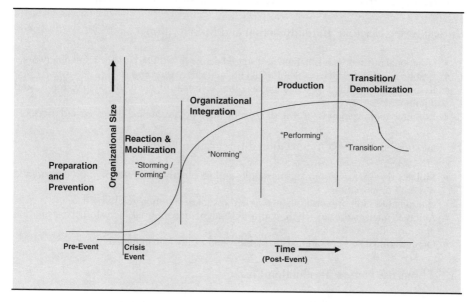

sary, things that must go right if the enterprise or operation is to succeed. Research-ers have developed a framework describing the critical success factors for the suc-cessful response to and recovery from an extreme event. This framework is based on observation and study of the responses to a series of extreme events and the con-duct of drills and exercises with U.S. and international response and relief organi-zations (Harrald and Mazzuchi 1993; Carley and Harrald 1997; Harrald and Stoddart 1998). These linked critical success factors illustrate how emergency management preparations, plans, structure, and organization enable a rapid transi-tion from the initial chaotic response and mobilization to the effective delivery of services during the production stage and during later recovery activities. Many of these critical success factors can only be achieved if the evolving emergency man-agement structure is an open organization, aware of and adjusting to the rapidly changing external environment, showing the importance of improvisation, adapt-ability, and creativity to the management of this transition from chaos to stability. Most important, these factors capture the essential need to anticipate future prob-lems, creating the potential for their solution before they occur, avoiding the reac-tive, bureaucratic response we saw during Hurricane Katrina.

Critical success factors: Preparedness and Prevention

- Domain awareness and detection capability are created and maintained
- Mobilization and response plans are based on realistic scenarios

- Mobilization capacity and capability is adequate to meet expected needs
- Adequate resources are available for initial response in high threat areas
- Interorganizational coordination is preplanned; stakeholders are identified

Critical success factors: Initial Reaction and Mobilization

- Situational awareness is obtained and shared across distributed organizational network
- Resources in place are capable of initial life and safety response
- Resource mobilization is based on accurate estimate of need for people, funds, and equipment
- Resource mobilization is governed by preplanned organizational structure and process

Critical success factors: Organizational Integration Phase

- Mobilized response resources are rapidly and efficiently integrated into predetermined response organization
- Coordinated multiorganization, networked response system is established
- Ability to manage the collection, synthesis, analysis, and internal and external distribution of information is established
- Organizational and operational adaptability and agility is maintained

Critical success factors: Production Phase

- Organizational productivity and resources are sustained and supported
- Requirement and productivity metrics are developed and monitored
- Accountability is established
- Requirements for recovery are identified

Critical success factors: Transition/Demobilization Phase

- Continuing needs are identified
- Plan for transition to local support of continuing needs is developed and followed
- External resources are demobilized according to established plans and procedures
- Resources are provided to support economic and social recovery
- Organizational learning is accomplished

Agility and Discipline

Barry Boehm and Richard Turner in their recent book *Balancing Agility and Discipline: A Guide for the Perplexed* (2004) described how large software engineering project teams must be both agile and disciplined to build large systems. Webster's defines *discipline* as "self-control or orderly conduct, acceptance of or submission to authority and control" and *agility* as "able to move quickly and easily, deft and active" (*Merriam Webster's Collegiate Dictionary* 1993). Boehm and Turner (2004, 1) stated that "discipline is the foundation for any successful endeavor. Discipline creates well organized memories, history, and experience" and that "agility is the counterpart of discipline. Where discipline ingrains and strengthens, agility releases and invents . . . agility applies memory and history to adjust to new environments to react and adapt, to take advantage of unexpected opportunities."

[T]he case for adaptability, creativity, and improvisation during response to complex events has been made largely outside the emergency management community by the social science research community.

As captured in the critical success factors outlined above, response organizations must possess agility and discipline to respond to extreme events. It is interesting to note that the advancements in discipline (structure, organization, and procedures) have originated from within the emergency management profession. The Incident Command System (ICS) evolved within the wildfire community. During the 1970s, the U.S. Forest Service and the state of California developed the prototype ICS system FIRESCOPE (FIrefighting RESources of California Organized for Potential Emergencies). In 1982, FIRESCOPE evolved into the National Interagency Incident Management System (NIIS) for fighting wildfires (NIMS Integration Center 2004). ICS rapidly became a standard protocol for fire services and was adopted by the U.S. Coast Guard as a method for organizing for oil spill response after the *Exxon Valdez* spill.

Concerns that ICS was a relatively closed system that would not foster adaptability and creativity were expressed by Cohn, Wallace, and Harrald (1991). Mendonça (2005) noted that ICS is more than organizational structure; it is a decision-making protocol for emergency response organizations that places a coordinator in the central role of facilitating team decision making. Walker et al. (1994, 42) stated that "the traditional NIIMS was designed as a closed, command and control system" and that it historically operated effectively in emergency situations where like organizations (e.g., firefighters) with uniform goals and relatively homogeneous organizational cultures were integrated into a single organization.

The advantages of ICS in creating the necessary discipline for multiagency response led to its becoming the de facto standard for firefighting and emergency management. The ICS forms the basis for the NIMS adopted in 2004 (see discussion below) and provides the following elements of discipline to incident management (www.nimsonline.org):

Common Terminology
Modular Organization
Management by Objectives
Reliance on an Incident Action Plan
Manageable Span of Control
Pre-designated Incident Mobilization Center Locations & Facilities
Comprehensive Resource Management
Integrated Communications
Establishment and Transfer of Command
Chain of Command and Unity of Command
Unified Command
Accountability of Resources and Personnel
Deployment
Information and Intelligence Management

It is interesting to note that the case for adaptability, creativity, and improvisation during response to complex events has been made largely outside the emergency management community by the social science research community. Dynes and Quarantelli (1968, 1976) identified the phenomena of emergence during the aftermath of a disaster as new groups formed to address unresolved problems. The postdisaster self-organization of impacted populations and the emergence of creative individual and group behavior has been repeatedly observed and confirmed by social science researchers.

Dynes (1994, 2000) demonstrated that the assumptions inherent in closed-system, command and control organizational models have been absent in the aftermath of almost all natural and technological disasters. The closed system model (which Dynes termed the "military model") assumes environmental chaos and the need for command, control, and centralized decision making. The open-system, problem-solving model assumes an environment that supports continuity and recovery and a need for coordination, cooperation, and decentralized decision making.

Other researchers have noted that structured planning and organization were only effective if the ability to improvise is preserved. Kreps (1991, 33) in a publication intended for local emergency managers, stated, "Without improvisation, emergency management loses flexibility in the face of changing conditions. Without preparedness, emergency management loses clarity and efficiency in meeting external disaster related demands. Equally importantly improvisation and preparedness go hand in hand." Kendra and Wachtendorf (2002) saw improvisation as the combination of planning and creativity when meeting unexpected situations or unexpected constraints. Mendonça and Wallace (2004, 8) noted that while emergency preparedness and planning is structured, emergency managers must improvise and that "extreme events may perturb pre-disaster social networks leading to their extension, dissolution, reconfiguration, or construction. The connections among individuals that are implied by disaster plans or other data sources may then be compared to those that actually occur during the response to an actual or simulated event."

Walker et al. (1994, 43) described the necessity for open organizational response management systems that "rely on internal and external feedback, organizational learning from the reactions of the external environments to its decisions, distributed decision making by small ad hoc teams, and a high degree of flexibility and innovation." Comfort (1999) in her examination of responses to major earthquakes has identified the ability of response organizations to build adaptive organizational networks as a key predictor of success.

Karl Weick (1998; Weick and Sutcliffe 2001) has focused the need for high-reliability organizations to anticipate and manage the unexpected. He used the term "mindfulness" to describe the ability of organizations to organize themselves and to create an organizational culture that enables them to detect and react to the unexpected (Weick and Sutcliffe 2001, 3). He asserted that "a well developed capability for mindfulness catches the unexpected earlier, when it is smaller, comprehends its potential importance despite the small size of the disruption and removes, contains or rebounds from the effects of the unexpected" (Weick and Sutcliffe 2001, 17). A primary objective of training and preparedness is to facilitate the ability to detect and manage the unexpected. The resulting awareness and ability to improvise enables organizations to focus on "the interval between anticipation and resilience during which the unexpected is detected more or less swiftly and managed more or less successfully" (Weick and Sutcliffe 2001, 159).

Louise Comfort (2005, 8) pointed out that the Hurricane Katrina response was far from the ideal identified by Weick (1998; Weick and Sutcliffe 2001). In fact, "The inability to identify and correct errors as the event evolved was a striking characteristic of the disaster response system throughout this event." Comfort has shown (1999) that the creative ability of response organizations to become adaptive networks has been a notable factor in determining the relative success of response and relief operations.

The U.S. Experience since 9/11

The United States, in a reaction to the September 11, 2001, attacks has embarked on a massive attempt to coordinate the management of risks due to extreme events. This effort has produced an impressive set of Presidential Decision Directives, National Strategies, plans, and organizations. The most obvious initiative taken by the United States was the creation of the DHS, now the largest civilian agency of the U.S. government with extensive responsibility for preserving the safety and security of the United States. Perhaps the most significant accomplishment to date, however, is the attempt to create a truly integrated national system for the preparation for, response to, and recovery from extreme events. Table 1 shows that prior to the formation of the DHS, the type of triggering event determined which federal agencies led the response, the type of federal response and coordination, and how the federal agencies interacted with the states.

TABLE 1

U.S. DISASTER PLANS IN 2001

Type of Event	Federal Plan	Lead Agencies	State Role
Presidentially declared disaster (natural disaster, terrorist attack)	Federal Response Plan	Federal Emergency Management Agency; Federal Bureau of Investigation	Lead role, supported by federal resources
Environmental disaster (release of oil, toxic substances)	National Contingency Plan	Environmental Protection Agency; Coast Guard	Parallel federal and state roles
Nuclear/radiological release	Federal Radiological Emergency Plan	Department of Energy; Federal Emergency Management Agency	State and local support of federal response
Wildfire	National Interagency Incident Management System	Department of Agriculture	Federal lead in federal lands, state lead in state lands
Biohazard/epidemic	Medical Support Plan, National Disaster Medical System	Department of Health and Human Services; Centers for Disease Control and Prevention	Federal support of state and local medical and public health response

The DHS was tasked by Presidential Decision Directive Number Five to create an integrated National Response System for all types of incidents (The White House 2003). The implementing documents are the NRP and the NIMS. The NRP provides the common policy base and national coordinating structure; NIMS provides the ability to structure and manage the incident response. Together, they provide the structure and discipline necessary to achieve many of the critical success factors described above in the U.S. federal system. NIMS in particular can be seen as creating the discipline and structure necessary for a response to complex incidents. The NIMS objectives are stated as follows:

> This system will provide a consistent nationwide approach for Federal, State, and local governments to work effectively and efficiently together to prepare for, respond to, and recover from domestic incidents, regardless of cause, size, or complexity. To provide for interoperability and compatibility among Federal, State, and local capabilities, the NIMS will include a core set of concepts, principles, terminology, and technologies covering the incident command system; multi-agency coordination systems; unified command; training; identification and management of resources (including systems for classifying types of resources); qualifications and certification; and the collection, tracking, and reporting of incident information and incident resources. (DHS 2004a, 7)

The NRP and NIMS are intended to accomplish the following goals:

- align national coordinating structures, capabilities, and resources;
- ensure an all-discipline and all-hazard approach to domestic incident management;
- manage incidents at the lowest possible geographical, organizational, and jurisdictional level;
- incorporate emergency management and law enforcement into a single structure;
- provide one way of operating for all events; and
- provide continuity of management from preincident to postincident.

Hess and Harrald (2004), in a *Natural Hazard Observer* invited comment, raised questions about both the need for and future effectiveness of the new system. Hurricane Katrina provides preliminary answers to their questions:

> Will a centralized, highly structured, closed system entrusted solely to trained professionals work effectively for managing complex events? Was such a sweeping change necessary to achieve immediate policy goals? What will be the unintended consequences of this policy initiative? (P. 1)

An Organizational Typology

The discipline provided by the ICS and the improvisation required by a problem-solving, open-system response are often assumed to be opposite ends of a linear scale. Recent experience prior to Hurricane Katrina, however, suggests that these are not opposites, that agility and discipline can both be achieved. Successful improvisation and creativity during the response to the attacks on the World Trade Center are discussed by Kendra and Wachtendorf (2002), Mendonça (2005), and Mendonça and Wallace (2004). Improvisation in the context of a successful implementation of an ICS structure during the response to the Pentagon is described in Harrald, Renda-Tanali, and Coppola (2002). It is useful to think of discipline and agility as orthogonal scales. If this is done, an organizational typology consisting of four types of organizations can be created by combining the need for both discipline and agility and shown in Figure 2. The four organizational types may be summarized as follows:

Type 1: Dysfunctional

- Relatively unstructured, poorly defined processes and procedures
- Relatively rigid, unable to move or change
- Weaknesses—unable to create repeatable or predictable processes, unable to adjust to unexpected events or conditions

Type 2: Ad Hoc/Reactive

- Relatively unstructured, no defined processes and procedures
- Able to be creative and improvise

FIGURE 2
AN ORGANIZATIONAL TYPOLOGY OF RESPONSE ORGANIZATIONS

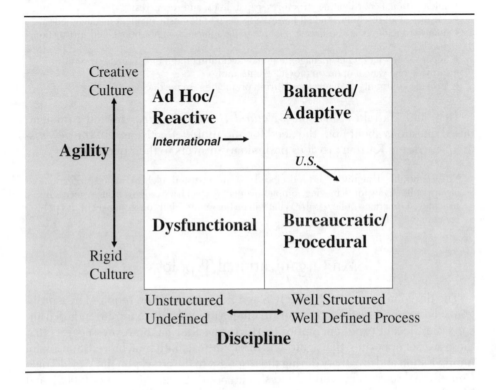

- Weaknesses—difficulty in creating and sustaining large organizations, difficulty in coordinating with other organizations
- Strengths—ability to change rapidly, to adjust to the unexpected
- Examples—many international relief organizations during 2004 Tsunami response

Type 3: Balanced/Adaptive

- Defined structure, well-defined processes and procedures
- Able to be creative and improvise
- Weaknesses—leaders must be innovative as well as technically competent, selection and training difficult
- Strengths—ability to mobilize and manage large, complex organizations, ability to change rapidly, adjust to other organizations
- Example—U.S. Coast Guard performance in Hurricane Katrina

Type 4: Bureaucratic/Procedural

- Defined structure, well-defined processes and procedures
- Relatively rigid, unable to change

- Weaknesses—inability to recognize and adapt to unexpected events, danger of becoming procedure-bound
- Strengths—ability to mobilize and coordinate large complex organizations, ability to develop consistent training
- Example—DHS performance in Hurricane Katrina

Where are we in this typology? Since its formation, the DHS has expended considerable effort on the dimension of increasing discipline by creating a true national system (federal, tribal, state, and local) to prepare for, respond to, and recover from extreme events. The motivation and focus has been terrorism, but the approach is all hazards. The DHS focus on defining policy, structure, and process is described above. Many disaster researchers believed that the ability to foster creativity, improvisation, and adaptability (the agility dimension) would suffer, as shown in Figure 2 (e.g., see Hess and Harrald 2004). The ponderous, bureaucratic response and recovery efforts following Hurricane Katrina show that these fears were not unfounded. The DHS must now make efforts to create flexibility and agility while preserving the structure and discipline it has achieved. In terms of the organizational framework, it must figure out how to make the national response system support a Type 3 organization.

Alternatively, the massive coordination problems encountered by governments and nongovernmental organizations during the international response to the Indian Ocean Tsunami exposed the limitations of existing coordinating authorities and mechanisms supported by minimal common structures and procedures. As reported by Gelling (2005, 7, col. 1), "The strongest international criticism of the relief effort in Aceh so far has been a lack of information-sharing and cooperation among private aid groups, donors, and the four levels of government. Eight months after the tsunami, in an effort to correct problems with coordination, the Indonesian government established the Aceh Rehabilitation and Reconstruction Agency as an umbrella organization that monitors every project." A long-overdue discussion about improving the structural linkages between organizations, and developing improved logistical and information systems has begun. The highly agile, international response community has recognized a need to increase its abilities along the discipline dimension, to move from a Type 2 to a Type 3 organization as shown in Figure 2.

Conclusions

The federal government's slow and ineffective response to Hurricane Katrina has raised many questions about the National Response System defined by the NRP and NIMS. It is doubtful that the extensive and expensive changes to the National Response System preserved the agility, flexibility, and creativity that have been essential in past response operations. It is a legitimate question to ask after Katrina if the National Response System is sufficiently resilient to ensure an adequate response to and recovery from a catastrophic event. Resilient systems avoid catastrophic failure by "failing gracefully," allowing time to adapt to unanticipated conditions and to recover system functions. The National Response System, consisting of organizations, plans, systems, technology, and people, could not adapt to unprecedented challenges and failed catastrophically during the initial response to Hurricane Katrina. Since its creation in 2002, the DHS has focused on increasing the discipline in the national system through an extensive development of doctrine, process, and structure and has neglected fostering the agility (creativity, adaptability, improvisation) that has historically been the key to success. The perceived failure of the federal, state, and local governments after Katrina has provoked intense criticism of leaders and response organizations. Responding to media reports of failures of leadership, political forces are mobilizing to fix the perceived problem prior to understanding the reasons for the failure of the system. Individual failures such as the inability to comprehend the reality presented by Katrina, the lack of critical competencies, and poor decision making occurred at all levels. However, we must separate these individual failures from organizational system problems.

> *The Department of Homeland Security*
> *must now make efforts to create flexibility*
> *and agility while preserving the structure*
> *and discipline it has achieved.*

The organizational systems that respond to extreme events must be open systems that allow information to be gathered from and transmitted to the public and nongovernmental organizations in addition to standard governmental sources. They must promote distributed decision making and improvisation in the face of unexpected events or conditions. We must recognize that the response to and recovery from a catastrophic event cannot be successful if only emergency managers and first responders are prepared and expect to operate within a closed system. We will fail if the only people who know emergency management plans and processes exist are the emergency managers and if we operate in a closed community with a closed language and protocol (the NRP contains an eight-page appendix of acronyms).

The president and others are proposing to move the responsibility for the preparedness and response to catastrophic events from the DHS to the Department of Defense. The militarization of homeland security and emergency management is a dramatic step with historic consequences. It assumes that the failure in Katrina was a failure of discipline—that civilian emergency management cannot effectively deploy and manage assets. The apparent conclusion is that because the military command and control system is effective in deploying resources, it must be capable of effectively and efficiently providing rescue and relief services. The military can maintain command, control, and order during times of chaos; move resources rapidly; occupy and hold territory; and sustain itself in adverse environments and will, therefore, continue to fill a critical role in response to extreme events. The military is not trained or structured for the complex tasks of intergovernmental coordination and collaboration needed when preparing for and responding to extreme events. Ultimately the response to and recovery from a catastrophic incident is about what V. A. D. M. Allen (2005) has termed "continuity of society": not only preserving life and property, but also sustaining the community, recovering the regional society and the economy, and mitigating the impacts of potential future disasters. These roles require federal, state, and local collaboration and leadership and a disciplined and agile national response system. This is not a time to attempt a simple fix by re-assigning responsibilities; it is a time to establish necessary competencies, systems, and relationships that will ensure that the next time a catastrophic event occurs we do not simply repeat the same mistakes with different people or organizations in charge.

References

Allen, V. A. D. M. Thad. 2005. Keynote address to the George Washington University School of Public Policy and Public Administration Symposium on Hurricane Katrina. George Washington University, Washington, DC, December 2.

Boehm, Barry, and R. Turner. 2004. *Balancing agility and discipline: A guide for the perplexed*. Boston: Addison-Wesley, Pearson Education.

Carali, Richard, J. R. Stevens, B. J. Wilke, and W. R. Wilson. 2004. *The critical success factor method: Establishing a foundation for enterprise security management*. CMU/SEI 2004-TR-010. Pittsburgh, PA: Carnegie Mellon University Press.

Carley, Kathleen M., and J. R. Harrald. 1997. Organizational learning under fire: Theory and practice. *American Behavioral Scientist* 40 (3): 310-32.

Cohn, Ruth E., W. A. Wallace, and J. R. Harrald. 1991. Organizing for response: The unresolved problem. In *Proceedings, 1991 International Oil Spill Conference*, 29-33. Washington, DC: American Petroleum Institute.

Comfort, Louise K. 1999. *Shared risk: Complex systems in seismic response*. Pittsburgh, PA: Pergamon.

———. 2005. Fragility in disaster response: Hurricane Katrina, 29 August 2005. *The Forum*, vol. 3, no. 3, article 1. http://www.bepress.com/forum/vol3/iss3/art1.

Dynes, Russell R. 1994. Community emergency planning: False assumptions and inappropriate analogies. *International Journal of Mass Emergencies and Disasters* 12:141-58.

———. 2000. *Governmental systems for disaster management*. Preliminary Paper no. 300. Newark: Disaster Research Center, University of Delaware.

Dynes, Russell R., and E. L. Quarantelli. 1968. Group behavior under stress: A required convergence of organizational and collective behavior perspectives. *Sociology and Social Research* 52:416-29.

———. 1976. *Organizational communications and decision making during crises*. Preliminary Paper no. 17. Newark: Disaster Research Center. University of Delaware.

Gelling, Peter. 2005. Bill Clinton finds better relief coordination in Tsunami area tour. *International Herald Tribune*, December 1.

Harrald, John R., and T. Mazzuchi. 1993. Planning for success: A scenario based approach to contingency planning using expert judgment. *Journal of Contingencies and Crisis Management* 1 (4): 189-98.

Harrald, John R., I. Renda-Tanali, and D. Coppola. 2002. Observing and documenting the interorganizational response to the September 11 attack on the Pentagon. In *Proceedings, 9th Annual Conference of the International Emergency Management Society (TIEMS)*, 32-43. Waterloo, Canada: TIEMS.

Harrald, John R., and Linda Stoddart. 1998. Scenario based identification and structuring of information needs for the response to complex international crises. In *Proceedings, Fifth Annual Conference of the Emergency Management Society*, 295-306. Washington, DC: Emergency Management Society.

Hess, Charles, and J. R. Harrald. 2004. The National Response Plan: Process, prospects, and participants. *Natural Hazards Observer* 28 (6): 1-2.

Kendra, James, and T. Wachtendorf. 2002. *Creativity in emergency response after the World Trade Center attack*. Preliminary Paper no. 324. Newark: Disaster Research Center, University of Delaware.

Kreps, Gary A. 1991. Organizing for emergency management. In *Emergency management: Principles and practice for local governments*, ed. T. E. Drabek and G. J. Hoetmer, 30-54. Washington, DC: International City Management Association.

Mendonça, David. 2005. Decision support for improvisation in response to extreme events: Learning from the response to the 2001 World Trade Center attack. *Decision Support Systems*.

Mendonça, David, and W. A. Wallace. 2004. Studying organizationally-situated improvisation in response to extreme events. *International Journal of Mass Emergencies and Disasters* 22 (2): 5-29.

Merriam Webster's Collegiate Dictionary, 10th ed. 1993. Springfield, MA: Webster, Inc.

National Incident Management System (NIMS) Integration Center, U.S. Department of Homeland Security. 2004. NIMS and the Incident Command System. November 18. Position Paper. Washington, DC: NIMS Integration Center, U.S. Department of Homeland Security.

Quarantelli, Henry. 2005. Catastrophe's are different from disasters: Some implications for crisis planning and managing drawn from Katrina. Working paper, Disaster Research Center, University of Delaware, Newark.

Roberts, Patrick. 2005. What Katrina means for emergency management. *The Forum* 3 (3): 4.

Rockhart, John R. 1979. Chief executives define their own data needs. *Harvard Business Review* 57 (2): 81-93.

———. 1981. The changing role of the information system executive: A critical success factor perspective. *Sloan Management Review*, winter, pp. 15-25.

Rockhart, John R., and C. V. Bullen. 1981. A primer on critical success factors. June. Working Paper 60, MIT Center for Information Systems Research, Cambridge, MA.

Tuckman, Bruce W. 1965. Developmental sequence in small groups. *Psychological Bulletin* 63:384-99.

U.S. Department of Homeland Security (DHS). 2004a. *National Incident Management System*. March 1. Washington, DC: U.S. Department of Homeland Security.

———. 2004b. National Response Plan. December. Washington, DC: U.S. Department of Homeland Security.

Walker, Ann Hayward, J. R. Harrald, D. L. Ducey, and S. J. Lacey. 1994. *Implementing an effective response management system*. Washington, DC: American Petroleum Institute.

Weick, K. E. 1998. Improvisation as a mindset for organizational analysis. *Organization Science* 9 (5): 543-55.

Weick, Karl E., and Kathleen M. Sutcliffe. 2001. *Managing the unexpected: Assuring high performance in an age of complexity*. San Francisco: Jossey-Bass.

The White House. 2003. Homeland Security Presidential Directive Number 5 (HSPD 5). Washington, DC: The White House.

Is the Worst Yet to Come?

By
DONALD F. KETTL

Following the 9/11 terrorist attacks on New York and Washington, public officials pledged that the nation would rise to the challenge and ensure that the country would not suffer such a disaster again. Almost exactly four years later, however, Hurricane Katrina inflicted a devastating blow on the Gulf Coast. Many of the problems that surfaced during 9/11 returned yet again to plague the Katrina recovery efforts. Moreover, as bad as the problems were in the Gulf, they could have been even worse had the storm been stronger or had it scored a direct hit on New Orleans. More disasters—from earthquakes and floods to bird flu and terrorist attacks—are likely and perhaps inevitable. Unless we take to heart the lessons that Katrina teaches, especially improved systems for communication and coordination, we are likely to repeat the Katrina problems. The worst is yet to come, without a substantial investment of political capital.

Keywords: Hurricane Katrina; disaster management; public management

Following September 11, 2001, public officials everywhere promised that the nation would learn the painful lessons the terrorist attack taught. But Hurricane Katrina not only revealed that we have failed to learn, it also showed that we have yet to build the capacity to deal with costly, wicked problems that leave little time to react.

More crises like September 11 and Katrina are inevitable. The next event might be a major California earthquake or a nasty flu virus, a terrorist attack or a megastorm. We cannot be sure what will happen; we can be certain that something will. And what each of these problems

Donald F. Kettl is the Stanley I. Sheerr Endowed Term Professor in the Social Sciences at the University of Pennsylvania, where he is director of the Fels Institute of Government and a professor of political science. He is the author of System under Stress: Homeland Security and American Politics; The Global Public Management Revolution, *2nd ed.; and* The Transformation of Governance: Public Administration for the 21st Century. *He is a fellow of the National Academy of Public Administration.*

DOI: 10.1177/0002716205285981

273

share is a common feature: they slop over the boundaries, in both public policy and public organizations, that the nation has created to deal with them. Nevertheless, the instinct is the same: to repeatedly draw boxes around problems that defy boundaries. If the nation does not learn the lessons that both Katrina and September 11 teach, we will suffer the same consequences, over and over. In that case, the worst is yet to come.

A Failure to Learn

When President Bush addressed the nation in the aftermath of Hurricane Katrina's devastating attack on the Gulf Coast, he promised the government would build on the lessons the storm taught, "This government will learn the lessons of Hurricane Katrina. We're going to review every action and make necessary changes, so that we are better prepared for any challenge of nature, or act of evil men, that could threaten our people" (Bush 2005b). Of course, after the September 11 terrorist attacks, top government officials also pledged that the nation would be far better prepared for crisis. Democrats pressed for the creation of a new department for homeland security. Bush embraced it and shaped it to his liking. Everyone promised the government would work better.

The 9/11 Commission, which spent months poring through the government's records on the attack, pointed to a "failure of imagination" as perhaps the most important underlying cause of the government's poor response to the attacks (National Commission on Terrorist Attacks 2004, 344, 350). Since then, that failure of imagination has continued. Top federal officials said in Katrina's wake that they had no idea that Katrina could cause such damage or that thousands of New Orleansians were marooned for days without food, water, shelter, or medical care. Local officials were marooned for days without telephone communication, while state officials could not connect to the federal officials about the help they needed.

The government's staggering recovery efforts in the Gulf raise deep, real worries about its ability to respond to other large-scale, high-consequence events. Disaster planners have a long list of possible events: a flu pandemic, a major California earthquake, a dirty bomb attack, a second megahurricane hit on the Gulf Coast or a major hurricane strike on Miami, or bioterrorism.

Some of these things are possibilities. Some are probable. But some major event like this is a certainty, and it is possible that the scale and impact could be even greater than for Katrina. Unless the nation, and especially its governments, quickly learn far better how to deal with such events, the consequences could well be even worse.

Think about the stress test that cardiologists administer to their patients. In day-to-day life, even diseased hearts often show little sign of problems. Cardiologists have discovered that, if they subject the heart to stress, they can discover—and treat—problems before they prove fatal. So the cardiologist wires up the patient with electrodes, fires up the treadmill, and gradually increases the speed and the incline to see how well the patient's heart responds to stress. If the patient fails the test—if it reveals blockages that weaken the heart's response—the doctor stops the test and prescribes treatment. If the patient collapses, there is nurse, a stretcher, and a bottle of oxygen at the ready.

Twice, the nation's homeland security system has been subjected to a stress test. Twice—first with September 11, second with Katrina—the patient has collapsed. So far, however, the nation has failed to learn the lessons the tests have taught—and has failed to treat the patient. That failure has unquestionably caused some Americans to die and others to suffer, and a third failed test might prove even more damaging. Most cardiac patients do not recover from heart damage that builds up over time.

The core of the problem lies in three puzzles: wicked problems, messy boundaries, and depleted intellectual capital.

---

*If all we have are backward-looking plans,
we doom ourselves to repeated failure.*

First, the nation is increasingly facing problems that, by their very nature, are *wicked* (see Rittel 1973). From megastorms to terrorist attacks, from nasty flu viruses to earthquakes, we face the virtual certainty of big events that provide *little time to react*, and where the *cost of failure* is enormous. The failure to respond to such problems can pose enormous, sometimes unthinkable, consequences.

Second, although we design standard bureaucracies to deal with routine problems, more of the problems we face *fail to match these boundaries*. Our large bureaucracies deal with routine problems, from mailing social security checks to managing air-traffic control, and they are pretty good at it. The wicked problems we increasingly face, however, fall outside normal routines. By their very nature, they slop over any boundary—political or organizational—that we can draw. Hurricanes pay no attention to the jurisdictional lines between Louisiana parishes. They ignore the boundary separating Louisiana from Mississippi and, for that matter, between the federal, state, and local governments. In Katrina, the governmental response was crippled by the instinct of government officials to stay within their boundaries while they tried to cope with problems that paid no attention to those boundaries. Moreover, terrorists certainly were watching the government's chaotic response and have learned. They know about the fragmentation of our system and are surely planning to exploit it. More problems slop over the boundaries we have created to deal with them. For the really wicked problems, it is impossible to draw a box around them. Moreover, any box we draw for a current problem is certain to prove a poor match for future problems. The mismatch between our boundaries and the problems we are trying to solve invites repeated failure and unacceptable consequences.

Third, the nation's intellectual capital for understanding, yet alone solving, these problems is seriously *depleted*. When they face big problems that demand quick responses, policy makers understandably retreat back to what they know or, at least, what they find comfortable. It is easy to blame terrorists in other countries, to suggest that other nations are either for us or against us, to rely on well-traveled governmental reorganization. For wicked problems that defy our organizational and policy boundaries, these past models provide a poor guide for future action. Attacking such problems with old, outdated tools is like trying to change a tire with a screwdriver and a hammer—while the car is moving down the highway at seventy miles per hour. If we cannot design new tools for society's toolbox, future failures are inevitable. Without a new toolbox for new problems, the nation will be constantly outmaneuvered by events—and by combatants who seek to exploit our weaknesses.

Learning Pathologies

Why did the nation fail to learn from September 11—and why are we likely to fail to learn yet again from Katrina? In brief, policy instincts are hardwired for obsolete approaches. That makes the system hardwired for failure. Better learning requires rewiring.

What are these obsolete strategies? Consider the following five pathologies.

1. An instinct to look back instead of looking forward

In observing the American response to the September 11 terrorist attacks, a European diplomat was puzzled. In its 2002 proposal for the new Department of Homeland Security (DHS), the Bush administration pointed backwards to the creation of the Department of Defense in 1947: a model of merging multiple organizations into one megadepartment. "I'm struck," the diplomat said, "that in charting a strategy for the future the nation focused on a model from the past" (interview with the author). In devising a new strategy for the most important problem of the twenty-first century, the nation relied on the best of 1940s technology. When Katrina put the new system to a stress test, it responded about as well as a 1947 Nash would respond on a twenty-first-century interstate highway.

Not only are many of the most important problems we face inherently wicked, many of them are *asymmetric*: broad and unpredictable events that, deliberately or not, take advantage of points of vulnerability in the system. On September 11, terrorists cleverly discovered and exploited weaknesses in the airline security system. Four years later, Hurricane Katrina inflicted enormous damage because of weaknesses in New Orleans's levee system.

It is one thing to deal with events that play to our strengths. That is why the battlefield engagements of both Gulf Wars lasted mere weeks. But when asymmetric events occur, backward-looking strategies doom us to enormous damage and injury. The nation needs to get much smarter, very quickly, in learning how to deal with asymmetric threats. Without learning in advance about how to deal with such threats, we tend to pull old game plans off the shelf to deal with new problems. If all we have are backward-looking plans, we doom ourselves to repeated failure.

2. An instinct to reform instead of to govern

The single most important fact about the creation of DHS in 2002 is that it emerged from political, not administrative, imperatives. Members of Congress worried about "connecting the dots"—bridging the gaps in the system to prevent such attacks from ever occurring again. In 2002, Sen. Chuck Grassley (R-Iowa) bluntly asked, "What will it take to 'connect the dots' necessary to piece together obscure clues and pursue leads to prevent another September 11 from devastating America all over again?" (Grassley 2002).

The conclusion: merge twenty-two agencies into a single new department. The Bush administration did not want to create a large new bureaucracy, and its top officials did everything they could to stop the plan. Not until it became clear that Congress was about to pass it did the administration embrace it. And in what proved one of the most brilliant tactical gambits of the George W. Bush years, the president then used the homeland security proposal to force congressional Democrats to accept a massive change in the new department's personnel system. They had little choice but to accept a department they had pressed on the president; in return, the president undermined a key part of the Democratic constituency.

The debate over creating the department in the end turned much less on how best to secure the homeland than on how to balance executive and legislative power. Bush turned the congressional initiative for the department into a clever tactic to shift the balance of power to the executive branch. Most broadly, the creation of the new department became a symbol of the nation's response to September 11, of the need to be seen to be responding, quite apart from the effectiveness of the response.

Despite the creation of the new department, key dots remained unconnected. Driving the debate was the need to coordinate intelligence, but the intelligence agencies successfully fought to remain outside the new department. How to make the new department work was largely an afterthought. It was huge, unwieldy, and beset by cross-pressures and bureaucratic turf wars. To make things worse, the Bush administration did not pay sufficient attention to staffing key positions, including FEMA, with officials skilled in emergency management. The department did not build skilled career administrators into key support positions, and too much of the department's intellectual capital was contracted out. Devising communication strategies linking federal, state, and local officials was largely an afterthought. It was little surprise, then, that when Katrina hit and DHS needed key people with the right instincts, no one was home at Homeland.

Some of these problems were inevitable, for any reorganization effort that vast was certain to face growing pains. Given the enormous breadth of the homeland security issue, the new department could only be viewed as a work in progress, and it was sure to take years for the department to settle into established routines. But Katrina revealed that a slow learning curve could impose enormous costs. The people of the Gulf Coast paid a price for FEMA's inability to respond effectively.

"When in doubt, reorganize!" is the usual catchphrase. Too often, elected officials declare victory as soon as the ink of the president's signature is dry and they win the symbol for which they were searching. Too often, elected officials neglect the job of making things work. Political candidates often put so much emphasis on the race that they forget to stop to ask themselves what they are going to do with the prize when they get it. Much of government's work is governing; Katrina demonstrates that periodically there are times when problems of capacity create serious problems. When we settle for bright political symbols instead of efficient public organizations, we inevitably pay the price.

3. An instinct to think vertically instead of horizontally

Battles over the chain of command erupted in the days after Katrina hit. New Orleans Mayor Ray Nagin complained that federal officials "don't have a clue what's going on down here" (CNN.com 2005b). Louisiana Governor Kathleen Babineaux Blanco said she could not get federal officials to respond. Army officials said they were on the scene with thirty-six hundred troops from the 82nd Airborne Division within eight hours of getting the request to respond—but that it took three days for that request to arrive. "If the first Cav and 82nd Airborne had gotten there on time, I think we would have saved some lives," explained Army Gen. (Ret.) Julius Becton Jr., who had served as FEMA director under Ronald Reagan. "We recognized we had to get people out, and they had helicopters to do that" (Brown, Borenstein, and Young 2005).

All along the vertical line, from local officials through the states to federal officials at the highest level, battles erupted. Officials were clearly confused about who ought, could, and should do what. The long vertical chain of command provided political cover, for in a tall hierarchy, the problem (and blame) always lies somewhere else.

The debate since has confused the inescapable need for a "unified command"—ensuring that the key decision makers are all on the same page—with the "chain of command"—the vertical links among decision makers, from top to bottom of the system. Someone has to be in charge of the response to events like Katrina. But that does not require a civil war among levels of government and between government organizations over just who that ought to be. Indeed, as long as we have a system of federalism, even thinking about "top" and "bottom" makes no sense. A coordinated response requires the subtle weaving together of forces from a vast array of functional areas and from different levels of government, not hierarchical control. American federalism preserves autonomy for officials at each level. They need to coordinate with each other. They surely do not need to fight over who is in charge.

In the aftermath of September 11, New York Mayor Rudolph Giuliani eventually established himself as the frontline spokesman. He gathered around him the resources he needed, from all levels of government. And New York's response began to emerge. It did not develop because Giuliani clawed to the top of a pyramid. It emerged because he became the conductor of a large and hugely complex symphony. He built a network of horizontal partnerships.

A coordinated response requires the subtle weaving together of forces from a vast array of functional areas and from different levels of government, not hierarchical control.

That, indeed, is the lesson of the first responders who worked so effectively together at the Pentagon on September 11. The jurisdictions that surrounded the Pentagon, and the government agencies that worked within them, agreed far in advance of the attack who would be in charge at the scene of any major problem. What happened? It worked. By deciding—and practicing—the incident command system in advance, the area governments were ready when the terrorists struck (Arlington County n.d.). They did not magnify the disaster by creating a bureaucratic disaster of their own. They worked effectively in a tightly knit horizontal network instead of struggling over a vertical chain of command.

Former congressman Lee Hamilton, who served as vice-chairman of the 9/11 Commission, put it bluntly in the days after Katrina struck. On creating a unified command, he concluded, "we're falling far short of where we would like to be four years after 9/11." He added that what has to be done "as quickly as possible after a disaster has struck is to have a unified command so that the hundreds of decisions—and hundreds of them have to be made quickly about personnel and equipment and rescuing people and alleviating suffering and all of the rest—can be made quickly. There was not a unified command in New York in 9/11. There was not a unified command quickly enough after Katrina." If the tough decisions are not made in advance, Hamilton concluded, "You have a disaster that will impact far more people then if you had the plan in place" (PBS *Newshour* 2005).

Effective response requires strong vertical lines in our organizations. Hierarchy provides the critical, unifying structure to the capacity of complex organizations. But effective response also requires strong horizontal relationships to put that capacity to work. We need to *organize vertically* and to *work horizontally*. If government officials fight over the baton instead of finding an effective orchestra conductor, Americans will needlessly suffer in any wicked problem.

4. An instinct to regulate instead of to perform

In case after case, rules, paperwork, and procedures stymied the government's response to Hurricane Katrina. President Bush said, "We will not allow bureaucracy to get in the way of saving lives" (Bush 2005a). But an infuriated Rep. Charlie Melancon (D-LA) told *Nightline*, "What I've seen the last several days is bureaucrats that were worried about procedure rather than saving lives. That's what I've seen" (ABC News, *Nightline*, September 2, 2005).

Hundreds of firefighters from around the country were stuck in Atlanta, receiving days of training on community relations and sexual harassment, before they reached the front lines. Truck drivers carrying thousands of water bottles were prevented from driving to New Orleans because they had not yet been assigned a "tasker number."[1] Sheriffs from other states simply ignored the paperwork. Wayne County, Michigan, Sheriff Warren C. Evans said he refused to stop his convoy of six trailer trucks, full of food and water, and thirty-three deputies. "I could look at CNN and see people dying, and I couldn't in good conscience wait for a coordinated response," he said (*New York Times* 2005).

Rules are invaluable. They help ensure that the same people in the same circumstances receive equitable treatment from government. For example, we would not want individual social security workers making their own individual judgment about the size of a senior citizen's check. But regulations can also create deep pathologies. They provide protection from blame and make it easy for officials to duck the responsibility for thinking about what they are trying to accomplish.

Rules matter. But they exist to foster superior performance. We cannot afford thousands of cowboys in the middle of a crisis, each setting policy on his own. When rules do not fit the situation, obedience to them can paralyze the capacity to act. The search for superior performance, not blind obedience to rules, must guide emergency response.

5. A misplaced veneration for outdated traditions instead of a focus on effective governance

In the midst of the post-Katrina problems, a senior state homeland security official (from far outside the region) said sadly that a major impediment to effective response is "our maniacally single-minded devotion to home rule" (interview with the author). We have governmental units that follow geographical lines, like river banks or lines on map. In many parts of the country, today's political boundaries reflect important seventeenth-century goals, such as ensuring that citizens live within a day's horseback ride of the county seat. These boundaries might have served the needs of centuries ago. They often prove a very poor match for twenty-first-century problems.

Self-government has always been the foundation of American democracy. That is as it should be, and the United States will survive any challenge it faces as long as self-government remains strong. But our government ought to empower effective action. The boundaries of government should not constrain our ability to act. Too often, even years after the September 11 attacks, first responders in neighboring jurisdictions have radios that operate on different frequencies. Communication problems in crises sometimes occur because of technical problems. Too often, as a report from the Century Foundation discovered in 2003, they persist because officials in neighboring communities simply do not want to talk to each other (Kettl 2003).

Not long after watching a television newsmagazine report on the risks of sports-utility vehicle (SUV) rollover accidents, I just missed witnessing just such an accident. I came upon the scene moments later, and there was an SUV on its roof on the side of the road. As luck would also have it, the occupants were not hurt—but they were hanging upside down by their seatbelts. But as luck would also have it, the accident was precisely at the intersection of two local governments. It was anything but clear whose job it was to get those people out.

In a case like that, two bad things could happen: neither government might respond, with each assuming the other would handle the call; or both governments would respond, with the full first-response arsenal, and with a big waste of taxpayer dollars. Because both communities had worked out these problems in advance, a third alternative occurred: emergency vehicles with sirens wailing converged on the scene from both directions—with just the right level of support. They managed to extract the occupants from the vehicle, and in the process they taught a critical lesson: when you are hanging upside down from your seatbelts in a rolled-over SUV, the last thing you care about is the name on the decal on the side of the emergency vehicle.

But bad things happened in Katrina's wake. In Louisiana, the "maniacal devotion to home rule" literally produced gunfire at the boundary between two communities. New Orleans authorities advised some of the tourists trapped at the city's convention center that the only way out of the city was across the Crescent City Connection, a bridge that led to neighboring Gretna City. Buses were waiting for them there, they were told. But when hundreds of bedraggled tourists dragged their suitcases to the bridge, they found police from the community across the bridge, Gretna City, waiting for them. When the tourists tried to cross the bridge, the Gretna City police fired over their heads to warn them back to New Orleans. They told the crowd that Gretna City "was not going to become New Orleans and there would be no Superdomes in their city." Some members of the crowd asked what choice they had. They reported later that the armed security officials told them "that was [their] problem" and that they had no water to give them. As two paramedics, caught amid the crowd, later wrote, "These were code words for if you are poor and black, you are not crossing the Mississippi River and you are not getting out of New Orleans" (Waterman 2005; ABC News Online 2005).

Too often throughout the struggle to deal with Katrina's aftermath, the boundaries separating neighboring jurisdictions—as well as the federal, state, and local governments—became barriers handicapping the government's response. These tales proved even more chilling than what occurred on September 11. People want their problems solved; they do not fuss over the patch on the arm of the person who solves them.

Lessons from Katrina

What general lessons does Katrina teach? First, we face a new generation of wicked problems that demand innovative solutions. Second, lessons of the past are important, but old lessons can hamstring our ability to look forward. Third, we need to govern instead of reaching for symbols. We need to plan, practice, implement—and learn. Fourth, we need public officials to lead. Communicating confidence to citizens and delivering on promises are both critical in crises. Fifth, we need to devise new strategies for effective horizontal coordination so that we are not handicapped by the pathologies of vertical bureaucracies. Sixth, we need good rules, but we cannot afford to allow them to undermine commonsense solutions or high performance at times of crises. Seventh, while we can—and must—protect our traditions of self-government, we cannot let boundaries drawn centuries ago handcuff our ability to respond.

But we can go much further. After September 11—and long before Katrina hit—careful analysis identified big problems. They plagued us in Katrina's wake. Determining how to prevent them from recurring is the key to defining the enduring public lessons.

Lessons for the federal government

As Katrina bore down on New Orleans, explains Leo Bosner, a twenty-six-year FEMA veteran, "We told these fellows [the agency's leaders] that there was a killer hurricane" taking aim on the city. "We had done our job, but they didn't do theirs" (CNN.com 2005a).

After September 11, Congress and President Bush joined in a fundamental restructuring of the nation's homeland security apparatus. FEMA, along with twenty-one other agencies, was moved into a new Department of Homeland Security. When Bush signed the bill creating the department on November 25, 2002, his promise was clear:

> Today, we are taking historic action to defend the United States and protect our citizens against the dangers of a new era. With my signature, this act of Congress will create a new Department of Homeland Security, ensuring that our efforts to defend this country are comprehensive and united.
>   The new department will analyze threats, will guard our borders and airports, protect our critical infrastructure, and coordinate the response of our nation for future emergencies. The Department of Homeland Security will focus the full resources of the American government on the safety of the American people. (Bush 2002)

But when it faced its first important test, the department failed. Indeed, the government's response to Katrina ranks as perhaps the biggest failure of public administration in the nation's history. While the storm was so immense that it surely would have swamped anything the government could have created in advance, the department's sluggish response simply did not match the promise that Democrats and Republicans, the president and members of Congress, made when they created it.

The boundaries of government should not constrain our ability to act.

However, the problems were not surprising. In March 2004, the Century Foundation issued a report card on DHS's first year that eerily outlined many of the issues that plagued the department's response to the hurricane (Kettl 2004). The Century Foundation report card graded the DHS on five areas: aviation security, intelligence, immigration, coordination with state and local governments, and departmental management. The overall grade was a C+. The lowest-graded areas? Coordination with state and local governments—a grade of C—and internal management—a grade of C.

In fact, a close look at the criteria for these two areas reveals chilling warnings. In supporting state and local governments, DHS received low grades for devising a national strategy to help state and local governments deal with homeland security issues, a failure to allocate grant funds according to risk, poor support for state training, and poor support for first responders. In managing its own operations, DHS struggled to integrate its vast collection of agencies into a single, coordinated department. It was little wonder, therefore, that when DHS faced its first big challenge, it fell far short in coordinating its own response and in dealing effectively with state and local governments. In late 2005, the 9/11 Commission issued a final report—and report card—that found recurring problems of intergovernmental communication (9/11 Commission 2005).

Straightforward steps could help DHS deal with this problem. First, the department could *work from the top down so that the system works from the bottom up*. Most of DHS's efforts have been focused in corralling its vast federal empire. Coordination with state and local governments has largely been an afterthought. But yet again, Katrina taught a fundamental lesson of homeland security. Just as was the case on September 11, all homeland security events start as local events. The federal response will fail if it is not part of an integrated national—federal, state, and local—plan.

Second, *structure matters—but not as much as leadership*. Katrina made clear that it was a mistake to move FEMA into DHS. Prevention of terrorist attacks—

the core mission of DHS—is closely related to managing response to events that do occur—the core mission of FEMA. But not all events that demand FEMA's response come from terrorism. Emergency planners have long worked to develop what they call an "all-hazard" approach: it does not matter whether the reason people are trapped in a building is because of a terrorist bomb, a tornado, an earthquake, or a hurricane—they just need to be rescued. The nation needs a much more agile emergency response system, and there is disturbing evidence that FEMA's response was crippled by internal problems within DHS. Even more important, however, is the recognition that good leaders can bridge the boundaries of any bureaucracy. But to improve the odds of success, they need a better structure.

Third, *every disaster is different*. Even more than a new structure, DHS needs top homeland security officials who understand their critical role in coordinating an integrated response from the vast collection of tools in the government's toolbox. Crucial to building that integrated response is developing a leadership, especially in FEMA, that understands its role. Every disaster is different, with different challenges, just as every piece of music is different. Homeland security leaders need to work like symphony conductors to bring the right collection of instruments together to make the right music to fit every situation.

Fourth, *the federal budget, especially its homeland security grants, can create incentives for a minimal level of preparedness of everywhere*. Major homeland issues, including natural disasters, can occur anywhere. Moreover, given the ease of travel throughout the nation, citizens from anywhere can easily find themselves deeply affected by problems somewhere else. Four tourists from York, Pennsylvania, were not paying much attention to the forecast when they set off for a New Orleans vacation—and then they found themselves stranded without electricity and struggling with New Orleanians for the basic needs of life. Some communities face far bigger risks than others—New Orleans (from hurricanes), San Francisco (from earthquakes), New York and Washington (from terrorist attacks)—and federal money needs to focus most there. But for the funds distributed elsewhere in the country, the federal government has missed the chance to use those grants as incentives to make sure that citizens everywhere have at least a minimum level of protection.

Lessons for state and local officials

State and local officials had their own struggles. The steady drumbeat of stories flowing out of the stricken area teaches, yet again, that state and local officials ought to follow these lessons.

First, *create a unified command*. Disaster management experts recommend that state and local officials establish unified command—bringing the full range of commanders together at a single location. Strong evidence shows that command, up and down the intergovernmental system, remained fragmented throughout much of the crisis.

Second, *create a single public face to encourage citizens' confidence*. Citizens need a voice of confidence from the scene. In the 1979 accident at the Three Mile Island nuclear power plant, near Harrisburg, Pennsylvania, Governor Dick Thornburgh and Harold Denton, from the Nuclear Regulatory Commission, brought unified command and constant communication with citizens. Their hard

---

Katrina made clear that it was a mistake to move FEMA into DHS [the Department of Homeland Security].

---

work helped steady nervous neighbors. Mayor Rudolph Giuliani underlined that lesson with his steady leadership following the September 11 terrorist attacks. One of the things that worsened Katrina's aftermath was the sense that no one was in charge because the public did not have steady communication from an official who could speak confidently about what was being done.

Third, *establish interoperable communication systems*. Just as in the aftermath of September 11, top officials found themselves cut off from other parts of the government because of failures in the communication system. New Orleans Mayor Nagin was stuck in the Hyatt Hotel for two days without a telephone. He resorted to sending pleas for help through CNN reporters. His staffers finally rigged a telephone line through an Internet long-distance account that a city technology team member had set up for his personal use (Rhoads 2005). Few things are more important than crisis communication, and job one for federal authorities ought to be to make sure that top officials can talk to each other in the inevitable future crises. Yet despite the recurring, inescapable message that effective emergency communication is the foundation of all emergency response, the nation still lacks an effective emergency communication system, especially one that is "interoperable"—one that allows officials in different jurisdictions to talk with each other.

These systems require technical elements: devices, like battery-powered satellite phones, that can continue to operate even if the power goes out and cell phone towers are blown down. People-based elements are an important part of this system, with a command system that links key decision makers so that they can make key decisions. But technology is not enough. In the crisis, many public officials could not communicate because they did not have established relationships on which they could draw. Coordination is not possible without preexisting trust.

Moreover, written plans are worthless unless everyone—including top officials—practices them regularly. Disturbing evidence indicates that many top officials at the federal, state, and local levels were unfamiliar with the disaster plans. As a result, the situation played out like a football game when the coach picks up the game plan for the first time on the way down the tunnel to the field on a Sunday afternoon.

But better disaster management is only one of the lessons that Katrina teaches. Recovery from the blow that Katrina struck will take years, and government has promised substantial aid likely to total far more than $100 billion. Without adequate management capacity, the federal, state, and local governments will struggle to spend the money well: to produce quick results without courting the evil trio of waste, fraud, and abuse. Evidence from the 2005 Government Performance Project (GPP), which measured the management capacity of American states, is not reassuring. The GPP produced grades for four management areas: money, people, information, and infrastructure (see http://results.gpponline.org).

The region facing the megareconstruction is the region graded lowest in the nation for its capacity in managing infrastructure. Louisiana and Mississippi received grades of C+. For Alabama, the grade was D. Moreover, the states are starting way behind. In all three states, officials say that they had postponed at least half of needed maintenance for at least the past four years. Deferred maintenance in Louisiana exceeds $3.8 billion. In Mississippi, it is $3.9 billion, and in Alabama, the total is $2.9 billion. Why? Officials in each state claim "lack of resources," although the three states rank among the lowest in tax burden. But even if the money began to flow, the infrastructure management systems in each of these states lags behind those of the nation's highest-performing states. Alabama does not have a capital plan. In Louisiana, the plan is heavily influenced by political factors, and the Department of Transportation and Development has not implemented a comprehensive maintenance and management system.

Thus, post-Katrina resources will flow to states that already have a substantial infrastructure backlog. All three states rank below the national average in capacity to manage infrastructure (and Alabama was ranked fiftieth). What is their capacity to handle the enormous influx of funds? And down the road, how can taxpayers be assured that the new facilities that are built with scarce tax dollars from around the nation will be maintained properly?

Is the Worst Yet to Come?

Two stress tests applied to the nation's homeland security system—the September 11 terrorist attacks and Hurricane Katrina—showed serious coronary blockages. That surely was serious enough. But in a sense, we were lucky: the events could have been even more serious, and the cost to the nation of our inability to respond could easily have been far bigger. We might not be even this lucky—if the word can possibly be used—the next time. Another hurricane might be a direct Category 5 hit. An earthquake could shatter a major West Coast city. And any of a variety of terrorist events could pose even larger consequences.

The results of the first two stress tests are not encouraging, and it is not clear how well the patient would survive a third test. Americans deserve better because we surely now know better. We need to learn from September 11 and Katrina—but we need to make sure we learn the right lessons.

But the consequences go far deeper than our response to terrorist events. Katrina also laid bare deep problems in the performance of American government that threaten to undermine the effort to rebuild the region, especially New Orleans. It was bad enough for the city to suffer catastrophic damage and loss of life. It would be worse for the city—and the nation—to suffer catastrophic failure amid the effort to rebuild it.

Note

1. For some of the Army's rules on "tasker numbers," see http://www.afsc.army.mil/im/rcdsmgt/admin/closetaskers.txt.

References

ABC News Online. 2005. September 2. http://www.abc.net.au/news/newsitems/200509/s1452073.htm.

Arlington County. N.d. *After-action report on the response to the September 11 terrorist attack on the Pentagon.* http://www.arlingtonva.us/departments/Fire/edu/about/FireEduAboutAfterReport.aspx.

Brown, Drew, Seth Borenstein, and Alison Young. 2005. Key military units' hurricane aid was stalled for 3 days. *Philadelphia Inquirer,* September 17, p. A1.

Bush, George W. 2002. President Bush signs Homeland Security Act. November 25. http://www.whitehouse.gov/news/releases/2002/11/20021125-6.html.

———. 2005a. Address to the nation. September 3. http://www.whitehouse.gov/news/releases/2005/09/20050903.html.

———. 2005b. Address to the nation. September 15. http://www.whitehouse.gov/news/releases/2005/09/20050915-8.html.

CNN.com. 2005a. A disturbing view from inside FEMA. September 17. http://www.cnn.com/2005/US/09/17/katrina.response/index.html.

———. 2005b. Mayor to feds: "Get off your asses." September 2. http://www.cnn.com/2005/US/09/02/nagin.transcript/.

Grassley, Chuck. 2002. Fixing the FBI. June 7. http://grassley.senate.gov/cgl/2002/cg02-06-7.htm.

Kettl, Donald F., ed. 2003. *The states and Homeland Security: Building the missing link.* New York: The Century Foundation. http://www.tcf.org/list.asp?type=PB&pubid=262.

———. 2004. *The Department of Homeland Security's first year: A report card.* New York: The Century Foundation. http://www.homelandsec.org/publications.asp?pubid=451.

National Commission on Terrorist Attacks upon the United States. 2004. *The 9/11 Commission report.* New York: Norton.

New York Times. 2005. Breakdowns marked path from hurricane to anarchy. September 11, sec. 1, pp. 1, 28, 29.

9/11 Commission. 2005. Final report on 9/11 Commission recommendations. December 5. http://www.9-11pdp.org/press/2005-12-05_report.pdf.

PBS *Newshour.* 2005. September 14. http://www.pbs.org/newshour/bb/fedagencies/july-dec05/hamilton_914.html.

Rhoads, Christopher. 2005. At center of crisis, city officials faced struggle to keep in touch. *Wall Street Journal,* September 9, p. A1.

Rittel, Horst W. J. 1973. *Dilemmas in a general theory of planning.* Berkeley: Institute of Urban and Regional Development, University of California.

Waterman, Shaun. 2005. Cops trapped survivors in New Orleans. *Washington Times,* September 9. http://washtimes.com/upi/20050908-112433-4907r.htm.

QUICK READ SYNOPSIS

Shelter from the Storm: Repairing the National Emergency Management System after Hurricane Katrina

Special Editor: WILLIAM L. WAUGH JR.
Georgia State University

Volume 604, March 2006

Prepared by Herb Fayer, Jerry Lee Foundation

DOI: 10.1177/0002716206286685

The Political Costs of Failure in the Katrina and Rita Disasters

William L. Waugh Jr., Georgia State University

Background

Hurricanes Katrina and Rita raise serious questions concerning the capacities of local, state, and federal governments to deal with major hazards and disasters. Several questions arise:

- How do we build the infrastructure, facilitate economic recovery, and move people into permanent homes?
- How will local, state, and federal governments help businesses, colleges, nonprofits, and families?
- How will we repair the flaws in the nation's support networks for the poor, elderly, and disabled that were revealed by the disasters?
- How can we deal with the racism that contributed to the slow response for African American communities?
- What flaws delayed the dispatch of emergency responders?
- How should "FEMA cities" sites be chosen for those who lost homes?
- How should we recruit and house workers for rebuilding?

Our system for dealing with disaster has to be repaired quickly.

Making Fixes
- State and emergency management officials strongly oppose expanding the use of the military in disaster management.
- Public administration experts say FEMA should be removed from the U.S. Department of Homeland Security (DHS).
- There is concern about how federal officials interfered with state disaster responses by delaying deployment of the National Guard.
- Some argue that collaborative structures be strengthened and others argue that the command structures be strengthened to assure better control and coordination during disasters.

The Gulf Coast
The vulnerability of New Orleans and the Gulf Coast were known well before Katrina—the scale of the disaster should not have been a surprise. There was
- too little regulation of coastal development to mitigate wind and storm surge,
- too little investment in strengthening the levees,
- too little attention to emergency planning to help vulnerable citizens and communities, and
- too little attention by public officials and the public to the risks of a strong hurricane.

Local Authorities
Local authorities are to blame for poor management of the levee system and poor decision making regarding mass evacuation and sheltering.
- Where there were plans, they were not implemented or only partially implemented.
- Many local agencies were simply overwhelmed, often reduced to saving themselves or releasing personnel to save their own families.

State Officials
State officials are to blame for being slow to understand the scale of the disaster and for the slow deployment of resources.
- Local emergency managers and first responders were left on their own.

Federal Authorities
Federal authorities are to blame for the slow response to state requests for aid and for their reactive posture.
- In spite of early warnings to DHS Secretary Chertoff, federal officials waited for states to request help rather than being proactive in assisting state officials.
- Once the need to act was recognized, federal agencies were slow to aid stranded victims, slow to rescue those trapped in homes and hospitals, slow to recover bodies, and slow to deliver FEMA trailers.
- The networks of governmental and nongovernmental organizations in the national emergency management system were in disarray.
- Volunteers were encouraged to wait for officials to tell them where the greatest needs were, and some waited for weeks.
- The lack of understanding of their emergency management roles was evident at all levels—officials failed to identify and address problems that were obvious to experts in professional disaster response.
NOTE: Had a major earthquake or terrorist attack struck during those weeks, the response capacities of the federal government might also have been overwhelmed.

Basic Problems
While partisan differences are driving some of the investigations, there appears to be consensus on some of the basic problems.
- Confusion over federal, state, and local roles was a problem.
- New federal procedures confused state and local officials.

- The National Response Plan (NRP) was newly adopted and not widely understood.

Major Problem   The poor emergency response was in many respects due to the sheer scale of the disaster.
- Roads were impassable, bridges were destroyed, and victims were scattered among hundreds of communities.
- Rescue and relief were delayed by water, downed lines, debris, and reports of violence.
- The unexpectedly large number of people needing assistance during and immediately after the levee breaches revealed a clear divide between those who had the resources to evacuate and the very large poor population lacking resources to evacuate or even to survive until help could arrive.
- It should always be expected that a significant percentage of the population will not evacuate for a variety of reasons and that they will not have prepared for surviving for days without food or water—many can only afford to live day to day in their normal lives.
- Local, state, and federal governments were confused about who would take the lead even though lead responsibility rested with state officials.

FEMA as Part   With the creation of DHS, the role of FEMA changed.
of DHS
- No longer cabinet level, FEMA is dependent upon DHS for its budget, spending priorities, and mission priorities.
- The agency is being dismantled and its parts moved into other parts of DHS where the focus is mainly on terrorism.

Gulf Coast   The situation along the Gulf Coast did not seem as dire as in New Orleans, but that was due to lack of news coverage.
- Rescue came late, and rural areas were slow to get supplies and other assistance.
- Local officials and emergency managers were overwhelmed and isolated and had few resources with which to help.
- Often they had no food or water for their own personnel.
- The slow state and federal response efforts, inadequacy of local resources, and limited availability of National Guard troops contributed to the frustration of local officials.

National Guard   Both Louisiana and Mississippi have large numbers of National Guard troops deployed in Iraq and Afghanistan.
- Ninety-two hundred Guard and reserve troops from these states were deployed during the disaster.
- Forty thousand more troops were brought in from all over the United States.
- The big problem was the Guard lacked up-to-date communications equipment and had insufficient trucks and engineering equipment because that equipment was being used overseas—many units were using Vietnam-era communications equipment.

Long-Term   Long-term recovery, hampered by partisan differences, may take many years.
Plans   Recommendations include
- rebuilding communities as they were before the disaster,
- not rebuilding large parts of New Orleans or moving most new development away from the coastlines,
- moving New Orleans to higher ground,
- buying out flood-prone areas,

- moving port facilities and other industry farther up the Mississippi,
- strengthening the levees, and
- planning for long-term housing and employment of evacuees.

NOTE: While plans may change, many likely will not return to their hometowns.

Observations   The assumptions upon which all agencies' disaster responses were based were seriously flawed.

- A large portion of the population was much more vulnerable than officials assumed.
- Poverty and racial distrust complicated the response.
- Confusion with emergency plans complicated the evacuations and everything that followed.
- Plans were not implemented or were only partially implemented.
- State officials requested aid early on but were slow to deploy their own resources.
- Evacuations highlighted the limited availability of gasoline along major routes.
- Confusion over the federal role complicated the process.
  - Poor communications were an issue.
  - The expectation that federal resources would only be needed in three or four days was disastrously wrong.
- There was a lack of effective coordination at state and federal levels.

NOTE: For the future, local and state officials have a political, legal, and ethical obligation to address the hazards that pose serious risks to their own communities, regardless of the priorities of the federal government. Officials must act now or the window of opportunity may close as the memories of the disaster fade.

The CEM   In emergency management, the standards for professional development can
Program   be found in the Certified Emergency Manager (CEM) program and the Emergency Management Accreditation Program (EMAP).

- The CEM requirements include breadth of experience, knowledge of emergency management roles, and functions and knowledge of management techniques.
- The EMAP standards provide benchmarks for professional emergency managers and emergency programs to assure they have the tools to manage risks as well as disasters effectively.

President Bush and Hurricane Katrina: A Presidential Leadership Study

Richard T. Sylves, University of Delaware

Presidency   The area of presidency studies involves analysis of presidential power and
Studies   attempts to understand the process of presidential policy making.

- This study takes a public policy analysis, organizational management, and leadership study approach toward the Bush administration's handling of Hurricane Katrina and its effects.

Incidents of National Significance

A new term, "incidents of national significance," now encompasses major disasters or emergencies declared by the president.

- Incidents of national significance under the National Response Plan (NRP) are defined as events that require coordination of federal, state, local, tribal, nongovernmental, and/or private sector entities in order to save lives and minimize damage.
- The secretary of the U.S. Department of Homeland Security (DHS) can use limited predeclaration authorities to move initial response sources—closer to a potentially affected area.
- All catastrophic incidents are considered incidents of national significance.
- Homeland security federal emergency management is focused on all-hazards management but with terrorism as the major threat.
- A presidential declaration of a major disaster or emergency activates the NRP and puts all federal, state and local agencies to work under the National Incident Management System (NIMS).

Presidential Authority

The 9/11 disaster centralized presidential authority, as did many catastrophic disasters before.

- Lawmakers granted the president greater powers to address crises.
- President Bush, acting on this opportunity, developed new forms of emergency management authority for his office.
- The president used this authority to put "major disasters" and "emergencies" under the terms "incidents" or "incidents of national significance"—as a result, emergency management (including FEMA) is today very much a matter of national security.
- Most of the changes reflect a preoccupation with homeland security that has had ramifications at the state and local levels.

NOTE: President Bush has had to cope with the size, complexity, and dispersion of power within the DHS—this mammoth, complex, and organizationally diffuse federal bureaucracy was less than two years old when Katrina struck. President-sanctioned reorganizations have compromised its ability to manage very large-scale, multistate disasters.

FEMA

The FEMA director, a de facto cabinet-level position under President Clinton, was folded into DHS, and many of the director's top management were transferred to DHS offices that had few, if any, emergency management responsibilities.

- FEMA has lost significant visibility as well as financial and human resources in the reorganization.
- Its activities are now overshadowed by much larger and better funded entities within DHS—FEMA no longer centrally manages disaster mitigation and preparedness.
- Under the above weakened position, Hurricane Katrina placed extraordinary demands on the emergency management system.
- Secretary Chertoff activated the NRP for Katrina, declaring it an incident of national significance.
  - The flaws revealed may instigate changes in the NRP and the NIMS.

Problems

The NIMS and the NRP no longer assign many predominant emergency management duties and leadership roles to FEMA.

- Before Katrina, experts in law enforcement, port security, intelligence, border control, immigration, and transportation security saw emergency management as an activity of secondary importance.
  - This situation could not have helped federal response.

- The response of government at all levels was not equal to the magnitude of Katrina's destruction—it is now clear that a challenge on this scale requires greater federal-state-local cooperation and in some ways a broader role for the U.S. Armed Forces.
- The nation's ability to respond to megadisasters has been weakened by the post-9/11 agency realignments and the loss of cabinet status for the director of FEMA.
- The new layers of DHS bureaucracy complicated FEMA's management response to Katrina, and complicating this further was the fact that five of eight top FEMA officials had virtually no experience in handling disasters before their appointments.

NOTE: History may prove that the Bush administration's handling of FEMA after 9/11, through the period of FEMA incorporation into DHS, and during Hurricane Katrina may be one major reason federal disaster management is unable to address catastrophic natural disasters.

Public Relations Debacle

For President Bush, Hurricane Katrina was a public relations debacle in almost all phases of the disaster. The president was perceived to have responded too slowly and ineptly.

- The president's actions disclose problems of mismanagement, slow response, poor federal-state and president-governor cooperation, and failure to provide needed relief in spite of promises made.
- The disaster revealed a president under siege who eventually apologized to the American public for the government's deficiencies.

Federal-State Relations

DHS has broad authority to respond to catastrophes, even if it means bypassing state and local governments.

- State and local governments have been induced, often through grants, to comply with the uniformity of federal standards governing homeland security–dominated emergency management.
- The NRP has a section that outlines how the government can rapidly deploy key essential resources.
  - It explains that response activities must begin without the benefit of a detailed assessment of disaster losses and that assessment might not be available for several days.
  - Certain emergency management assets may need to be deployed before they are requested via normal NRP protocols.
  - In Katrina, Secretary Chertoff refrained from using all the powers available to him, but this may not be the case in future disasters.
- Although predisaster plans were in place and a simulated Hurricane Pam exercise had been conducted months before Katrina, the president and his disaster management leadership had great problems working with governors in Louisiana and Mississippi.

Hurricane Wilma

A power struggle unfolded in Florida during Hurricane Wilma.

- The issue was about who is in control of recovery efforts, the state or the federal authorities.
- Governor Bush did not want federal intervention because he believes that it stifles innovation, creativity, and knowledge at the local level, but Chertoff was not taking any chances after his Katrina experience and had federal officials mobilizing in teams, and he had DHS send satellite phones to Florida.

- As Chertoff made his plans for Florida, the Fifth Army, under U.S. Northern Command (Northcom), was readied to take over the role of coordinating military assistance.
  - No one in Florida had requested Northcom's assistance, but Washington seemed to take control, and on October 18, General Clark of the Fifth Army called the Florida National Guard wanting to start flying in equipment to establish a Joint Command of federal and state officials.
  - In spite of Florida National Guard objections, federal officials announced the creation of "Wilma Command" to oversee the response.
- Craig Fugate, Florida's emergency manager, outmaneuvered the feds and immediately made Governor Jeb Bush the incident commander.

NOTE: President Bush needs to determine if federalizing disasters is worth alienating governors—the president's image, prestige, and historical legacy are at stake in the matter of disaster management.

Civil-Military Relations

The nation's experience with Hurricane Katrina highlighted the importance of the National Guard in disasters.

- However, changes since 9/11 have given the active military a greater domestic presence, and the Coast Guard, which now resides in DHS, has a much higher profile in disaster management.
- The president's plan to give the military a larger role in disaster relief faces a number of obstacles, including
  - laws against using active-duty troops for law enforcement,
  - questions about whether the National Guard is overextended, and
  - decisions about creating special military units for disasters.
- Northcom wants active-duty forces to be given complete authority for responding to disasters.
- Local and state officials fear that a federal takeover will worsen matters.
- Adding active military raises questions.
  - Should they have shoot-to-kill orders in areas where they encounter trouble or opposition?
  - Who is in charge? Is it the governor-controlled National Guard or president-directed active military?
  - What authority would governors have in military operations to address disasters?

NOTE: The government's slowness in responding to Katrina has sparked renewed interest in militarizing emergency response.

Conclusion

Hurricane Katrina tested the capacity, adequacy, and limits of administration-led disaster policy and management changes since 9/11.

- It was the supreme test of a president and his administration to effectively provide help and relief for victims and their devastated state and local governments and, thus, garner political credit.
- The Katrina disaster, perceived by the media and the public to have been badly managed, may produce political losses for the president.
- The nation is better served by those who learn the lessons of disaster management.

Metaphors Matter: Disaster Myths, Media Frames, and Their Consequences in Hurricane Katrina

Kathleen Tierney, Christine Bevc, and Erica Kuligowski,
University of Colorado

QRS

Background

Disaster research shows that both the general public and people in government and other organizations tend to believe in various disaster myths.
- Notions that disasters are accompanied by looting, social disorganization, panic, and deviant behavior are such myths.
- The media reported on Hurricane Katrina in ways that reinforced myths about antisocial behavior in disasters. Media initially employed a "civil unrest" frame and later characterized victim behavior as equivalent to urban warfare.
  - In Katrina, the media promoted false images even though they had little ability to verify what was actually happening.
  - They focused on dramatic, unusual, and exceptional behavior that reinforces the public beliefs about disaster behavior.
  - Behavior such as widespread looting is assumed by the media even though it is rare—such reporting leads to armed response by both law enforcement and the public.
- In reality, evidence shows that victims respond and adapt well.
  - Panic is not a problem in disasters—people help each other.
  - Social cohesiveness and informal mechanisms of social control increase during disasters.
  - Earlier community conflicts are suspended as communities unite under extreme stress.

Panic Myth

The assumption that the public will panic in the event of a terrorist attack, especially one involving weapons of mass destruction, has been taken for granted in media and public policy and is now reflected in discussions among emergency management professionals.
- In reality, people respond with normal and understandable responses to risk and uncertainty by actively seeking information, which, although sometimes an inconvenience to authorities, is not panic.
- The panic myth has been consistently reinforced in the aftermath of 9/11 by government and disaster response organizations issuing information on how to avoid panic, even though panic is a myth.
- These erroneous ideas are harmful because they influence governmental, organizational, and public responses during disasters.
  - For example, concerns with public panic can lead officials to avoid issuing timely warnings and to keep information from the public.

The Media

Why media portrayals of disasters so often deviate from what is actually known about behavior in emergencies highlights a number of factors.
- The focus on dramatic, unusual, and exceptional behavior can lead to the belief that such behavior is common and typical.
- The use of standard frames reinforces myths such as looting—the media publicize the use of the "National Guard to prevent looting," implying that if

not for the National Guard there would have been a serious looting problem.
- These themes and content make such a strong impression in part because they reflect and are consistent with other popular media portrayals of disaster behavior, such as in disaster movies.
- The media have a record of portraying minority group members in stereotypical ways and, in Katrina, portrayed African Americans as looting and whites as "finding supplies."
- Media-reinforced myths serve to justify policy stances adopted by law enforcement and other institutions concerned with social control.

NOTE: Media stories influence officials to adopt unproductive and outright harmful response strategies during an emergency. In Katrina, media depictions during the disaster provided strong evidence for later arguments that strict social control should be first priority during disasters and that the military is the only institution capable of managing disasters.

Looting Myth

Research has shown repeatedly that looting is highly unusual in U.S. disasters.
- Unlike looting during civil disorders, actual and potential disaster-related looting is widely condemned by the residents of affected communities.
- Despite the fact that actual looting is rare, many community residents still believe looting myths, arm themselves, and often refuse to evacuate to protect their property.

Military Role

The inability of federal, state, and local authorities to respond rapidly and effectively to Hurricane Katrina became a major scandal and led to the resignation of FEMA Director Michael Brown.
- Even before Brown's resignation, some government officials had argued that civil authorities were incapable of responding to major disasters and that the military would have to play a larger role than normal in a disaster.
- Although the initial response was incompetent, the federal government ultimately did mobilize, and a large part involved military and security forces.
- These forces were characterized as helping to restore public order, joining Louisiana National Guard forces that Governor Blanco described as "locked and loaded" to put down looting and violence.
  - Once the looting and civil unrest were perceived to have exceeded the capabilities of local police, the Guard was described as having been brought in to "restore and maintain law and order."
  - The media emphasized lawlessness, and an image of a new "war zone" began to emerge. This metaphor was quickly reflected in the discourse of public and military officials.
  - Within a few days, President Bush and government officials described themselves as determined to regain control and protect the people with military forces.
- Within two weeks, military deployment was more than seventy-two thousand troops.

Myths and Their Consequences

Initial evidence suggests that the media's relentless adherence to disaster myths and to frames emphasizing civil unrest and urban insurgency had a number of immediate negative consequences.
- By calling for curfews and viewing all victims' movements as suspect, authorities likely interfered with people assisting each other.

- Because of the focus on violence and looting, officials may have failed to take advantage of the good will and spirit of residents and community resources such as churches and local organizations.
- By reassigning emergency responders from lifesaving to law enforcement, those involved placed law and order above the lives of the hurricane survivors.
- By viewing survivors as "lawless thugs," responding agencies created conflicts between themselves and victims and ruined the collaborative partnership needed in disasters.
- Images of lawlessness might have caused help from outside the affected region to hesitate before mobilizing to disaster sites.

Racial Issues

The treatment of disaster victims in New Orleans and other areas has also reinforced the nation's racial divide.
- There are stark differences between white and African American perceptions of the governmental response to the disaster.
- Comparisons of black and white responses to a Pew Center poll revealed very significant opinion differences about racial equality and how blacks are treated by the government.
- With people of color having low regard for national leaders and crisis response agencies, there is a question of how they will respond in future national emergencies such as an avian flu epidemic.
- With government leaders, the media, and members of the white majority seeing people of color as lawless elements, what extreme measures are they likely to advocate during future emergencies?

Militarism

Predictably, the failed government response to Hurricane Katrina has led to new calls for stronger military involvement in disaster response activities.
- Disasters are now being characterized as events best managed by force to put down civil unrest and restore order.
- The military is widely viewed as possessing the resources, logistics capability, and strategic insights to "get things done" in disasters.
- This militaristic approach stands in contrast with assumptions concerning how disasters should be managed, which emphasize community resilience, building public-private partnerships, reaching out to marginalized residents and their institutions, and developing consensus-based coordinating mechanisms at all levels.
- The distorted images disseminated by the media and public officials have served to justify calls for greater military involvement in domestic policing.
- One consequence of the war on terrorism is a growing acceptance of the military's involvement in a wide variety of domestic missions, including providing security at Olympic Games and policing disasters.

NOTE: Disasters can become "focusing events" that bring about changes in laws, policies, and institutional arrangements. Hurricane Katrina may well prove to be the focusing event that moves the nation to place even more faith in military solutions for a wider range of social problems than ever before.

Rising to the Challenges of a Catastrophe: The Emergent and Prosocial Behavior following Hurricane Katrina

Havidán Rodríguez, Joseph Trainor, and Enrico L. Quarantelli, Disaster Research Center, University of Delaware

Background

This article looks at how people, groups, and organizations in Louisiana reacted to the impact of Hurricane Katrina in September 2005. This event was not just a crisis—it was a catastrophe that created emergent behaviors.

- One of the issues affecting the community was the negative imagery that developed through the media and word of mouth indicating a state of anarchy, disorganization, regression to animal-like behavior, and a collapse of social control, agencies, and personnel.
- In addition, the media disseminated actual comments from the mayor and police chief stating that snipers were staked out and that rival gangs were engaged in shootouts at the Superdome. They also quoted the FEMA director who said his agency was working "under conditions of urban warfare."
- The major thesis of this article is that emergent activities showed a different and opposite pattern to that suggested by the media.
  - People engaged in new but relevant coping behavior.
  - The same was true of outside groups trying to help.

The DRC

The establishment of the Disaster Research Center (DRC) has led to an analytical approach to emergent behavior.

- The DRC model states that organized behavior can involve either regular or nonregular tasks and that the structures to carry out these tasks can either already exist or come into being after impact.
- They show four types of groups:
  - established groups—regular tasks and old structures;
  - expanding groups—regular tasks and new structures;
  - extending groups—nonregular tasks and old structures; and
  - emergent groups—new tasks and new structures.
- About three weeks after Katrina, the DRC deployed eight researchers.
- In addition to other research methods, special attention was paid to first-hand personal accounts of individuals' own behavior.
- Even some of the DRC responses can be characterized as emergent behavior as they had to arrange for camping facilities as a substitute for lodging and they had to develop evacuation plans in anticipation of Hurricane Rita.

Hotels

The major hotels decided that they would not take hurricane-related reservations from local residents.

- Rooms were held for guests who were stranded; those who could evacuate were urged to do so.
- Hotels had many more guests than anticipated due to airline cancellations and employees' families moving into the facility.
- After the flooding, there was soon a scarcity of food and water, and guests began "looting" for basic necessities in nearby stores.
- Rumors of widespread antisocial behavior in the city did not deter guests and staff from helping one another.

- Hotels were able to rely on other hotels in their chains for resources as local resources were scarce, which eased some of their problems.
- When FEMA began to use the rooms for federal employees, the hotels had to then adapt to a long-term housing operation.

Hospitals   The DRC found that although hospitals had disaster plans covering an expected four-day situation, these plans did not include evacuation.
- Hospitals discharged less critically ill patients prior to the storm.
- Extra supplies were stocked, including fuel for generators.
- After the flooding, staff had to operate with dwindling supplies, poor communications, and extreme heat—this initiated massive but erratic improvisations.
- There was concern for personal safety as outsiders sought shelter in the hospitals. The staff feared for their safety after they heard the rumors of antisocial behavior in the city—some were given weapons.
- Private hospitals with more resources were able to arrange for helicopter evacuations while public hospitals could not do the same.

Local Neighborhoods   At the local neighborhood level, there was very extensive emergent behavior in informal groupings.
- One group named itself the "Robin Hood Looters" and commandeered boats, food, and supplies to help neighbors.
- They established norms of operation such as retrieving survivors but not bodies, and they agreed not to carry weapons.
- Another group took over a school, and after hearing the stories from the Superdome and the Convention Center, they decided *not* to evacuate to those locations.
- Some residents in Uptown armed themselves in response to stories of invading armed gangs of young black men.
NOTE: The widely circulating inaccurate stories added the perceived threat to personal safety to the problems already being faced in the flood crisis.

Search and Rescue Teams   The massive storm and subsequent flooding created a need for a response that many search and rescue agencies had never planned for.
- Many agencies had to improvise. The police and fire departments decided to make grids of the community to organize rescue efforts. They adopted the symbols used by federal agencies to mark every structure.
- The second phase involved initiating water rescue, which was unplanned and relied on local familiarity and the availability of boats.
- Other emergent behavior included breaking into a Wal-Mart to create a shelter.
- The formal and informal groups had to deal with nontraditional search and rescue actions, and all had to improvise to some degree.

The JFO   The establishment of the Joint Field Office (JFO) was an emergent action in light of a massive mobilization that was neither visualized nor planned for.
- The JFO was to coordinate federal, state, and volunteer agencies. Space was set aside for all participating groups, including volunteers.
- This unplanned office was established in an abandoned mall in Baton Rouge as an improvisation to try to coordinate all agencies.
  - The mall facilities were not equal to the high-tech demands of the operations. FEMA was not prepared to maintain such an outmoded facility; they had to improvise.

- After two weeks, the office was fully operational, and after four weeks, with about 2000 employees, the operation ran 24/7.
- A very complex, multifaceted, multipurpose, dynamic, and relatively large bureaucracy emerged in an extremely short time period.
  - Most of what went on was traditional and preplanned, but much done in the first weeks was of an emergent nature.

Looting

Emergent behavior is not always legal—looting of any kind is rare, and when it occurs it has certain distinctive patterns.
- Mainly it is done covertly, is strongly condemned in the community, is engaged in by just a few, and involves taking advantage of the chance opportunities that occur.
- Another pattern emerged in a disaster in St. Croix—it was overt, socially supported, engaged in by many, and targeted specific places.
- Elements of both of the above patterns emerged in the wake of Hurricane Katrina.
  - As many as twenty thousand people were involved in the drug culture before the storm. Thus, some of the behavior was not emergent but simply people continuing do to what they had already been doing.
  - Others engaged in the emergent stealing of necessities like food and water and boats. They did not consider this looting to be criminal behavior.

NOTE: Researchers of looting and criminal behavior should examine the obvious complexities of emergent behavior, especially in catastrophes rather than crises, a theoretical difference that is crucial to understanding much of what goes on in events like Hurricane Katrina.

Emergent Behavior

A subtle implicit bias assumes that emergent behavior is always a good thing, in the sense that it provides a better coping mechanism.
- The work on Katrina shows instances that do not support the bias, such as where evacuees refused housing offered on cruise ships and residents took refuge in attics and sometimes died.
- Overall, emergent behavior is usually good, but not always. It is a different way of acting, but not necessarily a better way.

Conclusion

The examination of the five groupings illustrates the range of emergent behavior that surfaced in New Orleans.
- Generally, most of the improvisations helped in dealing with the problems that continued to emerge.
- The various social systems and the people in them rose to the challenges of a catastrophe.
- Equally as important, behaviors that did appear were overwhelmingly prosocial, making the antisocial behavior seem relatively minor in terms of frequency and significance.

Moral Hazard, Social Catastrophe:
The Changing Face of Vulnerability along the Hurricane Coasts

Susan L. Cutter and Christopher T. Emrich,
University of South Carolina

Social Vulnerability

Social vulnerability is the differential susceptibility of social groups to the impacts of hazards, as well as their abilities to adequately respond to and recover from hazards.

- Social vulnerability is the product of social inequalities—it is not only a function of the demographics of the population but also of more complex constructs such as health care, social capital, and access to lifelines such as emergency response and goods and services.
- The nature of the built environment and sociodemographic interactions also play a role.
  - More generalized characteristics of the built environment such as urbanization, economic vitality, and development help define the livability and quality of life of the community, which in turn influence hazard susceptibility, response, and resilience in the aftermath of a disaster.
  - What a community is like before a disaster continues after the event—disasters magnify the existing social and economic trends; they do not fundamentally change them.
- The social vulnerability index (SoVI), a measure of vulnerability, provides an understanding of the dynamics that factor into the computation of social vulnerability—some factors more, some less.
- The relative importance of each indicator in the SoVI provides the pathway for vulnerability reduction and resiliency improvements.
  - Socioeconomic status, development density, population age, race, and gender account for nearly half of the variation in social vulnerability among all U.S. counties.
  - SoVI is a tool that will enable planners and developers, city governments, and individuals to make more informed decisions for hazard mitigation, preparation, and recovery.

Suburban Communities

Most of our experience with hurricane preparedness, response, and recovery is within a suburban context, not an urban central city.

- Suburbs have lower population and housing densities, and transportation is primarily by private automobile.
- Evacuations from suburbs are relatively straightforward, with most residents able to drive away from the area to a safe place to stay.
- Evacuations from coastal Mississippi and Alabama reflected mostly the suburban experience and went relatively smoothly compared to New Orleans.

Urban Communities

Urban places create new and complex emergency management challenges.

- Large city problems such as segregation, neighborhood decline, socioeconomic deprivation, and inequities in health care have now become central issues for many emergency managers.

- There is a need for more focus on improving the resiliency of the community and its residents—enhancing skills and other attributes known to minimize loss or to strengthen the capacity to recover.
- Many inner-city residents rely almost exclusively on public transportation— in New Orleans, 27 percent did not own a car.
- Orleans Parish had the highest SoVI score of all Katrina-impacted coastal counties.
  - It is the only county whose score had risen since 1960.
  - This means these people currently have less ability to cope with disasters and less ability to rebound than they did in 1960.

Moral Hazards   Moral hazards occur when society fails to protect the public from the adverse impacts of hazards and disasters either through inaction or through policies that reward risky behavior.

- The availability of flood insurance in high-risk, flood-prone areas encourages individuals to build in high-risk areas where otherwise they might not.
- The failure of the nation's emergency social safety net despite emergency preparations also created a moral hazard.
  - Rescue was slow.
  - Relief supplies were delayed up to a week.
- The preexisting social vulnerabilities in and around New Orleans gave rise to the social catastrophe, while the moral hazard occurred with our collective inability to respond.
- Emergency managers know too little about the disadvantaged communities that need the most help—the SoVI can provide this knowledge for planning, response, and recovery efforts.

Vulnerability   Two dominant sets of driving forces behind vulnerability are physical condi-
Forces   tions and social indicators or some combination of the two.

- The social vulnerability of urban places like Orleans Parish are the following:
  - race, gender, and class;
  - rural agriculture and debt/revenue ratio.
    - With a single sector economic base such as agriculture, there is no alternative source of employment if that sector suffers long-term damage.
    - Local debt/revenue ratio indicates vulnerability if the county debt is greater than its revenue, which suggests a place in economic distress.
- Pairing social indicators with physical indicators such as flood potential, storm surge, or coastal erosion provides slightly different results.
  - Boruff and colleagues combined a coastal erosion index with a variant of SoVI and found that along the Gulf Coast, coastal erosion vulnerability is more heavily influenced by social characteristics.
  - For the Atlantic and Pacific coasts, vulnerability was more influenced by physical characteristics.

Curbing Losses   Simply understanding the characteristics of people and places that lead to increased vulnerability is not enough to curb rising losses from disasters.

- What is needed is knowledge about who the most socially vulnerable people are and where they reside.
- Knowledge of who and where the most vulnerable populations reside allows protocols to be put in place before an event occurs to minimize the impact, saving lives and reducing property losses.
- We need proactive approaches to vulnerability reduction.

Enhancing
Resiliency

Although many expensive houses were destroyed along the coastline, the impact to the west and north from the storm surge area exemplifies the differences in social vulnerability in the Katrina disaster.

- Three miles inland from the exclusive Grand Strand in Mississippi, people are still trying to live in condemned houses while their affluent counterparts on the beach are able to live elsewhere while waiting for roads and utility repairs.
- In New Orleans, after three months, residents of the 9th Ward were allowed in to recover belongings, while more affluent parts of the city already had power and water restored for months.

Conclusion

For policy purposes, decreases in overall social vulnerability can be achieved locally by focusing mitigation and planning efforts on the most important component for each community.

- The recovery and reconstruction needs to proceed, but a "one-size-fits-all" strategy is not going to work and may exacerbate the preexisting social vulnerabilities found in the region.
- Greater care and consideration must be taken to derive a socially just recovery of the Gulf Coast.

Hurricane Katrina and the Flooding of New Orleans: Emergent Issues in Sheltering and Temporary Housing

Joanne M. Nigg, John Barnshaw, and Manuel R. Torres,
University of Delaware

Purpose

This article addresses the adequateness of governmental efforts to provide shelter and housing for evacuees displaced by Hurricane Katrina.

- A comparison of pre-Katrina planning documents with actual actions will show expectations compared to what actually occurred.
- The evacuation and sheltering/housing processes are a context for explaining how the failure of the unintegrated emergency management system exacerbated threats to health, welfare, and emotional well-being of the evacuees.

Background

On August 28, 2005, Mayor Nagin ordered the first mandatory evacuation in the history of the city of New Orleans.

- It was estimated that 100,000 to 120,000 did not evacuate prior to Hurricane Katrina.
- The state plans had the Superdome to be used as a refuge of last resort and not necessarily as a mass shelter.
- Planned use of school buses in the Southeast Hurricane Task Force plan did not happen because the city was unable to find drivers.
- On August 29, about nine thousand were in the Superdome and three thousand others in forty-five predesignated shelters—at this point all looked okay.
- On August 30, the levees started to fail and thirty-eight thousand more people were moved to the Superdome and the Convention Center.

  • Despite widespread media reports, Michael Brown and Michael Chertoff claimed to have no knowledge of the situation.
  • It was announced that Houston would take in evacuees, which caused another thirty to sixty thousand to converge on the Superdome.

NOTE: Although the complete evacuation of New Orleans was only expected to take two days, it took longer due to damaged infrastructure and overwhelming numbers of victims seeking exodus. By September 30, evacuees were in every state and almost half the U.S. zip codes.

Evacuation Planning

Evacuation planning is one of the tools emergency managers use to anticipate removing people from harm's way in a disaster.
  • Very little research has actually investigated *internal evacuation*, which is moving people to local shelters rather than out of the area.
  • Planning guidance focuses on the identification of safe structures in low-risk areas expected for short-term use.
  • Virtually no planning guidance is available to assist in transportation strategies, including how to communicate timely information.

NOTE: Without this type of planning, the transportation, medical, social service, and emergency sheltering needs can be adequately assessed, leaving the most vulnerable facing severe deprivation, worsening physical and health conditions, potential violence, and even death. In New Orleans, once the flooding began, the weaknesses of the state and local plan became apparent.

Sheltering and Housing

Planning for shelter and housing for victims falls along a continuum in the following order:
  • emergency shelters planned for short stays;
  • temporary shelters to provide for those who cannot go back to their homes—planned for several days to several weeks;
  • temporary housing, which allows victims to return to normal functions and tasks in new quarters—usually apartments or rentals; and
  • permanent housing for victims who will never be able to return to their original homes.

Katrina created a fifth category called long-term sheltering, which is out of the local area, for victims who do not know if or when they will return home.

Dynamic Needs

The catastrophic aftermath of Katrina reveals the fluid and dynamic sheltering process rendering the above continuum somewhat arbitrary.
  • The Superdome was a refuge of last resort, then it was an emergency shelter, and then an unplanned temporary shelter due to slow evacuation.
  • Hurricane Katrina provided significant deviation from traditional ideas of shelters because of
    • extended dislocation of victims from the impacted area,
    • moving victims to other states, and
    • extended duration of the evacuation.
  • The transition along the sheltering continuum was not in step order, as victims moved back and forth between types of shelters and housing.

NOTE: The above highlights emergent areas in sheltering and housing not previously observed and shows that further refinement of the typology is needed.

Intergovernmental Relations

Understanding intergovernmental relations is useful for providing a context for the political structure of decisions, and understanding how preexisting arrangements facilitate or exacerbate provisions and assistance to victims.

- According to the U.S. Department of Homeland Security's (DHS's) National Response Plan (NRP), a coordinated federal response can be started in two ways:
  - a request from a governor for a disaster declaration, and
  - an announcement by the secretary of DHS declaring a storm or event an incident of national significance (INS).
- The success of the NRP is predicated on the implementation of the National Incident Management System (NIMS) at all governmental levels to provide coordination and command structure.
- Although the implementation of the above was expected to facilitate information gathering and resource provision, as of May 2005 no date had been set for government compliance.

FEMA and DHS

Although FEMA and DHS have been engaged in catastrophe planning since 2001, there has been no consideration for long-term sheltering in distant locations; nor has there been any guidance issued.
- Based on the 2004 hurricane experiences in Florida, FEMA established a Housing Area Command (HAC) to expedite the process of developing emergency shelters for those displaced by Katrina.
  - The HAC was composed of FEMA and other agencies, the Red Cross, and members of the private sector.
- Katrina also provided FEMA with an opportunity to establish the Joint Housing Solution Center (JHSC), a loosely organized, coordinating group to work with local communities to assess their need for temporary shelter and temporary housing.
  - The ultimate goal of the JHSC is to provide resources and housing options with the intent to foster long-term community recovery and redevelopment.
  - It is intended to build capacity and develop policy at a regional level, while providing resources to assist them in their rebuilding and planning efforts.

JHSC in the Field

The JHSC is the field information gathering and operational arm of the HAC.
- JHSC teams worked with local government and community members to identify sheltering and temporary housing needs and to begin to implement solutions.
- While it sounded promising, it did not work effectively when dealing with a new program in four different states at the same time and with people who had no knowledge in the performance of these efforts.
- There also was no linkage between the JHSC, FEMA's Individual Assistance program, or the Red Cross.

Louisiana

In attempting to understand why an integrated emergency management system failed to exist before, during, and after Katrina, it is important to understand the sociopolitical context of intergovernmental politics at all levels from the city of New Orleans to the state and the federal government.
- The mayor, the governor, and FEMA's Michael Brown had varying expectations of the other's roles, which created ambiguity, confusion, and misappropriation or underutilization of resources.
- The unique tradition of consolidated power in parish presidents, coupled with the volatile nature of Louisiana state politics, served as barriers for resource allocation.
- All of this was further exacerbated by the introduction of President Bush and Michael Brown, who were promising support but not delivering on their

promises—Mayor Nagin said, "They don't have a clue what's going on down here."

- In a harsh media spotlight, the preexisting political traditions in Louisiana caused tensions among the different levels of government, further imperiling victims and facilitating a breakdown of intergovernmental coordination.

Conclusion   Hurricane Katrina severely taxed the emergency management system of this country and provided insight into how it can be improved.

- Increased attention must be paid to identifying safe refuges of last resort and emergency shelters.
- Plans are needed to prepare a region to accommodate the mass, albeit temporary, migration of homeless evacuees.
- The confusion in response to Katrina suggests that one plan may not fit all states—this may be a worthwhile challenge for FEMA to create individualized plans by area.

Weathering the Storm: The Impact of Hurricanes on Physical and Mental Health

Linda B. Bourque, Judith M. Siegel, Megumi Kano, and Michele M. Wood, University of California, Los Angeles

Introduction   Hurricane Katrina provides an example of what happens when evacuation is not handled appropriately.

- Vulnerable elderly people were substantially overrepresented among the dead.
- Evacuees represent a population potentially predisposed to a high level of psychological distress, exacerbated by severe disaster exposure, lack of economic and social resources, and an inadequate government response.
- This article reviews
  - deaths, injuries, and diseases attributed to hurricanes in the United States prior to Katrina;
  - recent studies of evacuation and the potential of evacuation to reduce death, injury, and disease;
  - preliminary data on Katrina death, injury, and disease; and
  - psychological distress attributed to hurricanes.

Statistics   According to statistics on hurricanes reported by the National Oceanic and Atmospheric Administration (NOAA) for 1970 to 1999,

- only 1 percent of deaths in the United States were caused by storm surge;
- fifty-nine percent drowned in inland, fresh-water flooding;
- twelve percent of deaths were caused by wind;
- most common injuries were lacerations, abrasions, sprains, and fractures; and
- in Florida in 2004, the most prevalent risk factor for indirect morbidity and mortality following four hurricanes was improper use of portable generators, which resulted in carbon monoxide poisoning and sometimes death.

Evacuation	While evacuations have the potential to save lives and reduce injuries, they are costly in time, money, and credibility.

- If an evacuation is ordered too early, the hurricane may change direction and make the effort unnecessary or move people to areas that are more dangerous.
- Late evacuations expose many to danger.
- The result is an evacuation policy that is, by design, precautionary but that raises concerns about the credibility of the information and its source.
- Hurricanes in 1998 and 1999 resulted in traffic jams throughout the Carolinas, Florida, and Virginia with some spending as many as 20 hours on the road.
  - Despite problems, South Carolinians support evacuations and consider life safety the primary goal of evacuation.
- It appears that mandatory evacuation orders are more effective than voluntary, but only rarely are persons forcibly removed from their home.
- Where several previous evacuations have taken place, people rely more on local media and the Weather Channel than on what officials say.
- Decisions not to evacuate are influenced by not knowing where to go, lack of transportation, cost of evacuation, care for pets, perceived delays in returning home, and the belief that homes are safe havens.

New Orleans

Prior to Hurricane Katrina, in 2002, the New Orleans *Times-Picayune* said that efficient evacuation was the key to survival in a major hurricane.

- To be successful, more than a million people have to travel over at least eighty miles of aging, low-capacity roads.
- They noted that such an evacuation would require a seventy-two- to eighty-four-hour window, which is substantially longer than the window within which forecasters can accurately predict a storm's track and strength.
- Such an evacuation is highly dependent on private automobiles, but 27 percent of households in Orleans Parish did not have a car.
- The total number of buses available could only evacuate 10 percent of those without cars—in fact no buses were assigned to evacuate residents of New Orleans before Hurricane Katrina, and mandatory evacuation was ordered just twenty hours before landfall.

Risks

Some have speculated that vulnerable, poor African Americans in New Orleans were most at risk of death during Katrina.

- When compared with census estimates for 2004, African Americans are somewhat underrepresented and males are overrepresented.
- Vulnerable elderly are substantially overrepresented among deaths.
- Although the media and others are quick to suggest that survivors are at increased risk of infectious diseases, detectable increases have rarely been documented.

Evacuees in Houston

Ninety-eight percent of the adults in the Houston Astrodome and the Reliant Center were from New Orleans.

- Most did not evacuate before the storm, either because they did not have a car or other way to leave, or because they underestimated the storm and its aftermath.
- One-third said they had experienced health problems as a result of the hurricane or the flooding.
- Eighteen percent had symptoms of acute gastroenteritis, with 50 percent of those positive for the common norovirus—no confirmed cases of *Shigella* dysentery, typhoid fever, or toxigenic cholera were identified.

Floodwater Toxicity

Considerable concern has been expressed about the potential toxicity of the New Orleans floodwaters.
- Floodwater tested in early September was similar to normal storm water runoff.
- Of concern are the large volume of floodwaters and the extent of human exposure to the floodwaters.

Psychological Distress

Postdisaster distress is determined by the characteristics of the disaster, cognitive processing of the event, individual characteristics, and qualities of the environment such as social support predisaster and postdisaster.
- Consistent predictors of distress are the severity of exposure and previous mental health problems.
- Internal resources, such as optimism, and external resources, such as social support, are important in reducing distress.
- Most children score in the normal range of distress, and their recovery tends to be rapid.
- Vulnerable persons are particularly prone to postdisaster stress, with vulnerability determined by prior distress, social class, gender, and linguistic or social isolation.
- The overwhelming majority of residents in the most severely affected areas of New Orleans were poor. This alone would predict high rates of psychological morbidity following Katrina.
- Disasters generate new, secondary stressors that serve as reminders of the trauma, including lack of food and shelter, relocation, crowding, financial strain, and coping with insurance companies and social services.
- Separation from family and friends and not knowing what happened to them increases stress and decreases social support.
- Lack of timely assistance and response from governmental agencies increases psychological distress.
- Beyond the lack of prediction and control that is seen in all disasters, human elements in disasters shatter fundamental beliefs about personal vulnerability, mortality, human nature and control over one's life.

Achieving Normalcy

To achieve normalcy, resources should be devoted to facilitating a quick return to predisaster conditions and routines.
- This includes restoring utilities, reopening businesses, and reestablishing social services.
- In the immediate aftermath, survivors of disasters need concrete and timely information on how to find shelter and assistance.
- In the longer term, the focus is on the process of rebuilding both the physical and social infrastructure.
- Because Katrina evacuees appear to be predisposed to a high level of psychological distress from the disaster, it will be important to document postdisaster experiences (including evacuation) to identify factors that exacerbate or diminish psychological distress following a major disaster.

Summary

Deaths that occur during the impact phase could be prevented if officials issued timely evacuation orders and provided transportation for those who need it and if coastal residents evacuated.
- Requirements that residents stay out of evacuated areas until utilities are restored and preliminary cleanup has been completed probably would reduce some postimpact injuries and deaths, but that conflicts with evacuees' desire to return home quickly in a search for normalcy.

• Distress is shown to increase in both adults and children, and it diminishes with time—the wide dispersion of Katrina evacuees and lack of timely assistance may exacerbate the mental health problems.

Challenges in Implementing Disaster Mental Health Programs: State Program Directors' Perspectives

Carrie L. Elrod, consultant; Jessica L. Hamblen,
Dartmouth Medical School; and Fran H. Norris,
Dartmouth Medical School

Background

Disaster study results highlight the importance of
• including mental health in state-level disaster plans;
• fostering collaborative relationships across institutions;
• clarifying program guidelines, sharing innovations; and
• building state capacity for needs assessment and program evaluation.
NOTE: The purpose of the present study was to increase understanding of the challenges involved in providing disaster mental health services by capturing the experiences and perspectives of a sample of state program directors.

CCP

The Crisis Counseling Assistance and Training Program (CCP) aims to meet the short-term metal health needs of disaster communities through a combination of outreach, education, brief counseling services, and referral.
• Outreach and education serve primarily to normalize reactions and to engage people who might need further care.
• Crisis counseling assists survivors to cope with stress and to refer clients to other services if they have more serious psychiatric problems.
• To be eligible to participate, states must establish that the need for the services is greater than state and local governments can meet.

Challenges

Numerous challenges interfere with the timely or effective delivery of mental health services.
• Unsolicited groups of well-meaning volunteers create chaos in disaster-stricken settings.
• Less experienced providers may suffer from vicarious trauma, leading to distress, absenteeism, and erosion of staff morale.
• Staff may self-segregate into those who are directly affected personally by the disaster and those who are not.
• Turf boundaries, communication gaps, confusion, the stressful nature of the work, suspicion regarding outsiders, funding gaps, lack of long-term care, and survivor stigma are other problems and challenges.

Planning

State directors' comments about predisaster planning and preparation clustered around three main topics:
• The presence or absence of a plan—low priority for disaster policy left few states with a disaster plan in place prior to facing their disaster.

- Preparatory activities—directors saw designation of provisions, establishing relationships with other agencies, and a strategic command post as necessary for an effective response.
- Predisaster training—FEMA training was perceived as vital with its experienced staff being able to discuss real-life situations.

Response

The initial phase of a disaster response was described as chaotic due to the many competing needs and priorities of the first week.

- Submitting the grant application for aid while handling local needs was referred to as "the second disaster."
- The Center for Mental Health Services (CMHS) officer was cited as an important source of support.
- Being part of a multidisciplinary team helped states gather information and implement the disaster response.
- Assessing multiple sources such as news media, Chamber of Commerce people, and public safety representatives helped with getting information.
- Contacting people who had previously been involved in disaster response was said to be positive and helpful in fulfilling the response.

NOTE: After the first week, attentions were drawn to a longer-term response.

Outreach

Outreach was a key component of every CCP and was generally thought to be effective by the state directors.

- The outreach workers go out into the community to educate victims about what responses they can expect, the types of services available, and where services may be obtained.
- The directors noted the importance of carefully identifying target populations and employing workers indigenous to those populations.
- There were several outreach challenges:
  - staff turnover was frequent;
  - the uncertainty of how to use paraprofessionals who might be untrained in mental health roles;
  - locating victims;
  - illiteracy and multiple languages in part of the population;
  - trying to provide one level of outreach to large groups, as not everyone in the group had the same needs; and
  - hostility and resistance from people who did not want help.

Counseling

Counseling is not intended to be therapy; the boundaries of crisis counseling remain blurred across programs and across states.

- Counseling ranges from active listening to a "wellness model" to therapeutic interventions.

Referrals

Referrals pose a number of challenges.

- First is the issue of when to refer—mostly, when someone accesses the system multiple times, they get referred to a professional service.
- One strategy is the identification of "red flags" that signal trouble.
- Most clinical directors were sensitive to the overloaded mental health system, while nonclinical directors were quicker to refer.

Training

Training was undertaken to ensure compliance with federal programs and to give a quality response.

- Directors mentioned there was a lot of disorganized material.
- Matching training needs to each individual in a short time is difficult.
- Timing of training was a factor:

- If too soon, staff turnover came into play.
- If too late, the people were already in the field without training.
- The strength of the program was that since the training was federal, people in different locations all got the same training.

The CCP Model

The CCP model focuses on providing community-level response. The primary challenges are
- establishing effective and accurate communication,
- developing collaborative relationships with other agencies,
- resolving turf issues, and
- developing a system for acquiring and transferring funds from the federal authority to the state and then into the CCP and out to the direct service providers and agencies.

Phasing Out the Response

Typically, the decision to end a CCP was based on funding or diminished need, and the actual length of the intervention was described as adequate.
- Extensions were requested when deemed necessary, which kept staff hanging, not knowing if the extension would be granted.
- Phasing down resulted in job losses for most of the CCP staff, which prompted many to leave for other jobs before the CCP ended.
  - In some cases, directors felt that staffs' desire to continue stemmed more from their own needs than the community's.

Evaluating the Program

Evaluation attempts of any kind were acknowledged as critical but were conducted by only about half of the CCPs.
- Most evaluations were anecdotal reports.
- Often, there was resistance by program members to be evaluated.
- Other resistance came from the fact that evaluations were not part of the federal grant.

Recommendations

The findings yielded recommendations that may improve the rapidity and effectiveness of responses aimed at the psychosocial needs of victims.
- Mental health should be an integral part of disaster plans.
- Plans should include dedicated resources that can be mobilized and accessed immediately.
- Written plans may help the knowledge transfer from one event to another and one person to another.
- Plans should include a designated disaster mental health coordinator with
  - a clear job description,
  - mechanisms to build capacity by developing collaborative relationships (with written contracts), and
  - communication venues.

Training Recommendations

There are four key recommendations regarding federal training for mental health coordinators.
- Establish a curriculum that progresses through the process of disaster mental health response.
- Follow up grant writing courses with advanced grant training.
- Develop online courses.
- During an event, states should be provided with a list of trainers matched to their event and their audience.

NOTE: Directors want to see the grant process streamlined since grant requests are prepared during a crisis.

Implementation   Several actions would facilitate the implementation and ongoing administra-
Recommend-   tion of programs:
ations
                     • program manuals to define and clarify the components of outreach, coun-
                       seling, and referral;
                     • training to facilitate the understanding of manuals; and
                     • clear guidelines regarding the training and use of paraprofessionals.

Fiscal   Fiscal management was an area of difficulty.
Management   • States should be required to address fiscal issues as part of their applications
                       and to have mechanisms in place for distributing federal funds to the CCP
                       and its providers.
                     • Federal program administrators should increase their capacity to provide
                       technical assistance in this management area.

General   The authors recommend a standardized approach to CCP evaluation that
Recommend-   depends less on the initiative and expertise of specific programs.
ations
                     • There should be a set of common tools and procedures and a process of
                       using the evaluation to help guide services.
                     • Exit interviews with state directors would help capture and transfer lessons
                       learned from past responses.

Caveats   Two caveats about recommendations are as follows:
                     • The nature of qualitative research is to explore issues surrounding a pro-
                       gram—this often highlights the feedback that needs attention, but one
                       should not lose the positive responses and aspects of a program.
                     • It should be acknowledged that several changes are in process at the federal
                       level that are consistent with the author's recommendations.
                       ◦ An operations manual is in production.
                       ◦ A standardized evaluation protocol was enacted across twenty state pro-
                         grams after Katrina.
                       ◦ States now have common tools, manuals, and procedures.
                       ◦ For the first time, there is the capability for cross-site analysis of program
                         reach and outputs.

Hurricane Katrina and the Paradoxes
of Government Disaster Policy:
Bringing About Wise Governmental
Decisions for Hazardous Areas

Raymond J. Burby, University of North Carolina at Chapel Hill

Background   Disaster losses can be blunted if local governments prepare comprehensive
                     plans that pay attention to hazard mitigation.
                     • The federal government can take steps to increase local government com-
                       mitment to planning and hazard mitigation by making relatively small
                       adjustments to the Disaster Mitigation Act of 2000 and the Flood Insurance
                       Act.
                     • A major change needed is to reorient the National Flood Insurance Pro-
                       gram from insuring individuals to insuring communities.

Paradoxes   The damage in New Orleans and the trend in increasing numbers and severity of disasters are the wholly predictable outcomes of well-intentioned, but short-sighted, public policy decisions at all levels of government. These decisions create two paradoxes.

- One is the *safe development paradox*, showing that in trying to make hazardous areas safe for development, government policies instead have made them targets for catastrophes.
- The other is the *local government paradox*, showing that while citizens bear the brunt of losses in disasters, local public officials often fail to take actions necessary to protect them.
- The consequences of each paradox reinforces the other and in combination lead to a never-ending cycle of ever-more-unsafe urban development and ever larger, catastrophic losses.
- The pork-barrel politics that sustain the safe development paradox are unlikely to change in the face of continuing, severe natural disasters.
- What can change is uninformed local government decision making about urban development that results in millions occupying at-risk structures in vulnerable locations. We need federal policies that
  - require local governments to prepare comprehensive plans that give consideration to natural hazards and
  - require them to assume greater financial responsibility for the consequences of their urban development decisions.

NOTE: Comprehensive planning requirements adopted by state governments already have resulted in lower per capita losses from flooding, but less than half of the states require plans and fewer than ten states require that they pay attention to natural hazards.

Flood Program   If the government reorients the National Flood Insurance Program (NFIP) so more of the burden of responsibility for insurance coverage is borne by local governments, local officials may become more committed to limiting development in hazardous areas and to mitigating the hazard to existing at-risk developments.

Safe Development   For some time the federal government has pursued a policy toward the use of hazardous areas that is part of the paradox of safe development.

- The basic idea is that land exposed to natural hazards can be profitably used if steps are taken to make it safe for human occupancy.
- To achieve this, measures are taken to mitigate the likelihood of damage and to deal with the residual financial risk.
- The development stimulus of these policies is further augmented by federal aid that reduces the cost to localities of providing infrastructure in hazardous areas.

New Orleans   The two biggest parishes in New Orleans (Jefferson and Orleans) provide examples of federal safe development policies in action.

- Knowing the high level of risk in New Orleans, the federal government in 1947 authorized levees to make ninety-six hundred acres from wetlands useable.
- Following Hurricane Betsy in 1965, Congress authorized construction of the Lake Pontchartrain and vicinity Hurricane Protection Project to protect the two parishes from major hurricanes (up to Category 3).
- Then Congress passed the National Flood Insurance Act (FIA; 1968), which provided more federal underpinning for the conversion of wetlands.

- Convinced that the area was reasonably safe, people did not hesitate to join in a major building boom and settle in the former wetlands to the east of the Industrial Canal.
- In 1999, oblivious to the danger, the City Planning Commission promoted these areas for growth. Six years later the entire area was under water.
NOTE: The paradox is that trying to make the most hazardous areas safe had the unintended effect of contributing to the devastation of Katrina.

NFIP

The NFIP tries to limit flood losses by imposing construction standards based on a 1 in 100 flood chance.

- The program has had difficulty because flood insurance rate maps are not up-to-date to take into account the new risks from building on wetlands, coastal erosion, and so on.
- Flood insurance is available, but buildings are not required to be elevated in areas of risk from either dam or levee failure.
- As a consequence of the above problems, the NFIP has not been able to cover its costs from paid premiums.
- To the degree the program fails to reflect risk in rates and operates at a loss, it subsidizes the occupancy of hazardous areas and facilitates more development than is economically rational.
- The basic standard of protection used by the NFIP, the one-hundred-year flood event, may need to be changed to the five-hundred-year event since most flood losses in the United States stem from less frequent flood events.
- The current program provides little incentive for property owners to take steps on their own to reduce flood vulnerability.

Local Paradox

Given that the incidence of disaster losses is primarily borne by local residents and businesses, one would expect avoidance of losses to be a high priority for local officials.

- Prior to being coerced by the requirements of the NFIP into adopting floodplain management regulations, virtually no local governments had done anything in building or zoning regulations to minimize losses, and even after the NFIP many did not enforce them seriously.
- Few local governments are willing to reduce natural hazards by managing development since they see it as a minor problem compared to unemployment, crime, housing, education, and other problems.
- Also, the costs of mitigation are immediate while the benefits are uncertain, may not occur during their tenure, and are not visible.
- In addition, a lack of citizen concern stifles local initiatives.
- Federal encouragement of the use of areas exposed to natural hazards also may discourage local governments from taking action as they believe the federal government will meet their needs in every disaster. Efforts to deal with these issues are only recently under way, and the degree to which these efforts have any effect is not known at this time.

Avoiding the
Two Paradoxes

Unless the two paradoxes are addressed in federal policy, devastation similar to Katrina will be repeated across the United States.

- Appropriate land-use planning and oversight of development can reduce risks.
- Some states have established building codes to be enforced by local governments, and some require local governments to prepare comprehensive plans. NFIP claims payments in coastal areas of states with state planning mandates are lower than in states that leave these decisions to local govern-

ment discretion. The three states hit hardest by Katrina had left decisions about planning and enforcement entirely to local governments.
- The Gulf states have been noteworthy for their reluctance to interfere in land-use and development decision making—this in contrast to Florida's demands for local action resulting in much lower losses.
- Comparing Florida, which requires local plans, to Texas, which does not, shows twenty times the NFIP claims in Texas.

Sharing the Burden

The two paradoxes help account for the upward spiral in the frequency and magnitude of natural disasters.
- To reverse this trend, it will be necessary for local governments to share more of the burden through careful management of development in hazardous areas and by assuming more of the financial responsibility for risk.
- The Disaster Mitigation Act could be amended to require mitigation plan updates be integrated into local comprehensive plans.
- The FIA could be amended to add the preparation of local comprehensive plans with hazard mitigation sections as a condition for participation in the program.

Policy Changes

The two policy changes suggested above would be beneficial, but given the lack of concern for hazard mitigation revealed by the local government paradox, a major change in government policy is likely to be needed before the increasing trend in disaster losses can be halted.
- This would involve amendment of the FIA to shift from insuring individuals to insuring communities.
- Flood insurance coverage and premiums would be based on the degree of exposure to loss.
- Local governments could pay the premiums from general fund revenues or they could set up special assessment districts or other mechanisms to raise the funds from properties that benefit from the insurance coverage.
- In cases where local governments refuse to participate, state governments could take responsibility for acquiring the coverage and requiring that both local governments and property owners take steps to reduce the risk of flood damages.

New Policy Benefits

The revolutionary change to the flood insurance program might have a number of benefits.
- All flood-prone buildings would be covered.
- Incentives for community participation could be created with disaster assistance coverage penalties for those who do not participate.
- The cost of the coverage could create incentives for state and local governments to reduce current risks and think twice before allowing more risky development.
- It would make it possible for the NFIP to more closely align premium amounts with risk and allow stronger incentives for lowering risk.

NOTE: Potential state and local opposition might be muted if Congress passes the Safe Communities Act, which authorizes significant financial assistance to help communities integrate hazard mitigation into their comprehensive planning and urban development decision making.

Conclusion

Before they could seriously be considered, the policy initiatives suggested here would require examination of the procedural changes needed to bring them about and an in-depth analysis of costs and benefits and the potential for unintended consequences.

Q
R
S

Q
R
S

- The increased costs in the short run would be offset by improved financial security for local citizens and governments.
- Federal assistance could be provided to particularly poor communities to help get the program in place without severe financial burdens.
- The suggested programs would speed recovery after disasters.
- The hope is to halt and possibly reverse the trend in increasingly serious natural disasters.

Planning for Postdisaster Resiliency

Philip R. Berke and Thomas Campanella,
University of North Carolina at Chapel Hill

Background

In the aftermath of Hurricanes Katrina and Rita, government officials, residents, real estate developers, business owners, and urban designers became engaged in a debate about rebuilding. Items discussed include

- how to plan for more resilient places that are socially just, economically vital, ecologically compatible, and less vulnerable;
- how to give the hundreds of thousands of displaced residents a voice in determining their future; and
- what federal and state reforms are needed that facilitate rather than impede questionable intensive development of hazardous areas.

NOTE: Postdisaster resiliency applies to the process of recovery planning in which all stakeholders, rather than a powerful few, have a voice in rebuilding.

Planning

To take advantage of the short open window of opportunity after a disaster, a community should have a recovery plan in place before a disaster strikes.

- A recovery plan guides short-range emergency and rehabilitation actions and long-range redevelopment decisions.
- It conveys a sense to the public that local officials are organized and in charge.
- By involving residents in all phases of planning, the predisaster planning helps create a knowledgeable constituency that is more likely to support redevelopment policies and programs after a disaster.
- The core purposes of the plan are to
  - offer a vision of the future after a disaster,
  - provide a direction-setting framework to achieve the vision,
  - inject long-range resiliency into short-term recovery actions, and
  - represent a big picture of the community that is related to broader regional, state, and national response policies.
- In the case of mitigation, a predisaster plan can identify potential sites, free of hazards, that could serve as relocation zones for areas likely to be damaged in hazardous areas.

Plans

Local governments have used two approaches in preparing a predisaster recovery plan.

- Stand-alone plan—easier to revise, has more technical sophistication, is less demanding of coordination, and is simpler to implement.
- Integrated plan—the recovery plan is just one element integrated into a broader comprehensive plan for an entire municipality, county, or region.

　　　　◦ It brings more resources together, broadens the scope of understanding about interactive effects of recovery issues with other local issues, and provides access to a wider slate of tools.

　　　　◦ It has the advantage of linking recovery to the broader economic, social, and environmental community resiliency.

NOTE: The most effective choice is likely to be a stand-alone plan in collaboration with preparation of a comprehensive plan—a combination.

Q R S

Plan Research　　Evidence is emerging that well-conceived plans have a positive influence on more robust mitigation practices and reduction in damage.

- Studies also found that recovery and mitigation plans are frequently of low quality.
- Also, many communities have not given any attention to disaster recovery and mitigation planning.
- This shows that planners are aware of hazards but put a low priority on taking action—they view natural hazards as facts of life that are often inexplicable and completely unavoidable.
- The evidence suggests a need for strong federal and state actions to stimulate local planning for postdisaster recovery and mitigation.

Planning　　There are significant barriers to effective local planning for mitigation and
Barriers　　resiliency, especially in the Katrina impact region.

- As of the late 1990s, only twenty-five states mention that natural hazards should be accounted for in local comprehensive plans.
- The idea of planning as a means for creating more resilient places in the Gulf Coast states is practically nonexistent.
　　◦ This inaction has deterred sensible controls on development in high-hazard areas that might have prevented much of the destruction from Katrina.
- The federal government has a history of weak support for planning and strong support for encouraging development in exposed areas.
　　◦ This has been encouraged by generous disaster relief payments; income tax write-offs for lost property; and the National Flood Insurance Program, which does not charge high enough premiums to cover storm losses and is now in deficit.
- Given the nonsupportive federal and state mitigation policies, prospects for quality plans are low in many parts of the United States. It is not surprising that plans for recovery are nonexistent on the Gulf Coast.

New Urbanism　　New Urbanism mixes land uses, including homes, shops, schools, offices, and public open spaces—modeled after small towns of the nineteenth century and intended to counter the negative societal impacts caused by sprawl including the widespread development of hazardous areas.

- The major benefit is to maximize open space without reducing the number of dwellings with an aim to concentrate building in safe areas.
- There is a mix of housing prices to bridge socioeconomic divides.

Rush to　　In the rush to prepare recovery plans, officials may overlook the shortcomings
Recovery　　of New Urban development codes, which do not now include design standards for natural hazards mitigation, as well as other environmental concerns.

- Placing high-density, compact urban forms in harm's way can lead to greater risks than the current low-density development.
- New Urbanism, however, holds considerable promise when development practices account for environmentally sensitive areas.

*Citizen
Involvement*

A duty of democratic governance is to consult citizens and involve them in decisions and plans that will affect them.

- This did not happen with evacuation planning in New Orleans.
- Research shows prospects for well-conceived plans increase with broader participation and support of stakeholders.
- The wider the range of participants, the greater the opportunity to educate a wider array of stakeholders about problems and solutions.
- Early and continuous involvement generates increased commitment and a sense of ownership and control over policy proposals, which can offset the influence of traditionally powerful groups with ties to the real estate industry.
- Research shows that when plans lack involvement of locals, decisions are made without the benefit of local knowledge and capacities and may not be consistent with local values, needs, and customs.
  - This may create opposition to plans.

Social Repair

While restoring infrastructure is critical, it is also important to repair the torn social fabric—a process that entails reconnecting severed familial, social, and religious networks, neighborhood by neighborhood.

- Recovery involves reconstructing the myriad social relations embedded in schools, workplaces, child care arrangements, shops, places of worship, and places of play and recreation.
- In New Orleans, the likelihood that displaced residents will not return home carries profound implications for the recovery of a robust metropolis rather than a kind of theme park celebrating its former self.

*Changes
Needed*

We can only hope that Hurricane Katrina will wrench us to our senses in building more resilient places.

- Federal and state governments should play a stronger role in encouraging local planning for postdisaster recovery and mitigation.
- We need to look at federal strategies that remove the monetary loss risk from local governments and look at risk avoidance instead.
  - These current strategies discourage local governments from adopting controls on development in hazardous areas.
- Without proper planning, the New Urban model will expose more people and buildings to harm.
- Any change will need meaningful consultation and participation of citizens in recovery decisions and plans that affect them—something that will be difficult on the Gulf Coast until the social fabric is repaired.

Federal Reform

The nation needs a more sustainable approach and a reformed federal-state-local relationship for recovery planning and mitigation.

- Federal policy should focus on performance-based environmental risk-reduction targets.
- Emphasis should be placed on land-use planning aimed at relocating existing development from high-hazard zones to low-hazard zones, and avoidance of new development in high-hazard zones.
- Local governments must pay a greater share of public infrastructure repair costs through insurance—the premium should be structured to encourage mitigation and avoid risky development.

*Facilitate
Participation*

The federal government should require communities to take citizen participation—serious application of the principles below should be required in any local planning process.

- Apply grassroots organizing in new ways to encourage participation and encourage local people to lead civic institutions that tackle disaster recovery problems.
- Help people acquire new civic skills, with special attention given to those with low status in communities.
- Build more extensive networks to accomplish disaster resiliency goals.
- Build new norms—a culture that values and enables collective action.

Disaster Mitigation and Insurance: Learning from Katrina

Howard Kunreuther, University of Pennsylvania

Background

Hurricane Katrina has highlighted challenges associated with reducing losses from hurricanes and other natural hazards.
- Before a disaster, most homeowners, businesses, and the public sector do not voluntarily adopt cost-effective loss-reduction measures.
- The magnitude of a storm leads the government to provide liberal relief to victims even if it claimed it had no intention of doing so prior to the disaster.
- This combination of underinvestment in mitigation and the liberal use of taxpayer funds after a disaster does not auger well for the future.

NOTE: One of the reasons for this disaster syndrome is that many individuals perceive a disaster as something unlikely to happen to them.

Voluntary Mitigation

Extensive evidence indicates that residents in hazard-prone areas do not undertake loss-prevention measures voluntarily.
- In the case of flood-prone areas, actions by the federal government, such as building levees, makes residents feel safe.
- This problem is reinforced by local officials who do not enforce building codes or land-use restrictions.
- Also, if developers do not design homes resistant to disasters, large-scale losses, as seen in Katrina, can be expected.
- Many people see the risk as being sufficiently low that they cannot justify investing in mitigation even if it may be cost-justified—there is evidence that individuals do not seek out information on probabilities.
  - Those who do seek out information on the likelihood of a severe disaster may find that experts disagree, and they may focus on the lowest-probability estimate.
- Individuals are often myopic and hence take only into account the potential benefits of such investments over the next year or two. This is one of the most documented failings in human decision making.
- Those with limited disposable income will not even consider mitigation and often do not buy insurance either.

Peer Influence

How actions of others impact one's own decisions relates to the broader question of interdependencies.
- For example, if most homes in flood-prone neighborhoods were elevated, then others would likely follow, and vice versa.
  - Some suggested solutions are to subsidize mitigation efforts, provide tax breaks, and enforce building codes.

Disaster Assistance

Federal disaster assistance may create a type of Samaritan's dilemma: providing assistance after hardship reduces incentives to manage risks.
- If a family expects to receive government assistance after a loss, it will have less incentive to invest in mitigation and insurance.
- The increased loss due to lack of protection serves to amplify the government's incentive to provide greater assistance.
- In spite of the above, evidence shows that individuals or communities have *not* based their decisions on expectation of future relief.
  - Most had not expected to receive aid after a disaster.
  - Local governments that received disaster relief undertook more efforts to reduce losses than those that did not.
  - This behavior seems counterintuitive; the reasons for it are not fully understood.

Cost-Benefit Analysis

A simplified five-step procedure for conducting a cost-benefit analysis (CBA) includes the following:
- Specify the nature of the problem, the options being considered, and the interested parties in the process.
- Determine direct costs of mitigation alternatives.
- Determine the expected benefits of mitigation alternatives.
- Calculate the attractiveness of mitigation alternatives by comparing the expected benefits to each party to the upfront costs.
- Choose the best alternative.

Banks' Role

The challenge in developing a disaster management plan that encourages mitigation measures is to develop approaches that will encourage individuals to want to undertake these measures.
- Banks can play a key role if they require homeowners in hazard areas to purchase insurance against natural disasters and they make sure the premiums reflect the risk of living in the area.
- Banks could also require that a third-party inspector ensure that structures meet the building codes.
- Banks could encourage owners by providing home improvement loans with payback that occurs over the life of the mortgage.
- These efforts would lower the cost of insurance by lowering the costs for reinsurers who help insurance companies spread losses.
- Banks could provide a seal of approval to each structure that meets or exceeds building code standards.

Tax Incentives

One way for communities to encourage residents to pursue mitigation measures is through tax incentives.
- A taxpayer could get a rebate on state taxes to reflect the lower costs of disaster relief.
- Property taxes could also be reduced for the same reason.
- Some disincentives may come into play.
  - Improved property may get a higher assessment value and hence have a higher tax bill—this could be addressed with exemptions for such improvements.

Conclusions

If we, as a society, are to commit ourselves to reducing future losses from natural disasters and limit government assistance after the event, we have to engage the private and public sectors in a creative partnership.
- This requires well-enforced building codes and land-use regulations coupled with insurance protection.

- Economic incentives via long-term mitigation loans and subsidies to low income residents are needed.
- In addition, if structures are well-designed and land-use regulations are in place, there will be fewer injuries and fatalities and less need for large evacuations.
- CBA can play an important decision-making role.
- We may want to rethink the type of disaster insurance provided in hazard-prone areas.
  - It might be an idea to provide protection against all hazards under a home-owners policy rather than continuing with separate current programs.

The Primacy of Partnership: Scoping a New National Disaster Recovery Policy

James K. Mitchell, Rutgers University

Background

Hurricane Katrina is widely perceived as a threshold-crossing event, capable of bringing about changes in public policy akin to the policy response to 9/11.
- Of great importance is the nourishment of partnerships among stakeholder groups.
- Such partnerships have previously been organized around common material interests, but these might be more enduring if they also are based on ideas that capture shared ambiguities of hazard.
  - These partnerships, in many forms, bring together different levels of government, bridge the divide between public and private sectors, merge contributions of disciplines and professions, and close the gaps between experts and laypersons.
  - These partnerships have proved to reduce hazards.
- Lay publics need to be engaged in the partnerships and discussions.
NOTE: The process of recovery from Katrina presents social scientists an opportunity to extend inquiry and partnerships into new arenas that have the potential to sharpen understanding as well as to address policy reforms.

Recovery

The size and complexity of post-Katrina recovery tasks is daunting, combining a major urban catastrophe with general regionwide devastation.
- These tasks are probably on par with post–World War II reconstruction of European and Japanese cities.
- In this situation, recovery generally becomes a national rather than a state or local priority. A comprehensive national policy is needed that lays out a broad clear path for the Gulf Coast and the whole nation.
- It is time to institute a formal national policy for disaster recovery—such a policy discussion has largely been missing after Katrina.

Leadership

Prominent among discussions for coping with threats are calls for improved leadership via a single person or entity through which all important decisions would flow.
- While skillful leadership is helpful during emergencies, its significance is easy to misinterpret and to overstate.

- Humans tend to attach disproportionate importance to individuals as causal agents and to downplay the role of structural or contextual factors.
- Crises tend to constrain decision choices, while predisaster hazard mitigation has greater payoffs.
- Planning for leadership prior to a disaster is highly problematic. During a disaster, there may be conflict between the interests of the public and the interests of the leader.
- Disasters require flexibility, but leaders may fall back on rigid militaristic command and control.
- While it is foolish to ignore the importance of leadership, it is both facile and misleading to view leadership as a panacea for what is already, and for other reasons, a faltering public interest and engagement with natural hazards and disasters.

Partnership

Partnership is at the heart of American hazards management policies and is the pivotal concept in reforms of these policies that have been proposed and less often implemented.
- One of the biggest barriers to improved policies is the fleeting interest after the initial abundant response to major disasters.
- In quiet times, there is usually no great public clamor for more effective programs to reduce risks, and the effort is left to a relatively small range of interested people including experts in government agencies, academia, and nongovernmental entities as well as a few in institutions such as utilities, real estate firms, and insurance companies.
- These groups, by joining forces, have managed to persuade public leaders to work for mitigation more so than disaster relief.
- It is now commonly accepted that policy making and management should involve all stakeholders.

NOTE: Since the late 1990s, public-private partnerships have been widely touted as a path-breaking innovation that brings a wide range of stakeholders to a table once dominated by bureaucrats, disaster professionals, and scientists.

Sustainable Development

For all its potency, the notion of partnership is interpreted in a way that robs it of its potential to be a sustaining instrument for change.
- Interest-centered forms of partnerships tend to last only as long as the groups that have come together continue to share those interests.
- *Sustainable development* is an idea that synthesizes the concerns of two important fields of endeavor—ecology and economics—that look at long-term survival options.
  - Partnerships based on this kind of divergent but synthetic thinking are likely to be more resilient than those that rest on simpler notions of self-interest.
  - These partnerships address the desire for environmental stability and the desire for economic growth—a better fit between society and nature.

Beyond Sustainability

There are now several possibilities for thinking beyond sustainability.
- *Linking recovery to other national policy goals*—public institutions are being reinvented to better cope with future hazards and disasters, and new programs and policies are being negotiated.
  - Shifts toward mitigation are facilitated by situating recovery in the context of policy goals that address issues of constitutionality, morality, sustainability, sociocultural change, technological revolution, and geopolitical transformation.

- *Surprises complicate recovery*—disaster planning needs to address many different kinds of unexpected contingencies.
- *Diverse functions need to be recovered*—hazardous places where people live serve different functions that are vulnerable to risk in different ways.
  - The most important are material and economic, metabolic (air, water, waste), information exchange networks, artistic and performance roles, creative expression, and power and regulatory functions.
  - These function areas are vulnerable to the extent that they are not capable of accommodating surprises and/or resolving the multiple contending demands of urban constituencies.
  - These vulnerabilities are mobilized, if not directly by the extreme event, then indirectly by cascading consequences.
- *Accommodating contradictory interpretations of hazard*—partnerships need to recognize that different people or groups see hazards and disasters through different lenses.
  - The potential for making common cause between groups that view hazard through the lens of science and those that employ paradigms of aesthetics, entertainment, risk stimulation, and cathartic therapy have not been well explored.
  - The way is open for a major constituency-building effort by proponents of hazard management if the potential for new partnerships of different interpretive paradigms are grasped.

Partnerships will become more important everywhere as humankind faces new kinds of threats, reemerging old risks, new vulnerabilities, and surprises.

Conclusions
- To address challenges, we need to increase the importance and prominence of hazard as an item on the human agenda.
- Far from narrowing and specializing, we need to maintain and expand the range of alternative coping measures—as a result, we can put together many different ways to prevent, avoid, and reduce disasters.
- What is needed most is broadening the discourse about recovery and bringing more people into it.
- In support of the above ends, we must harness the enormous potential of partnerships.
- Changes to existing policies for hazard management are needed, and the momentum to bring them about is present.

NOTE: We need to use the broad-based, partnership-based approaches that have served so well and not retreat to narrower expediency-driven alternatives.

Agility and Discipline: Critical Success Factors for Disaster Response

John R. Harrald, George Washington University

Background
It is appropriate to ask how to organizationally prepare for, respond to, and recover from extreme events to minimize the disruption and maximize the

resiliency of our social and economic systems. This article reviews the following:
- The nature of the challenge presented by extreme events.
- The recent experience in developing plans and procedures.
- A critical success factor approach to preparing, responding, and recovering.
- Organizational typology based on dimensions of discipline and agility.
- Three themes from the emergency management literature are as follows:
  - There is a trade-off between command and control requirements in managing a large organization and in the need to ensure broad coordination and communication.
  - There is a need to be able to adapt, be creative, and improvise while demanding efficient and rapid delivery of services under extreme conditions.
  - Diverse organizations must be able to operate together with common structure and process while interacting with thousands of volunteers.
- This article proposes that all of the above are needed and that the implied trade-offs are false choices—there must be both discipline and agility in emergency response conditions.

Response Plan

The Catastrophic Incident Annex to the National Response Plan describes the attributes of an extreme event from the perspective of its demands on emergency management—these were the actual attributes experienced in Katrina.
- Local response capabilities may be quickly overwhelmed.
- The area's critical infrastructure will be disrupted.
- It may take up to forty-eight hours or longer to assess what is needed.
- Federal support must be timely to save lives, prevent suffering, and mitigate severe damage.
- A large number of people may need to be housed in long-term temporary housing.
- The environmental impacts can severely challenge the ability and capacity to achieve a timely recovery.
- Responses must be flexible enough to address emerging needs.
- There may be a large number of casualties.
- The event may occur with little or no warning.
- Large-scale evacuation strategies may be complicated by health-related implications.

Event Attributes

Henry Quarantelli describes the attributes of a catastrophic event:
- Most or all of the community built environment is heavily impacted.
- Local officials are unable to undertake their usual work role.
- Help from nearby communities cannot be provided.
- Most, if not all, everyday community functions are sharply interrupted.
- The mass media filter less incoming information than during disasters and serve to define the catastrophe as they see it.
- The political arena becomes even more important.

Response Phase

The response phase can be subdivided into four phases reflecting the evolution of objectives and functions over time.
- First, the response is conducted by resources on the ground while external forces are mobilized.
- An integration phase structures these resources into a functioning organization capable of assessing needs and providing services.
- A production phase is where the response organization is fully productive, delivering services as a matter of routine.

- Finally, the external presence is diminished during a transition to recovery stage.

Critical Success Factors

Critical success factors are those few key areas in which favorable results are absolutely necessary if the operation is to succeed. Critical success factors are identified for each phase:
- Preparedness and Prevention
- Initial Reaction and Mobilization
- Organizational Integration Phase
- Production Phase
- Transition/Demobilization Phase

NOTE: The critical success factors identify attributes of agility and discipline that must be developed by response organizations to meet the critical needs and allocate resources.

Incident Command System

The Incident Command System (ICS) evolved within the wildfire fighting community as a system of discipline and rapidly became a standard protocol for fire services and was also adopted by the Coast Guard.
- The ICS forms the basis for the National Incident Management (NIM) system and provides the following elements of discipline:
  - Common terminology
  - Management by objectives
  - Manageable span of control
  - Resource management
  - Establish and transfer command
  - Unified command
  - Information and intelligence management
  - Modular organization
  - Incident Action Plan
  - Predesignated locations
  - Integrated communications
  - Chain and unity of command
  - Deployment
  - Accountability of resources and personnel

Improvising

Researchers show that structured planning and organization are only effective if the ability to improvise is preserved.
- Improvisation and preparedness go hand in hand.
- Response management must rely on internal and external feedback.
- Organizations must anticipate and manage the unexpected.
- Organizational "mindfulness" is the quality to detect and react to the unexpected to catch and manage the unexpected earlier.

NOTE: In Katrina, the inability to identify and correct errors as the event evolved was a striking characteristic.

Changes since 9/11

The United States, in reaction to the September 11, 2001, attacks, has embarked on a massive attempt to coordinate the management of risks due to extreme events.
- First was the creation of the U.S. Department of Homeland Security (DHS).
- Then was the attempt to create a truly integrated national system for the preparation for, response to, and recovery from extreme events.
- The implementing documents are the National Response System (NRS) and the National Incident Management System (NIMS)—together they

provide the structure and discipline necessary to achieve many of the critical success factors.
- The above are intended to accomplish the following:
  - align national coordinating structures, capabilities, and resources;
  - ensure an all-discipline and all-hazard approach;
  - incorporate emergency management and law enforcement into a single structure;
  - provide one way of operating for all events; and
  - provide continuity of management from preincident to postincident.

NOTE: The ponderous, bureaucratic response to Katrina shows that DHS must now make efforts to create flexibility and agility while preserving the structure and discipline it has achieved—it must support a balanced/adaptive organization.

Conclusions   The federal government's slow and ineffective response to Hurricane Katrina has presented many challenges.
- The organizational systems that respond to extreme events must be open systems that allow information to be gathered from and transmitted to the public and to nongovernment organizations.
- There must be improvisation and distributed decision making in the face of the unexpected—we will fail if the only people who know emergency management plans and processes are the emergency managers who operate in a closed community with a closed language.
- We must remember that the military can be used to maintain command, control, and order and to move resources rapidly, but they are not trained or structured for the complex intergovernmental coordination and collaboration needed when preparing for or responding to extreme events.
- What is needed is federal, state, and local collaboration and leadership and a disciplined and agile national response system—it is time to establish necessary competencies, systems, and relationships that will ensure we do not repeat the same mistakes with different people.

Is the Worst Yet to Come?

Donald F. Kettl, University of Pennsylvania

Background   If the nation does not learn the lessons that both Katrina and September 11, 2001, have taught us, we will suffer the same consequences, over and over.
- The government's staggering recovery efforts in the Gulf Coast raise deep worries about its ability to respond to other large-scale, high-consequence events.
- We face the virtual certainty of more big events that provide little time to react and where the cost of failure is enormous.
- These wicked problems we increasingly face fall outside normal routines and slop over any boundary, political or organizational.
  - The mismatch between our boundaries and the problems we are trying to solve invites repeated failure.
  - The nation's intellectual capital for understanding, yet alone solving, these problems is seriously depleted.

- Policy makers, when facing big problems that demand quick responses, understandably retreat to what they know, or, at least, what they find comfortable. These past models provide a poor guide for future action.
- We need new tools for new problems or we will be constantly outmaneuvered by events and combatants who exploit our weaknesses.

Looking   We have not learned from 9/11, and we are likely to fail to learn yet again from
Backward   Katrina.
- We have an instinct to look back instead of forward—in response to 9/11, the nation focused on a model from the past (creation of the U.S. Department of Defense in 1947) in devising a new strategy in the creation of the U.S. Department of Homeland Security (DHS).
- Many of the problems we face are broad and unpredictable events that, deliberately or not, take advantage of weak points in our system.
  - In 9/11, it was weak points in airline security, and in Katrina it was weaknesses in the levee system.
- The nation needs to get much smarter in dealing with unpredictable events; if all we have are backward-looking plans, we doom ourselves to repeated failure.

DHS Problems   The single most important fact about the creation of the DHS is that it emerged from political, not administrative, imperatives.
- What the administration felt it would take to prevent another 9/11 was to merge twenty-two agencies into a single new department.
- Creation of DHS turned much less on how best to secure the homeland than on how to balance executive and legislative power.
- Driving the debate was the need to coordinate intelligence, but the intelligence agencies successfully fought to remain outside the DHS.
- The department was unwieldy and beset by cross-pressures and bureaucratic turf wars—staff skills, as seen in FEMA, were poor.
- Communication strategies linking federal, state and local officials was largely an afterthought—when Katrina hit, key people with the right instincts were not in place.
- Katrina shows that when we settle for bright political symbols instead of efficient public organizations, we inevitably pay the price.

Thinking   Battles over the chain of command erupted in the days after Katrina hit.
Vertically
- All along the vertical line, from local officials through the states to federal officials at the highest levels, battles erupted and confusion reigned.
- Some one person has to be in charge of events like Katrina, but a coordinated response requires the subtle weaving together of forces from a vast array of functional areas and from different levels of government, not hierarchical control. Officials need to coordinate with each other.
- Hierarchy provides the critical, unifying structure to the capacity of complex organizations, but effective response also requires strong horizontal relationships to put that capacity to work.
  - We need to organize vertically and to work horizontally.

Regulations   In case after case, rules, paperwork, and procedures stymied the government's response to Hurricane Katrina.
- Rules are invaluable, but they can create deep pathologies by providing protection from blame and making it easy for officials to duck the responsibility for thinking about what needs to be done.
- When rules do not fit the situation, obedience to them can paralyze action.

Home Rule

A senior DHS official said that a major impediment to effective response is "our maniacally single-minded devotion to home rule."
- Old political boundaries of authority prove to be a very poor match for twenty-first-century problems. Boundaries should not constrain the ability to act.
- In New Orleans, the devotion to home rule literally produced gunfire at the bridge that refugees were told to use to evacuate from the Superdome to Gretna City—the police fired warning shots to turn the people away.
- In Katrina's aftermath, local, state, and federal boundaries handicapped the government's response.

Lessons Learned

What general lessons does Katrina teach?
- We face a new generation of wicked problems that demand innovative solutions.
- Lessons of the past are important, but old lessons can hamstring our ability to look forward.
- We need to govern instead of looking for symbols—we need to plan, practice, implement, and learn.
- We need public officials to lead and communicate confidence.
- We need new strategies for horizontal coordination.
- We need good rules, but they should not undermine common sense.
- We must not let old boundaries handcuff our ability to respond.

Federal Lessons

After 9/11, Congress and the president joined in a fundamental restructuring of the nation's homeland security apparatus.
- FEMA and twenty-one other agencies merged into DHS, with the administration saying it was to ensure that the efforts to defend this country are comprehensive and united.
- But when it faced the first important test, the department failed.
- DHS received low grades for devising a national strategy to help state and local governments, for allocating grant funds according to risk, for poor support for state training, and for poor support for first responders.

Federal Solutions

Straightforward steps could help DHS deal with its problems.
- The department could work from the top down so that the system works from the bottom up—it must be part of an integrated national plan involving federal, state, and local resources.
- Structure matters, but not as much as leadership—there must be a much more agile emergency response system.
- DHS needs top homeland security officials who understand their critical role in coordinating an integrated response.
- It will be crucial to develop a leadership, especially in FEMA, that recognizes that every disaster is different, with different challenges.
- The federal budget, especially in grants, can create incentives for a minimal level of preparedness everywhere in the United States.

State and Local Lessons

State and local officials had their own challenges, and they learned they need to do the following:
- Create a unified command—bringing the full range of commanders together at a single location.
- Create a single public face to encourage citizen's confidence by communicating about what is being done by people ably in charge.
- Establish interoperable communications so officials are not cut off from one another.

- Establish relationships among commanders so they are familiar with working with one another.
- Practice what is in the written plans so everyone is familiar with what is in the plan and what needs to be done.

Without adequate management capacity, governments will struggle to spend recovery money well and without waste, fraud, and abuse.
- The Gulf Coast is the region graded lowest in the nation for its capacity to manage infrastructure.
- Local officials blame lack of resources in the postponement of maintenance on mitigation infrastructure, but the infrastructure management systems in these states lag well behind other states.
- Thus, post-Katrina resources will flow into states that already have a substantial infrastructure backlog—can taxpayers be assured that new facilities will be maintained properly?
- After such a catastrophe of damage and loss of life, it would be worse to suffer catastrophic failure amid the effort to rebuild.

Q
R
S

Disaster Mitigation and Disaster Response Recommendations

Background

The "Shelter from the Storm" research articles in the March 2006 issue of *The Annals of the American Academy of Political and Social Science* make clear that the 2005 hurricane damage on the Gulf Coast could have been lessened considerably, and that lives did not have to be lost.

- Several things have led people and businesses to feel personally and financially secure about being in hazardous areas:
  - cheap federal flood insurance programs;
  - the expectation of substantial federal aid to disaster victims;
  - lack of restrictions on construction in hazardous areas;
  - encouragement by local governments who see this construction as good for the economy and for creating jobs; and
  - the belief that the risks must be low if government endorses construction in these areas.

Recommendations for Mitigation

To mitigate the potential for natural disasters, we need to change the way we control new construction in hazardous areas.

- The ideal would be to stop construction in hazardous areas and not to rebuild in high risk flood-prone areas and coastal areas.
- Where construction is allowed, special building codes must be required and enforced by local governments.
- Banks need to restrict construction loans and mortgages to those structures that meet the new codes.
  - Banks must insist on inspections by skilled inspectors.
  - Banks should require owner-paid insurance for these properties, which can be made affordable by including it as part of the monthly payments over the life of the loan.
- The federal government should stop subsidizing flood insurance (this is a major incentive to build in flood-prone areas)..
  - All community related disaster insurance should be at unsubsidized premiums and paid by the communities involved so they have an incentive to enforce codes.
- Predisaster planning should involve residents, thereby helping to create a knowledgeable constituency that is more likely to support redevelopment policies and programs after a disaster.
- We need to provide the poor with financial incentives to either move out of hazardous areas or to do mitigation.

Evacuation

Evacuation is the most powerful tool to prevent loss of life.

- The public in each community must be educated in how the evacuation plan will work.
  - They need to know the best routes.
  - They need to know where to get gas and supplies on the evacuation routes.
  - They need a complete emergency supply kit even if it means that officials have to provide supplies for all who evacuate.
- The evacuation plan must be realistic—to evacuate an entire community may take twice as long as or longer than most current plans have allowed for.
- A plan must be in place for the evacuation of people who have no means of transportation, are infirm, are elderly, are in hospitals and nursing home,

and who refuse to voluntarily evacuate because they won't leave their pets or are just belligerent about evacuating.

- The public must be made aware that looting of homes does not normally occur in natural disasters.
    - In addition they should be made to feel secure that the focus of National Guard deployment in the disaster area is to help emergency workers with things like downed power lines and fires. Looting is not a major problem and therefore is not a major concern of the National Guard.

Planning for Response

The response to almost all previous disasters has been slow and disorganized in the first few days. We must clarify roles at local, state, and federal levels.

- Local governments must stockpile supplies, vehicles, and personnel at strategic locations before a natural disaster strikes.
- Local disaster plans must be in place and must have been tested with practice drills.

Relationships among first responders and emergency organizations must be developed.

- There must be one command center for all heads of emergency teams with a single leader in place.
- All levels of responders must have compatible communication systems.
- States must have a plan for using the National Guard.
    - This plan must take into account the possible destruction of roads, bridges, and other infrastructure.
    - The leader of the state emergency command post must have authority to use the National Guard as needed.
- A system of feedback from local areas to advise the command post on needs must be in place—satellite phones may be an answer.
- The federal level requires structure, but also freedom to improvise based on unexpected needs at the scene and to respond with agility when the need to improvise arises.
    - People on the ground need to be able to decide what's needed and call for support when and where needed without red tape.
    - Grant writing for emergency relief and support must be streamlined, so it can be in federal hands in one day.
    - FEMA must be a stand-alone agency staffed with people experienced in emergency management.
    - Trucks and helicopters (whether they be U.S. military or National Guard equipment) must be available for release by the state emergency command post leader without having to go through a written requisition—one call should do it.
    - We should adapt the Incident Command System (ICS) evolved within the wildfire fighting community as a system of discipline as outlined in John R. Harrald's article [this volume].

Shelters

A plan must be in place to shelter evacuees out of harm's way during the disaster and in the short- and long-term after the disaster where needed.

- Sites for FEMA "trailer cities" should be preselected as part of a plan.
- Shelters are needed for emergency workers and relief crews.
- A shelter plan must include medium-term housing for evacuees until they can go back to their houses or into a FEMA trailer city.
- Shelters must be able to handle pets as well as people.

Volunteers

Well meaning volunteer groups and individuals need to be included in disaster plans so they are not in the way of government responders.

Use of the Military

Although there has been a clamor for more involvement of the U.S. military in disaster relief efforts, two other options may prove more important:
- Reestablishment of FEMA as a separate entity outside of DHS; and
- use of the National Guard under the command and direction of the leader in the central command post.

Florida as an Example

A final recommendation would be to look at how Florida's emergency management system is organized and work to improve it and make it the model for the entire United States.